Collins

WATERWAYS GUIDE 6

Nottingham, York & the North East

CONTENTS

Published by Nicholson
An imprint of HarperCollins*Publishers*
Westerhill Road, Bishopbriggs, Glasgow G64 2QT
www.harpercollins.co.uk

HarperCollins*Publishers*
1st Floor, Watermarque Building, Ringsend Road, Dublin 4, Ireland

Waterways guides published by Nicholson since 1969
This version first published by Nicholson and Ordnance Survey 1997
New editions published by Nicholson 2000, 2003, 2006, 2009, 2012, 2014, 2017, 2021

Wildlife text from *Collins Complete Guide to British Wildlife* and *Collins Wild Guide*.

The representation in this publication of a road, track or path is no evidence of the existence of a right of way.

Researched and written by Jonathan Mosse.

The publishers gratefully acknowledge the assistance given by Canal & River Trust and their staff in the preparation of this guide. Grateful thanks are also due to the Environment Agency, members of the Inland Waterways Association, and CAMRA representatives and branch members.

A catalogue record for this book is available from the British Library

Printed and bound in Poland by Dimograf

ISBN 978-0-00-843082-5

10 9 8 7 6 5 4 3 2

INTRODUCTION

Wending their quiet way through town and country, the inland navigations of Britain offer boaters, walkers and cyclists a unique insight into a fascinating, but once almost lost, world. When built this was the province of the boatmen and their families, who lived a mainly itinerant lifestyle: often colourful, to our eyes picturesque but, for them, remarkably harsh. Transporting the nation's goods during the late 1700s and early 1800s, negotiating locks, traversing aqueducts and passing through long narrow tunnels, canals were the arteries of trade during the initial part of the industrial revolution.

Then the railways came: the waterways were eclipsed in a remarkably short time by a faster and more flexible transport system, and a steady decline began. In a desperate fight for survival canal tolls were cut, crews toiled for longer hours and worked the boats with their whole family living aboard. Canal companies merged, totally uneconomic waterways were abandoned, some were modernised but it was all to no avail. Large scale commercial carrying on inland waterways had reached the finale of its short life.

At the end of World War II a few enthusiasts roamed this hidden world and harboured a vision of what it could become: a living transport museum which stretched the length and breadth of the country; a place where people could spend their leisure time and, on just a few of the wider waterways, a still modestly viable transport system.

The restoration struggle began and, from modest beginnings, Britain's inland waterways are now seen as an irreplaceable part of the fabric of the nation. Long-abandoned waterways, once seen as an eyesore and a danger, are recognised for the valuable contribution they make to our quality of life, and restoration schemes are integrating them back into the network. Let us hope that the country's network of inland waterways continues to be cherished and well-used, maintained and developed as we move through the 21st century.

If you would like to comment on any aspect of the guides, please write to Nicholson Waterways Guides, Collins, Westerhill Road, Bishopbriggs, Glasgow G64 2QT or email nicholson@harpercollins.co.uk.

Also available:

Collins NICHOLSON

Waterways guides and map

1 **Grand Union, Oxford & the South East**

2 **Severn, Avon & Birmingham**

3 **Birmingham & the Heart of England**

4 **Four Counties & the Welsh Canals**

5 **North West & the Pennines**

7 **River Thames & the Southern Waterways**

Norfolk Broads

Inland Waterways Map of Great Britain

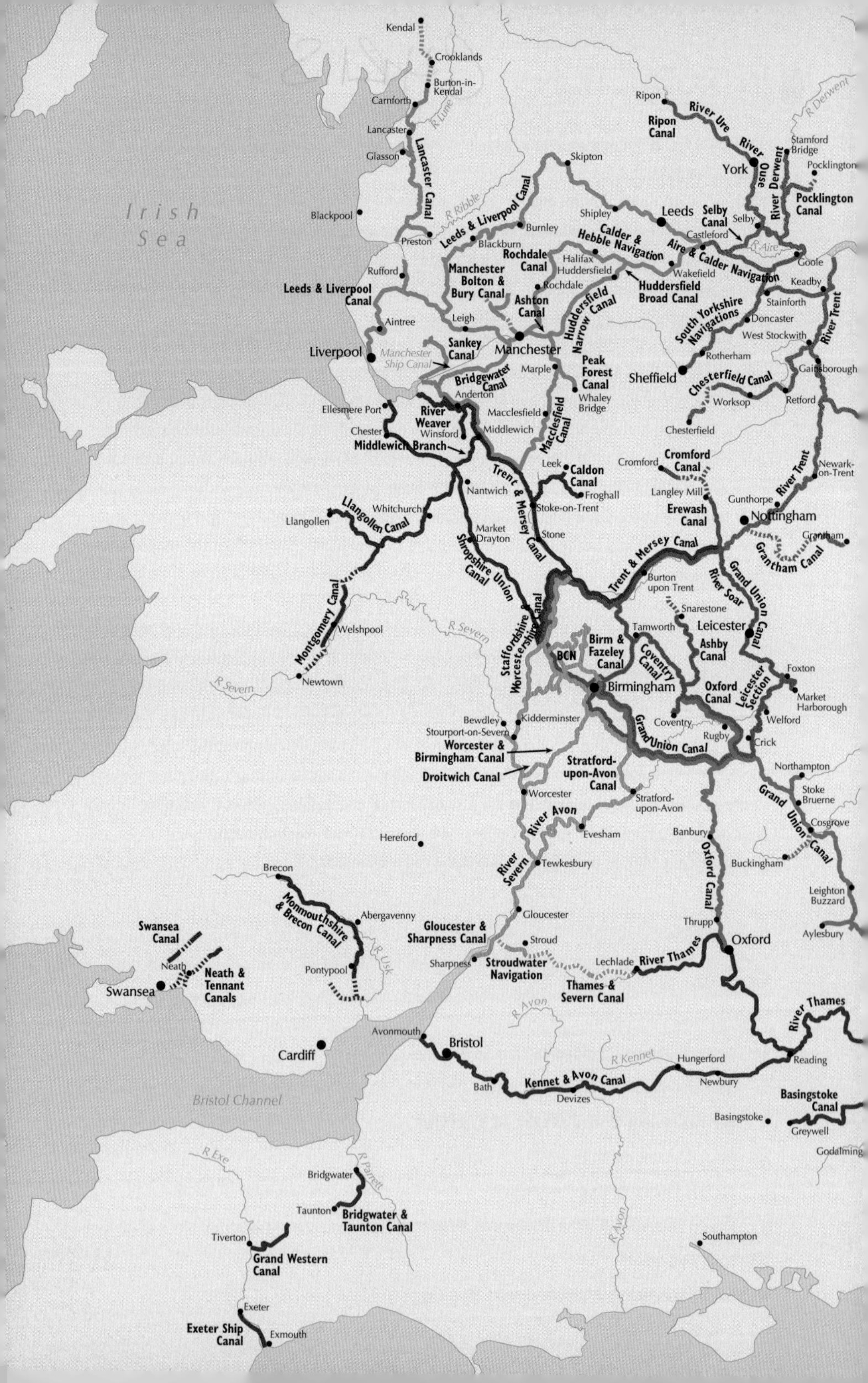

Kendal
Crooklands
Burton-in-Kendal
Carnforth
R Lune
Lancaster
Glasson
Lancaster Canal
Irish Sea
Blackpool
R Ribble
Preston
Leeds & Liverpool Canal
Burnley
Blackburn
Skipton
Shipley
Leeds
Ripon
River Ure
Ripon Canal
River Ouse
York
R Derwent
Stamford Bridge
Pocklington
River Derwent
Pocklington Canal
Selby Canal
Selby
Castleford
R Aire
Calder & Hebble Navigation
Aire & Calder Navigation
Goole
Rochdale Canal
Halifax
Huddersfield
Wakefield
Rufford
Manchester Bolton & Bury Canal
Rochdale
Huddersfield Broad Canal
Leeds & Liverpool Canal
Ashton Canal
Huddersfield Narrow Canal
Keadby
Stainforth
South Yorkshire Navigations
Doncaster
Aintree
Leigh
West Stockwith
River Trent
Liverpool
Manchester Ship Canal
Sankey Canal
Manchester
Peak Forest Canal
Rotherham
Gainsborough
Bridgewater Canal
Marple
Sheffield
Chesterfield Canal
Anderton
Whaley Bridge
Worksop
Retford
Ellesmere Port
River Weaver
Macclesfield
Macclesfield Canal
Chester
Winsford
Middlewich
Chesterfield
Middlewich Branch
Cromford
Cromford Canal
Leek
Caldon Canal
Trent & Mersey Canal
Newark-on-Trent
Nantwich
Froghall
Langley Mill
River Trent
Gunthorpe
Whitchurch
Llangollen Canal
Stoke-on-Trent
Erewash Canal
Nottingham
Llangollen
Market Drayton
Stone
Grantham
Shropshire Union Canal
Trent & Mersey Canal
Grantham Canal
Burton upon Trent
Grand Union Canal
River Soar
Snarestone
Montgomery Canal
R Severn
Staffordshire & Worcestershire Canal
Leicester
Welshpool
Tamworth
Birm & Fazeley Canal
Ashby Canal
BCN
Coventry Canal
R Severn
Newtown
Birmingham
Oxford Canal
Leicester Section
Foxton
Market Harborough
Coventry
Bewdley
Kidderminster
Rugby
Welford
Stourport-on-Severn
Grand Union Canal
Crick
Worcester & Birmingham Canal
Stratford-upon-Avon Canal
Northampton
Droitwich Canal
Worcester
Stratford-upon-Avon
Stoke Bruerne
Grand Union Canal
River Avon
Evesham
Banbury
Cosgrove
Hereford
Brecon
River Severn
Tewkesbury
Oxford Canal
Buckingham
Monmouthshire & Brecon Canal
Leighton Buzzard
Abergavenny
Gloucester
Swansea Canal
Gloucester & Sharpness Canal
Thrupp
Oxford
Aylesbury
R Usk
Stroud
Neath
Neath & Tennant Canals
Sharpness
Stroudwater Navigation
Lechlade
River Thames
Swansea
Pontypool
Thames & Severn Canal
R Avon
River Thames
Avonmouth
Bristol
Cardiff
R Kennet
Hungerford
Reading
Bath
Kennet & Avon Canal
Newbury
Devizes
Bristol Channel
Basingstoke Canal
Basingstoke
Greywell
Godalming
R Exe
R Parrett
Bridgwater
Taunton
Bridgwater & Taunton Canal
R Avon
Tiverton
Southampton
Grand Western Canal
Exeter
Exeter Ship Canal
Exmouth

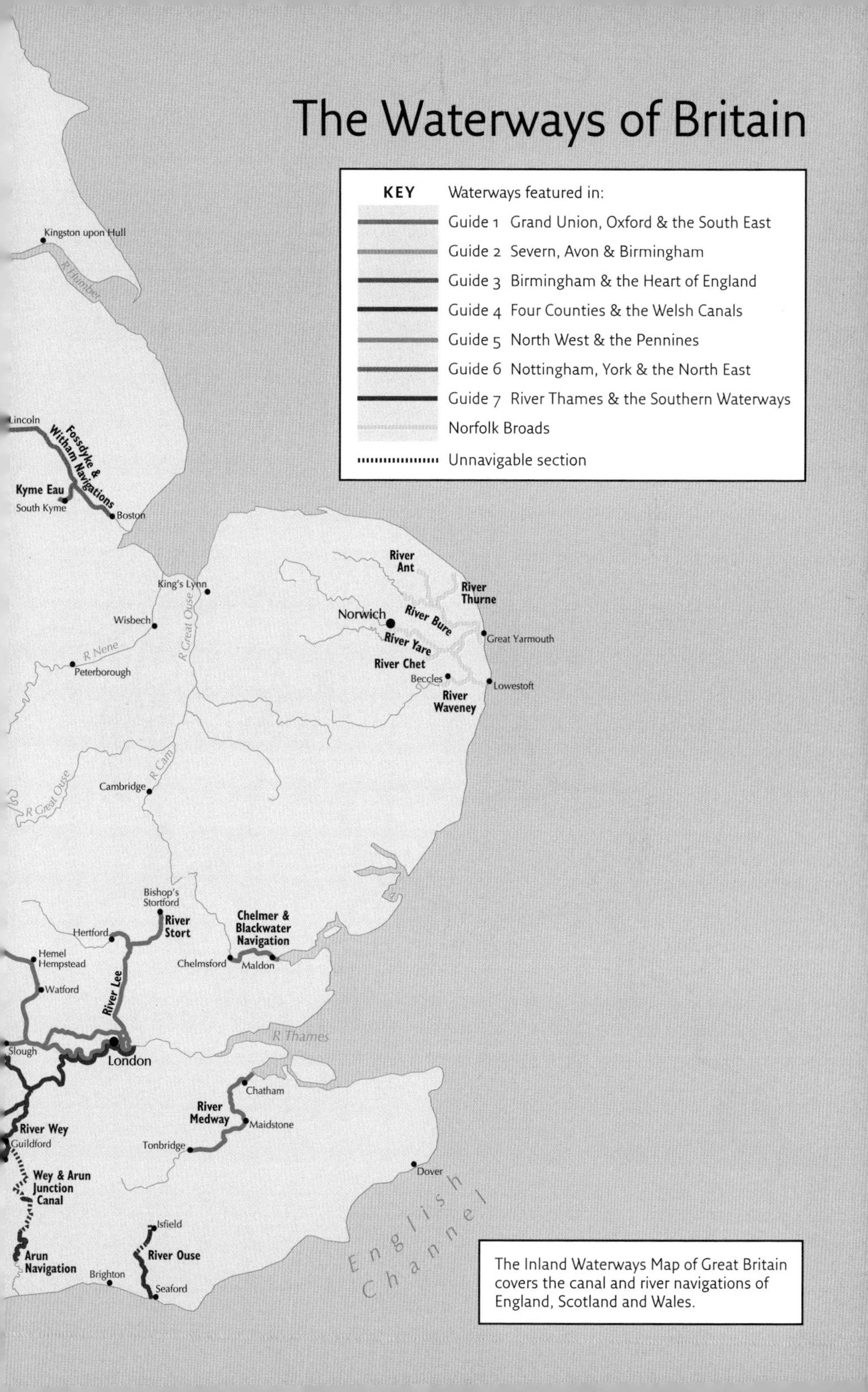
The Waterways of Britain
KEY
Waterways featured in:
Guide 1 Grand Union, Oxford & the South East
Guide 2 Severn, Avon & Birmingham
Guide 3 Birmingham & the Heart of England
Guide 4 Four Counties & the Welsh Canals
Guide 5 North West & the Pennines
Guide 6 Nottingham, York & the North East
Guide 7 River Thames & the Southern Waterways
Norfolk Broads
Unnavigable section
Kingston upon Hull
R Humber
Lincoln
Fossdyke & Witham Navigations
Kyme Eau
South Kyme
Boston
King's Lynn
Wisbech
R Nene
Peterborough
R Great Ouse
River Ant
River Thurne
Norwich
River Bure
River Yare
River Chet
Great Yarmouth
Beccles
Lowestoft
River Waveney
R Cam
Cambridge
Bishop's Stortford
River Stort
Hertford
Chelmer & Blackwater Navigation
Hemel Hempstead
Chelmsford
Maldon
Watford
River Lee
R Thames
Slough
London
Chatham
River Medway
Maidstone
River Wey
Guildford
Tonbridge
Dover
Wey & Arun Junction Canal
English Channel
Isfield
River Ouse
Arun Navigation
Brighton
Seaford
The Inland Waterways Map of Great Britain covers the canal and river navigations of England, Scotland and Wales.

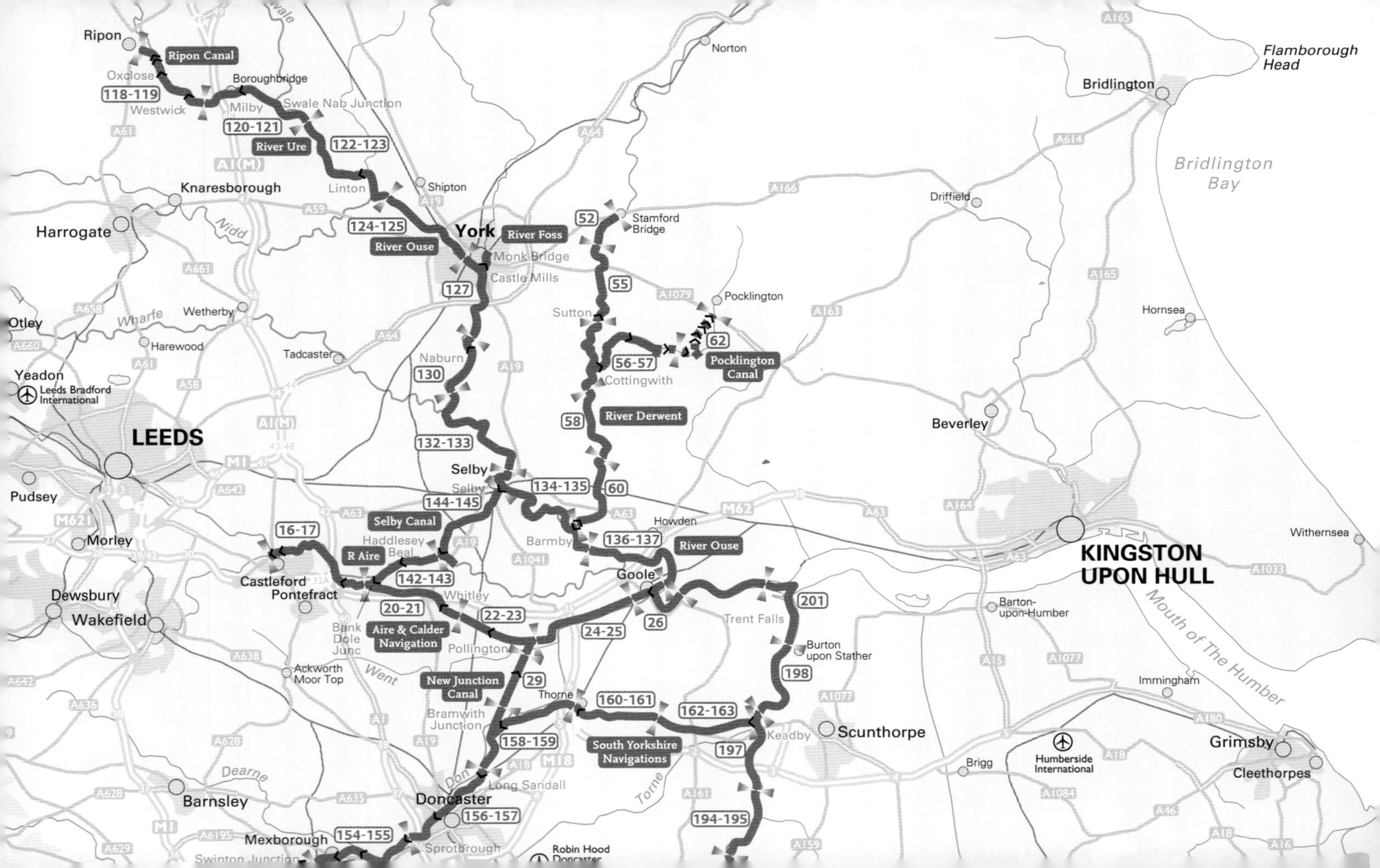

Ripon
Ripon Canal
Oxclose
Boroughbridge
118-119
Westwick
Milby
Swale Nab Junction
120-121
River Ure
122-123
Norton
Flamborough Head
Bridlington
Bridlington Bay
Knaresborough
Linton
Shipton
Harrogate
124-125
York
River Foss
River Ouse
Monk Bridge
Castle Mills
127
52
Stamford Bridge
55
Sutton
Pocklington
62
56-57
Pocklington Canal
Cottingwith
River Derwent
58
Driffield
Beverley
Hornsea
Wetherby
Wharfe
Nidd
Otley
Harewood
Tadcaster
Naburn
130
Yeadon
Leeds Bradford International
LEEDS
132-133
Selby
134-135
60
144-145
Pudsey
Selby Canal
Morley
16-17
Haddlesey
Beal
R Aire
142-143
Barmby
136-137
Howden
River Ouse
Goole
KINGSTON UPON HULL
Withernsea
Castleford
Pontefract
Dewsbury
Wakefield
20-21
Whitley
22-23
24-25
26
201
Trent Falls
Barton-upon-Humber
Mouth of The Humber
Bank Dole Junc
Aire & Calder Navigation
Pollington
Burton upon Stather
198
Ackworth Moor Top
Went
New Junction Canal
29
Thorne
160-161
162-163
Immingham
Bramwith Junction
158-159
South Yorkshire Navigations
197
Keadby
Scunthorpe
Brigg
Humberside International
Grimsby
Cleethorpes
Dearne
Barnsley
Don
Long Sandall
Doncaster
156-157
Torne
194-195
Mexborough
154-155
Sprotbrough
Swinton Junction
Robin Hood Doncaster

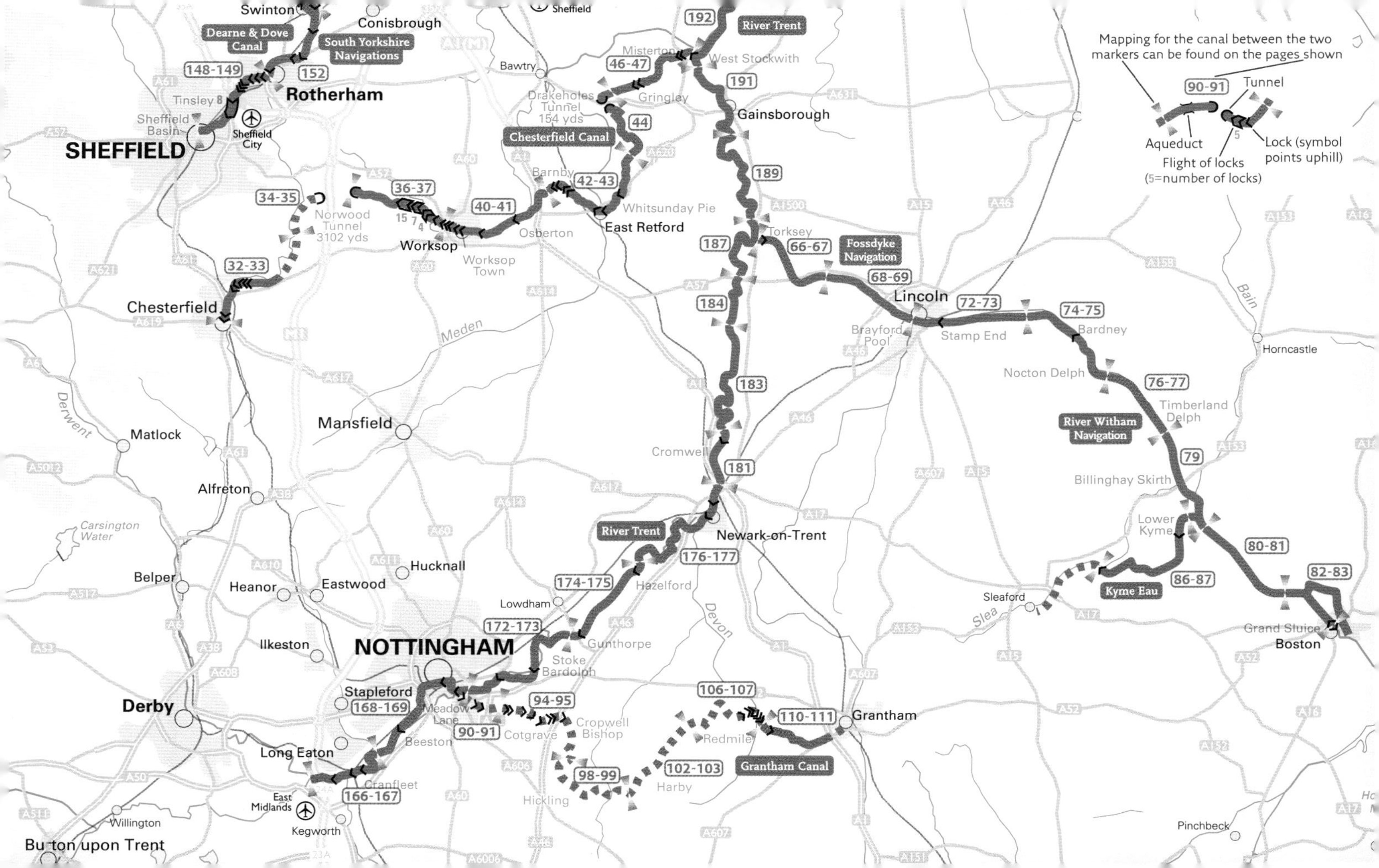
Mapping for the canal between the two markers can be found on the pages shown
90-91
Tunnel
Aqueduct
Flight of locks
(5=number of locks)
Lock (symbol points uphill)
SHEFFIELD
Sheffield Basin
Tinsley 8
Sheffield City
Rotherham
Swinton
Conisbrough
Dearne & Dove Canal
South Yorkshire Navigations
148-149
152
34-35
Norwood Tunnel 3102 yds
32-33
Chesterfield
36-37
Worksop
Worksop Town
40-41
Osberton
Barnby
42-43
East Retford
Whitsunday Pie
44
Chesterfield Canal
Drakeholes Tunnel 154 yds
Gringley
46-47
Misterton
Bawtry
West Stockwith
192
River Trent
191
Gainsborough
189
Torksey
187
184
183
181
Cromwell
Newark-on-Trent
176-177
River Trent
Hazelford
174-175
Lowdham
Gunthorpe
Stoke Bardolph
172-173
NOTTINGHAM
Meadow Lane
90-91
Stapleford
168-169
Beeston
Long Eaton
Cranfleet
166-167
East Midlands
Kegworth
94-95
Cotgrave
Cropwell Bishop
98-99
Hickling
102-103
Harby
106-107
Redmile
110-111
Grantham
Grantham Canal
66-67
Fossdyke Navigation
68-69
Lincoln
Brayford Pool
72-73
Stamp End
74-75
Bardney
Nocton Delph
76-77
Timberland Delph
River Witham Navigation
79
Billinghay Skirth
Lower Kyme
86-87
Kyme Eau
Sleaford
Slea
80-81
82-83
Grand Sluice
Boston
Horncastle
Bain
Pinchbeck
Mansfield
Matlock
Derwent
Alfreton
Carsington Water
Belper
Heanor
Eastwood
Hucknall
Ilkeston
Derby
Willington
Burton upon Trent
Meden
Devon

GENERAL INFORMATION FOR WATERWAYS USERS

INTRODUCTION

Boaters, walkers, fishermen, cyclists and gongoozlers (on-lookers) all share in the enjoyment of our quite amazing waterway heritage. Canal & River Trust (CRT) and the Environment Agency, along with other navigation authorities, are empowered to develop, maintain and control this resource. It is to this end that a series of guides, codes, and regulations have come into existence over the years, evolving to match a burgeoning – and occasionally conflicting – demand. Set out in this section are key points as they relate to everyone wishing to enjoy the waterways.

The *Boater's Handbook* is available from all navigation authorities. It contains a complete range of safety information, boat-handling know-how, warning symbols and illustrations, and can be downloaded from www.canalrivertrust.org.uk/enjoy-the-waterways/boating/a-guide-to-boating/boaters-handbook. It is complimented by this excellent video: www.youtube.com/watch?v=lXn47JYXs44.

CONSIDERATE BOATING

Considerate Boating gives advice and guidance to all waterway users on how to enjoy the inland waterways safely and can be downloaded from www.canalrivertrust.org.uk/boating/navigating-the-waterways/considerate-boating. It is also well worth visiting www.considerateboater.com. These publications are also available from the Customer Services Team which is staffed *Mon-Fri 08.00-21.00; Sat and B Hols 08.00-19.00 & Sun 09.00-19.00*. The helpful staff will answer general enquiries and provide information about boat licensing, mooring, boating holidays and general activities on the waterways. They can be contacted on 0303 040 4040; customer.services@canalrivertrust.org.uk; Canal & River Trust, Head Office, First Floor North, Station House, 500 Elder Gate, Milton Keynes MK9 1BB. Visit www.canalrivertrust.org.uk for up to date information on almost every aspect of the inland waterways from news and events to moorings.

Emergency Helpline Available from Canal & River Trust outside normal office hours on weekdays and throughout weekends. If lives or property are at risk or there is danger of serious environmental contamination then immediately contact 0800 47 999 47; www.canalrivertrust.org.uk/contact-us/contacting-us-in-an-emergency.

ENVIRONMENT AGENCY

The Environment Agency (EA) manages around 600 miles of the country's rivers, including the Thames and the River Medway. For general enquiries or to obtain a copy of the *Boater's Handbook*, contact EA Customer Services on 03708 506 506; enquiries@environment-agency.gov.uk. To find out about their work nationally (or to download a copy of the *Handbook)* and for lots of other useful information, visit www.gov.uk/government/organisations/environment-agency. The website www.visitthames.co.uk provides lots on information on boating, walking, fishing and events on the river.

Incident Hotline The EA maintain an Incident Hotline. To report damage or danger to the natural environment, damage to structures or water escaping, telephone 0800 80 70 60.

LICENSING – BOATS

The majority of the navigations covered in this book are controlled by CRT and the EA and are managed on a day-to-day basis by local Waterway Offices (details of these are in the introductions to each waterway). All craft using the inland waterways must be licensed and charges are based on the dimensions of the craft. In a few cases, these include reciprocal agreements with other waterway authorities (as indicated in the text). CRT and the EA offer an optional Gold Licence which covers unlimited navigation on the waterways of both authorities. Permits for permanent mooring on CRT waterways are issued by CRT.

Contact Canal & River Trust Boat Licensing Team on 0303 040 4040; www.canalrivertrust.org.uk/boating/licensing; Canal & River Trust Licensing Team, PO Box 162, Leeds LS9 1AX.

For the Thames and River Medway contact the EA. River Thames: 0118 953 5650; www.gov.uk/government/organisations/environment-agency; Environment Agency, PO Box 214, Reading RG1 8HQ. River Medway: 01732 223222 or visit the website.

BOAT SAFETY SCHEME

CRT and the EA operate the Boat Safety Scheme aimed at maintaining boat safety standards and featuring four-yearly testing, primarily intended to identify third party risks. A Boat Safety Scheme Certificate (for new boats, a Declaration of Conformity) is necessary to obtain a craft licence from all navigation authorities. CRT also requires proof of insurance for Third Party Liability for a minimum of £2,000,000 for powered boats. The scheme is gradually being adopted by other waterway authorities. Contact details are: 0333 202 1000; www.boatsafetyscheme.org; Boat Safety Scheme, First Floor North, Station House, 500 Elder Gate, Milton Keynes MK9 1BB. The website offers useful advice on preventing fires and avoiding carbon monoxide poisoning.

TRAINING

The Royal Yachting Association (RYA) runs one and two day courses leading to the Inland Waters Helmsman's Certificate, specifically designed for novices and experienced boaters wishing to cruise the inland waterways. For details of RYA schools, telephone 023 8060 4100 or visit www.rya.org.uk. The practical course notes are available to buy. Contact your local boat clubs, too. The National Community Boats Association (NCBA) run courses on boat-handling and safety on the water. Telephone 0845 0510649 or visit www.national-cba.co.uk.

LICENSING - CYCLISTS

You no longer require a permit to cycle on those waterways under the control of Canal & River Trust. However, you are asked to abide by the ten point Greenway Code for Towpaths available at www.canalrivertrust.org.uk/see-and-do/cycling which also provides a wide range of advice on cycling beside the waterways. Cycling along the Thames towpath is generally accepted, although landowners have the right to request that you do not cycle. Some sections of the riverside path, however, are designated and clearly marked as official cycle ways. No permits are required but cyclists must follow London's Towpath Code on Conduct at all times.

TOWPATHS

Few, if any, artificial cuts or canals in this country are without an intact towpath accessible to the walker at least and the Thames is the only river in the country with a designated National Trail along its path from source to sea (for more information visit www.nationaltrail.co.uk). However, on some other river navigations, towpaths have on occasion fallen into disuse or, sometimes, been lost to erosion. The indication of a towpath in this guide does not necessarily imply a public right of way. Horse riding and motorcycling are forbidden on all towpaths.

INDIVIDUAL WATERWAY GUIDES

No national guide can cover the minutiae of detail concerning every waterway, and some CRT Waterway Managers produce guides to specific navigations under their charge. Copies of individual guides (where available) can be obtained from the relevant CRT Waterway Office or downloaded from www.canalrivertrust.org.uk/enjoy-the-waterways/boating/planning-your-boat-trip. Please note that times - such as operating times of bridges and locks - do change year by year and from winter to summer. For free copies of a range of helpful leaflets for all users of the River Thames - visit www.visitthames.co.uk/about-the-river/publications.

STOPPAGES

CRT and the EA both publish winter stoppage programmes which are sent out to all licence holders, boatyards and hire companies. Inevitably, emergencies occur necessitating the unexpected closure of a waterway, perhaps during the peak season. You can check for stoppages on individual waterways between specific dates on www.canalrivertrust.org.uk/notices/winter, lockside noticeboards or by telephoning 0303 040 4040; for stoppages and river conditions on the Thames, visit www.gov.uk/river-thames-conditions-closures-restrictions-and-lock-closures or telephone 0845 988 1188.

NAVIGATION AUTHORITIES AND WATERWAYS SOCIETIES

Most inland navigations are managed by CRT or the EA, but there are several other navigation authorities. For details of these, contact the Association of Inland Navigation Authorities on 0844 335 1650 or visit www.aina.org.uk. The boater, conditioned perhaps by the uniformity of our national road network, should be sensitive to the need to observe different codes and operating practices.

The Canal & River Trust is a charity set up to care for England and Wales' legacy of 200-year-old waterways, holding them in trust for the nation forever, and is linked with an ombudsman. CRT has a comprehensive complaints procedure and a free explanatory leaflet is available from Customer Services. Problems and complaints should be addressed to the local Waterway Manager in the first instance. For more information, visit their website.

The EA is the national body, sponsored by the Department for Environment, Food and Rural Affairs, to manage the quality of air, land and water in England and Wales. For more information, visit its website.

The Inland Waterways Association (IWA) campaigns for the use, maintenance and restoration of Britain's inland waterways, through branches all over the country. For more information, contact them on 01494 783453; iwa@waterways.org.uk; www.waterways.org.uk; The Inland Waterways Association, Island House, Moor Road, Chesham HP5 1WA. Their website has a huge amount of information of interest to boaters, including comprehensive details of the many and varied waterways societies.

STARTING OUT

Extensive information and advice on booking a boating holiday is available from the Inland Waterways Association, www.visitthames.co.uk and www.canalrivertrust.org.uk/boating/boat-trips-and-holidays. Please book a waterway holiday from a licensed operator – this way you can be sure that you have proper insurance cover, service and support during your holiday. It is illegal for private boat owners to hire out their craft. If you are hiring a holiday craft for the first time, the boatyard will brief you thoroughly. Take notes, follow their instructions and do ask if there is anything you do not understand. CRT have produced a 40 min DVD which is essential viewing for newcomers to canal or river boating. Available to view free at www.canalrivertrust.org.uk/boatersdvd or obtainable (charge) from the CRT Customer Service Centre 0303 040 4040; www.canalrivertrust.org.uk/shop.

PLACES TO VISIT ALONG THE WAY

This guide contains a wealth of information, not just about the canals and rivers and navigating on them, but also on the visitor attractions and places to eat and drink close to the waterways. Opening and closing times, and other details often change; establishments close and new ones open. If you are making special plans to eat in a particular pub, or visit a certain museum it is always advisable to check in advance.

MORE INFORMATION

An internet search will reveal many websites on the inland waterways. Those listed below are just a small sample:

National Community Boats Association is a national charity and training provider, supporting community boat projects and encouraging more people to access the inland waterways. Telephone 0845 0510649; www.national-cba.co.uk.

National Association of Boat Owners is dedicated to promoting the interests of private boaters on Britain's canals and rivers. Visit www.nabo.org.uk.

www.canalplan.org.uk is an online journey-planner and gazetteer for the inland waterways.

www.canals.com is a valuable source of information for cruising the canals, with loads of links to canal and waterways related websites.

www.ukcanals.net lists services and useful information for all waterways users.

GENERAL CRUISING NOTES

Most canals and rivers are saucer shaped, being deepest at the middle. Few canals have more than 3-4ft of water and many have much less. Keep to the centre of the channel except on bends, where the deepest water is on the outside of the bend. When you meet another boat, keep to the right, slow down and aim to miss the approaching craft by a couple of yards. If you meet a loaded commercial boat keep right out of the way and be prepared to follow his instructions. Do not assume that you should pass on the right. If you meet a boat being towed from the bank, pass it on the outside. When overtaking, keep the other boat on your right side.

Some CRT and EA facilities are operated by pre-paid cards, obtainable from CRT and EA regional and local waterways offices, lock keepers and boatyards. Weekend visitors should purchase cards in advance. A handcuff/anti-vandal key is commonly used on locks where vandalism is a problem. A watermate/sanitary key opens sanitary stations, waterpoints and some bridges and locks. Both keys and pre-paid cards can be obtained via CRT Customer Service Centre.

Safety

Boating is a safe pastime. However, it makes sense to take simple safety precautions, particularly if you have children aboard.

- Never drink and drive a boat – it may travel slowly, but it weighs many tons.
- Be careful with naked flames and never leave the boat with the hob or oven lit. Familiarise yourself and your crew with the location and operation of the fire extinguishers.

- Never block ventilation grills. Boats are enclosed spaces and levels of carbon monoxide can build up from faulty appliances or just from using the cooker.
- Be careful along the bank and around locks. Slipping from the bank might only give you a cold-water soaking, but falling from the side of, or into a lock is more dangerous. Beware of slippery or rough ground.
- Remember that fingers and toes are precious! If a major collision is imminent, never try to fend off with your hands or feet; and always keep hands and arms inside the boat.
- Weil's disease is a particularly dangerous infection present in water which can attack the central nervous system and major organs. It is caused by bacteria entering the bloodstream through cuts and broken skin, and the eyes, nose and mouth. The flu-like symptoms occur two-four weeks after exposure. Always wash your hands thoroughly after contact with the water. Visit www.leptospirosis.org for details.

Speed

There is a general speed limit of 4 mph on most CRT canals and 5 mph on the Thames. There is no need to go any faster - the faster you go, the bigger a wave the boat creates: if your wash is breaking against the bank, causing large waves or throwing moored boats around, slow down. Slow down also when passing engineering works and anglers; when there is a lot of floating rubbish on the water (try to drift over obvious obstructions in neutral); when approaching blind corners, narrow bridges and junctions.

Mooring

Generally you may moor where you wish on CRT property, as long as you are *not causing an obstruction*. Do not moor in a winding hole or junction, the approaches to a lock or tunnel, or at a water point or sanitary station. On the Thames, generally you have a right to anchor for 24 hours in one place provided no obstruction is caused, however you will need explicit permission from the land owner to moor. There are official mooring sites along the length of the river; those provided by the EA are free, the others you will need to pay for. Your boat should carry metal mooring stakes, and these should be driven firmly into the ground with a mallet if there are no mooring rings. Do not stretch mooring lines across the towpath and take account of anyone who may walk past. Always consider the security of your boat when there is no one aboard. On tideways and commercial waterways it is advisable to moor only at recognised sites, and allow for any rise or fall of the tide.

Bridges

On narrow canals slow down well in advance and aim to miss one side (usually the towpath side) by about 9 inches. *Keep everyone inboard when passing under bridges and ensure there is nothing on the roof of the boat that will hit the bridge.* If a boat is coming the other way, the craft nearest to the bridge has priority. Take special care with moveable structures - the crew member operating the bridge should be strong and heavy enough to hold it steady as the boat passes through.

Going aground

You can sometimes go aground if the water level on a canal has dropped or you are on a particularly shallow stretch. If it does happen, try reversing *gently*, or pushing off with the boat hook. Another method is to get your crew to rock the boat from side to side using the boat hook, or move all crew to the end opposite to that which is aground. Or, have all crew leave the boat, except the helmsman, and it will often float off quite easily.

Tunnels

Again, ensure that everyone is inboard. Make sure the tunnel is clear before you enter, and use your headlight. Follow any instructions given on notice boards by the entrance.

Fuel

Diesel can be purchased from most boatyards and some CRT depots. To comply with HMRC regulations you must declare an appropriate split between propulsion and heating so that the correct level of VAT can be applied. However, few boatyards stock petrol. Where a garage is listed under a town or village's facilities petrol (and DERV) are available.

Water

It is advisable to top up daily.

Pump out

Self-operated pump out facilities are available at a number of locations on the waterways network. These facilities are provided by CRT and can be operated via a 25-unit prepayment card. Details of how to buy a pump out card either online, by phone or in person are available from www.canalrivertrust.org.uk. The cards provide for one pump out or 25 units of electricity. Cards can be obtained from CRT Waterway Offices, some Marinas and boatyards, shops and cafés.

Boatyards

Hire fleets are usually turned around at a weekend, making this a bad time to call in for services.

VHF Radio

The IWA recommends that all pleasure craft navigating the larger waterways used by freight carrying vessels, or any tidal navigation, should carry marine-band VHF radio and have a qualified radio operator on board. In some cases the navigation authority requires craft to carry radio and maintain a listening watch. Two examples of this are for boats on the tidal River Ouse wishing to enter Goole Docks and the Aire & Calder Navigation, and for boats on the tidal Thames, over 45ft, navigating between Teddington Lock and Limehouse Basin.
VHF radio users must have a current operator's certificate. The training is not expensive and will present no problem to the average inland waterways boater. Contact the RYA (see Training) for details.

PLANNING A CRUISE

Don't try to go too far too fast. Go slowly, don't be too ambitious, and enjoy the experience. Mileages indicated on the maps are for guidance only. A *rough* calculation of time taken to cover the ground is the lock-miles system:

Add the number of *miles* to the number of *locks* on your proposed journey, and divide the resulting figure by three. This will give you an approximate guide to the number of *hours* your travel will take.

TIDAL WATERWAYS

The typical steel narrow boat found on the inland waterways is totally unsuitable for cruising on tidal estuaries. However, the adventurous will inevitably wish to add additional 'ring cruises' to the more predictable circuits of inland Britain. Passage is possible in most estuaries if careful consideration is given to the key factors of weather conditions, tides, crew experience, the condition of the boat and its equipment and, perhaps of overriding importance, the need to take expert advice. In many cases it will be prudent to employ the skilled services of a local pilot. Within the text, where inland navigations connect with a tidal waterway, details are given of sources of advice and pilotage. It is also essential to inform your insurance company of your intention to navigate on tidal waterways as they may very well have special requirements or wish to levy an additional premium. This guide is to the inland waterways of Britain and therefore recognizes that tideways – and especially estuaries – require a different approach and many additional skills. We do not hesitate to draw the boater's attention to the appropriate source material.

LOCKS AND THEIR USE

A lock is a simple and ingenious device for transporting your craft from one water level to another. When both sets of gates are closed it may be filled or emptied using gates, or ground paddles, at the top or bottom of the lock. These are operated with a windlass. On the Thames, the locks are manned all year round, with longer hours from April to October. You may operate the locks yourself at any time.

If a lock is empty, or 'set' for you, the crew open the gates and you drive the boat in. If the lock is full of water, the crew should check first to see if any boat is waiting or coming in the other direction. If a boat is in sight, you must let them through first: do not empty or 'turn' the lock against them. This is not only discourteous, and against the rules, but wastes precious water.

In the diagrams the *plan* shows how the gates point uphill, the water pressure forcing them together. Water is flooding into the lock through the underground culverts that are operated by the ground paddles: when the lock is 'full', the top gates (on the left of the drawing) can be opened. One may imagine a boat entering, the crew closing the gates and paddles after it.

In the *elevation*, the bottom paddles have been raised (opened) so that the lock empties. A boat will, of course, float down with the water. When the lock is 'empty' the bottom gates can be opened and the descending boat can leave.

Remember that when going *up* a lock, a boat should be tied up to prevent it being thrown about by the the rush of incoming water; but when going *down* a lock, a boat should never be tied up or it will be left high and dry.

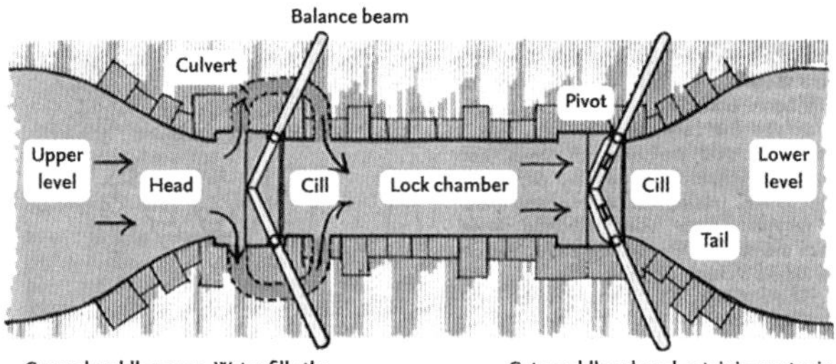

A plan of a lock filling.

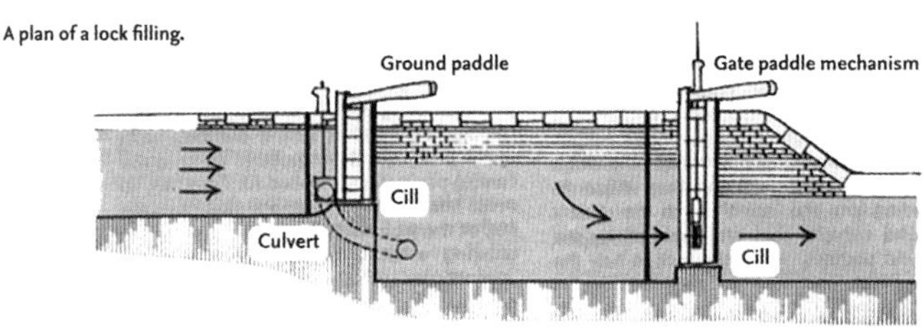

An elevation of a lock emptying.

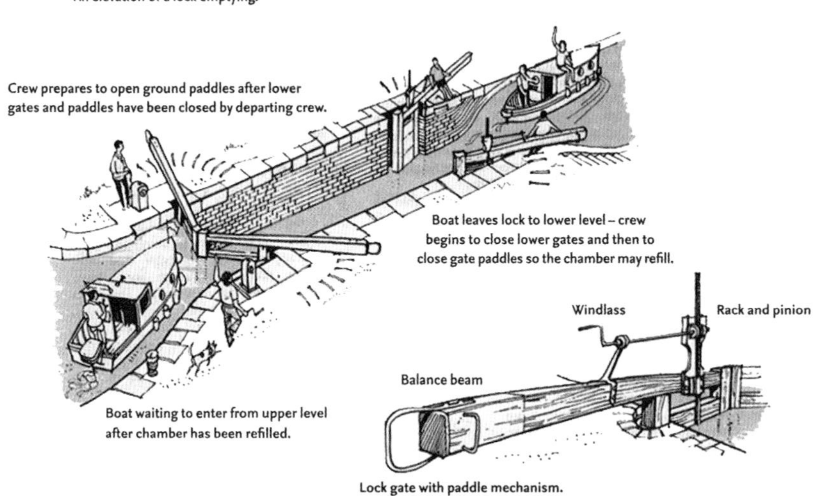

Lock gate with paddle mechanism.

- Make safety your prime concern. *Keep a close eye on young children*.
- Always take your time, and do not leap about.
- Never open the paddles at one end without ensuring those at the other end are closed.
- Keep to the landward side of the balance beam when opening and closing gates. Whilst it may be necessary to put your back behind the balance beam to gain a better purchase when starting to close a gate, always move to the correct position as soon as possible.
- Never leave your windlass slotted onto the paddle spindle – it will be dangerous should anything slip.
- Keep your boat away from the top and bottom gates to prevent it getting caught on the gate or the lock cill.
- Never drop the paddles – always wind them down.
- Be wary of fierce *top gate* paddles, especially in wide locks. Operate them slowly, and close them if there is *any* adverse effect.
- Always follow the navigation authority's instructions, where given on notices or by their staff.

Farndale H entering Bulholme Lock, Castleford

AIRE & CALDER NAVIGATION

MAXIMUM DIMENSIONS

Castleford to Goole
Length: 200'
Beam: 20'
Headroom: 11' 9" (see note 2 on page 23 and note 5 on page 27)
Draught: 8' 2"

MANAGER

0303 040 4040; enquiries.yorkshirenortheast@canalrivertrust.org.uk

MILEAGE

CASTLEFORD to:
Bank Dole: 7 miles, 3 locks including Castleford
New Junction Canal: 16½ miles, 5 locks
Goole: 24 miles, 5 locks

SAFETY NOTES

CRT produce a Boaters Guides for pleasure boaters using this (and many other) waterway(s) downloadable from www.canalrivertrust.org.uk/enjoy-the-waterways/boating/a-guide-to-boating/boaters-handbook. This is both a commercial waterway and one developed from a river navigation: both pose their own disciplines highlighted in the notes.

Each lock on the waterway has a set of traffic lights both upstream and downstream of the lock chamber. The purpose of these lights is to convey instructions and advice to approaching craft.

Red light
Stop and moor up on the lock approach. The lock is currently in use.

Amber light *(between the red and green lights)*
The lock keeper is not on duty. You will need to self-operate.

Green light
Proceed into lock.

Red & green lights together
The lock is available for use. The lock keeper will prepare and operate the lock for you.

Flashing red light
Flood conditions – unsafe for navigation.

Most lock approach moorings are immediately upstream and downstream of the lock chamber; however, **please note:**

Ferrybridge Lock upstream approach mooring is located on the river side of the lock island.

Locks at Castleford, Bulholme, Ferrybridge and Bank Dole allow access to river sections of the navigation. River level gauge boards indicate conditions as follows:

GREEN BAND – Normal river levels safe for navigation.

AMBER BAND – River levels are above normal. If you wish to navigate the river section you are advised to proceed on to and through the next lock.

RED BAND – Flood conditions unsafe for navigation. Lock closed.

All locks between Castleford and Goole (except Bank Dole) are equipped with VHF Marine Band Radio. They monitor and operate on channel 74.

See page 21 for details of self-operation of these locks.

In an emergency non-VHF users should contact the manager's office.

The River Aire was first made navigable to Leeds in 1700 and rapidly became a great commercial success, taking coal out of the Yorkshire coalfield and bringing back raw wool, corn and agricultural produce. Improvements were then made to the difficult lower reaches, with first Selby and later Goole becoming Yorkshire's principal inland port. The opening of the New Junction Canal in 1905 further secured its suitability for commercial traffic, which until recently amounted to some 2 million tons, mainly coal, sand and petroleum. In 2015 the closure of Kellingley Colliery brought coal-carrying to the three Ferrybridge Power Stations along the navigation to an abrupt close. At a single stroke 1½ million tons of coal were transferred annually onto road and rail transport, together with the associated environmental cost. Fortunately, a year later the decision was made to close the final power station on the site – Ferrybridge C – so ending 50 years of energy production at this high-profile, riverside location. Opened in 1966, Ferrybridge C became the first power station in Europe to succeed in generating electricity from 500-megawatt plant. It also entered the record books in 1973 when one of its generators set a world record, running non-stop for over 5,400 hours and generating 2,999 gigawatt hours of electricity.

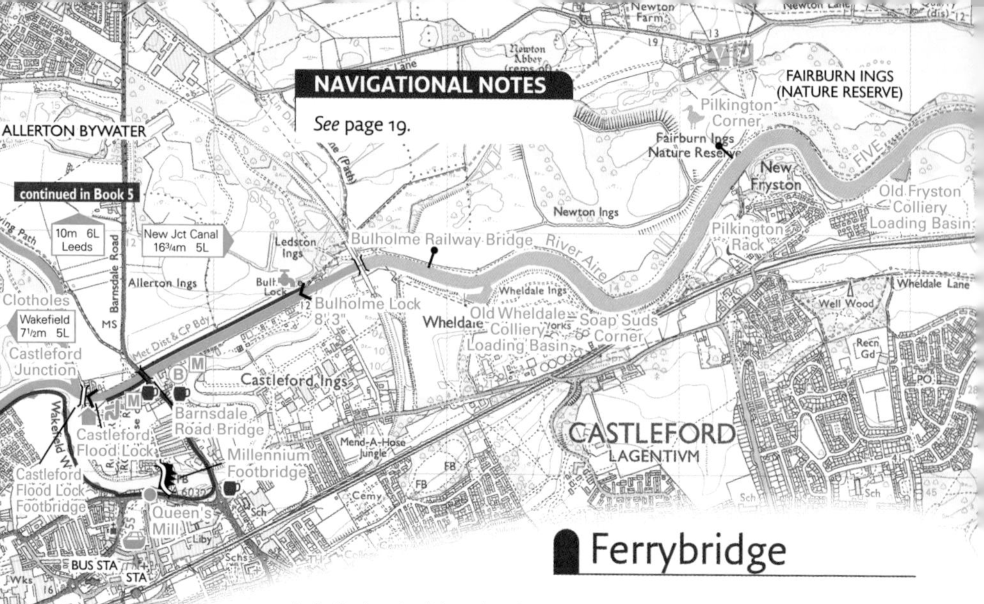

NAVIGATIONAL NOTES
See page 19.

Ferrybridge

At Bulholme Lock is a sign directing walkers to Newton. This walk should not be attempted in wet weather as the footpath becomes waterlogged. The lock keeper's bungalow, built on stilts, replaces a traditional canalside cottage. At this point the canal enters the river which is surrounded by large areas of derelict land. Landscaping of the now-abandoned Fryston and Wheldale collieries is still being undertaken but will, no doubt, lead to the establishment of plants and trees in the area. The lower land to the north of the navigation forms the Ings, a word dating back to Viking times which denotes areas of riverside water meadows which are subject to seasonal flooding. Mining subsidence in the area, particularly over the last 50 years, has meant that much of this land has now become permanently waterlogged, resulting in the loss of a considerable area of agricultural land. These wetlands have, however, provided a habitat for all forms of wildlife, the area between the river and the village of Fairburn being recognised as a nature reserve since 1957. Owned by the Coal Authority, formerly the National Coal Board, and leased to the RSPB, the 618-acre site was designated a statutory bird sanctuary in *1968* – 251 species of birds have been recorded, of which about 170 are regular visitors. Originally the land was acquired in order to provide space for tipping spoil from the collieries. The Coal Authority still retains tipping rights in the area but, in the interest of wildlife, has restricted its activities. Continued work on the spoil heaps prevents the natural establishment of vegetation, although tree planting on the mature spoil heaps between Castleford and Ferrybridge has proved most effective. This stretch of river, known as Five Mile Pond, traces a surprisingly pretty course as it meanders through banks now well established with silver birch, larch and alder. Just before the skew railway bridge are some sluice gates, installed in order to regulate the water levels within the washland areas of the reserve. These levels can vary considerably, often having a disastrous effect on nesting birds. Boaters should note that the only recognised access to the reserve is from the Fairburn to Allerton Bywater road to the north of Castleford. On no account should visitors try to gain access from the river, as the land here is the property of the Coal Authority and is prone to subsidence. The village of Fairburn is a good walk from Castleford but would provide a useful refreshment point for anyone visiting the bird sanctuary. On arrival at the three disused Ferrybridge Power Stations one is reminded of the river's industrial character. Originally seven cooling towers stood on the site, together with a vast tippler to lift the loaded coal pans out of the water, tipping them into what was then a vast storage site. Four cooling towers were demolished in *October 2019*, leaving just three, in case the site should ever be adapted for gas-fired electricity production. Coal has been transported to Ferrybridge from over 30 collieries throughout the north east and until fairly recently approximately 25 per cent of this was carried by water. Hargreaves alone carried well over 1,000,000 tons of coal to Ferrybridge C each year. Leaving behind the remaining gaunt buildings of the power stations, the graceful 18th-C

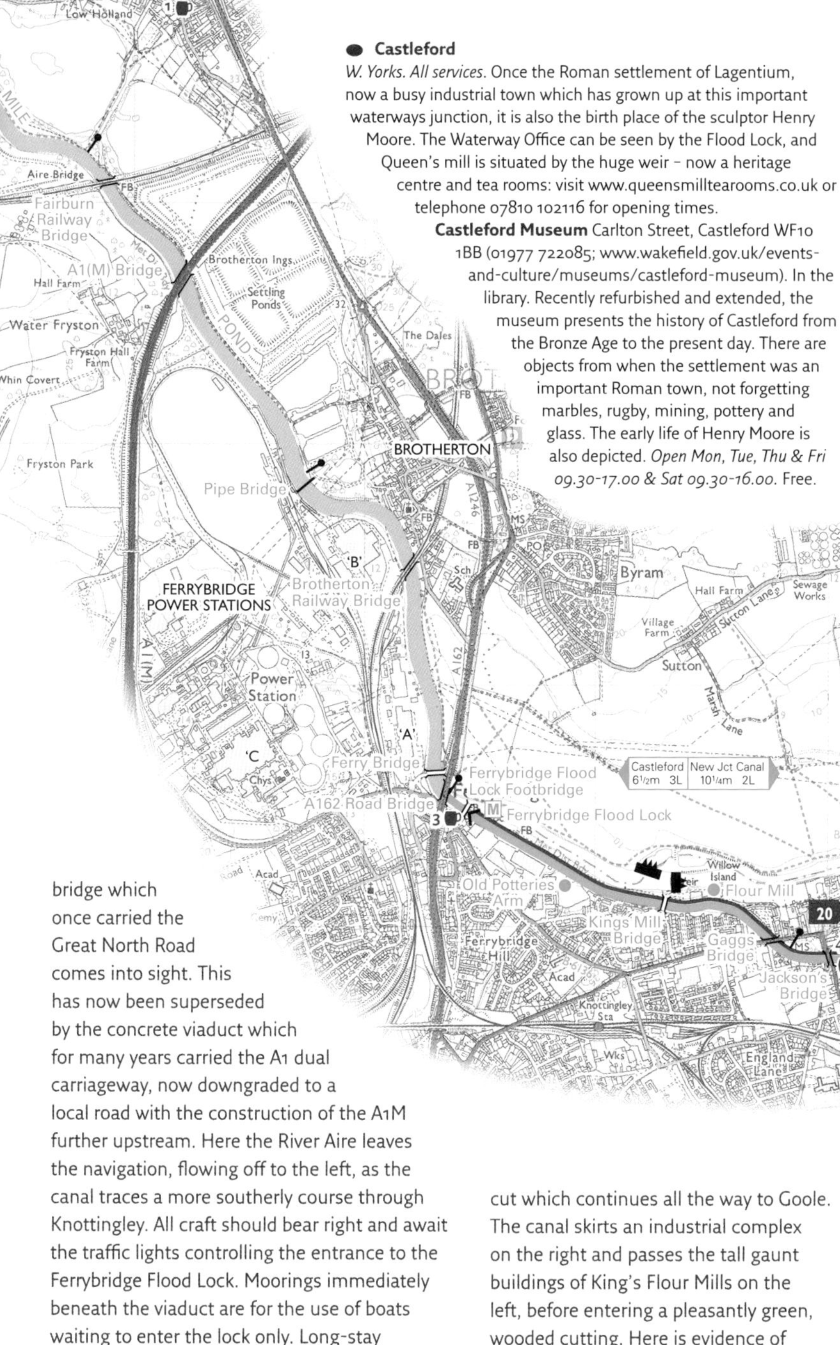

Castleford

W. Yorks. All services. Once the Roman settlement of Lagentium, now a busy industrial town which has grown up at this important waterways junction, it is also the birth place of the sculptor Henry Moore. The Waterway Office can be seen by the Flood Lock, and Queen's mill is situated by the huge weir – now a heritage centre and tea rooms: visit www.queensmilltearooms.co.uk or telephone 07810 102116 for opening times.

Castleford Museum Carlton Street, Castleford WF10 1BB (01977 722085; www.wakefield.gov.uk/events-and-culture/museums/castleford-museum). In the library. Recently refurbished and extended, the museum presents the history of Castleford from the Bronze Age to the present day. There are objects from when the settlement was an important Roman town, not forgetting marbles, rugby, mining, pottery and glass. The early life of Henry Moore is also depicted. *Open Mon, Tue, Thu & Fri 09.30-17.00 & Sat 09.30-16.00.* Free.

bridge which once carried the Great North Road comes into sight. This has now been superseded by the concrete viaduct which for many years carried the A1 dual carriageway, now downgraded to a local road with the construction of the A1M further upstream. Here the River Aire leaves the navigation, flowing off to the left, as the canal traces a more southerly course through Knottingley. All craft should bear right and await the traffic lights controlling the entrance to the Ferrybridge Flood Lock. Moorings immediately beneath the viaduct are for the use of boats waiting to enter the lock only. Long-stay *moorings* are to be found on the river to the left of the lock. Care should be exercised on this section as the river terminates in a weir. *Pubs and shops* in Ferrybridge can be reached from the lock. The navigation now enters an artificial cut which continues all the way to Goole. The canal skirts an industrial complex on the right and passes the tall gaunt buildings of King's Flour Mills on the left, before entering a pleasantly green, wooded cutting. Here is evidence of limestone quarrying over and above the need to make passage for the waterway and indeed the approaches to both Gaggs and Jacksons bridges remain as solid rock.

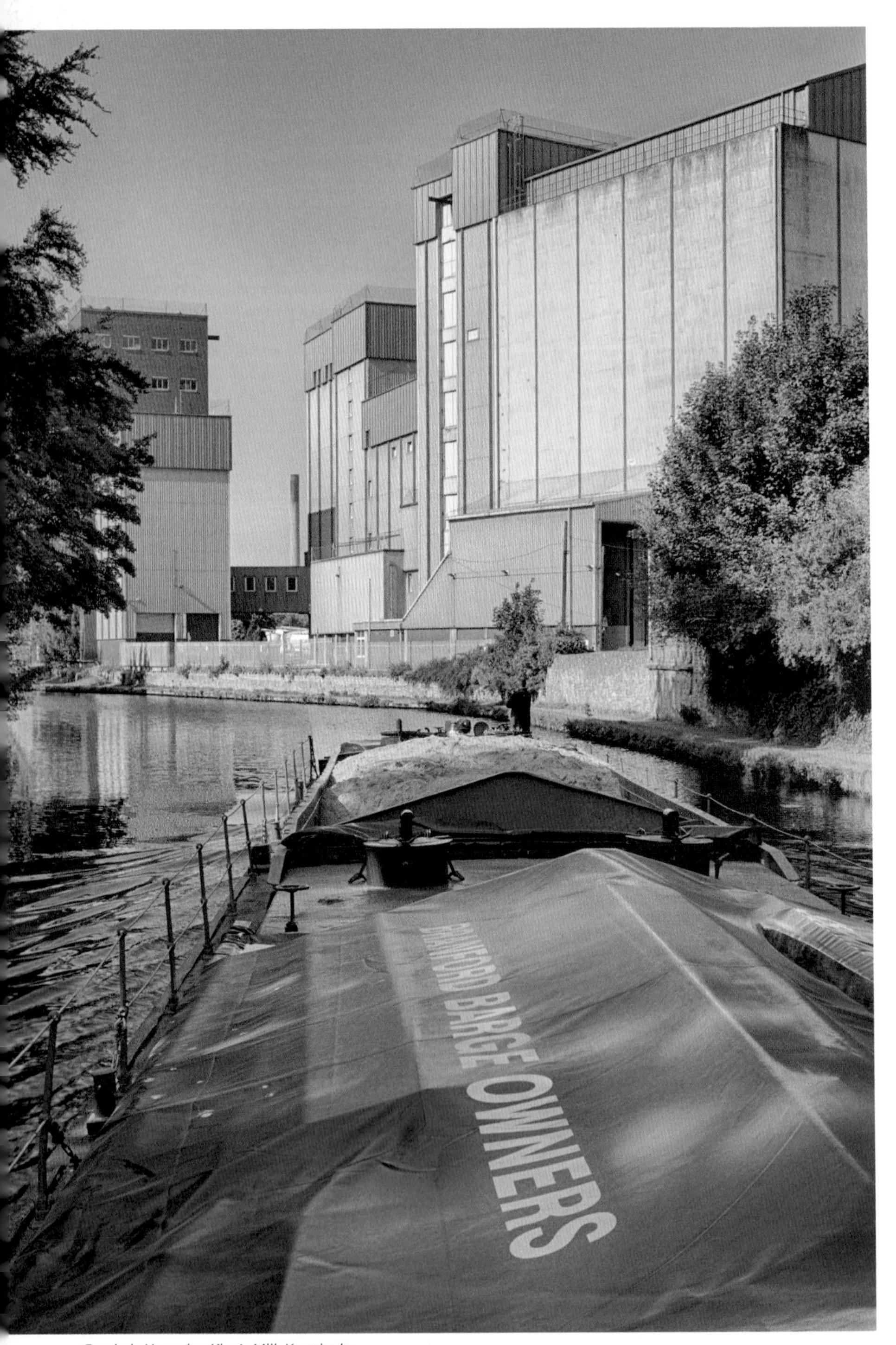

Farnhale H passing King's Mill, Knottingley

Fairburn

W. Yorks. Limestone and alabaster were once quarried here. There is also a record of a tunnel, 350yds long, which extended under the village connecting it to the river. Perched on the hillside and once divided by the busy Great North Road the village, now relatively peaceful, overlooks the Ings.

Ferrybridge

W. Yorks. Tel, stores, chemist, fish & chips, off-licence, butcher, baker, takeaway, garage. The town takes its name from the bridge over the River Aire which was built at the point where, for many centuries, travellers were ferried across the water. Possession of the site has been contested in the past by the Romans and much later by the armies of York and Lancaster. The area is still dominated by the remains of the three power stations that once supplied a significant proportion of the electricity distributed by the National Grid. Three of the seven cooling towers linger on against the day when a new gas-fired plant could be built on the site. The scale of the original, diminutive, brick-built Ferrybridge A power station, fronting the river, is a reminder of how our demand for energy has grown over the past 50 years.

NAVIGATIONAL NOTES

1 All the locks on the Aire & Calder are hydraulically controlled and are usually only operated by the mobile lock keepers for commercial traffic. Pleasure boaters can operate these locks themselves using a Watermate key. Always obey the traffic light signals (see page 15 for details).

2 Remember that this is a river navigation. Many of the locks are accompanied by large weirs, so keep a sharp lookout for the signs which direct you safely into the locks.

3 When the river level rises after prolonged heavy rain, the flood locks will be closed. Pleasure craft should stay put until they are advised by a lock keeper that it is safe to proceed.

4 This is a commercial waterway, used by 600-tonne tanker and sand barges. Keep a lookout for them, and give them a clear passage, especially on the many bends that the river describes on this stretch. Moor carefully on the canal sections of the navigation, using bollards or fixed rings rather than mooring stakes, since the wash from these craft can be substantial.

5 The Ferrybridge Power Stations are no longer in operation but navigators should still keep a good look out for 600-ton gravel barges operating along the Five Mile Pound, especially approaching the sharp bends that the river prescribes. Craft movement can be monitored on VHF Channel 74.

6 There is nowhere suitable to moor on this part of the river.

Boatyards

Ⓑ**Castleford Boatyard Ltd** The Boat Yard, Lock Lane, Navigation Road, Castleford WF10 2LG (01977 513111/07415 833995; www.castlefordboatyard.co.uk). D E Gas, solid fuel, short and long-term moorings, boat fitting out, engine sales and repairs (including outboards), boat sales and repairs, cranage, welding and fabrication, GRP repairs, winter storage, slipway, dry dock, wet dock, chandlery, DIY facilities, books, maps and gifts.

Pubs and Restaurants (page 17)

1 The Three Horseshoes Silver Street, Fairburn, Knottingley WF11 9JA (01977 672543; www.thethreehorseshoesfairburn.co.uk). Close to the Fairburn Ings Nature Reserve, this friendly pub serves real ales and freshly prepared meals *Mon-Thu L & E; Fri-Sun 12.00-21.00 (Sun 18.00).* Real ales and beer garden. Children welcome. Wi-Fi. *Open daily 12.00-23.00 (Sun 22.30).*

2 The Waggon & Horses Great North Road, Fairburn, Knottingley WF11 9JY (01977 675459). Welcoming, traditional real ale pub serving bar meals *L and E and Sun roasts.* Beer garden. Children welcome.

3 The Golden Lion 1The Square, Ferrybridge, Pontefract WF11 8ND (01977 674028). Riverside at Ferrybridge Lock. A friendly pub overlooking the River Aire. Real ale. Meals available *L.* Children welcome. Outside seating. B&B.

4 Steampacket Inn The Bendles, 2 Racca Green, Knottingley WF11 8AT (01977 672093; www.the-steam-packet-inn.business.site). Lively welcoming local serving real ale and food *daily until 19.00 (Sun 16.00).* Child- and dog-friendly. Outdoor play area. *Open 11.00-23.30 (Sat-Sun 00.00).*

WALKING AND CYCLING

At the present time there is no recognisable towpath beyond Bulholme Lock. It is possible to follow a series of footpaths and/or the minor road to Brotherton on the north bank of the river, to reach the canal towpath at Ferrybridge.

Whitley Bridge

Immediately through Shepherds Bridge the navigation forks: straight ahead leads to Bank Dole Lock into the River Aire and thence to the Selby Canal, while the main line bends right. Care should be exercised here on account of both moored commercial craft and laden barges approaching under Skew Bridge. They require first call on the available water to line up for Shepherds Bridge. For much of this journey the canal is steel-piled to accommodate the continuing mining subsidence, thus preventing the softening of its banks by vegetation. *Moorings, a picnic area* and *BBQ facilities* are available at Whitley Lock. Boaters should keep to the east to enter the lock and avoid the bypass weir.

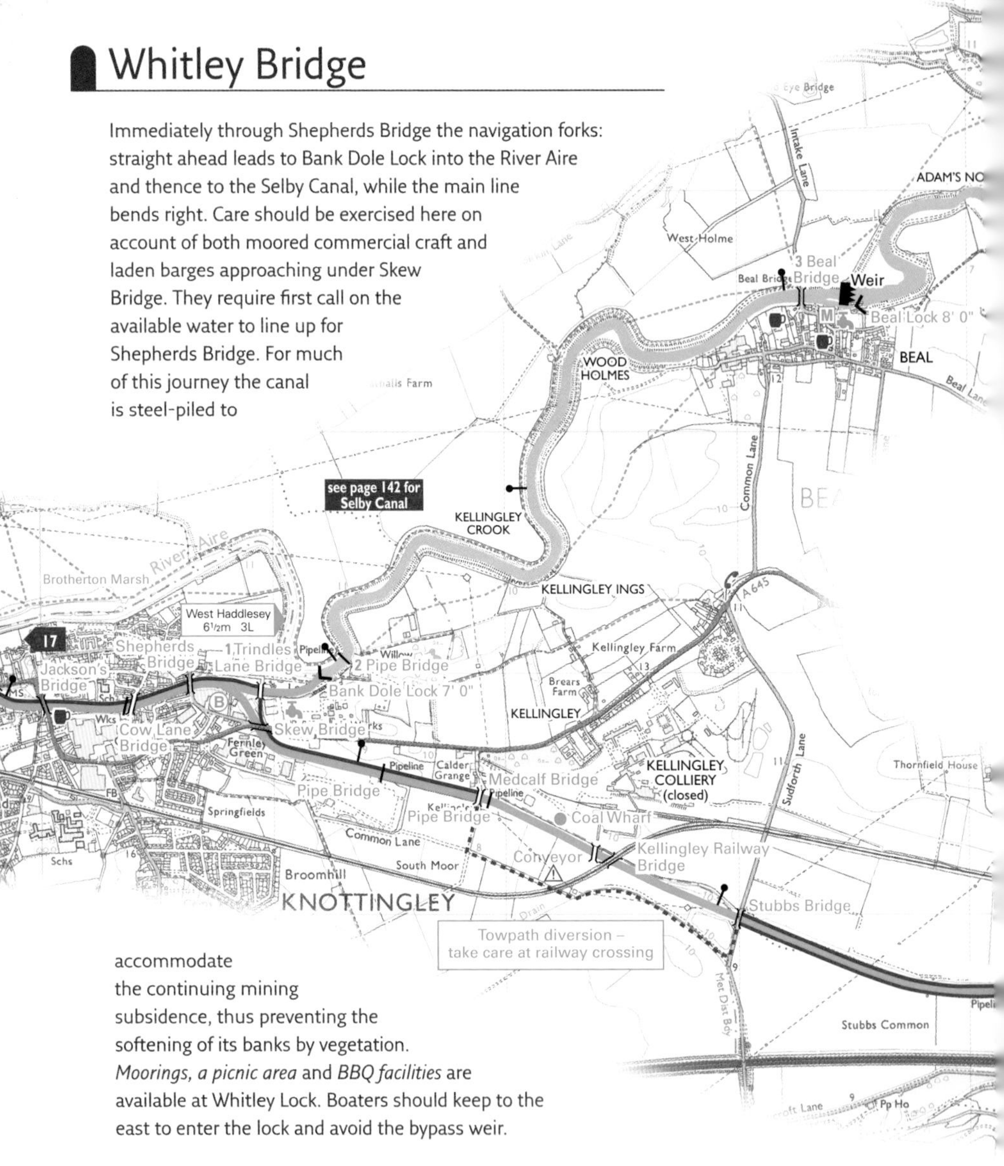

Knottingley

W. Yorks. All services. Once famous for the making of clay tobacco pipes and for its pottery, Knottingley now depends on the manufacture of synthetic chemicals, hydrocarbons, cosmetics and glassware. The local glassworks, its production now limited to scent bottles, once manufactured the majority of the glass containers found in our homes and supermarkets. The pretty church of St Botolph can be seen at the north end of Jacksons Bridge. The church has some impressive carvings around the doorway and an interesting campanile tower. The area next to the church was once the site of Knottingley Old Hall, an Elizabethan residence demolished in 1830 'for the sake of the limestone beneath it'.

Eggborough

N.Yorks. PO, tel, stores, chemist, butchers, off-licence, takeaway, fish & chips, station (limited service). The original settlement of Whitley Bridge has now been lost amidst a sprawling development of new housing in Low Eggborough. There are two feed mills in the area.

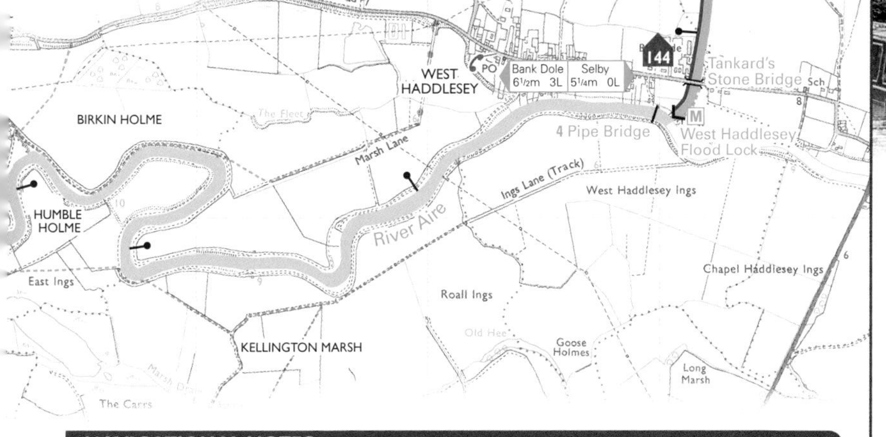

NAVIGATIONAL NOTES

1. **Lock operation** Lock gate and sluice operating pedestals are located adjacent to the upstream and downstream gates. You will need to insert a Watermate key into the pedestal to activate the system and allow use. Follow the step by step instructions on the operating panel in order to open the gates/sluices safely. Each pedestal can only be used to operate the adjacent gate/sluice.
2. **Emergency breakdown telephone** In the event of a breakdown in the operating system a red fault light will illuminate. Should this occur an emergency telephone is located in the front of the lockside control building. The cabinet door will automatically unlock or use your Watermate key. Dial 0800 47 999 47 and advise of your location and fault details. Remain by the telephone in case the duty engineer calls back for further information.

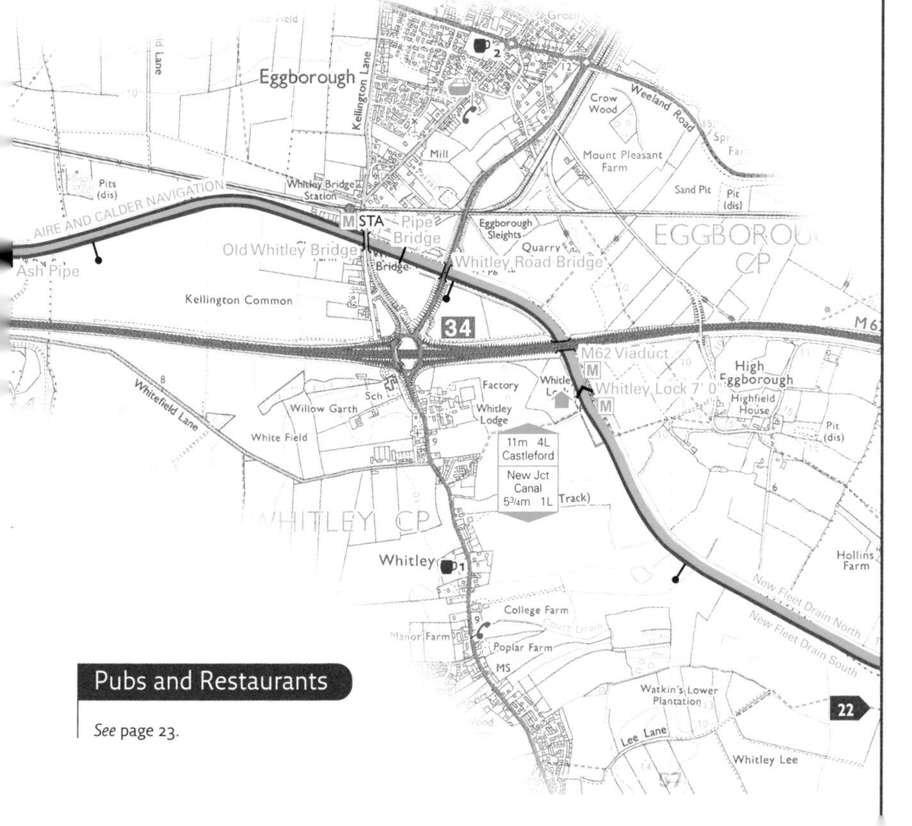

Pubs and Restaurants

See page 23.

Pollington

Soon Heck Bridge appears, giving access to a local *pub*. There used to be a quaint village shop, where only the sign outside gave the visitor any indication of its function. Once inside it soon became apparent that the shop was no more than a room set aside in someone's house. Sadly this is yet another whimsical feature of English village life that has passed away. Just beyond Heck Bridge is the home of the South Yorkshire Boat Club, making use of the basin once excavated to provide transhipment of stone to Goole from the local quarry. Immediately beyond the village the east coast main railway from London to Edinburgh crosses the navigation. Now electrified, this line carries the Class 800 series Hitachi Avanti trainsets capable of hauling passenger trains at speeds of up to 140mph yet still restricted to 125mph pending a viable signalling system and an ever-receding line upgrade. To the north stand the twin chimneys of the disused quarry, now the site of a concrete pipe works. The navigation now adopts a fairly bleak and monotonous course through a flat but fertile landscape. Trees are scarce, and hedges and livestock are nowhere to be seen. There are numerous drainage ditches. The straggling village of Pollington lies to the north of Pollington Bridge where there is now just a single *pub*. The school and a brick-built chapel with a bell tower are on the south side of the bridge. To the west of the village, facing the canal, stands Pollington Hall, an attractive 18th-C house with pleasingly proportioned narrow windows and a door pediment. Beyond the lock is Manor Farm where there is evidence of a moat. These buildings, along with Pollington Grange to the south of the navigation, indicate a former prosperity. At Pollington Lock the lock keeper's pretty cottage is one of the best examples of its type, with attractively rounded brick arches above the windows and a particularly deep overhang to the roof at the gable ends. Beyond Crow Croft Bridge the demolished abutments of an old

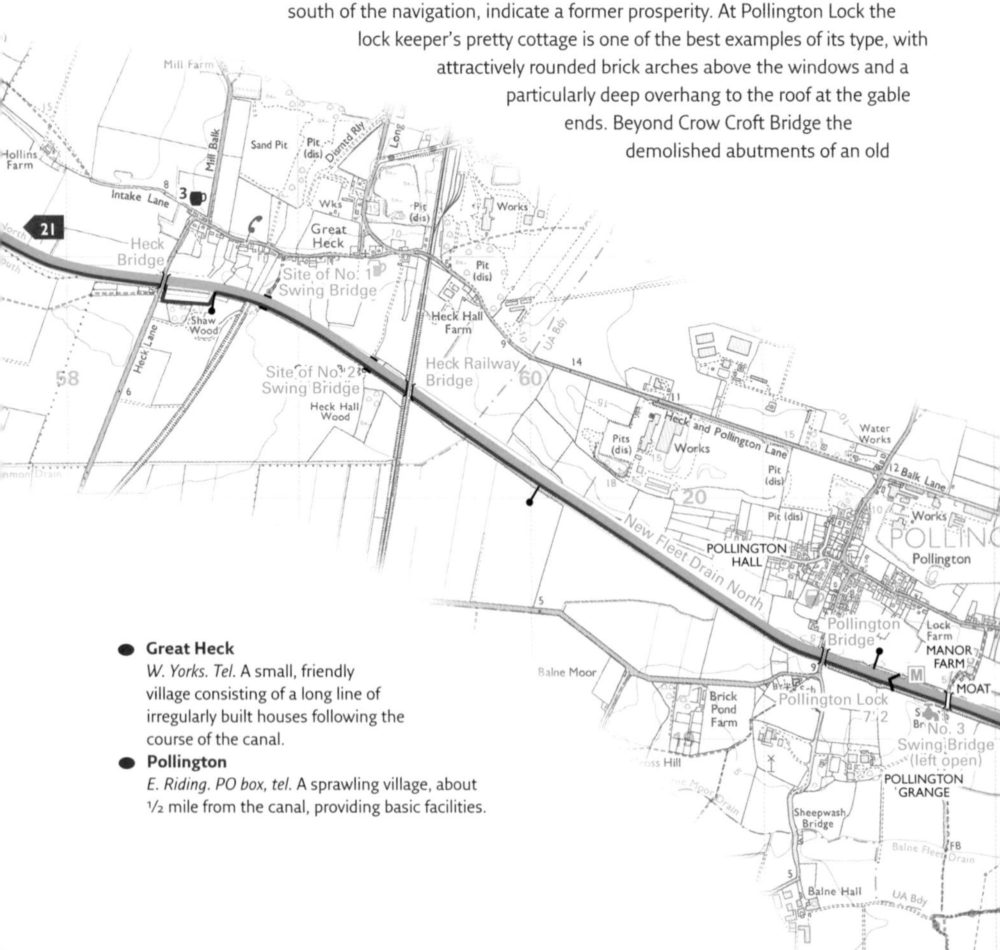

- **Great Heck**
  W. Yorks. Tel. A small, friendly village consisting of a long line of irregularly built houses following the course of the canal.
- **Pollington**
  E. Riding. PO box, tel. A sprawling village, about 1/2 mile from the canal, providing basic facilities.

railway bridge can be seen, unusual in that it once pivoted upwards at one end. At this point the River Went draws close and follows the line of the navigation towards Goole. The dinghies of the Beaver Sailing Club at Southfield Reservoir add an unexpected and welcome splash of colour to the landscape. The 120-acre reservoir, built at the turn of the century, marks the beginning of the New Junction Canal leading south to Sheffield. Its construction provided a water supply to meet the needs of the much larger locks installed on the navigation, and it effectively maintains the water levels of the docks at Goole.

NAVIGATIONAL NOTES

1 *See* page 21 for details of self-operation of locks.
2 Heck Bridge is reputed to be suffering from mining subsidence and skippers of craft with an air draft greater than 10' 3" should consult the Boaters Guide available on www.canalrivertrust.org.uk.

Pubs and Restaurants (pages 21-23)

1 George & Dragon Doncaster Road, Goole DN14 0HY (01977 277374; www.georgeanddragondn14.co.uk). 1 mile south west of Whitley Lock. A family-friendly pub that prides itself on fresh food based on locally sourced ingredients, available *daily L and E*. Real ale and real cider. Dog- and family-friendly, patio garden. Sports TV. Wi-Fi. *Open daily 12.00-23.00 (Sat 01.00).*

2 Horse & Jockey Weeland Road, Eggborough, Goole DN14 0RX (01977 661295; www.facebook.com/horseandjockeynewpage). Family-run local serving real ales and homemade food *L and E. Regular* quiz nights and live TV sports coverage. Children welcome. *Open Mon-Fri 16.00-23.00 & Sat-Sun 12.00-00.00.*

3 The Bay Horse Main Street, Great Heck DN14 0BQ (01977 301468; www.bayhorsegreatheck.co.uk). 300yds north of Heck Bridge. A cosy pub, popular with boaters, serving real ale and excellent homemade food *Fri-Sat E & Sun L*. Children and dogs welcome, patio seating. Real fires and Wi-Fi. *Open Mon-Sat mid-afternoon and Sun 12.00-20.00.*

4 The King's Head 6 Main Street, Pollington, Goole DN14 0DN (01405 861507; www.kingsheadpollington.co.uk). At the east end of the village. Friendly pub serving real ale and highly-thought-of food *Tue-Sat 17.30-20.30; Sat 12.00-14.00 & Sun 12.00-16.30.* Children welcome, garden. Traditional pub games. Wi-Fi. B&B. *Open Mon-Fri 17.00-23.00 (Fri 00.00) & Sat-Sun 12.00-00.00 (Sun 23.00).*

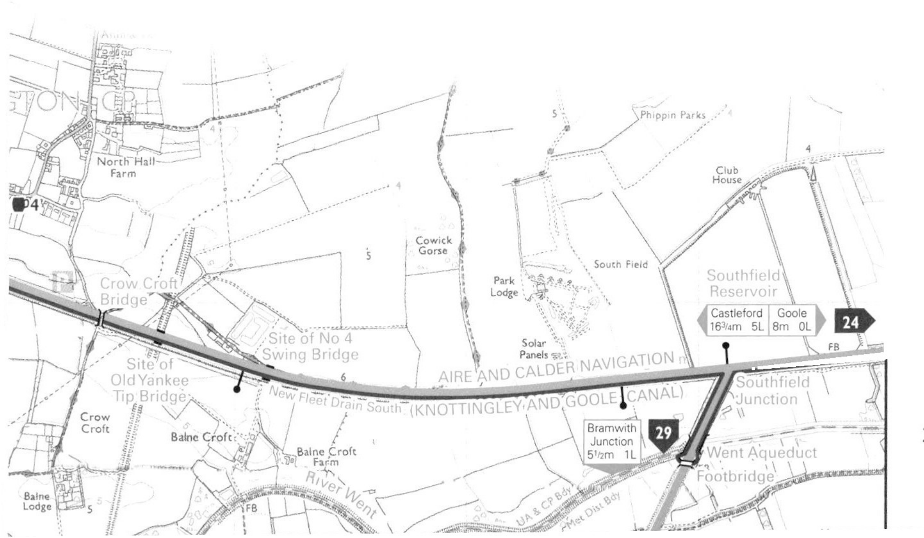

Rawcliffe Bridge

Beyond the turning to Keadby and Sheffield, up the unerringly straight New Junction Canal, the Aire & Calder performs an exaggerated dogleg and then sets off on an equally straight course for its terminus in Goole Docks. This manoeuvre is brought about by the appearance of the River Don from the south, joined near Beever Bridge by the diminutive River Went. In times of high rainfall the Went becomes more aggressive, flooding the surrounding farmland and leaving large deposits of silt in its wake. The turf-growing enterprise in this area bears witness to the inherent fertility of this regular fluvial performance and to man's ability to capitalise on one of nature's excesses. Having swung hard left, the boater is now in alignment with the Dutch River, the artificial channel cut by Cornelius Vermuyden to contain the River Don's previous exuberance. Before his intervention the Don had two mouths: one across the Isle of Axholme into the Trent near Trent Falls and a second into the River Aire, little more than a mile north of here. Were the boater not to swing right, under New Bridge, but to carry on straight ahead (with the addition of the odd wiggle or two) he would, in fact, be following the Don's old course. As the tidal Dutch River, Vermuyden's Don now accompanies the canal all the way to Goole.

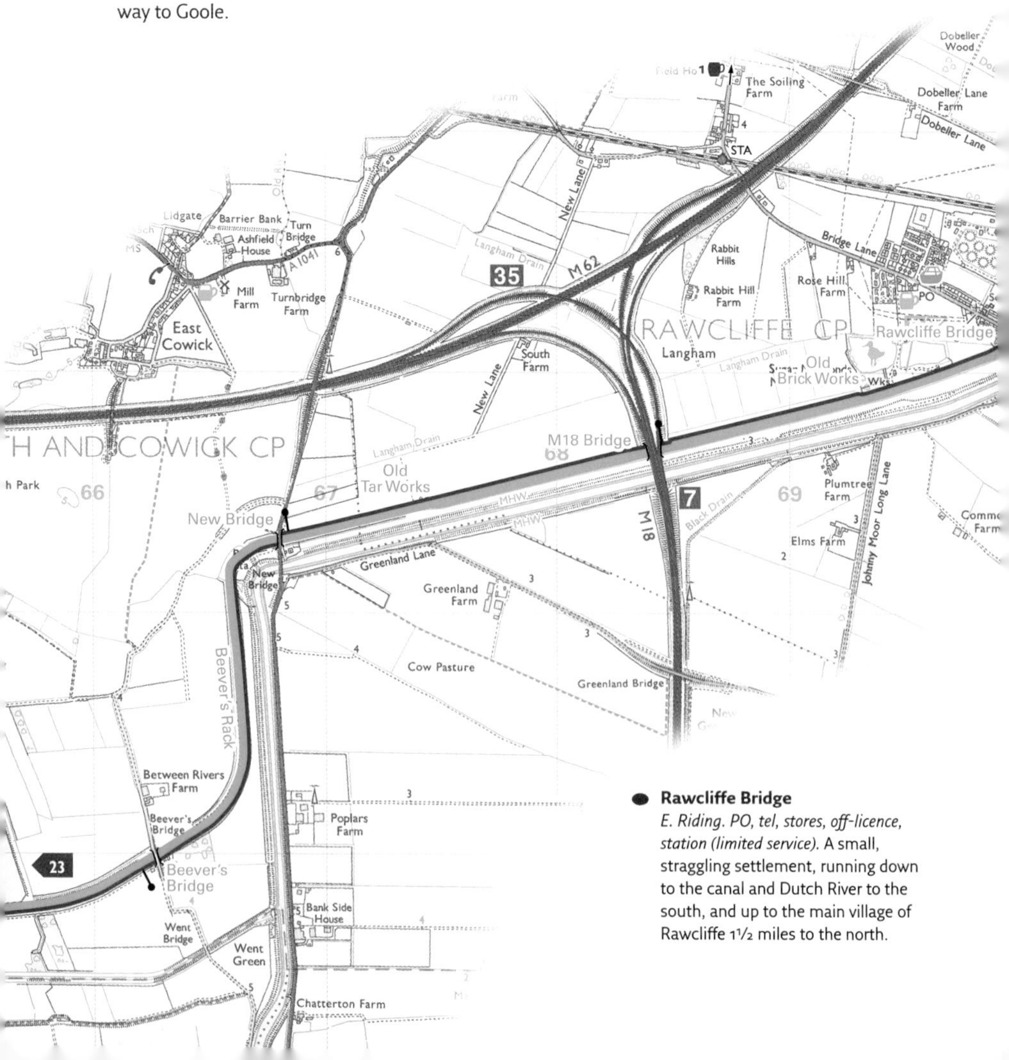

23

Rawcliffe Bridge
E. Riding. PO, tel, stores, off-licence, station (limited service). A small, straggling settlement, running down to the canal and Dutch River to the south, and up to the main village of Rawcliffe 1½ miles to the north.

Both navigations – the Dutch River is used by experienced skippers – duck under the M18 (a sheltered 'berth' much fancied by local barge owners for painting their boats) and passes the site of both an old tar works and of a disused brickworks. Both works used to rely heavily on the canal for raw materials and the export of their finished products.

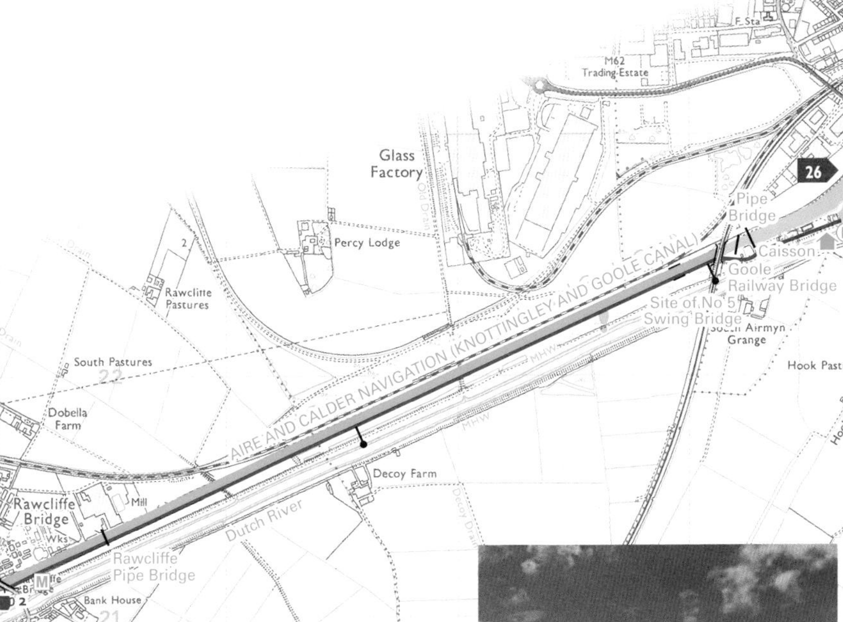

Pubs and Restaurants

1 Jemmy Hirst at the Rose & Crown 26, Riverside, Rawcliffe DN14 8RN (01405 837902; www.facebook.com/JemmyHirst2019). Approximately 1 mile north from the canal, through Rawcliffe Bridge and well worth the walk. Boldly declaring that 'No one is perfect but if you're from Yorkshire you're pretty close' this traditional, award-winning pub serves well-kept real ales and occupies an attractive location beside the River Aire. Dog- and family-friendly. Riverside beer garden. Traditional pub games and real ales. *Open Mon-Wed 16.00-22.00; Thu-Fri 16.00-23.00 & Sat-Sun 12.00-23.00.*

2 The Black Horse Hotel Bridge Street, Rawcliffe Bridge, Goole, DN14 8PN (07947 867966; www.theblackhorsehotelgoole.com). Sandwiched between the canal and Dutch River this pub has re-invented itself as a hotel. Family-friendly. Wi-Fi. B&B.

Goole Docks

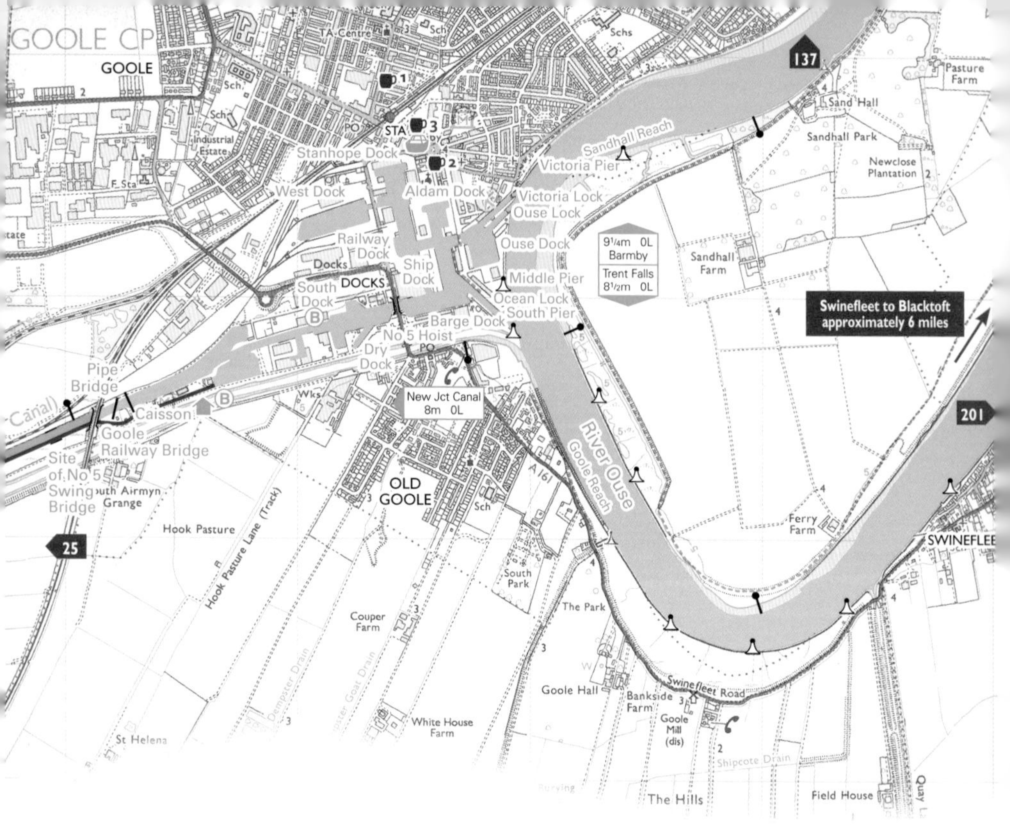

Goole

Immediately before the railway bridge, marking the effective start of Goole Docks, is the site of the old No 5 swing bridge, replaced by a device replicating the stop planks found on narrow canals. A 'curtain' resting in the bottom of the waterway was winched across from one bank to the other. It was originally installed at the outbreak of World War II in anticipation of the docks being bombed. Once through the bridge, it can be plainly seen that there is far more boat capacity than there is waterborne traffic to fill it. To the north is a small basin, the remains of what was a proposed connection to the West Dock. It was here that Humber keels removed their lee-boards, masts and cog boats before heading inland. Fuel barges used to berth beside a boatyard in the first basin on the left (known as the 'dog and duck'), followed by John Branford's sand barges (cargoes from Hull to Leeds) at the aggregate wharf, and the occasional Waddington's boat. On the right is a concrete plant, commercial wharves and finally William Bartholomew's No 5 Boat Hoist, now restored. Bartholomew devised the system of trains of floating tubs – known as Tom Puddings – towed in a long snaking line (as many as 19 at a time) behind a tug, to be up-ended into a coaster, via the Boat Hoist, on their arrival in the docks.

Boatyards

Ⓑ **Goole Boathouse** The Timber Pond, Dutch Riverside, Goole DN14 5TB (01405 763985; www.gooleboathouse.co.uk). **DE** Gas, pump out, secure overnight and long-term moorings *(6' max draught)*, chandlery, dry dock, slipway, winter storage, engine repairs, blacking, welding, licensed clubhouse.

Ⓑ **Viking Marine** Albert Street, Goole DN14 5SY (01405 765737; www.vikingmarine.co.uk). **D** Gas, mooring, boat sales, 16-tonne hoist, winter storage, maintenance and repair service, chandlery, Wi-Fi. Approved Honda main dealer (outboards and generators). *Closed Sun.*

NAVIGATIONAL NOTES

1. There are CRT visitor moorings at the sanitary station, by Goole Boathouse.
2. At the west end of South Dock the navigation ceases to be the responsibility of CRT and comes under the jurisdiction of Associated British Ports (ABP). They may be contacted on VHF radio channel 14 – call *Goole Docks* – or by telephoning 01482 327171. **Boats using the tideway and Ocean Lock must carry VHF radio and have at least two persons on board.**
3. Beyond this point ocean-going shipping is manoeuvring and contact must be made with Ocean Lock Control before continuing.
4. Overnight mooring in this area will incur a substantial charge and temporary mooring, whilst awaiting a lock or bridge swing is only permitted if the crew are in attendance. Mooring on any pier whilst on the tideway (unless awaiting a lock) will also incur a charge.
5. Headroom under the swing bridge is approximately 11' 6" (the level of the dock can vary) and contact should be made with the lock keeper to arrange for it to be opened.
6. Lock operating times are *2½ hours before high tide and 1 hour after* for which no charge is made. Outside these times special pens are always available on payment of a fee, which is in turn dependent on the time of day or night.
7. The lock keeper will willingly offer advice and information on navigating the tideway. For his part the boater must inform ABP that he is on the river and make his position known. ABP maintain a continuous watch on Channel 14. **At high tide the River Ouse is a busy navigation, carrying ocean-going shipping.**
8. It is approximately 7 miles from Swinefleet to Trent Falls. ABP's jurisdiction extends from the mouth of the Humber to Gainsborough on the Trent and Skelton Railway Swing Bridge (aka Hook Railway Bridge) on the Ouse – approximately ¾ mile up river from Goole. The bridge keeper can be contacted on VHF channel 9 – or by telephoning 01430 430012. Above this point the river falls under the jurisdiction of CRT who publish useful guidance for boaters at www.canalrivertrust.org.uk/about-us/our-regions/north-east-waterways/planning-a-safe-passage-on-river-tees-and-river-ouse. This includes contact details for all moveable bridges and the manned locks.

Goole

E. Riding. All services. When the Aire & Calder Navigation applied for an Act to build a canal from Knottingley to Goole in 1819, Goole was no more than a few cottages scattered around the marshes on the banks of the Ouse. Work commenced on cutting the canal in 1822 and by the following year a new town was developing rapidly as dwellings were built for the employees of the company. By 1828 foreign trade had begun with Hamburg and the local people entertained themselves by going down to the docks in the evening to await the arrival of foreign vessels on the spring tides. It is said of Goole that it was 'born under Victoria and died with her'. The docks are still very much the focal point of Goole, handling cargoes from Europe and Scandinavia. Lock Hill, near the Leisure Centre, is a good vantage point for watching vessels manoeuvring.

Goole Leisure Centre North Street, Goole DN14 5QX (01405 769005; www.eastriding.gov.uk/leisure/leisure-centres-and-fitness/leisure-centres). Excellent facilities for the whole family.

Goole Museum and Art Gallery Carlisle Street, Goole DN14 5DS (01405 768963; www.eastridingmuseums.co.uk/find-a-museum/?entry=goole_museum). The museum house an interesting exhibition depicting the development of Goole and the surrounding area, with an emphasis on the docks and shipping. *Open Tue, Thu, Fri 10.00–17.00, Wed 10.00–19.00, Sat 09.00–16.00.* Free.

Pubs and Restaurants

1 The Tom Pudding 20 Pasture Road, Goole DN14 6EZ (07762 525114; www.facebook.com/TomPuddingMicropub). Cosy micropub with exposed brick walls and ceiling beams, this ex-newsagents serves four rotating real ales (always one gluten free) and three ciders. Dog-friendly and traditional pub games. Acoustic live music *Thu. Open Mon-Thu 16.00-23.00 & Fri-Sun 12.00-23.00 (Sun 14.00).*

2 The Drake 58 Aire Street, Goole DN14 5QE (01405 767444). Originally a late 19th-C bank, this recently restored pub serves real cider. The handsome interior features Minton tiles, striking glasswork, replica Venetian ceilings and the original joinery. Beer garden, family-friendly, newspapers, pool, sports TV and Wi-Fi. B&B. *Open Sun-Fri 11.00-23.00 (Fri 02.00) & Sat 16.00-02.00.*

3 City and County Market Square, Goole DN14 5DR (01405 722600; www.jdwetherspoon.co.uk/home/pubs/city-and-county). Bustling, value-for-money establishment in the town's former HSBC bank premises. Wide range of real ales and inexpensive food available *from breakfast through 'til 00.00.*

See also **Pubs and Restaurants** on page 136

New Junction Canal

The New Junction Canal provides a link between the Aire & Calder and the South Yorkshire Navigations and was one of the last canals to be constructed in this country. The waterway is 5½ miles long and completely straight all the way, the monotony being broken only by a series of bridges and a lock. There are aqueducts at each end of the long corridor formed by the navigation, the first carrying the canal over the River Went; the more southerly over the River Don. Two smaller aqueducts are to be found at Chequer Lane and Westfields. Although the countryside here is flat, it is not without character. *Moorings* are available beside Sykehouse Lift Bridge and from here the village of Sykehouse and its *pub* may be reached, approximately ¾ mile to the west of the canal. Further *moorings* are available close to Sykehouse Lock. Beyond Top Lane Lift Bridge is Low Lane Swing Bridge, carrying the road leading into Kirk Bramwith, with its interesting Norman church. Then the Don aqueduct appears. It presents a rather forbidding feature, bracketed at either end by large guillotine gates, designed to contain the waters of the river when in flood, preventing them from inundating the navigation. Passing boats, although protected by a barrier on one side, have no more than railings on the other side, to prevent their descent into the river below. Once over the aqueduct, the canal is joined by the Stainforth & Keadby section of the navigation meeting at a very fine angle from the left. Its junction is masked by trees growing on the narrow spit of land formed between the two canals.

NAVIGATIONAL NOTES

1. All locks and moveable bridges can be boater-operated using a Watermate key.
2. Sykehouse Lock: when locking upstream keep away from the top gates to avoid excessive turbulence. Similarly, boats below the lock should keep well clear of the bottom gates when it is emptying. The swing bridge is interlocked with the operation of the lock so follow the instructions on the pedestal.

Sykehouse
S. Yorks. PO box, tel. A linear settlement which sprawls extensively to either side of the canal. A pub can be found to the west where there is attractive housing, much of which has been thoughtfully constructed of old brick. Holy Trinity Church has an attractive brick tower which was added to the original stone structure in 1724. The stone was subsequently replaced by a Victorian brick edifice. The village virtually closes down during the winter months.

Pubs and Restaurants

1 **The Old George Inn** Broad Lane, Sykehouse DN14 9AU (01405 785635; www.facebook.com/The-Old-George-Inn-342486445899916). It is a brave man who would interfere with a Yorkshireman's cricket! Once the home of the local cricket team, the adjoining field now contains an adventure playground which has made this a popular pub with families from the surrounding towns and villages. The building dates back some 500 years, the pub having been formed from what was once a terrace of cottages consisting over the years of a shop, a dame school, a farrier, a butcher and a slaughter house. The original wheel for hoisting the animals aloft for slaughter still hangs in the dining area. Real ale and real cider are served here and food *L and E, daily.* Large patio seating area and children's play area. Open fires and Wi-Fi. Also traditional pub games, newspapers and sports TV. Camping. *Open daily 12.00-00.00 (Sun 11.30).*

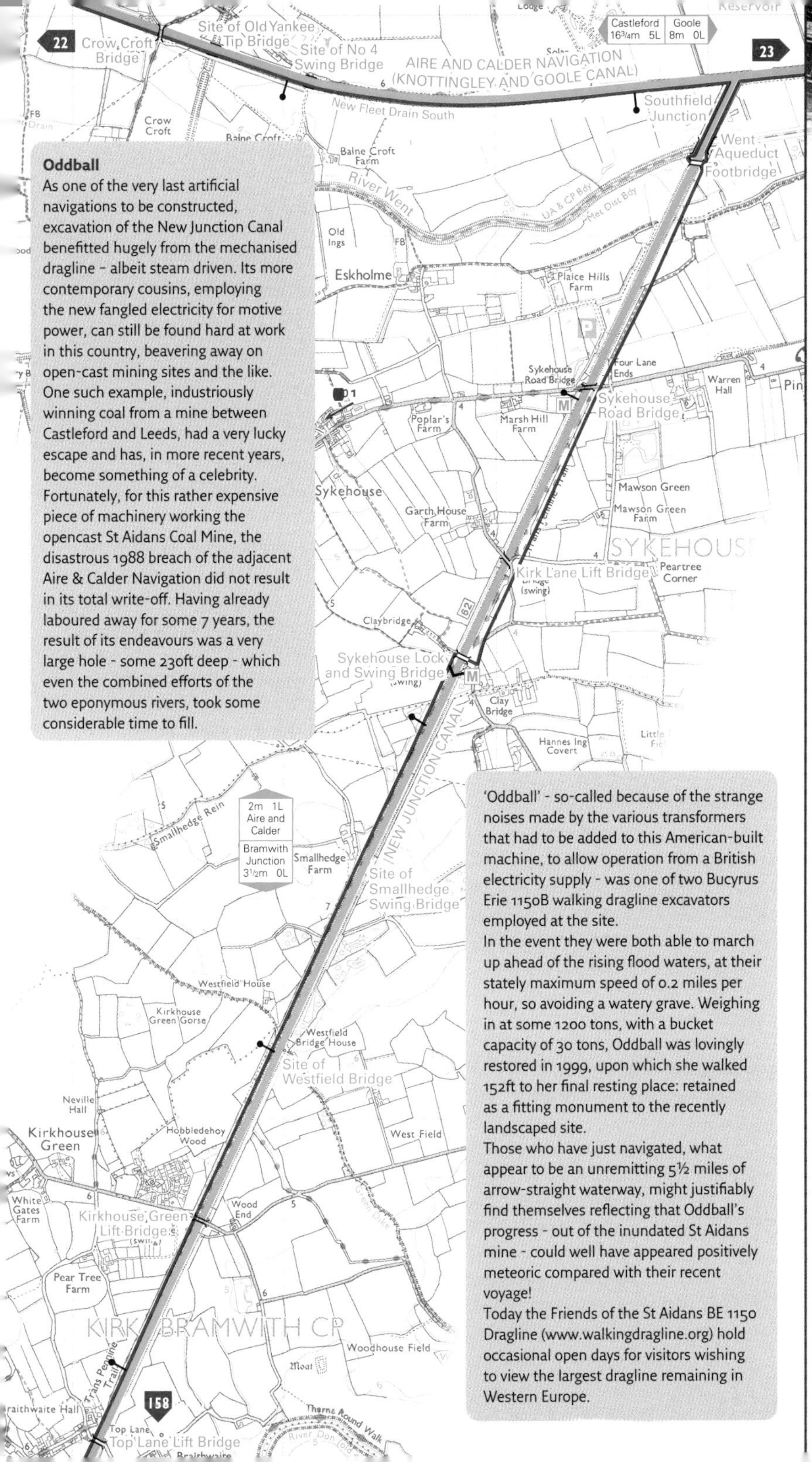

Oddball

As one of the very last artificial navigations to be constructed, excavation of the New Junction Canal benefitted hugely from the mechanised dragline - albeit steam driven. Its more contemporary cousins, employing the new fangled electricity for motive power, can still be found hard at work in this country, beavering away on open-cast mining sites and the like. One such example, industriously winning coal from a mine between Castleford and Leeds, had a very lucky escape and has, in more recent years, become something of a celebrity. Fortunately, for this rather expensive piece of machinery working the opencast St Aidans Coal Mine, the disastrous 1988 breach of the adjacent Aire & Calder Navigation did not result in its total write-off. Having already laboured away for some 7 years, the result of its endeavours was a very large hole - some 230ft deep - which even the combined efforts of the two eponymous rivers, took some considerable time to fill.

'Oddball' - so-called because of the strange noises made by the various transformers that had to be added to this American-built machine, to allow operation from a British electricity supply - was one of two Bucyrus Erie 1150B walking dragline excavators employed at the site.

In the event they were both able to march up ahead of the rising flood waters, at their stately maximum speed of 0.2 miles per hour, so avoiding a watery grave. Weighing in at some 1200 tons, with a bucket capacity of 30 tons, Oddball was lovingly restored in 1999, upon which she walked 152ft to her final resting place: retained as a fitting monument to the recently landscaped site.

Those who have just navigated, what appear to be an unremitting 5½ miles of arrow-straight waterway, might justifiably find themselves reflecting that Oddball's progress - out of the inundated St Aidans mine - could well have appeared positively meteoric compared with their recent voyage!

Today the Friends of the St Aidans BE 1150 Dragline (www.walkingdragline.org) hold occasional open days for visitors wishing to view the largest dragline remaining in Western Europe.

CHESTERFIELD CANAL

MAXIMUM DIMENSIONS

Length: 72'
Beam: 6' 10"
Headroom: 7' 1"
Draught: 2' 6"
(Craft of 7' 6" beam, on leaving the River Trent, *may* be able to proceed as far as Clayworth, depending on the height of the superstructure - Bridge 78 is the most restrictive overall structure.)

MANAGER

0303 040 4040;
enquiries.yorkshirenortheast@canalrivertrust.org.uk

MILEAGE

CHESTERFIELD to:
Staveley: 5 miles
Killamarsh: 10 miles
Norwood Tunnel West End: 12 miles
Norwood Tunnel East End: 14 miles
Ryton Aqueduct: 17½ miles
Worksop Town Lock: 20 miles
Osberton Lock: 23½ miles
Retford Town Lock: 30½ miles
Clayworth Bridge: 36 miles
Drakeholes Tunnel: 39 miles
WEST STOCKWITH, junction with River Trent: 45½ miles

Locks: 65 (Nos 6–19 derelict)

The Chesterfield Canal was initially surveyed in 1768 by John Varley to follow a line between Chesterfield and Bawtry on the River Idle, as an improvement on the trade route already in use. However, both Worksop and Retford were anxious to benefit from the proposed waterway, so Varley undertook a second survey a year later along a route to West Stockwith that bypassed the Idle altogether.

In 1769 James Brindley who had, due to pressure of other work, delegated the initial survey to Varley, called a public meeting at the Red Lion in Worksop. Here he proposed a draft line, terminating near Gainsborough and costing £105,000. This was later re-amended, on the grounds of cost and speed of construction, to meet the Trent at West Stockwith.

Work started in October 1771 with John Varley as resident engineer, Brindley being still too busy with other schemes to be permanently on site. Most of the work, including digging the 2893yds long Norwood Tunnel, constructing the summit level reservoir and building the lock flights, was let as separate contracts and carried out by individual contractors. Brindley's method was to make each section of the canal navigable as soon as it was completed to enable the company to benefit from the carriage of the heavy construction materials.

Brindley's death in September 1772 was a sad blow to the project and led to Varley being placed in overall charge of this, his first large project. Ultimately Hugh Henshall, Brindley's brother-in-law, was made inspector of works, later to become chief engineer with a salary of £250 per annum. In the following year he discovered work, carried out by John Varley's father and two brothers, in the construction of Norwood Tunnel, to be unsatisfactory. Soon other examples of dubious contractual arrangements and slack management came to light, all reflecting badly on the Varley family. The extent of John Varley's complicity in these matters remains to this day a matter for debate.

On 4 June 1777 the canal was officially opened from West Stockwith to Chesterfield. Norwood Tunnel caused problems from the outset, as did the shortage of water to the summit pound. Boats travelling less than 12 miles empty, or lightly laden, were penalised when using a lock. Over the next 25 years a more satisfactory solution was provided by the building of three large reservoirs at Killamarsh, Woodhall and Harthill.

As had always been envisaged by the canal's promoters, coal was the principal cargo carried, followed by stone, corn, lime, lead, timber and iron. Pottery and ale were also regular cargoes. Traffic peaked at over 200,000 tons in 1848, when records show the average load as 22 tons.

Early in 1841 a cargo of Anston stone, bound for the construction of the new Houses of Parliament, was carried for transhipment at West Stockwith, the first of approximately 250,000 tons despatched over a period of four years. As always, amalgamation with a railway company, in this case the Manchester & Lincoln Union Railway, led to a steady decline in the canal's fortunes and a reduction in maintenance. By 1904 it was reported that the minimum headroom in Norwood Tunnel was reduced to 4' 10", owing to subsidence, while a roof collapse on 18th October 1907 led to its final closure. Between the wars, now under London & North Eastern Railway (LNER) ownership, the canal was reasonably maintained, while the tidal lock into the Trent was enlarged and repaired in 1923-5. Attempts were also made to reduce the weed which had appeared in 1852 and remains, to some extent, a problem today. The navigation was temporarily resuscitated by the transport of munitions during World War II, but traffic virtually came to an end in 1955 when the small trade from Walkeringham brickworks (near Gringley) to the Trent finished. One cargo that did linger on into the early 1960s was that of warp: a fine natural silt dredged from the Trent at Idle Mouth and used as a metal polishing material in the Sheffield cutlery trade. To the end all boats - known as 'Cuckoos' - remained horse-drawn.

WALKING AND CYCLING

To find the start of the navigation in Chesterfield, take the B6543 Brimington Road north east from its junction with Malkin Street, close to the Railway Station's main forecourt. Where this road crosses the river, walkers can access the towpath to the north west via Holbeck Close. Cyclists should, however, continue along Brimington Road to a point just south of the sharp bend under the railway. Here a waymarked path leads down to the junction of river and canal. From here the towpath is in excellent condition for both walkers and cyclists to a point just north of Staveley, as it is both the Cuckoo Way and a spur leading down from the Trans Pennine Trail - National Cycle Network Route 67. The waymarked Bluebank Loop, commencing at bridge 3, offers a very worthwhile diversion, or a separate walk in its own right. This is depicted on a most attractive, incised interpretation board. To the east of Eckington Road Bridge, the trail divides, with a second spur heading south whilst the main route turns almost due north. The Cuckoo Way follows the line of the canal in a north easterly direction and this section is only suitable for walkers. Cyclists should use the trail at least as far as Renishaw. For further details on the coast to coast Trans Pennine Trail telephone (01226) 772574 or visit www.transpenninetrail.org.uk.

North of Barlborough Road Bridge the Trans Pennine Trail still remains the easiest way of following the line of the canal - part in water, part infilled - certainly as far as cyclists are concerned. At Forge Bridge the line can be followed east into Killamarsh, as far as Bridge Street, without too much difficulty. At this point the faint-hearted are best advised to head north to Sheffield Road (the B6058) and then turn right and rejoin the somewhat overgrown towpath towards the top of the hill at Nether Green, where a Cuckoo Way finger post points due north. The purist may wish to stick, as far as possible, to the old line of the canal, avoiding the housing development alongside Kirkcroft Avenue and, via a section of Pringle Drive, meeting the aforementioned finger post at Belk Lane Lock (now very much an ornamental garden feature). At Norwood the path, although on private property, is a public right of way and leads to a stile above the tunnel mouth. From here, skirt along the right hand field boundary to a tunnel under the motorway, beyond which the path runs steadily downhill, finally meeting Hard Lane beyond newly landscaped open-cast workings. It continues east of the road, crossing a meadow to rejoin the fully navigable waterway at the eastern tunnel portal. When in doubt look out for the Cuckoo Way waymarking.

Chesterfield

The canal itself begins at Tapton Mill Bridge, where it leaves the River Rother above a weir. The original intention was to cross over the river at this point and continue the waterway into Chesterfield. However, a shortage of funds dictated that the cheaper option, provided by a short section of river navigation, was chosen, hence the present terminus south of Wharf Lane Changeover Bridge. This in fact superseded the original terminal basin and warehouse (slightly further north) that were severed from the river by the building of the Manchester, Sheffield and Lincolnshire Railway in the late 19th C – which has, in turn, been replaced by the Inner Relief Road. Currently there are plans to develop 40 acres either side of the waterway, close to its present terminus, giving the navigation pride of place, complete with a new mooring arm. A single floodgate protects the canal at its junction with the Rother and before long the navigation becomes embroiled in a group of road crossings, bracketing the first lock and the excellent Tapton Lock Visitor Centre. Beyond are two further bridges – this time carrying the main line railway junction – as the waterway turns north east and heads for open countryside. There is little to remind the boater of the proximity of town and industry as the canal enters a side cutting overhung with the trees of Bluebank Wood. Dixon's Lock was newly reconstructed in a position some 200yds below the original to avoid the ravages of open-cast mining, and newly planted spoil tips are still very much in evidence as the waterway enters a shallow cutting. Hollingwood and Staveley (once the home of a vast canalside iron foundry) maintain a discrete distance from the navigation, separated by a tract of gently rising pastureland, and it is a matter of wonder how rapidly nature (with a little assistance from the bulldozer) regains control. Hollingwood Hub, beside Works Road Bridge 8c, is very much a focus for the activities of the Chesterfield Canal Trust and houses a *coffee shop*. Outside there is an audio post with eight recorded messages from people with first hand experience of the canal. Just to the east of Eckington Road Bridge, waterway and Trans Pennine Trail diverge: the trail heads north along an abandoned railway line, while the largely infilled course of the canal wanders off across the fields towards Mastin Moor.

Pubs and Restaurants

See page 38.

BOAT TRIPS

The Chesterfield Canal Trust Hollingwood Hub, 22 Works Road, Hollingwood, Chesterfield S43 2PF (01246; 477569; www.chesterfield-canal-trust.org.uk/trip-boats) operate four trip boats based at Chesterfield, Hollingwood, Worksop and Ranby. For details of days and times of public trips visit their website. Also available for charter – telephone for more information.

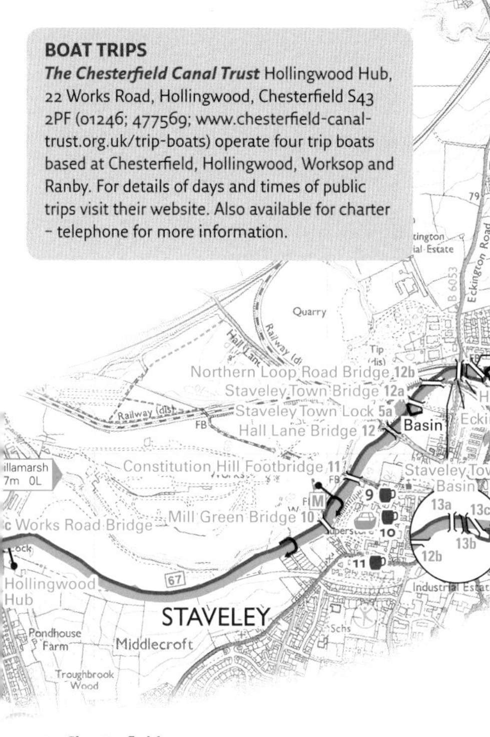

● **Chesterfield**

Derbyshire. All services. Probably best known as the town with the crooked spire (*see* St Mary and All Saints Church below), Chesterfield prospered well before the relatively recent wealth introduced by local metalworking industries and coal mining. It was known as Cestrefeld by the Anglo-Saxons, the 'Cestre' prefix indicating that the Romans were active here well before them. In this important market town many street names are of ancient origin and hint at a range of medieval trades that were once dominated by industries linked to the plentiful supply of wool produced on the surrounding hills. George Stevenson lived at Tapton for more than a decade, moving to the area whilst surveying a route for the North Midland Railway between Derby and Leeds. While digging the 'Mile Long' tunnel at Clay Cross, just south of Chesterfield, extensive iron and coal deposits were discovered in 1837, which Stevenson went on to exploit, launching the 'Clay Cross Company'. Today Chesterfield is a prosperous market town, retaining excellent railway connections but with little of its former industry.

The **Chesterfield Canal Trust** (www.chesterfield-canal-trust.org.uk) runs boat trips (*see* above) and promotes the canal and its full restoration. Visit the website for information about their work and events.

Barrow Hill Roundhouse Campbell Drive, Barrow Hill, Chesterfield S43 2PR (01246 472450; www.barrowhill.org). Built in 1870, this is in fact a square building constructed to house, maintain, coal and water and, in many cases, to turn steam locomotives. With the demise of steam haulage, most roundhouses were demolished, but, thanks to its continuing use for diesel traction and the dedication of the Barrow Hill Engine Society, this example survives and now houses one of the largest collections of electric, diesel and steam engines in the country. *Open Sat, Sun 10.00–16.00* and there is a calender of special events (when there is a free bus service) – telephone for details or visit their website. Café. 1 mile north of Hollingwood Lock or buses 56, 80 or 90 from Chesterfield bus station. Charge.

Chesterfield Museum and Art Gallery St Mary's Gate, Chesterfield S41 7TD (01246 345727; www.chesterfield.gov.uk/explore-chesterfield/museums.aspx). The museum houses the actual builders' wheel used in the construction of the crooked spire, left inside the tower when building was completed. Also insights into Chesterfield life and George Stevenson's preoccupation with growing straight cucumbers. The art gallery contains Impressionist work by local artist Joseph Syddall. *Open Mon & Thu-Sat 10.00-16.00.* Free.

Revolution House High Street, Old Whittington, Chesterfield S41 9JZ (01246 345727; www.visitchesterfield.info). Once an alehouse, known as the Cock & Pynot (magpie), this cottage was the meeting place for three local noblemen intent on overthrowing King James II in favour of William and Mary of Orange. Today the ground floor houses a display of 17th-C furniture; there is a video telling the story of the Revolution and upstairs are changing exhibitions relating to local themes. *Open Easter-Sep & B Hol Mon, Sat-Sun 11.00-16.00.* Free. Bus service from Chesterfield.

St Mary and All Saints Church St Mary's Gate, Chesterfield S41 7TJ (01246 206506; www.chesterfieldparishchurch.org.uk). Whether viewed from near or far, most attention is focused on the spire rather than upon the church itself. Standing 228ft from ground to weathervane, leaning 9½ft out of plumb and grotesquely twisted, the whole edifice is constructed from 150 tons of wood and 32 tons of lead; and nothing secures it to the tower save its own mass. Legends abound as to the cause of its twist,

Killamarsh

When the Great Central Railway built their line from Sheffield to Nottingham in 1890, its straight-as-a-die route between Staveley and Killamarsh conflicted on a very regular basis with the contoured course of the Chesterfield Canal. Rather than incur the substantial cost of building a succession of bridges, the Railway Company straightened the line of the canal, excavating cuttings as required, and it is for this reason that both canal and the now-disused railway run in tandem north and west of Renishaw. Here the navigation makes a second sweep to the east, passing through what was once a vast foundry complex, now demolished and built upon. Moulding sand had, over the years, been tipped into the canal bed and the waterway has only recently been re-excavated. At Forge Bridge and almost doubling back on itself, the navigation finally settles on a more easterly course, picking its way through the houses of Killamarsh. Vociferous protest in the 1970s failed to prevent a part of the canal being built upon and now, in places, the original line is difficult to follow. However, alternative routes are under investigation to link in with future plans at Norwood, where 13 locks await restoration. Here a superb flight of staircase locks – three groups of three and one of four – lift the canal to the bricked-up western portal of Norwood Tunnel. The building at the bottom of the flight was once the Boatman Inn; the large decorative 'lakes' were side pounds: storage for the considerable quantity of water needed to operate the locks, and in turn connected to reservoirs in the hills above. Between the top two staircase lock groups a dwelling has been converted from an old sawmill. This very early example of waterway construction dates, in the main, from 1775 and within ⅓ mile encapsulates some of the very best in canal engineering, all within an idyllic setting.

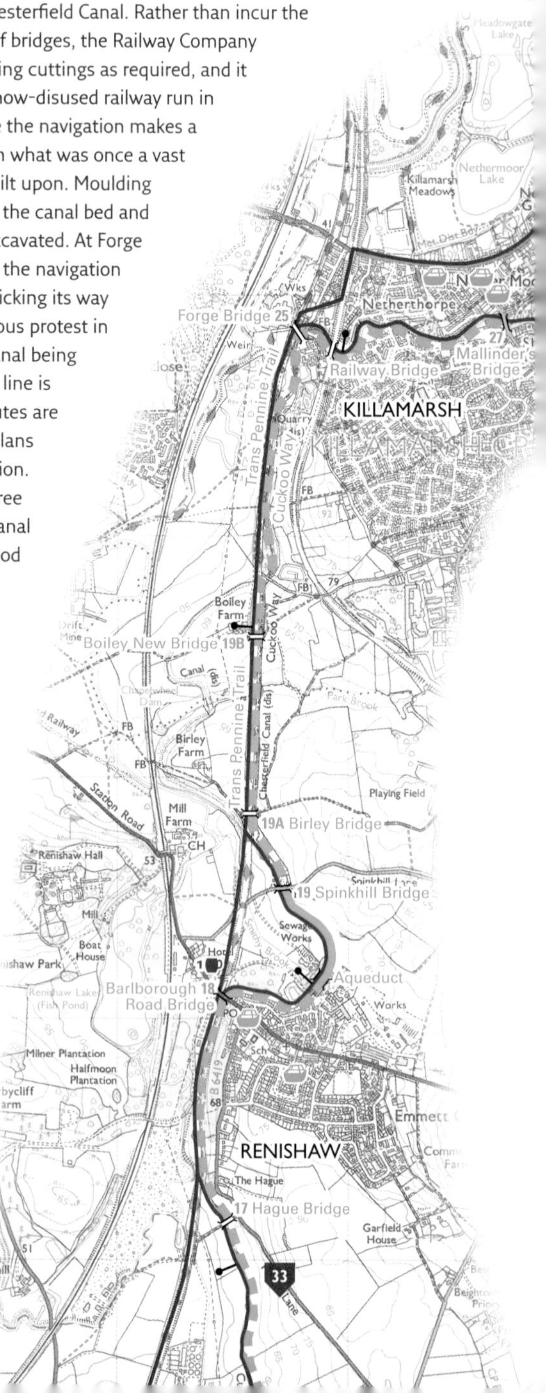

Pubs and Restaurants

See page 39.

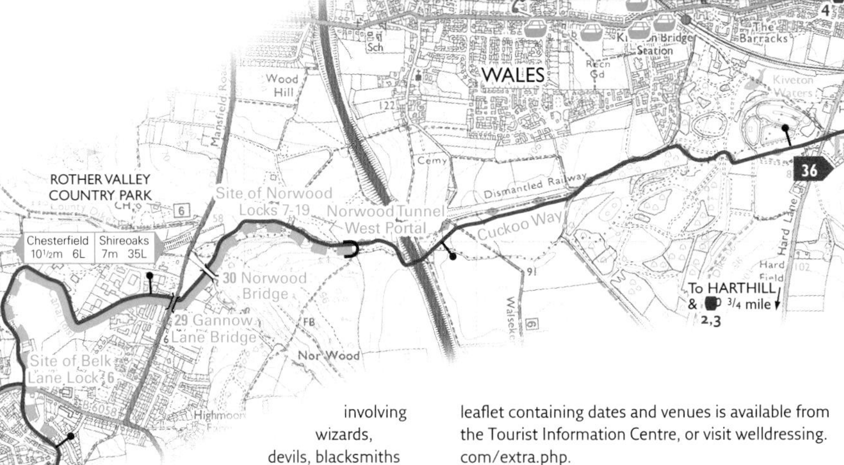

involving wizards, devils, blacksmiths and virgins, though not necessarily all at once. More reasonably, the nature of the green oak from which it was constructed over 600 years ago, shrinking as it seasoned *in situ*, is the most likely culprit, aided and abetted by a design that eschews cross-bracing and allowed the bottom timbers to gradually decay over the years. A holy building in one form or another has stood on the site since the middle of the 7th C; the present building was dedicated in 1234 and completed in 1360, when the spire was added. The Norman font was dug up in the vicarage garden in 1848, although the cause of its migration remains a mystery. The spire almost fell prey to a serious fire in December 1961 and was within minutes of total destruction.

Tapton Visitor Centre Lockoford Lane, Chesterfield S41 7JB (01629 533020; www.chesterfield-canal-trust.org.uk/off-the-water/tapton-lock-visitors-centre). Focus for much activity along the canal and within the Three Valleys area, the centre is a fund of information and has a well-stocked shop selling a range of useful publications, guides and maps together with free walks leaflets and an exhibition area. Also snacks and hot and cold drinks. *Open daily 10.00-16.00. Closed for lunch 13.00-13.45.* Free.

Tourist Information Centre Rykneld Square, Chesterfield S40 1SB (01246 345777; www.visitchesterfield.info). *Open daily Mon-Sat 09.30-18.00.*

Well Dressing Derbyshire. While its origins remain something of a mystery, but undoubtedly pre-dating Christianity, this decorative art thrives in the area *throughout the summer* in a variety of forms. A leaflet containing dates and venues is available from the Tourist Information Centre, or visit welldressing.com/extra.php.

Staveley

Derbyshire. PO, tel, stores, greengrocer, hardware, chemist, butcher, takeaways, fish & chips, library, garage. Mentioned in the Domesday Book, part of the Frecheville family estates in the 16th C and more recently owned by the Dukes of Devonshire, Staveley has, post Industrial Revolution, been the focus for the iron and coal industries in the area, with large foundries beside the canal at Hollingwood. The shop is *open Mon-Sat 08.00-22.00 & Sun 10.00-16,00.*

Renishaw

Derbyshire. PO, tel, stores, chemist, off-licence, garage. Another foundry town once producing a vast array of complex castings for a wide range of industries. Shop *open daily 07.00-22.00.*

Renishaw Hall Renishaw, near Sheffield S21 3WB (01246 432310; www.renishaw-hall.co.uk). 3/4 mile north west of Barlborough Road Bridge. The 300-year-old home of the Sitwell family who established themselves as coal magnates and iron founders long before displaying their literary credentials. Gardens, museum, tearoom, craft centre and galleries *open Apr-Sep, Wed-Sun & B Hols 10.30-16.30.* Tours of the Hall *Fri 13.00-14.30 (also Sat-Sun in Aug).* Advanced booking advisable. Charge.

Killamarsh

Derbyshire. PO, tel, stores, chemist, fish & chips, takeaway, off-licence, library. Known as Chinewoldemaresc at the time of the Domesday survey, with a manor held by the tenure of providing a horse to the value of five shillings, with a sack and a spur, for the King's army in Wales. More recently and much more prosaically, a coal-mining centre, its deposits now exhausted. Shop *open daily 06.30-21.30 (Sun 07.30).*

WALKING AND CYCLING

The Derbyshire Countryside Service (01629 533190; www.derbyshire.gov.uk/leisure/countryside/countryside.aspx) produce excellent walks leaflets (downloadable from the website) covering the Three Valleys area around the western end of the canal. **Crags Museum and Prehistoric Gorge** (01909 720378; www.creswell-crags.org.uk). Visit their website for a fascinating insight into the rich cultural and natural heritage of a former coalfield area. The **Dronfield 2000 Rotary Walk** is 'a countryside walk for all' to the north west of the canal – visit www.walkingenglishman.com/ldp/dronfield2000rotarywalk.html – for further details. Cycle hire from Rother Valley Country Park – see page 39.

Shireoaks

Leaving the eastern tunnel portal, the waterway settles into an open cutting before gliding through woodland coppice to emerge beside the Anston stone quarries, the source of the stone used in the construction of the Houses of Parliament. Nothing can prepare the boater for the magic of the next few miles: it is pure waterway witchcraft as beyond, set against rolling farmland to the north, the canal heads for the first of the treble locks, followed immediately by three single locks and another treble. So begins a truly awesome length of waterway and an amazing feat of early canal engineering. Two double and two single locks take the navigation down into Turnerwood Basin, ringed by a charming collection of waterside cottages. Thence by seven locks, following in quick succession, the waterway tunnels into a delightful ribbon of woodland on its approach to Ryton Aqueduct and Boundary Lock, newly constructed to accommodate mining subsidence in the area. At Shireoaks the navigation ducks under the rebuilt road bridge sitting beside the local cricket field – a perfect replica of a county ground in miniature. Beyond is the *marina*, dug out on the site of an abandoned colliery and offering *short-term moorings, a slipway, showers and toilets, a self-operated pump out* and *electrical hook up*, together with *recycling facilities*, and a post box.

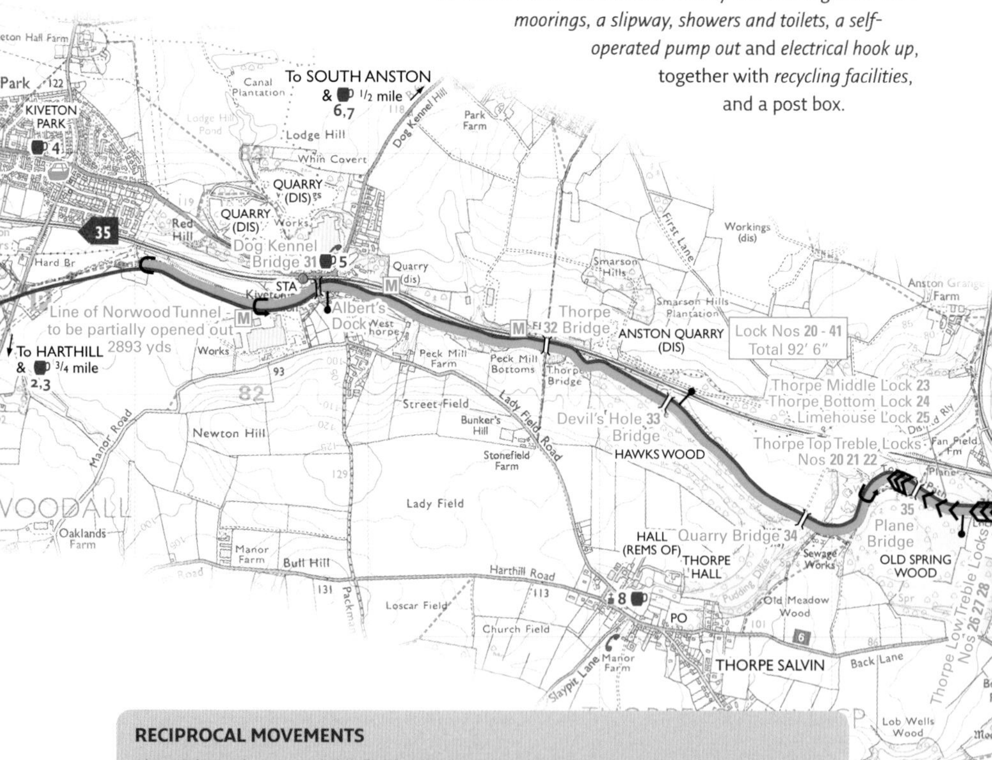

> **RECIPROCAL MOVEMENTS**
>
> Above John Varley's remarkable flights of locks are woods and stone quarries, areas where natural resources have been exploited in the developments of our age. Anston Quarries not only offered a ready source of stone for the locks and bridges along the canal, they were also the source of almost 250,000 tons of stone used to rebuild the Houses of Parliament when they burnt down in 1834. However the traffic has not been entirely one way. The small community of Shireoaks lost 24 young men in World War I (who are commemorated by a Calvary Cross) and exactly half that number in World War II. In their memory a clock was installed in the turret of St Luke's parish church with a double, three-legged gravity escapement. The significance of this mechanism is that, not only will it resist outside influences – such as wind pressure on the hands – but that it is also a direct copy of Edmund Becket Denison's design for Big Ben.

- **Wales**
  Derbyshire. PO, tel, stores, hardware, chemist, takeaways, library, bank, off-licence, fish & chips, garage, station. A mining community that now sits above the M1. The older area is set around the church. It was here that the body of Sir Thomas Hewitt, the somewhat eccentric owner of Hewitt Hall at Shireoaks, was eventually laid to rest. A confirmed atheist, Sir Thomas had begun to build an elaborate mausoleum at his home but died before it was completed. His servants tried to outwit the family's wishes to bury him at the church in Wales and one night filled the coffin with stones and set off with his body through the local woods at dead of night. Rumour has it that a strong wind blew out their torches and the servants were so frightened that they returned hastily to the hall with the body, which was then buried according to the family's plan. Scratta Wood was eventually felled and burned following reputed hauntings! The village shop is *open Mon-Sat 06.30-22.30 & Sun 06.30-20.00.*
  Rother Valley Country Park Mansfield Road, Wales Bar, Sheffield S26 5PQ (0114 247 1452; www.rvcp.co.uk). Entrance just north of Gannow Lane Bridge 29. One thousand acres of parkland catering for a wide variety of leisure pursuits on both land and water. There is an 18th-C working mill, craft centre, and **Old Mill and Stables Café** - *open daily* for appetising, inexpensive meals and snacks. For enquiries about leisure pursuits including boats, canoes, windsurfers and bicycles, telephone 0114 247 1452. For access by bus, telephone Traveline 01709 515151 or visit www.derbysbus.info. *Open daily dawn to dusk (except Xmas).*
- **Kiveton Park**
  Derbyshire. PO box, tel, stores, off-licence, station. A cluster of houses and industrial units where once there were major stone quarries.
- **Harthill**
  Derbyshire. PO, tel, stores, butcher, baker, off-licence, greengrocer, takeaway, launderette. An attractive village whose main street is described in Scott's *Ivanhoe*. Mentioned in the Domesday Book, the first church was established here in 1078 by the son-in-law of William the Conqueror. Its successor houses some fine wooden carvings and an imposing timber roof. It is here that the body of John Varley was buried in1809. *Shop open Mon-Sat 06.45-19.00 & Sun 07.15-18.30.*
- **South Anston**
  Derbyshire. PO, tel, stores, chemist, butcher, off-licence, takeaway, garage. A sprawling settlement overlooked by the pretty church of St James with its elegant spire. The shop is *open daily 06.00-21.00 (Sun 07.00).*
- **Thorpe Salvin**
  Derbyshire. A tiny village which has several times been winner of Britain in Bloom and had the onerous task of representing England in the European competition. The small nucleus of attractive stone houses is dominated by the now-ruined Elizabethan Thorpe Hall and the church. A very fine Norman doorway, a chained bible and a font depicting the four seasons are some of the treasures which can be seen within.

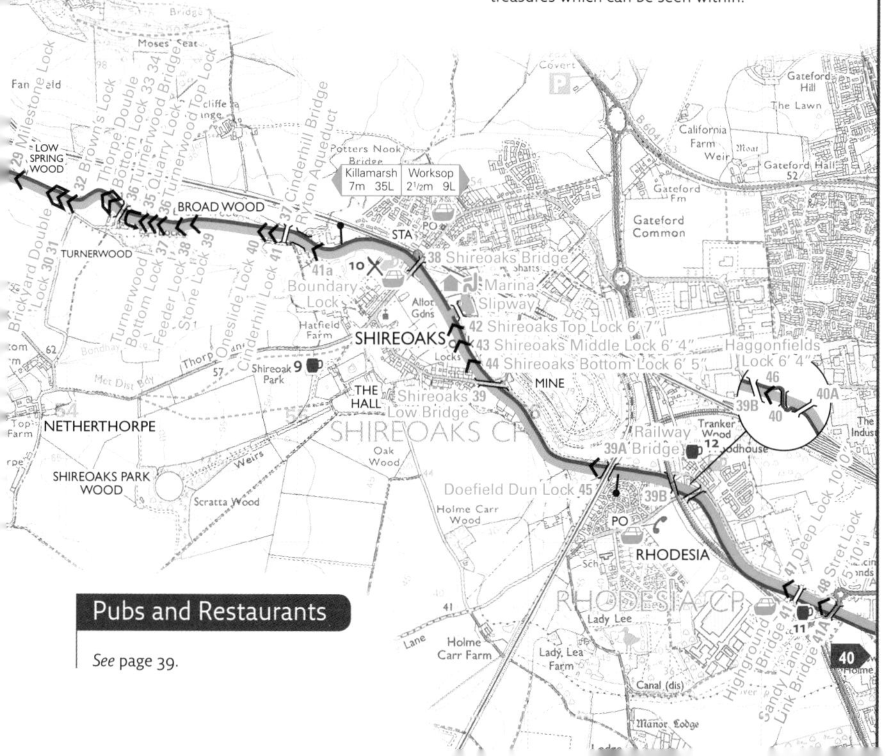

Pubs and Restaurants

See page 39.

Shireoaks

Notts. PO, tel, stores, off-licence, fish & chips, station. It is worth taking the time to explore this village whose splendid terrace of miners' cottages leads down the hill to the church. The village takes its name from a giant oak tree which cast its shade into Yorkshire, Derbyshire and Nottinghamshire and which was said to have measured 94ft in circumference. The money for both the church and the cottages was given by the 5th Duke of Newcastle following the sinking of the pit. The presence of coal in the area brought work for up to 600 men and it is easy to imagine the impression that the newly-built colliers' cottages of Shireoaks Row must have made on the village. It is still possible to identify some of the original window casements and doors with their elaborate strap hinges, although many of the dwellings have cast history aside for more comfortable 20th-C fitments. The foundation stone of the church was laid in 1861 by Edward VII, then Prince of Wales. The quill pen which he used at the ceremony can still be seen in the church. Dedicated to St Luke, the building houses a beautiful altar, commemorating the Duke of Newcastle, and a painted ceiling. In 1975 the spire of the church had to be removed following subsidence caused by the mining in the area. A miner's lamp hangs above the pulpit as a poignant reminder of the industry which was the lifeblood of the village until the closure of the pit in 1990. The village has twice won the best-kept village award. Just beyond Shireoaks Row stands the impressive half-ruined Jacobean Hall, built in 1612, whose coach-house has been sensitively converted into a pub. The 45 acres of land behind the hall were laid out as a water garden to include a lake, cascade and ornamental canal.

Rhodesia

Notts. PO, tel, stores, off-licence. A small settlement to the south west of the A57 flyover. Gas is available at the village store which is *open Mon-Fri 06.30-20.00; Sat 07.00-20.00 and Sun & B Hols 09.00-16.00*

Pubs and Restaurants (pages 32-33)

1 The Market 95 New Square, Chesterfield S40 1AH (01246 273641; www.themarketpub.co.uk). Large town hostelry serving an excellent and ever-changing range of real ales together with Bar food *L & E daily*. Also real cider. Outside seating and children are welcome *when dining*. Quiz *Thu* and live music *Sun*. *Open 11.00-23.00 (Sun 12.00).*

2 The Rutland Arms 23 Stephenson Place, Chesterfield S40 1XL (01246 205857; www.facebook.com/Rutland-Arms-102034874671974). This pub incorporates the former vicarage and is overshadowed by the church-with-the-twisted-spire. Food is available *Mon-Fri L and E; Sat 12.00-20.00 & Sun 12.00-17.00.* Real ale and real cider. Garden, family-friendly and Wi-Fi. *Open 12.00.*

3 The Chesterfield Arms 40 Newbold Road, Chesterfield S41 7PH (01246 236634; www.chesterfieldarms.co.uk). A real ale (and cider) lovers' dream come true - the selection is breath-taking! Matched by a friendly welcome and a relaxed atmosphere and décor. Child- and dog-friendly, outside seating. Quiz *Wed*. Real fires. *Open daily 12.00-23.00 (Fri-Sat 00.00).*

4 The Derby Tup 387 Sheffield Road, Whittington Moor, Chesterfield S41 8LS (07930873072; www.facebook.com/Thederbytup). North west of Tapton Lock. Another pub with an ever changing selection of real ales offering a friendly welcome and a warm atmosphere. Also real cider. Dog-friendly, traditional pub games, newspapers, real fires and Wi-Fi. Quiz *Thu*. *Open daily 16.00 (Sun 14.00).*

5 Lock Keeper Tapton, Chesterfield S41 7NJ (01246 560700; www.brewersfayre.co.uk/en-gb/locations/derbyshire/lock-keeper). East of Tapton Lock. Boater-friendly establishment serving real ales and food available *from breakfast (Mon-Fri 06.30 & Sat-Sun 07.00) onwards.* Brewers Fayre with that wee bit extra. Children welcome. Outside seating. B&B. Bar *open 12.00.*

6 The Royal Oak 1 The Shambles, Chesterfield S40 1PX (01246 234886; www.facebook.com/royaloaktheshambles). Dating back to 12th C and reputed to be the town's oldest pub, this establishment has been both a rest house for the Knights Templar and a butcher's, although in its present incarnation it serves an excellent range of real ales. Dog-friendly and Wi-Fi. Food available *12.00-16.00. Open daily 11.30 (Sun 12.00).*

7 Nona's Coffee Shop 22 Works Road, Hollingwood Hub, Hollingwood, Staveley S43 2JP (07477 600141). Highly regarded coffee shop selling drinks, sandwiches, light meals, ice creams and a selection of cakes. Everything is home made. *Open daily 09.30-16.00.*

8 Speedwell Inn Lowgates, Staveley S43 3TT (01246 472252; www.facebook.com/pages/category/Pub/The-Speedwell-Inn-145106072324990). Home of Townes beers, this intimate local is free of piped music and electronic games, making it very much a hub of conversation. Dog-friendly, traditional pub games, sports TV and Wi-Fi. *Open Mon-Sat 17.00-23.00 (Fri-Sat 16.00) & Sun 12.00-22.30.*

Try also **9 Beechers Brook** High Street, Staveley S43 3UU (01246 471178), **10 The Elm Tree Inn** High Street, Staveley S43 3UU (01246 769146), and **11 Harleys** Market Street, Staveley S43 3UT (01246 477410).

SELF-DISCOVERY OR WATERWAYS RECOVERY?

Messing about in the mud has long been the pursuit of little boys (and girls) and is an occupation that some of us have great difficulty in shrugging off, even in later life. Imagine, then, having the opportunity to legitimise this sensory indulgence in the respectable form (in the eyes of some, at least) of canal restoration. There are still many muddy, overgrown ditches festering in their own private world of decay that were once illustrious watery highways. As the more straightforward canal restorations are successfully accomplished, so the more difficult ones become the targets for the doyens of dirty digging, namely the Waterways Recovery Group (www.wrg.org.uk). Formed with the express purpose of resurrecting fallen waterways and familiar to many a boater as the driving force behind the annual National Waterway Festivals, this organisation is able to dig the dirt with the best of them. The Chesterfield Canal is one of many navigations to have benefited from their unstinting ability to mix endeavour with cheerfulness, pleasure with muck and sand with cement.

Pubs and Restaurants (pages 34-37)

1 The Sitwell Arms Hotel 39 Station Road, Renishaw S21 3WF (01246 435226/0800 082 0804; www.sitwellarms.com). Hotel offering an extensive à la carte restaurant menu *L and E (not L Mon and Sat or E Sun)*. Bar meals available *Mon-Fri L and E; all day Sat & Sun*. Real ales. Children welcome; Garden. Live entertainment *last Sat of the month*. B&B.

2 The Beehive 16 Union Street, Harthill S26 7YH (01909 774573; www.thebeehiveharthill.com). Friendly village pub serving real ale and a good choice of reasonably priced food *L and E*. Quiz *Thu*. Patio seating and sports TV. *Open daily 12.00-23.00 (Sun 22.30)*.

3 The Blue Bell 4 Woodall Lane, Harthill S26 7YQ (01909 770391; www.facebook.com/TheBlueBellHarthill). Award-winning pub serving a wide range of real ales. Child- and dog-friendly, beer garden. Real fires and sports TV. Quiz *Thu & Sun. Open Sun-Fri 17.00-23.00 (Sun 12.00) & Sat 14.00-00.00*.

4 The Saxon Hotel Station Road, Kiveton Park S26 6QP (01909 770517). North of Kiveton crossroads. Busy modern local. Children welcome. Garden.

5 The Station Pub Redhill, Kiverton Park S26 6NP (01909 774677; www.thestationpubkivetonpark.co.uk). Refurbished pub-cum-eatery serving real ales and tasty home-cooked food. Family-friendly. Patio. Conservatory and pool table. Karoake *Fri*. Grill *open daily for breakfast 09.00-11.30; lunch 12.30-15.30 & evening meal 17.30-21.00*. Pub *open 12.00*.

6 The Loyal Trooper 34 Sheffield Road, South Anston S25 5DT (01909 562203; www.loyaltrooperpub.co.uk). Welcoming local serving real ale and reasonably priced, homemade food *Mon-Sat L and E & Sun 12.00-17.00*. Traditional pub games and sports TV. Wi-Fi. Well worth the 1 mile walk up from the canal. Beer garden. *Open 12.00-23.00 (Fri-Sat 00.00)*.

7 The Leeds Arms 29 Sheffield Road, South Anston S25 5DT (01909 567055; www.theleedsarms.co.uk). Village pub serving real ale and food *Tue-Thu L and E; Fri-Sat 12.00-20.00 & Sun 12.00-17.00*. Traditional pub games, real fires, a garden and sports TV. *Open 12.00-23.00 (Mon 16.00)*.

8 The Parish Oven Worksop Road, Thorpe Salvin S80 3JU (01909 774888; www.theparishoven.co.uk). Modern pub in the centre of the village, serving real ales and food is available *daily 12.00-20.00 (Sun 21.00)*. Child- and dog-friendly; garden and children's play area. Traditional pub games. Quiz *Wed. Open 12.00-23.00 (Fri-Sat 00.00)*.

9 The Hewett Arms Shireoaks Park, Thorpe Lane, Shireoaks S81 8LT (01909 500979; www.facebook.com//pages/Hewitt-Arms/151473074884303). ½ mile south west of the canal. A restrained conversion of the coach house and stables adjoining the hall. A good range of real ales can be enjoyed in comfort overlooking the landscaped park. *Open Tue-Fri 19.30-23.00 & Sun 13.30-23.00*.

10 Laura's Café 2A Shire Oak Row, Shireoaks S81 8LT (07946 042362). Beside Bridge 38. Laura's homemade cakes, toasties, bacon rolls and *all-day* breakfasts are more than sufficient to entice any canal users away from the navigation. Also teas, coffee and cold drinks. *Open Tue-Sun & B Hols 09.30-16.00*.

11 The Lock Keeper Sandy Lane, Rhodesia S80 1TJ (01909 532565; www.lockkeeperpub.co.uk). A family pub between Deep and Stret Locks serving real ale together with reasonably priced food available *12.00-22.00*. Children welcome, garden. Wi-Fi. B&B. *Open 11.00-23.00 (Sun 22.30)*.

12 The Woodhouse Inn Woodend, Rhodesia S80 3HD (01909 475358; www.woodhouseinn.co.uk). Real ale available and food *Wed-Sun 12.00-21.00 (Sun 18.00)*. Dog- and family-friendly, garden. Traditional pub games, real fires, sports TV and Wi-Fi. *Open 12.00-23.00 (Fri-Sat 00.00)*.

Boatyards

Ⓑ **Shireoaks Marina** Worksop S81 8NQ (0303 040 4040; www.watersidemooring.com/344-shireoaks-marina-l1/Vacancies). E Pump out, long-term mooring, slipway, toilets, showers, recycling facilities.

Worksop

Once below Worksop Town Lock, you will have descended one of the most splendid flights of locks anywhere on the waterways system: 31 in all over a distance of just four miles. Representing hard work for today's navigator, it also presented an amazing challenge to the canal's original builders and acts as a tantalising preview to the eventual resurrection of the spectacular (and currently derelict) 13 lock flight immediately to the west of Norwood Tunnel. On leaving the town (*recycling facilities* at the CRT Depot, Sandy Lane) just south of Bridge 44A, there is a useful *stores, several takeaways, an off-licence and a fish & chip shop* before the waterway heads out into open countryside and passes the attractive farm buildings of Osberton Hall. Beyond here it wanders eastward, passing beyond the hubbub of the A1 at Ranby, on its approach to the contrasting peace and isolation of Forest Locks.

Pubs and Restaurants

1 **The Shireoaks Inn** 81-83 Westgate, Worksop S80 1LT (01909 472118; www.shireoaksinn.co.uk). Once a row of cottages, now a welcoming hostelry, dispensing real ale and real cider. Excellent value, home-cooked food available *Mon-Fri L and E and Sat-Sun all day.* Family-friendly, traditional pub games and sports TV. *Open 11.30 (Sun 12.00).*

2 **The Greendale Oak** 41 Norfolk Street, Worksop S80 1LE (01909 423846; www.greendaleoak.co.uk). Just off Westgate. Cosy mid-terraced pub popular with the locals. Dog-friendly, traditional pub games and sports TV. *Open Mon-Fri 16.00-23.00 & Sat-Sun 12.00-00.00.*

3 **The Mallard** Station Approach, Carlton Road, Worksop S81 7AG (07973 521824;www.facebook.com/MallardPublicHouse). An exciting selection of ever-changing real ales from small breweries together with a comprehensive range of continental bottled beers. Outside seating and pub games. Real cider. Disabled access from station platform. Dog-friendly. Traditional pub games. *Open Mon-Thu 16.00-23.00; Fri-Sat 11.00-23.00 & Sun 12.00-22.30.*

4 **The Station Hotel** Carlton Road, Worksop S80 1PS (01909 474108; www.thestationhotelworksop.co.uk). Real ales and a comprehensive menu are available *Mon-Fri E & Sat-Sun L and E (not Sun E).* Dog-friendly, garden, traditional pub games, sports TV and Wi-Fi. Real cider. B&B. *Open Mon-Fri 15.00-23.00 & Sat-Sun 12.00-23.00.*

5 **The Dukeries Brewery Tap** 18 Newcastle Avenue, Worksop S80 1ET (07584 305027; www.facebook.com//dukeriesbrewerytap). Bar and micro-brewery, sharing the same building in the middle of the town, serving up to five real ales. Dog- and family-friendly. Traditional pub games and Wi-Fi. *Sat* live music. Camping nearby. *Open Tue 19.00-23.00 & Fri-Sat 16.30-23.00 (Sat 18.00).*

6 **The Liquorice Gardens** 1a Newcastle Street, Worksop S80 2AS (01909 512220; www.jdwetherspoon.com/pubs/all-pubs/england/nottinghamshire/the-liquorice-gardens-worksop). Named after the nearby Priory liquorice gardens, tended for their medicinal properties, this thriving establishment is today guaranteed to provide inexpensive food *from breakfast until 23.00.* There is always a good selection of reasonably priced real ales available and children are welcome. *Open 08.00.*

7 **The Chequers Inn** Old Blyth Road, Ranby, Retford DN22 8HT (01777 709090; www.thechequersatranby.co.uk). An attractive canalside pub, recently refurbished, serving real ale and food available *daily 12.00-21.00 (Sun 19.00).* Large outside terrace overlooking the waterway. Family-friendly, garden and real fires. Wi-Fi. Mooring. *Open 12.00-23.00 (Sun 22.30).*

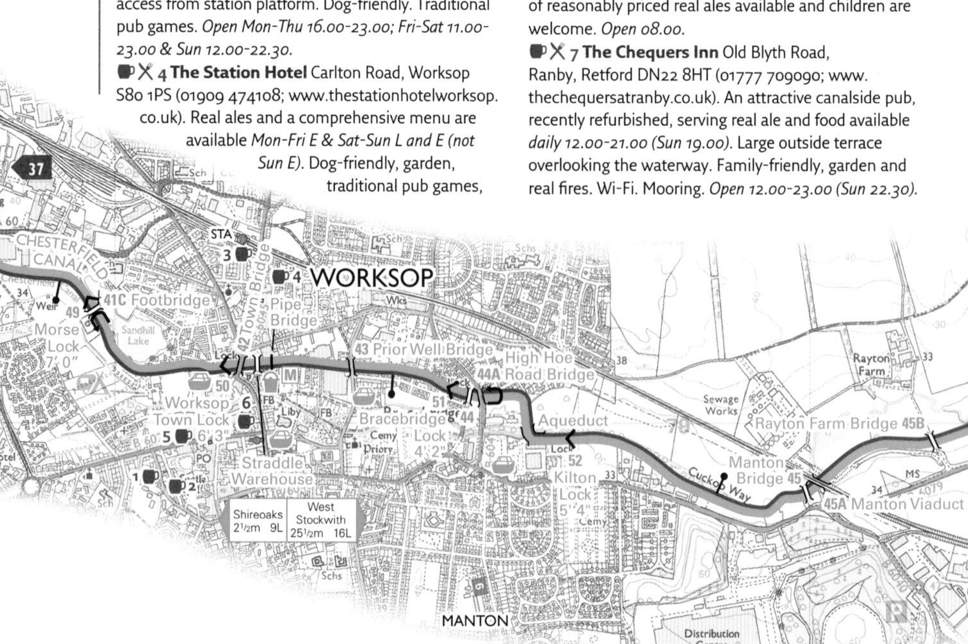

● **Worksop**

Notts. All services. Old buildings of note in Worksop are the Priory and its gatehouse.

Mr Straw's House 5-7 Blythe Grove, Worksop S81 0JG (01909 482380; www.nationaltrust.org.uk/mr-straws-house). When William and Walter Straw's father died in 1932, the brothers kept his house as a shrine and altered nothing. In 1991 William died and left the property, with a legacy of £1.5 million, to the National Trust. They have preserved this time capsule and opened it to visitors. *Open Apr-Oct, Tue-Sat 11.00-17.00.* Entrance by pre-booked timed tickets only - telephone or write for tickets.

The Priory Priorswell Road, Workshop S80 2BU (01909 472 180; www.worksoppriory.co.uk). Near Prior Well Bridge. The church dates from the 12th C. Much rebuilding has taken place since then: in fact from 1970-72 the superstructure was added to, incorporating a new spire. Interesting paintings and monuments are inside the church and a gruesome relic from Sherwood Forest - a skull with the tip of an arrow embedded in it. *Visits by appointment.*

Within a few miles of the town there are some interesting places and beautiful countryside to visit, although a car or a bicycle is needed to reach them. All around are the surviving woods of Sherwood Forest, while to the south of the town is the area called the Dukeries, each of the adjacent estates of Thoresby, Clumber and Welbeck having been owned by a duke. Welbeck is now an army college, Thoresby Park is open to the public. Clumber House was demolished in 1938 but the Park, owned by the National Trust, is one of its most visited properties. Three miles west of Worksop is an outstanding building well worth visiting - the tiny Steetley Chapel (PE28 5YE) - described as 'the most perfect and elaborate specimen of Norman architecture to be found anywhere in Europe'. *Open 10.00-16.00 during British Summer Time.* The quiet villages of north Nottinghamshire were once home to the Pilgrim Fathers.

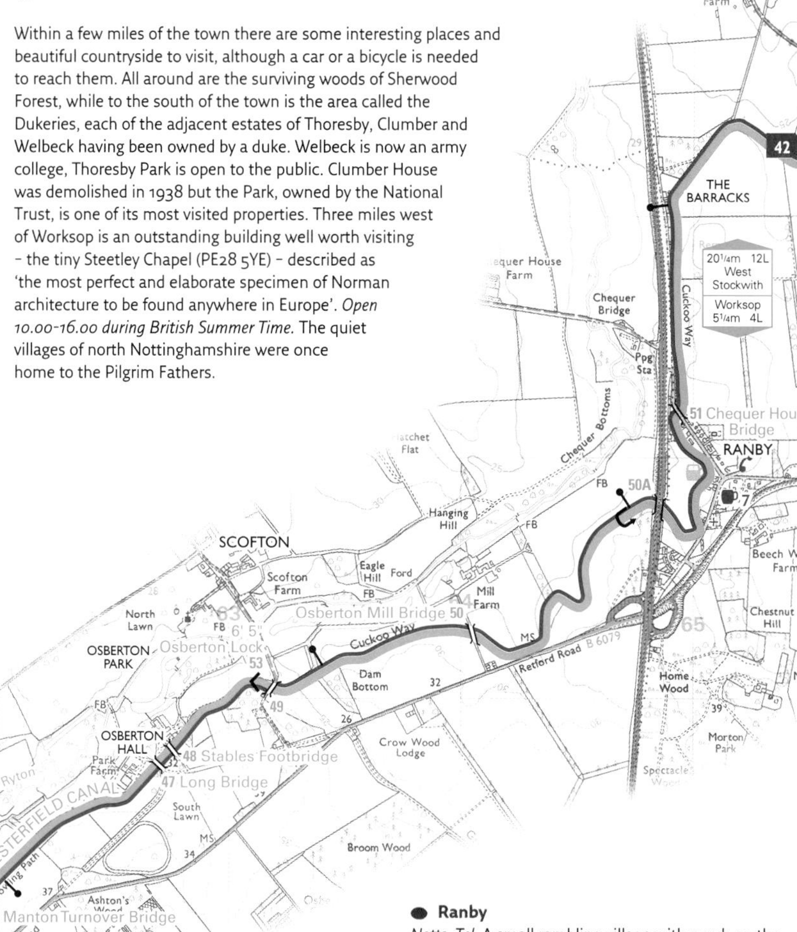

● **Ranby**

Notts. Tel. A small rambling village with a pub on the canal, the only one for miles in either direction.

Osberton Hall Built in 1806 by James Wyatt and enlarged and altered in 1853. Private.

● **Scofton**

Notts. This is the tiny estate village for Osberton Hall. The old stable block, sitting beside the canal, is impressive and is surmounted by a clock tower.

Retford

The straight road crossing the canal at Barnby Wharf Bridge was a Roman highway. It was, in fact, the original course of the Great North Road but 200 years ago the citizens of Retford got the road diverted to pass through their town, thereby increasing its importance and prosperity. They must now be equally relieved to have rid themselves of it again. In the open countryside around here are the four Forest Locks, complete with *all facilities* including *showers and toilets.* At the second lock there are good *moorings* and a *water point* right beside the top gate. Below the locks the outskirts of Retford are clearly visible as the waterway winds its way towards the town, passing through West Retford Lock and over three minute aqueducts, arriving close to the town centre beside a handy *supermarket.* Here is the last of the narrow locks with a large canal warehouse beside it.

WALKING AND CYCLING

Beside bridge 63 there is a nicely presented map setting out all the paths and bridleways within the parish of Hayton. These represent a wealth of walking (and cycling) opportunities throughout the local area.

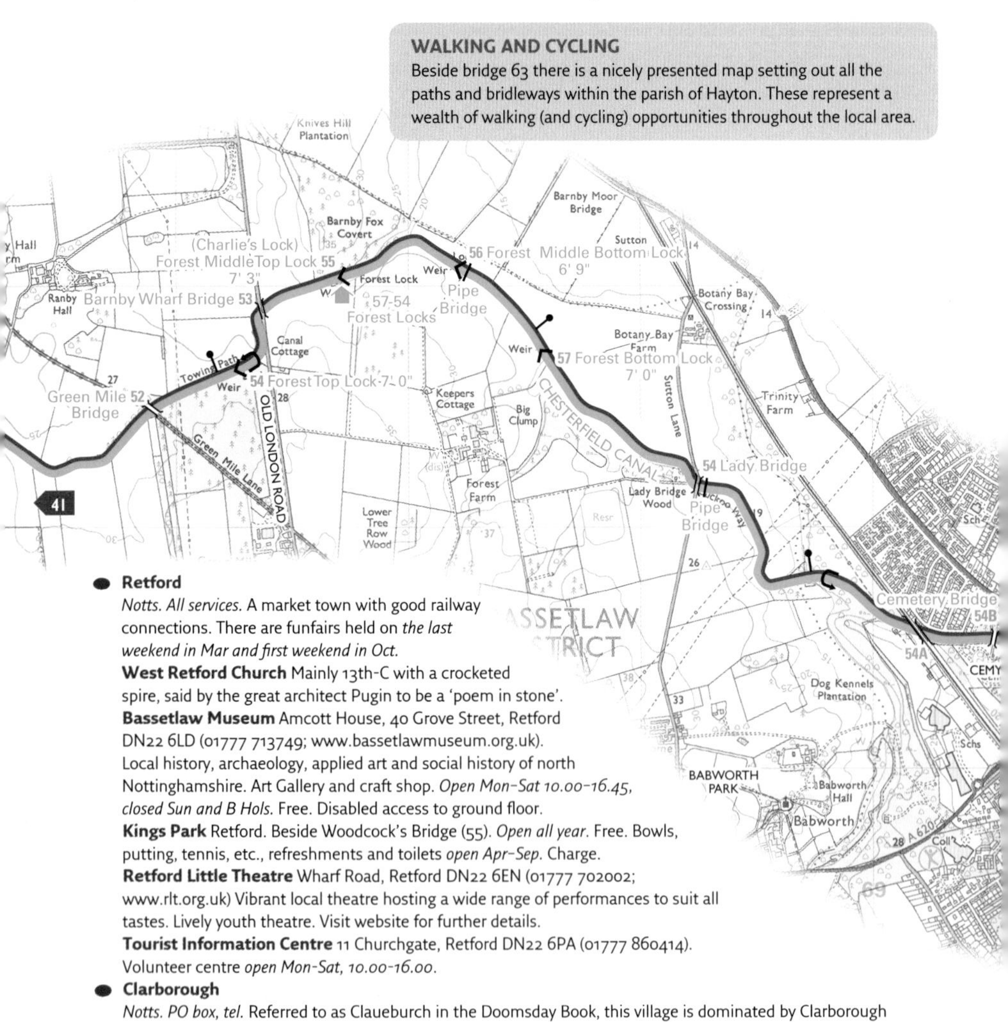

● **Retford**

Notts. All services. A market town with good railway connections. There are funfairs held on *the last weekend in Mar and first weekend in Oct.*

West Retford Church Mainly 13th-C with a crocketed spire, said by the great architect Pugin to be a 'poem in stone'.

Bassetlaw Museum Amcott House, 40 Grove Street, Retford DN22 6LD (01777 713749; www.bassetlawmuseum.org.uk). Local history, archaeology, applied art and social history of north Nottinghamshire. Art Gallery and craft shop. *Open Mon–Sat 10.00–16.45, closed Sun and B Hols.* Free. Disabled access to ground floor.

Kings Park Retford. Beside Woodcock's Bridge (55). *Open all year.* Free. Bowls, putting, tennis, etc., refreshments and toilets *open Apr–Sep.* Charge.

Retford Little Theatre Wharf Road, Retford DN22 6EN (01777 702002; www.rlt.org.uk) Vibrant local theatre hosting a wide range of performances to suit all tastes. Lively youth theatre. Visit website for further details.

Tourist Information Centre 11 Churchgate, Retford DN22 6PA (01777 860414). Volunteer centre *open Mon–Sat, 10.00–16.00.*

● **Clarborough**

Notts. PO box, tel. Referred to as Claueburch in the Doomsday Book, this village is dominated by Clarborough Hill. There is a yew tree, reputed to be over 1000 years old, growing in the parish churchyard of St John the Baptist.

● **Hayton**

Notts. Tel. In nearby Bolham, where the local inhabitants once lived in caves hewn in the rock, there are the remains of an ancient chapel.

Pubs and Restaurants

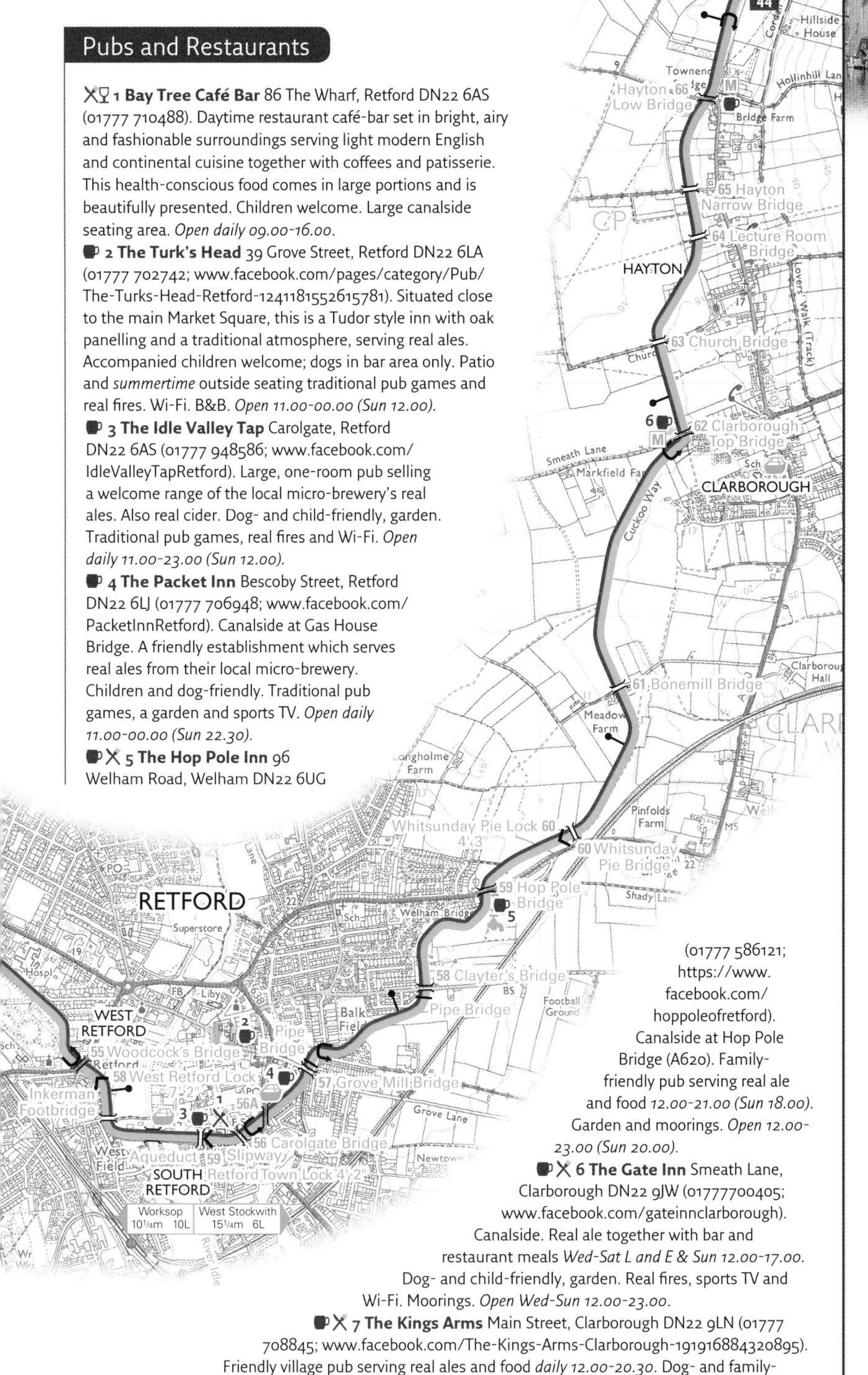

1 Bay Tree Café Bar 86 The Wharf, Retford DN22 6AS (01777 710488). Daytime restaurant café-bar set in bright, airy and fashionable surroundings serving light modern English and continental cuisine together with coffees and patisserie. This health-conscious food comes in large portions and is beautifully presented. Children welcome. Large canalside seating area. *Open daily 09.00-16.00.*

2 The Turk's Head 39 Grove Street, Retford DN22 6LA (01777 702742; www.facebook.com/pages/category/Pub/The-Turks-Head-Retford-124118155261578l). Situated close to the main Market Square, this is a Tudor style inn with oak panelling and a traditional atmosphere, serving real ales. Accompanied children welcome; dogs in bar area only. Patio and *summertime* outside seating traditional pub games and real fires. Wi-Fi. B&B. *Open 11.00-00.00 (Sun 12.00).*

3 The Idle Valley Tap Carolgate, Retford DN22 6AS (01777 948586; www.facebook.com/IdleValleyTapRetford). Large, one-room pub selling a welcome range of the local micro-brewery's real ales. Also real cider. Dog- and child-friendly, garden. Traditional pub games, real fires and Wi-Fi. *Open daily 11.00-23.00 (Sun 12.00).*

4 The Packet Inn Bescoby Street, Retford DN22 6LJ (01777 706948; www.facebook.com/PacketInnRetford). Canalside at Gas House Bridge. A friendly establishment which serves real ales from their local micro-brewery. Children and dog-friendly. Traditional pub games, a garden and sports TV. *Open daily 11.00-00.00 (Sun 22.30).*

5 The Hop Pole Inn 96 Welham Road, Welham DN22 6UG (01777 586121; https://www.facebook.com/hoppoleofretford). Canalside at Hop Pole Bridge (A620). Family-friendly pub serving real ale and food *12.00-21.00 (Sun 18.00).* Garden and moorings. *Open 12.00-23.00 (Sun 20.00).*

6 The Gate Inn Smeath Lane, Clarborough DN22 9JW (01777700405; www.facebook.com/gateinnclarborough). Canalside. Real ale together with bar and restaurant meals *Wed-Sat L and E & Sun 12.00-17.00.* Dog- and child-friendly, garden. Real fires, sports TV and Wi-Fi. Moorings. *Open Wed-Sun 12.00-23.00.*

7 The Kings Arms Main Street, Clarborough DN22 9LN (01777 708845; www.facebook.com/The-Kings-Arms-Clarborough-191916884320895). Friendly village pub serving real ales and food *daily 12.00-20.30.* Dog- and family-friendly, garden. Traditional pub games, real fires, sports TV and Wi-Fi. *Open 12.00-00.00.*

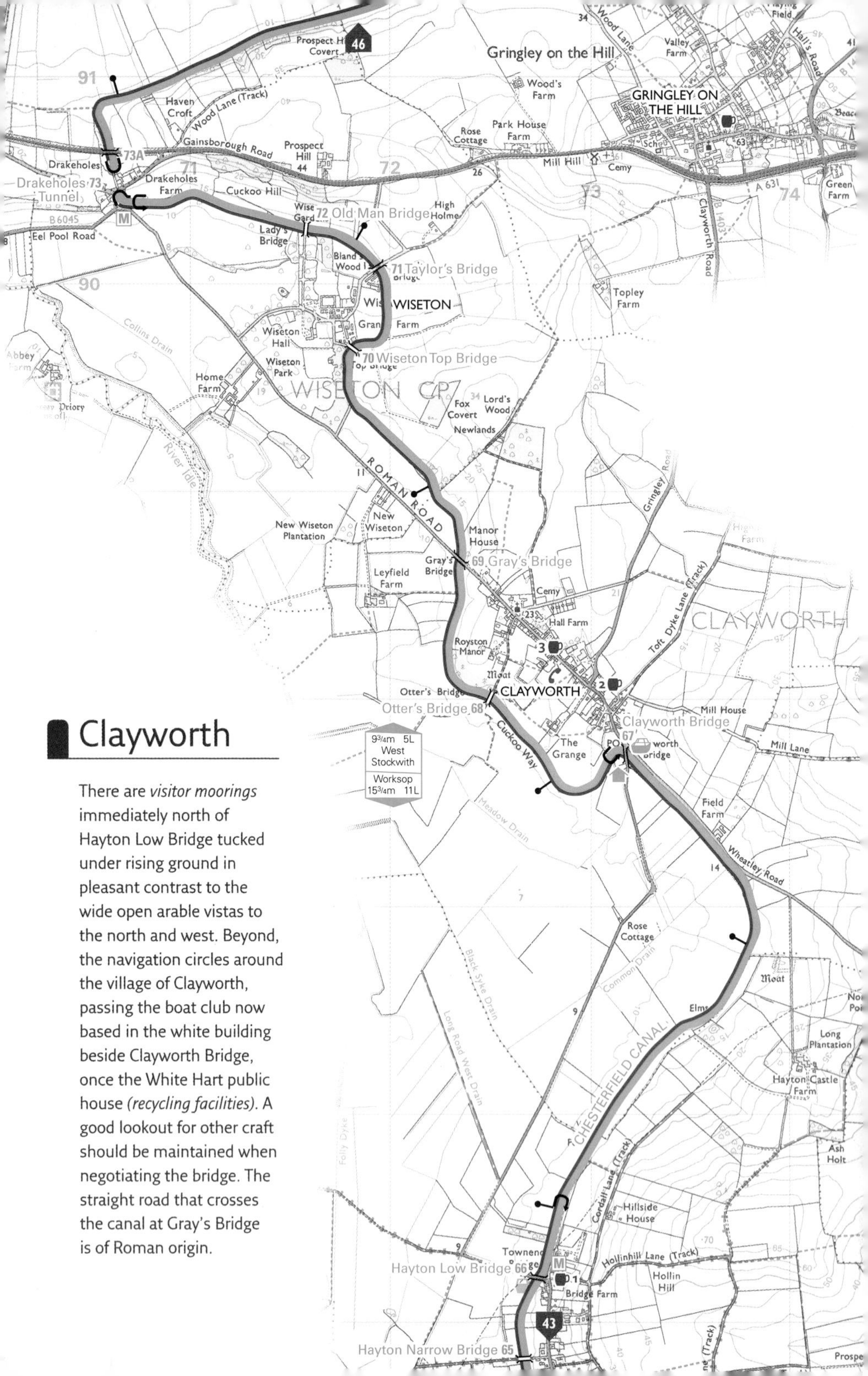

Clayworth

There are *visitor moorings* immediately north of Hayton Low Bridge tucked under rising ground in pleasant contrast to the wide open arable vistas to the north and west. Beyond, the navigation circles around the village of Clayworth, passing the boat club now based in the white building beside Clayworth Bridge, once the White Hart public house *(recycling facilities)*. A good lookout for other craft should be maintained when negotiating the bridge. The straight road that crosses the canal at Gray's Bridge is of Roman origin.

Again the waterway curls around the next habitation, skirting an attractive courtyard housing development built on the site of Wiseton Park's old walled kitchen garden. The brick from the enclosing walls has been put to good use in the construction of many of the houses. Heading towards Drakeholes *(moorings)*, the canal passes the stern features of a bearded man on the parapet of Old Man Bridge and, accompanied by woods, reaches the attractive moorings nestling beside the tunnel entrance. Drakeholes Tunnel (154 yds) is cut through rock and is mostly unlined with a *slipway* and *winding hole* immediately to the south. The navigation to the north is a thoroughly delightful stretch, heavily overhung with trees from Gringley to Drakeholes, running along the bottom of a ridge of hills. Wildlife near the water's edge includes coots, moorhens, water rats and bats. It is very secluded but the intimate feeling of the thickly wooded cutting beyond the tunnel has been ruined by the construction of a large road bridge.

Clayworth

Notts. PO, tel, stores. A quiet and pleasant village extending along a single main street. The houses are of all periods, the new blending well with the old. The Retford & Worksop Boat Club (01777 817546; www.rwbc.org.uk) is based at the old pub at Clayworth and welcomes visitors to the clubhouse. There are good *moorings* and *all facilities* here. In the old days a passenger boat used to run every Saturday from this pub to Retford, so that the villagers of Clayworth, Hayton and Clarborough could take their produce to Retford Market. The goods were loaded into the 'packet' boat on the Friday night, then the people would return early on Saturday morning, leaving at 06.30 to reach Retford by 08.30. The boat used to return in the evening when the market closed. A handsome sundial sits over the porch of the pretty village church, inscribed with the words 'Our days on earth are as a shadow'. Inside there is a series of beautiful wall paintings. The *post office* is in the village hall, *open Fri 13.00-16.00.*

Wiseton

Notts. Tel. A superbly elegant estate village set in a landscaped park, still clearly fulfiling its original manorial function. Trees and grass separate the various buildings, of which the large stable with its handsome clock tower is the most significant. The Hall, a modern red brick building, which replaced the original in 1962, is well hidden behind high walls.

Pubs and Restaurants

1 The Boat Inn Main Street, Hayton DN22 9LF (01777 862980; www.facebook.com/The-Boat-Inn-108485960741218). A popular and nicely kept pub offering real ales and a wide range of reasonably priced food available *Mon-Fri L and E & Sat-Sun 12.00-20.00 (Sun 17.00).* Real cider. Garden and children's play area. Traditional pub games, real fires, sports TV and Wi-Fi. *Open 12.00-00.00.*

2 The Brewers Arms Town Street, Clayworth DN22 9AD (01777 816107; www.brewersarmsclayworth.co.uk). Real ale. Traditional bar meals available *L and E Tue-Sun & Mon B Hols.* Dog- and family-friendly, patio. Real fires and Wi-Fi. *Open Mon-Fri L and E (Not Mon L) & Sat-Sun 12.00-01.00.*

3 The Blacksmiths Town Street, Clayworth DN22 9AD (01777 818171; www.blacksmithsclayworth.com). A 2012 facelift turned into a major rebuild to which the exposed interior steelwork bears testament. However, this culinary phoenix is now a gastro pub featuring locally sourced ingredients, fine wines and real ales. Food is available *Wed-Sun L and E (not Sun E).* Large garden, children welcome, dogs *until 17.30.* Real fires and Wi-Fi. B&B. *Open Wed-Sun 12.00-23.00 (Sun 19.00).*

West Stockwith Basin

West Stockwith

The course of the navigation is entirely rural and pleasant, passing well-established but often decaying farm buildings and two disused brickworks, one now the repository for canal dredgings. At Misterton there are two locks close together and between them there once stood the Albion Flour Mill, powered by canal water from a small reservoir beside the top lock. The church spire of East Stockwith stands opposite the point where the Chesterfield Canal enters the Trent. The lock here is keeper-operated. Just above the lock is a basin housing a *boatyard*, a *boat club, a hire boat company, a slipway (contact 07957 354915) and a waterpoint* and plenty of moored pleasure boats. Also *toilets and showers. Pump out* facilities are also available from the lock keeper when on duty. A *pub* and *a farm shop* are nearby.

NAVIGATIONAL NOTES

1 Entering the canal from the Trent can be tricky due to the tidal flow across the entrance to the lock. A leaflet is obtainable from CRT 0303 040 4040 (and from most Trent locks) with instructions on how to access the lock safely – or contact the lock keeper. The lock accepts craft up a maximum size of 72' x 17' 6". The lock is keeper-operated (give as much prior notice as possible by telephoning 01427 890204 or 07884 238780 and passage can usually be made *2½ hours before to 4½ hours after* high water. By coincidence, flood (when the tide ceases ebbing and turns to come back in) at Stockwith is almost the same time as high water at Hull. The flood runs for approximately 2½ hours and the direction of flow changes very rapidly. VHF radio frequencies: calling channel 16, working channel 74. The radio is not constantly manned. Commercial river traffic operates on channel 6 upstream of Keadby Bridge and it is useful for VHF users to monitor this channel to establish the whereabouts of large craft.

2 All subsequent locks on the waterway require a T-shaped key to release the anti-vandal mechanism.

3 The Trent series charts, published by The Boating Association (www.theboatingassociation.co.uk), are detailed charts of the tidal Trent (and the tidal Ouse and non-tidal Trent) and are available to buy online. Also from CRT lock keepers. Charge.

4 Your boat should be equipped with bow and stern lines of at least 30ft, although at some of the Trent locks these are now supplied.

5 The section of the river downstream of Gainsborough is under the jurisdiction of ABP Hull, who require that all boats should carry a marine band VHF radio and have a minimum crew of two.

6 CRT also publish useful guidance for boaters at canalrivertrust.org.uk/about-us/our-regions/north-east-waterways/planning-a-safe-passage-on-river-tees-and-river-ouse.

Pubs and Restaurants

1 The Blue Bell 1 High Street, Gringley on the Hill DN10 4RF (01777 816303; www.bluebellinngringley.co.uk). Well worth the walk up from the canal, this traditional village local serves real ales and bar food *daily*. Family-friendly, garden and children's play area. Real fires. *Open Mon-Fri 15.00-23.00 & Sat-Sun 11.00-00.00.*

2 The Waterfront Inn Canal Lane, West Stockwith DN10 4ET (01427 891223; www.waterfront-weststockwith.co.uk). Canalside at West Stockwith Basin. A good selection of real ales dispensed in a friendly pub together with excellent and inexpensive food available *Wed-Sun L and E (not Sun E)*. Dog- and family-friendly, garden. Traditional pub games, real fires, Wi-Fi and glamping pods. B&B. *Open Mon-Tue 16.00 & Wed-Sun 12.00 (Sat 10.00).*

3 The White Hart 36 Main Street, West Stockwith DN10 4EY (01427 892672; www.whiws.co.uk). By the junction of the rivers Idle and Trent. Friendly family country pub with a welcoming atmosphere, serving real ales from the Idle Brewery situated in a barn next door, together with food available *L and E (not Sun E)*. Children and dogs welcome. Traditional pub games, newspapers, real fires and sports TV. Camping nearby. *Open daily 11.00-23.00.*

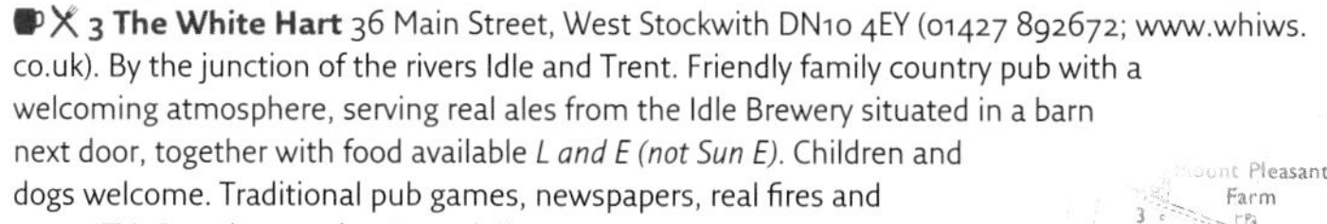

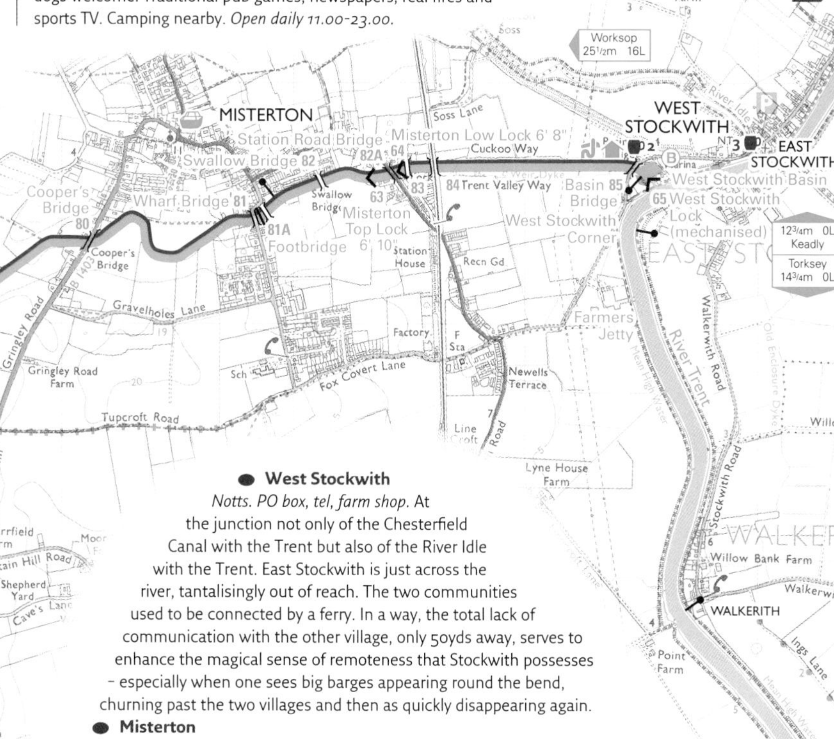

● **West Stockwith**
Notts. PO box, tel, farm shop. At the junction not only of the Chesterfield Canal with the Trent but also of the River Idle with the Trent. East Stockwith is just across the river, tantalisingly out of reach. The two communities used to be connected by a ferry. In a way, the total lack of communication with the other village, only 50yds away, serves to enhance the magical sense of remoteness that Stockwith possesses - especially when one sees big barges appearing round the bend, churning past the two villages and then as quickly disappearing again.

● **Misterton**
Notts. PO, tel, stores, chemist, off-licence, takeaways, fish & chips, butcher, library, camping. The village has a thriving Methodist church, as do most of the places in this area. John Wesley came from nearby Epworth.

● **Gringley on the Hill**
Notts. PO box, tel. The village is about a mile's walk up from the canal. A small rise on a level with the church tower gives a good view. On a clear day the pinnacles of Lincoln Cathedral can sometimes be seen, nearly 20 miles to the south east.

Boatyards

Ⓑ **Mick Ogden Boating** The Lock, Canal Lane, West Stockwith DN10 4ET (07591 436308).
D Gas. *Open daily 10.00-18.00 and at other times by arrangement.*

Ⓑ The following facilities are available in the basin and are obtained by telephoning the lock keeper on 01427 890204 or 07884 238780. Short- and long-term mooring, winter storage, slipway, toilets, showers.

WILDLIFE ON THE CHESTERFIELD CANAL

Wildlife flourishes along the Chesterfield Canal, as this diverse selection of birds you might see on the canal demonstrates.

The *Canada Goose* is a large, unmistakable goose with an upright stance and a long neck, giving it a swan-like silhouette. The goose has white cheeks on an otherwise black head and neck. Its body is mainly grey-brown except for a white under stern; the juveniles are similar but the markings are less distinct. The canada goose nests beside wetlands and sometimes in nearby arable fields. Outside the breeding season, sizeable flocks of geese will be seen. In flight the geese utter a loud, disyllabic trumpeting call.

Mallard Ducks are widespread and familiar. The colourful male has a yellow bill and a green, shiny head and neck, separated from the chestnut breast by a white collar. Its plumage is otherwise grey-brown except for a black stern and white tail. The female has an orange bill and mottled brown plumage. In flight both sexes have a blue and white speculum (patch on trailing edge of inner wing).

Lapwing breed in open, flat country, including undisturbed farmland and coastal marshes, and nest on the ground. After nesting, flocks form and travel to find suitable feeding areas free of frost. In winter the British population is boosted by an influx of continental birds. The lapwing looks black and white at a distance but in good light has a green, oily sheen on the back; winter birds have buffish fringes to their feathers on the back. The spiky crest feathers are longer in male birds that the females. In flight the lapwing has rounded, black and white wings and a flapping flight. Their call is a loud 'peewit'.

The *Green Woodpecker*, despite its size and bright, colourful plumage, can be surprisingly difficult to see. It is usually rather wary and often prefers to hide behind tree trunks rather than show itself. Sometimes it is seen feeding on lawns or areas of short grass when the green back, greenish buff underparts and red and black facial markings can be seen. It uses its long tongue to collect ants. If disturbed the green woodpecker flies off revealing a bright yellow-green rump. The spiky tail gives support when climbing tree trunks. Its presence is often detected by a loud and distinctive yaffling call. The stout, dagger-like bill is used to excavate wood for insect larvae and to create nest holes. It favours open, deciduous woodland.

Redshank A fairly common resident breeding species, numbers being boosted by an influx of continental birds in winter. A nervous bird, the loud, piping alarm call alerts observers to its presence. It is easily recognised by its red legs and long, red-based bill. Plumage is mostly grey-brown above and pale below with streaks and barring; plumage is more heavily marked in the breeding season. In flight the redshank shows a characteristic broad, white trailing margin to the wing. During the breeding season, the bird favours flood meadows, salt marshes and moors, nesting among grasses; in winter, coastal habitats, especially mudflats and estuaries. Its food includes shrimps, snails and worms. The redshank has an even-paced, jerky walk as it hunts its prey.

The *Moorhen* is a widespread and familiar wetland bird: often wary, in urban areas they can become rather tame. The adult has brownish wings but otherwise mainly dark grey-black plumage. It has a distinctive yellow-tipped red bill and a frontal shield on its head, with white feathers on the sides of the undertail and a white line along the flanks. Juvenile birds have pale brown plumage. The moorhen's legs and long toes are yellowish. It swims with a jerky movement, with tail flicking. In flight the moorhen shows dangling legs.

The *Grey Heron* is a familiar large, long-legged wetland bird. The adult has a dagger-like, yellow bill and a black crest of feathers. The head, neck and underparts are otherwise whitish except for black streaks on the front of the neck and breast. The back and wings are blue-grey. In flight, the wings are broad and rounded with black flight feathers; the heron employs a slow, flapping wingbeat and holds its neck folded in a hunched 's' shape close to its body. The juvenile is similar to the adult but the markings are less distinct and the plumage more grubby in appearance. The heron is often seen standing motionless for hours on end on long, yellow legs, sometimes with its neck hunched up. It will occasionally actively stalk prey which comprise mainly amphibians and fish, especially eels. The heron's call is a harsh and distinctive 'frank'. The heron nests in loose colonies mainly in trees but sometimes seen on coasts in winter.

Goldfinch A beautiful, small finch, with bright yellow wingbars and a white rump. The adult has red and white on face, a black cap extending down the sides of the neck, buffish back and white underparts with buff flanks. The juvenile has brown, streaked plumage but yellow wingbars as in the adult. Goldfinch favour wasteground and meadows where the narrow, pointed bill is used to feed on the seeds of thistles and teasel in particular. The goldfinch builds a neat, deep nest towards the end of a branch. They are usually seen in small flocks which take to the wing with a tinkling flight call. The male's song is twittering but contains call-like elements.

The *Great Tit* is a common woodland and garden species, appreciably larger than the blue tit alongside which it is often seen at bird feeders. The great tit has bold black and white markings on its head and a black bib forming a line running down its chest, broader in the male than the female. The underparts are otherwise yellow and upperparts mainly greenish. Juveniles have sombre plumage with no white on the head. Their song is extremely variable but a striking 'teecha teecha teecha' is rendered by most males. In summer the birds feed mainly on insects.

The *Kingfisher* is a dazzlingly attractive bird, but its colours often appear muted when the bird is seen sitting in shade or vegetation. It has orange-red underparts and mainly blue upperparts; the electric blue back is seen to the best effect when the bird is observed in low-level flight speeding along a river. It is invariably seen near water and uses overhanging branches to watch for fish. When a feeding opportunity arises, the kingfisher plunges headlong into the water, catching its prey in its bill: the fish is swallowed whole. Kingfishers nest in holes excavated in the river bank.

The *Mute Swan* is a large and distinctive water bird, the commonest swan in Britain. The adult has pure white plumage, black legs and an orange-red bill. The black blob at the base of the bill is smaller in the female than the male. Young cygnets are often seen accompanying the mother. While swimming, the bird usually holds the neck in an elegant curve.

Chesterfield Canal near Clayworth

RIVER DERWENT AND THE POCKLINGTON CANAL

RIVER DERWENT

Environment Agency Foss House, 1-2 Peasholme Green, Kingspool, York YO1 7PX (03708 560 560; enquiries@environment-agency.gov.uk).

MAXIMUM DIMENSIONS (at Barmby Lock)

Length: 62'
Beam: 16' 6"
Headroom: 10' 6"
Draught: 4'
A certificate must be purchased from the Barrage Control Centre if you are joining the Derwent, to certify that your craft complies with anti-pollution requirements. Navigation through or above Sutton Lock without riparian owners' permission is a matter of contention. **At the time of going to press the lock is inoperable.**

MILEAGE

STAMFORD BRIDGE to:
Sutton Lock: 6½ miles
Junction with Pocklington Canal: 10½ miles, 1 lock
Bubwith: 15 miles, 1 lock
Wressle: 19 miles, 1 lock
RIVER OUSE: 22 miles, 1 lock

POCKLINGTON CANAL

MAXIMUM DIMENSIONS

Length: 56' 9"
Beam: 14'
Headroom: 8'
Draught: 4'

MANAGER

0303 040 4040;
enquiries.yorkshirenortheast@canalrivertrust.org.uk

MILEAGE

RIVER DERWENT to:
Melbourne: 5 miles
Bielby: 7 miles
CANAL HEAD: 9½ miles

RIVER DERWENT

Prior to 1702 the River Derwent was navigable to Stamford Bridge. A 'publick' act in that year allowed locks to be built to make the river navigable to Scarborough Mills, although works were never carried out above Yedingham, and little trade developed above Malton. Following the repeal of the 1702 Act in 1935, the navigation fell into disrepair, although pleasure craft continued to use sections of the river. New lower gates were fitted to Sutton Lock in 1972, and these are now owned by the Yorkshire Wildlife Trust (1 St George's Place, York YO24 1GN; 01904 659570; www.ywt.org.uk). Consult them **before** making a passage through the lock, and also contact the Environment Agency on 01757 638579 for passage through the top gates of the lock. Entry into the lower part of the river from the River Ouse is by way of Barmby Barrage Lock, controlled by the Environment Agency. The whole of the waterway covered by this book is a Site of Special Scientific Interest (SSSI), being considered one of the finest examples of a lowland river in the country. The seasonally flooded meadows around the lower reaches, known as the Derwent Ings, are of international importance for traditionally managed grassland communities and the species of wildfowl and wading birds supported.

THE POCKLINGTON CANAL

This canal was promoted in a bill of 1814 by merchants in Pocklington and was originally intended to join the River Ouse at Howden. However Earl Fitzwilliam, then owner of the Derwent Navigation, intervened and the canal was connected with the River Derwent. The opening of the York & North Midland Railway in 1847 started the canal's demise, and traffic ceased in 1932. Restoration has been completed on structures as far as Coates Lock, although the canal is currently only navigable to the Melbourne Arm, with an extension eastwards to the Bielby Arm now in the pipeline.
The area surrounding Canal Head has also been put in good order. Virtually all of the route is designated an SSSI, and rich communities of aquatic plants and the invertebrates they support are well established in the disused section. The Pocklington Canal Amenity Society campaigns and works for its complete restoration.

Stamford Bridge

The presently navigable River Derwent leaves the moorings by Stamford Bridge, and approaches a large railway viaduct with a sturdy central iron span, built in 1846. Although the tracks have now been lifted, it has been preserved as an ancient monument, and you can walk across it for a splendid view. Access is from the old station in Stamford Bridge (in Church Road). Beyond the viaduct the river flows into a shallow valley amongst gentle rolling countryside, which persists until East Cottingwith. The village of Low Catton can be seen to the east, its Norman church standing quite close to the river.

NAVIGATIONAL NOTES

The best place to moor at Stamford Bridge is in the old lock cut. Ensure that your craft is well into the chamber and completely clear of the bridge, in case of a change in water level.

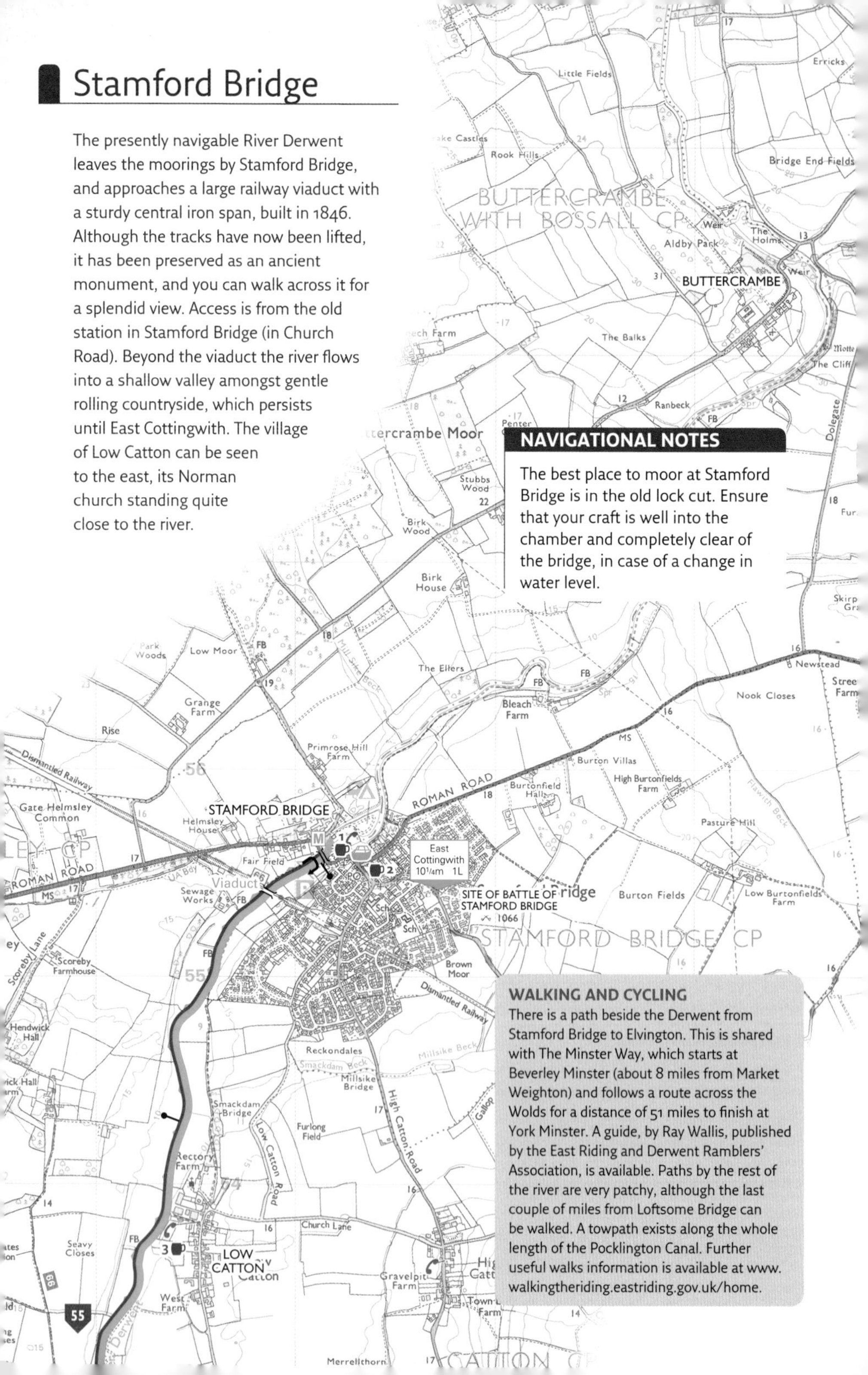

WALKING AND CYCLING

There is a path beside the Derwent from Stamford Bridge to Elvington. This is shared with The Minster Way, which starts at Beverley Minster (about 8 miles from Market Weighton) and follows a route across the Wolds for a distance of 51 miles to finish at York Minster. A guide, by Ray Wallis, published by the East Riding and Derwent Ramblers' Association, is available. Paths by the rest of the river are very patchy, although the last couple of miles from Loftsome Bridge can be walked. A towpath exists along the whole length of the Pocklington Canal. Further useful walks information is available at www.walkingtheriding.eastriding.gov.uk/home.

Stamford Bridge
N. Yorks. PO, tel, stores, chemist, butcher, baker, off-licence, takeaways. An unremarkable but pleasant village centred to the east of the bridge, which was built in 1727 by William Etty. There are several small pleasant pubs to visit, and a picnic area immediately downstream of the road bridge, on the east bank. This is also a popular area for camping and caravanning. In recent years it has suffered the effects of flooding.

Whiskys.co.uk 7 The Square, Stamford Bridge, York YO41 1AG (01759 371356; www.whiskys.co.uk). A truly amazing selection of over 400 single-malt whiskies, from a bottle to an ancient cask.

Battle of Stamford Bridge, 1066 Taking place on the morning of 25 September, this battle was to mark the end of Scandinavian influence over the politics of England. Harald Hardrada had joined forces with the King's brother Tostig and together they had taken York. In response King Harold's army marched the 185 miles from London, in an astonishing six days, to take Hardrada's forces by surprise. Attacking across the river, they broke through the Viking lines and killed Hardrada. Harold then offered a truce, but this was rejected and the fighting continued until Tostig was also killed. With the now-depleted English army in York, William of Normandy (William the Conqueror) seized his opportunity and landed unopposed on the south coast. The Battle of Hastings followed.

Low Catton
N. Yorks. PO box, tel. A plain village lying to the south east of All Saints Church. Originally Norman, later additions include the north aisle and south doorway, both built in the 13th C. The font also dates from this time. The stained-glass east window is worth a look. It depicts the crucifixion, dates from 1866, and is by Morris.

Barmby Tidal Barrage

Pubs and Restaurants

1 **The New Inn** 12-13 The Square, Stamford Bridge, York YO41 1AF (01759 371307). Large, rambling, comfortable and friendly riverside pub serving real ale, and substantial bar meals *L and E.* Children welcome. *Open 11.00-23.00 (Sun 12.00).*

2 **The Bay Horse** 6 Main Street, Stamford Bridge, York YO41 1AB (01759 373028; www.facebook.com/BayHorse.Stamford). A handsome brick-built pub with a small garden, serving real ale and food *E.* Traditional pub games, sports TV and *occasional* live music. *Open 15.00-00.00 (Sat-Sun 12.00).*

3 **The Gold Cup Inn** Low Catton, Stamford Bridge, York YO41 1EA (01759 371354; www.goldcuplowcatton.com). Traditional village inn with open fires, and booth seating and tables, all made from a single oak tree. Real ale. Bar and restaurant meals, all home-made with local ingredients *Mon-Fri L and E (not Mon L) & Sat-Sun 12.00-21.00.* Pretty garden. *Open Mon-Fri L and E (Not Mon L) & Sat-Sun 12.00-23.00.*

AN ELECTION TAKES ITS TOLL

The Derwent Navigation was owned between 1782 and 1833 by Earl Fitzwilliam, and it became quite prosperous. But when, in 1807, the local electors did not return both of the Earl's nominees to Parliament, and voted instead for an independent, he gave vent to his displeasure by raising tolls on the river:

'Take Notice, That from and after the First Day of July next, you are hereby required to deliver ... to the lock keeper ... a full Account, in Writing, of all the Coals, Corn, Goods, Wares, Merchandize (sic), or Commodities, that shall be carried up or down the said River ... and to pay to the said lock keeper ... at Stamford Bridge, such sum of Money as shall be demanded, for every ton weight ... that shall be carried or conveyed in any such Boat, barge or Vessel, up the said River Derwent ... or down the said River Derwent ... not exceeding Eight Shillings ... *Dated this 16th Day of June, 1807*'

When the independent's election to Parliament was later declared to be invalid, he was replaced by the Earl's nominee. Tolls were then brought back to their original rates.

Elvington

Discreetly hiding away in its shallow valley, the River Derwent proceeds virtually due south, gently meandering and avoiding all settlements, which have sensibly been kept well away from the flood plain. The countryside is pleasantly old-fashioned, being divided into many small fields, each separated by a substantial hedge. The meadow known as the Mask, on the eastern bank, is particularly pretty. Hedges here are rich with hawthorn, crab apple, dog rose and oak.

Kexby

N. Yorks. There is nothing much of note in this village. The church of St Paul, constructed in 1852, lies to the west of the river. The main road now bypasses the original bridge, which dates from the 17th C.

Elvington

N. Yorks. Tel, stores, bakery, off-licence. There are moorings below Sutton Lock, so you can leave your boat here and walk up to the village, which is particularly pretty around the green. Holy Trinity Church, built in 1877, is well worth a look. It has a large nave and aisle, a substantial square tower with a clock, and a timber bell-stage. Sutton Bridge was built around 1700: just downstream is the lock, which was constructed in 1878 and more recently restored in memory of E.L. who was, apparently, 'a true gentlemen'. The water abstraction plant above the village, and another at Barmby on the Marsh, take as much as 20 per cent of Yorkshire's water supply from the river.

Yorkshire Air Museum Halifax Way, Elvington, York YO41 4AU (01904 608595; yorkshireairmuseum.org). About 2 miles north west of Elvington, off the B1228. A fascinating and dynamic museum, authentically based on a World War II Bomber Command Station. The unique displays include the original Control Tower, Air Gunners' Collection, Barnes Wallis' prototype 'bouncing bomb' and a superb new Airborne Forces Display. The rapidly expanding collection of historical aircraft depicts aviation from its earliest days, to World War II with the awesome and unique Halifax rebuild through to postwar jets, including Lightning, Mirage and Hunter fighters, a Buccaneer bomber and a Victor tanker. The British land speed record was broken here in May 1999. *Open Apr-Oct 10.00-17.00, daily; Nov-Mar 10.00-16.00 daily.* Allow *3-4 hours* for your visit. Charge.

Sutton upon Derwent

N. Yorks. PO, tel. The church of St Michael and All Angels stands above the lock on the east bank, and dates from the early Norman period. Indeed the organ arch, discovered in 1927, is the original arch of a church without aisles. The arches of the arcades are also Norman. Other details, and the aisle windows, date from the 14th C. The substantial remains of an 11th-C cross shaft is still to be seen, with carved beasts' heads, the Virgin and child and other Viking work. The rest of the village is scattered away from the river. *Part-time PO* in the village hall.

The Ings

Wheldrake, York. By the river, and extending downstream past Wheldrake Ings Nature Reserve, these areas are a showpiece for local traditional farming methods - flooding in winter, never ploughed and never treated with artificial fertilisers.

NAVIGATIONAL NOTES

Please refer to the notes *on page* 51 **before** making a passage through Sutton Lock. The lower gates have substantial leaks. **At the time of going to press Sutton Lock is inoperable.**

Pubs and Restaurants

1 The Grey Horse Inn Main Street, Elvington, York YO41 4AG (01904 608335; www.ourlocal.pub/pubs/the-grey-horse-elvington). A cosy and friendly village pub serving real ale. Food is served *Tue-Sat L and E (not Tue L) and Sun 12.00-16.00.* Dog- and child-friendly, garden. Traditional pub games, newspapers, real fires and Wi-Fi. B&B. *Open Mon-Tue 16.30 & Wed-Sun 11.30 until midnight.*

2 St Vincent Arms Main Street, Sutton upon Derwent, York YO41 4BN (01904 608349; www.stvincentarms.co.uk). Traditional village pub with no music or machines, serving real ale and meals *L and E.* Children welcome. Garden. *Open L and E from 11.30.*

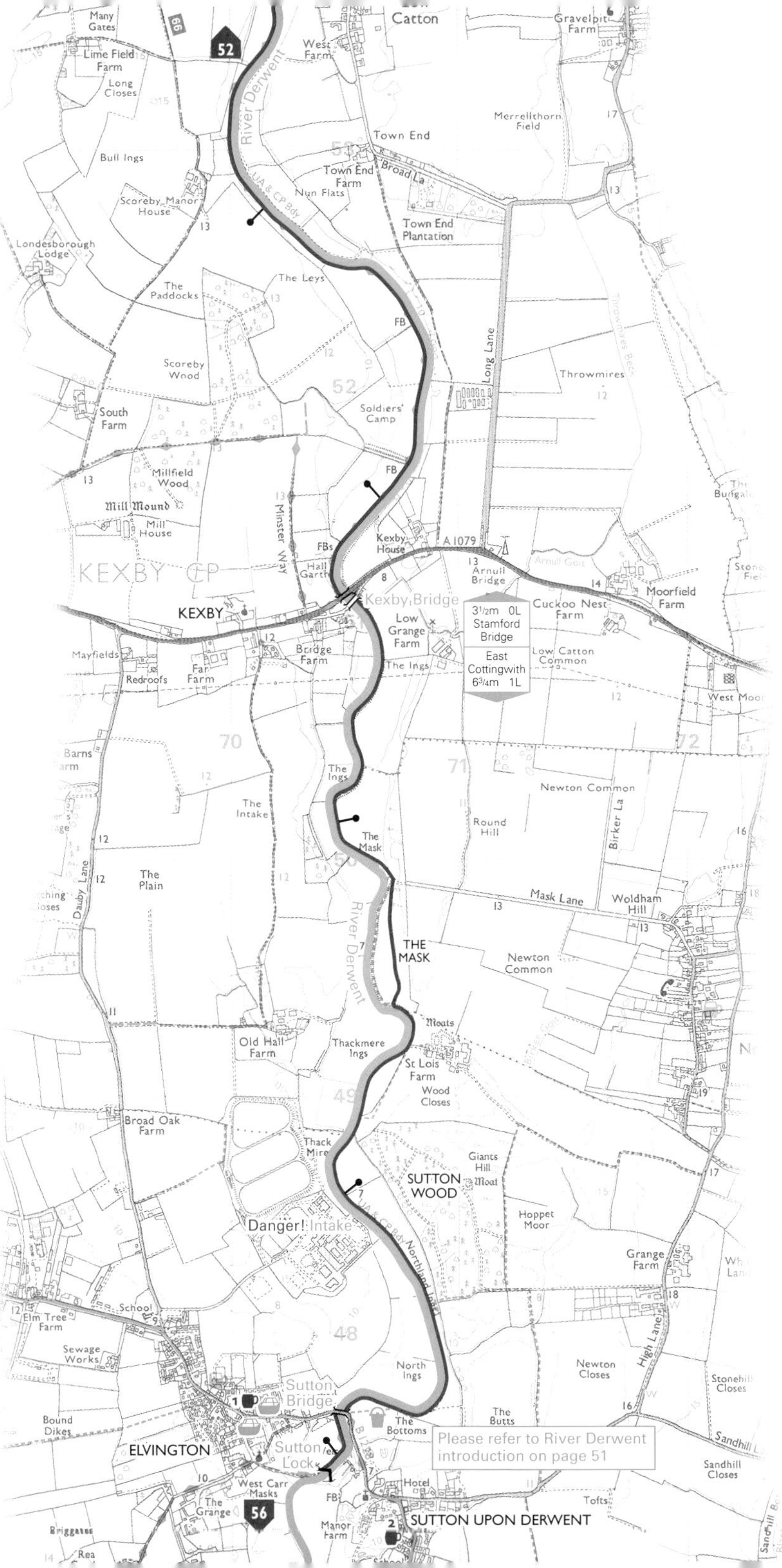

Many Gates
52
Catton
Gravelpit Farm
West Farm
Lime Field Farm
Long Closes
River Derwent
Merrellthorn Field
Town End
Bull Ings
Town End Farm
Broad La
Nun Flats
Scoreby Manor House
Town End Plantation
Londesborough Lodge
The Leys
The Paddocks
FB
Long Lane
Throwmires
Scoreby Wood
Soldiers' Camp
South Farm
Millfield Wood
Mill Mound
Mill House
Minster Way
Kexby House
A 1079
FBs
Hall Garth
KEXBY CP
Arnull Bridge
Moorfield Farm
Kexby Bridge
KEXBY
3½m 0L Stamford Bridge
East Cottingwith 6¾m 1L
Cuckoo Nest Farm
Low Grange Farm
Mayfields
Bridge Farm
Low Catton Common
Far Farm
Redroofs
The Ings
West Moor
Barns Farm
The Ings
Newton Common
The Intake
Round Hill
The Mask
Birker La
The Plain
Dauby Lane
Mask Lane
Woldham Hill
THE MASK
Newton Common
Moats
Old Hall Farm
Thackmere Ings
St Lois Farm
Wood Closes
Broad Oak Farm
Thack Mire
Giants Hill
SUTTON WOOD
Moat
Hoppet Moor
Danger! Intake
Northland Ings
Grange Farm
School
Elm Tree Farm
Sewage Works
North Ings
Newton Closes
High Lane
Stonehill Closes
Sutton Bridge
Bound Dikes
The Butts
The Bottoms
Please refer to River Derwent introduction on page 51
Sandhill Closes
ELVINGTON
Sutton Lock
West Carr Masks
Hotel
The Grange
56
Tofts
Manor Farm
SUTTON UPON DERWENT
Briggates

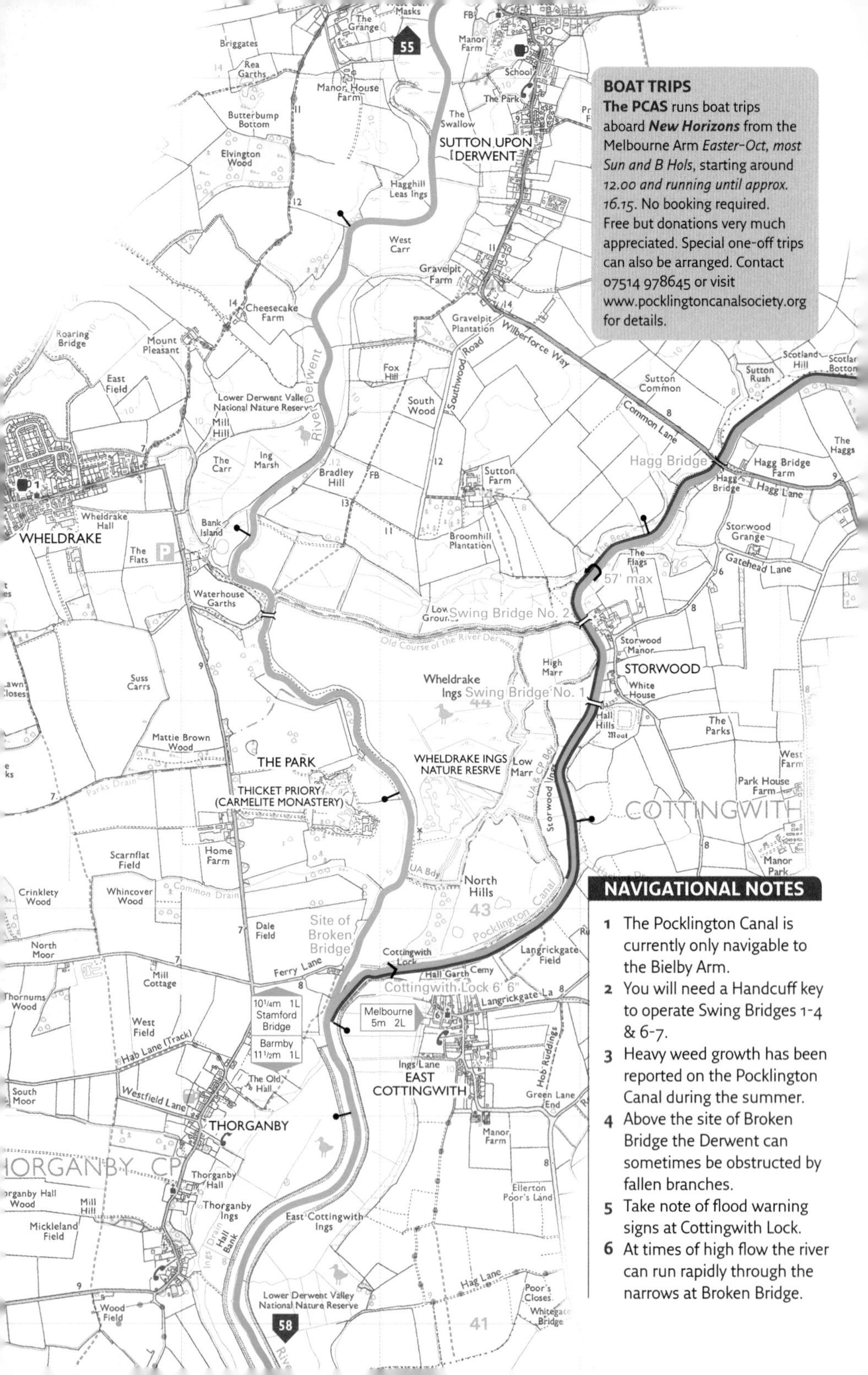

BOAT TRIPS

The PCAS runs boat trips aboard ***New Horizons*** from the Melbourne Arm *Easter–Oct, most Sun and B Hols*, starting around *12.00 and running until approx. 16.15*. No booking required. Free but donations very much appreciated. Special one-off trips can also be arranged. Contact 07514 978645 or visit www.pocklingtoncanalsociety.org for details.

NAVIGATIONAL NOTES

1. The Pocklington Canal is currently only navigable to the Bielby Arm.
2. You will need a Handcuff key to operate Swing Bridges 1-4 & 6-7.
3. Heavy weed growth has been reported on the Pocklington Canal during the summer.
4. Above the site of Broken Bridge the Derwent can sometimes be obstructed by fallen branches.
5. Take note of flood warning signs at Cottingwith Lock.
6. At times of high flow the river can run rapidly through the narrows at Broken Bridge.

East Cottingwith

Just beyond a tiny and hardly recognisable riverside *pub* the river splits: the Beck heads north east and is joined by the Pocklington Canal at Cottingwith Lock. The towpath can be picked up to the north of East Cottingwith, via the path (Canal Lane) beside the village's old cemetery or via another path from the end of Church lane. Continuing through the flat farmland the canal reaches Melbourne, where there is an Arm with *services, toilets* and *moorings*. The canal beyond here has been restored as far as the Bielby Arm. You can, however, walk along the remaining stretch of waterway to Canal Head, to enjoy the scenery and view the restoration works. The terminus is especially attractive.

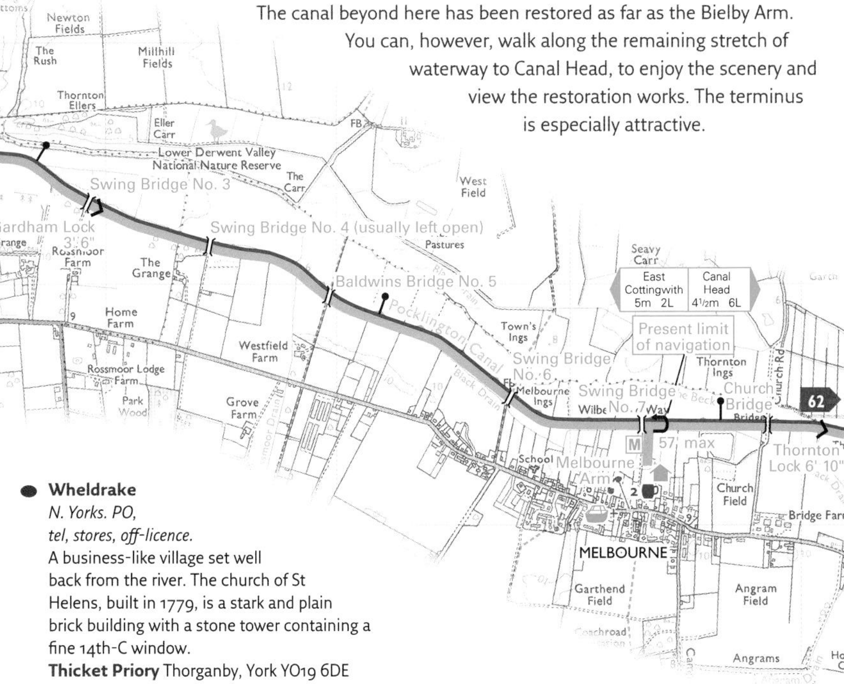

● **Wheldrake**
N. Yorks. PO, tel, stores, off-licence. A business-like village set well back from the river. The church of St Helens, built in 1779, is a stark and plain brick building with a stone tower containing a fine 14th-C window.
Thicket Priory Thorganby, York YO19 6DE (01904 448277; www.thicketpriorycarmel.org). A new Carmelite priory has been built in the grounds of the previous priory. Nestling in trees to the west of the river, opposite Wheldrake Ings, the red-brick house dates from 1847.

● **Thorganby**
N. Yorks. PO box, tel. A pleasant village. The church of St Helens is brick-built with a stone tower, the base of which dates from the 12th C. The church registers date from 1653.

● **East Cottingwith**
E. Riding. PO box, tel. A simple red-brick village built just above the flood plain of the river. The handsome church of St Mary dates from 1780: look for the plaque on the outside wall dedicated to Robert Grey, full of lines of type which don't quite fit.

● **Melbourne**
E. Riding. PO box, stores, off-licence. Linked to the canal by an arm, the village is enlivened by handsome Georgian houses and a delightful corrugated-iron church, dating from 1882. Shop *open Mon-Sat 08.00-18.00 (Sat 16.00).*

Pubs and Restaurants

1 The Wenlock Arms 73 Main Street, Wheldrake YO19 6AA (01904 448240; www.thewenlockarms.co.uk). Welcoming local serving real ales and home-made meals and bar snacks *Mon-Sat L and E & Sun 12.00-16.00.* Dog- and family-friendly, garden. *Open Mon-Fri L and E & Sat-Sun 12.00-00.30 (Sun 23.00).*

2 The Melbourne Arms Main Street, Melbourne, York YO42 4QJ (01759 319457; www.facebook.com/Melbournepub). Friendly, welcoming hostelry in the centre of the village serving real ales and good value food *Mon-Fri E; Sat-Sun L and E (not Sun E).* Outside seating, traditional pub games and Wi-Fi. *Open Mon-Fri 17.00-00.00 & Sat-Sun 12.00-00.00.*

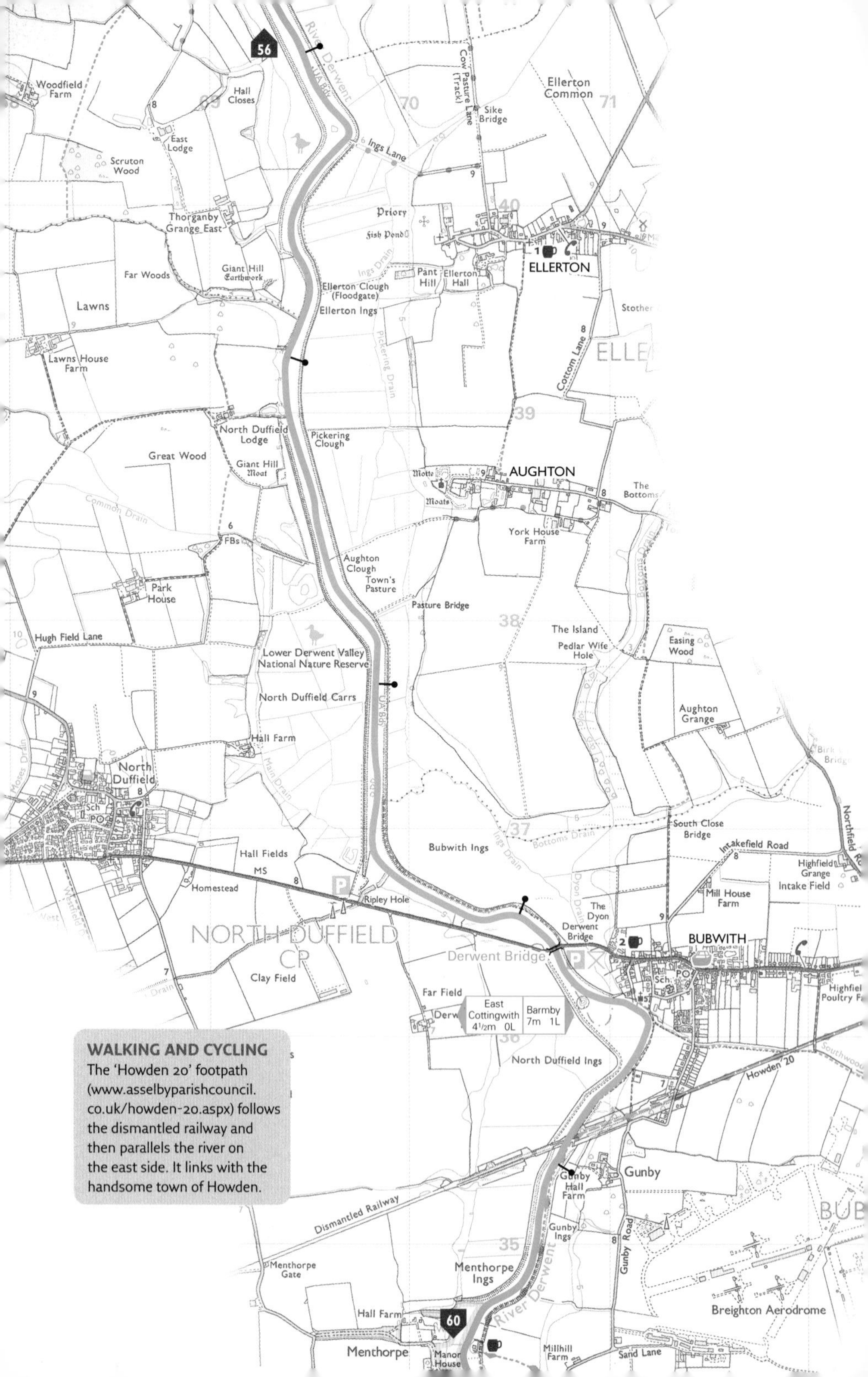

WALKING AND CYCLING

The 'Howden 20' footpath (www.asselbyparishcouncil.co.uk/howden-20.aspx) follows the dismantled railway and then parallels the river on the east side. It links with the handsome town of Howden.

Bubwith

Firmly enclosed by floodbanks, the River Derwent, more substantial now, continues its business-like progress towards its junction with the Ouse. The countryside is quite flat, with the few buildings which are to be seen providing landmarks and an odd group of trees here and there giving a little colour. Just one road crosses on this section: the A163 between North Duffield and Bubwith.

Ellerton
E. Riding. PO box, tel. A small village of old and new brick houses, with a pretty chapel and a duck pond. A windmill, standing separately to the east, has been converted into a dwelling. At the far west end of the village is the site of a priory, but little remains to be seen. The church of St Mary, built in 1848, stands nearby, once abandoned but now beautifully restored.

Aughton
E. Riding. PO box. At the western end of this small farming village, beyond the substantial remains of a motte and bailey, is the splendid church of All Saints. Before you enter, it is worth having a good look from the outside: the tower slopes unreasonably and the chancel appears to have been sliced in half through a doorway, which is now bricked up. The Perpendicular tower has fine gargoyles and sinuous carvings of newt-like creatures crawling over the wall. These are the sign of the Aske family, who have long associations with the village. On the south side there is a sundial. The chancel arch is Norman, as is the south doorway. Brasses of Richard Aske and his wife date from 1466. Robert Aske, leader of the Pilgrimage of Grace, and executed in 1536, was born in the village.

North Duffield
E. Riding. PO, tel, stores, off-licence. Solid, East Riding village, west of the river, much swollen by new housing.

Bubwith
E. Riding. PO, tel, stores, butcher, baker, delicatessen, takeaway, garage. A pleasant village with several attractive Georgian houses facing the street, which is just a short walk along from the bridge, built in 1793. The large church of All Saints is tucked away right by the river. It is Norman in origin, with a chancel arch topped by a Norman gable end. The fine tower is Perpendicular. Fragments of Norman work can be seen built into the church, including a tiny winged figure, dating from c.1200.

Pubs and Restaurants

1 The Boot & Shoe Inn Main Street, Ellerton, York YO42 4PB (01757 288346). A pretty country pub near the chapel, serving real ale. Bar meals are served *Fri-Sat E & Sun L* – booking *advisable.* Dogs welcome, garden. Traditional pub games and real fires. *Open Mon-Thu 17.30; Fri-Sat 16.00 & Sun 12.00.*

2 The White Swan 9 Main Street, Bubwith, Selby YO8 6LT (01757 289981; www.bubwithwhiteswan.com). This pleasant village pub serves real ale and appetising, home-made food *L and E Tue-Sun.* Children welcome; dogs on patio area only. Traditional *Sun L. Open Tue-Sun 11.30-00.00.*

ECOLOGY AND THE BARRAGE

A five-year trial is underway, designed to help the Environment Agency's understanding of the impact of Barmby Barrage on the hydrology of the lower Derwent – and to promote the protection and enhancement of the grasses of the flood plain meadow – whilst safeguarding the wider nature conservation interests. The intention is that, when flows in the river Derwent are 848 cubic feet per second, 700 cubic feet per second and 565 cubic feet per second (as measured by the Agency's gauging station on the Derwent at Buttercrambe) – and when there is standing water on the Meadows – they will:

a) Open the gates at Barmby Barrage such that the Derwent level is allowed to follow the Ouse level to its minimum at low tide, then closing them on the rising tide to avoid Ouse water flowing back in.

b) This will be operated over a half tidal cycle (once over each day).

c) With this opening and closing regime repeated over different flow bands, on different days.

The Environment Agency will gather data from recorders at Bubwith, Elvington, East Cottingwith, Loftsome Bridge and Barmby Barrage. Further details are available at www.gov.uk/government/publications/environment-agency-notice-of-proposal/environment-agency-notice-of-proposal#details-of-the-proposal.

Barmby on the Marsh

A few moored boats mark the presence of the pub at Breighton Ferry. Of course boating is a pleasure reserved just for the summer months, as during winter the situation can change radically, and high flood banks on the lower reaches of both the Derwent and the Ouse are a constant reminder of the potential power of these rivers. The Derwent finally enters the Ouse at the Barmby Tidal Barrage. There are pontoon *moorings* available here, on the Derwent, at the boaters' own risk due to the (faint) possibility of the river level dropping suddenly, in the event of a failure of the barrage's automatic gate control mechanism. The lock keepers are very accommodating and happy to explain their critical role in water management on the waterway, so it is worthwhile stopping to talk and explore. This is also a good opportunity to tell them of an intended passage through Sutton Lock and establish it's current status. Boaters can either head upstream (right) *with the tide* towards York, or downstream (left) towards Goole, the Trent and ultimately Hull and the North Sea.

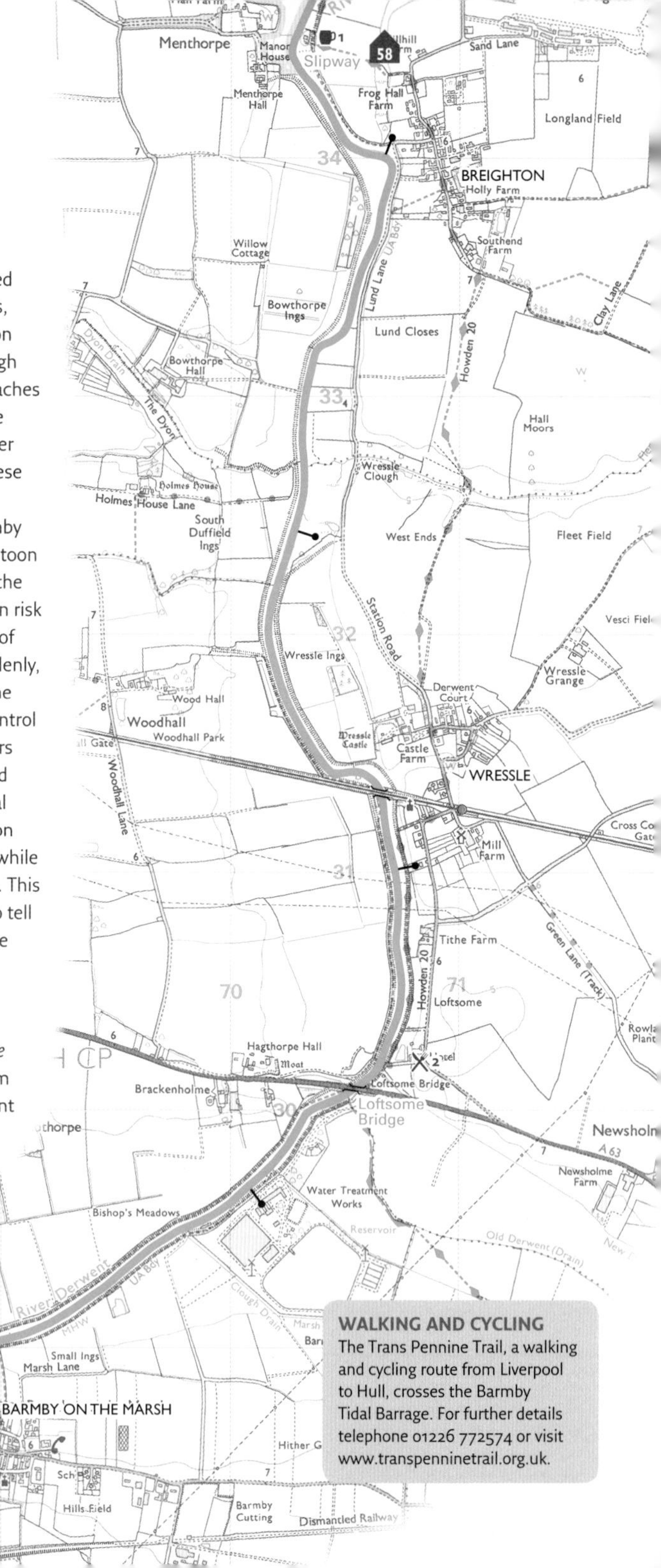

WALKING AND CYCLING

The Trans Pennine Trail, a walking and cycling route from Liverpool to Hull, crosses the Barmby Tidal Barrage. For further details telephone 01226 772574 or visit www.transpenninetrail.org.uk.

NAVIGATIONAL NOTES

1 Entry to (or exit from) the River Derwent is through the lock at Barmby. Telephone and check your passage on 01757 638579 (answerphone) or call on VHF channel 74. In the unlikely event that you are obliged to arrive unannounced (and out of hours) ring the bell on the Ouse jetty. However, where possible always give *24 hrs* notice.
2 The maximum craft size is 62' x 16' 6" at Barmby and 60' x 14' at Sutton Lock. This may be reduced on high tides so, if pertinent, mention your craft's length on initial contact.
3 High water Barmby is *approximately 1hr 40mins after HW Hull.*

Breighton
E. Riding. PO box, tel. A small, quiet agricultural settlement.
The Real Aeroplane Company
The Aerodrome, Sand Lane, Breighton, Selby YO8 6DS (01757 289065; www.realaero.com). Entrance off Gunby Road. This enthusiastic working museum, airfield and runway has a splendid collection of aircraft, including a Supermarine Spitfire PR11, a Hawker Hurricane Mk12, a Messerschmitt Bf 109 and many others. There are plenty of exciting events during the summer where you will see, weather permitting, these planes, or others, in the air! Café. *Open Sat and Sun 10.30–16.00 (or you can try on weekdays as well);* telephone or visit website for events calendar and for details of membership/season ticket required to access airfield. Charge.

Wressle
E. Riding. PO box, tel. A farming village scattered either side of the station and level crossing. Standing prominently to the north west, by the river, are the impressive towers of Wressle Castle, built for Sir Thomas Percy, Earl of Northumberland, around 1380. Beautifully constructed from fine stone, two of the four original towers still remain containing fragments of rooms, spectacular windows, fine fireplaces and, at the top, a stone crucifix. You can admire the remains of the castle from the river or the road, *but there is no public access.* Just to the south, over the railway crossing, is the handsome church of St John of Beverley. This was built wholly of brick in 1799. There is a pretty chapel house just down the road.

Barmby Tidal Barrage
Barmby on the Marsh Goole DN14 7HX (01757 638579). Constructed between 1974 and 1975 at a cost of £750,000, the barrage excludes the tide from the River Derwent, thus allowing more water to be extracted for domestic supply. The Environment Agency has, however, been quick to grasp the amenity value of the site, and there are excellent leisure facilities. Bird watching can be conducted from the wetland hide, which is *open daily 08.00–20.00.* Here you can expect to see the usual waders, plus herons, kingfishers, mallard, teal and swans, amongst others. Coarse fishing is free at the site and specially constructed platforms provide angling facilities for the disabled. There are several waterside *picnic areas, toilets,* and *facilities for the disabled.*

Barmby on the Marsh
E. Riding. PO box, tel. A straggling red-brick village with some fine Georgian houses, hemmed in by the rivers Ouse and Derwent. St Helen's Church was built in the 18th C, and has a handsome brick tower, with some medieval work in the nave.

Pubs and Restaurants

1 **The Breighton Ferry** Breighton, Selby YO8 6DH (01757 288407; www.facebook.com/breightonferry). In a fine riverside position, this homely pub serves bar meals, as well as more elaborate restaurant meals *L and E.* Children will enjoy the playthings in the large garden. Live music *Sat.* Camping and caravanning. Permanent moorings are maintained, there is launching for day boats, and fishing rights are held.

2 **The Loftsome Bridge Hotel** Wressle YO8 6EN (01757 630070; www.loftsomebridge.co.uk). An attractive riverside hotel serving excellent food including breakfast/brunch *06.30–11.00* together with *L and D daily.* B&B. Bar *open from 11.00.*

3 **Lorenzos** High Street, Barmby on the Marsh, Goole DN14 7HT (01757 633827; www.lorenzositalian.co.uk). Italian restaurant and bar serving classic Italian cuisine including highly-thought of pizzas. Vegan and gluten-free options. Food served *Sun–Thu 12.00–21.00 and Fri–Sat 12.00–22.00.*

Canal Head, Pocklington Canal

This last section of the Pocklington Canal is really very attractive, flanked on the east side by overhanging bushes and trees, and on the west by a low towpath hedge, through which rambling farms with grazing animals can be seen. The canal beyond the Bielby Arm is currently being restored: when this remaining section of the waterway is open, it will provide a worthy addition to the network (subject to a satisfactory agreement between Canal & River Trust and Natural England). Here the waterway turns through 90 degrees towards Pocklington while the Arm would once have served the nearby village. To the north are the Wolds, low hills forming the horizon as the final locks are climbed and Canal Head is reached. The basin area here has been restored, and there are *picnic tables* overlooked by a canal warehouse, now tastefully converted into dwellings. The Pocklington Canal Amenity Society (PCAS) was formed in 1969 with the objective of safeguarding and restoring the canal and today (amongst many other activities) they operate an Information Centre at Canal Head *on Sundays and bank holidays throughout the summer.* For more information contact 07514 978645; www.pocklingtoncanalsociety.org.

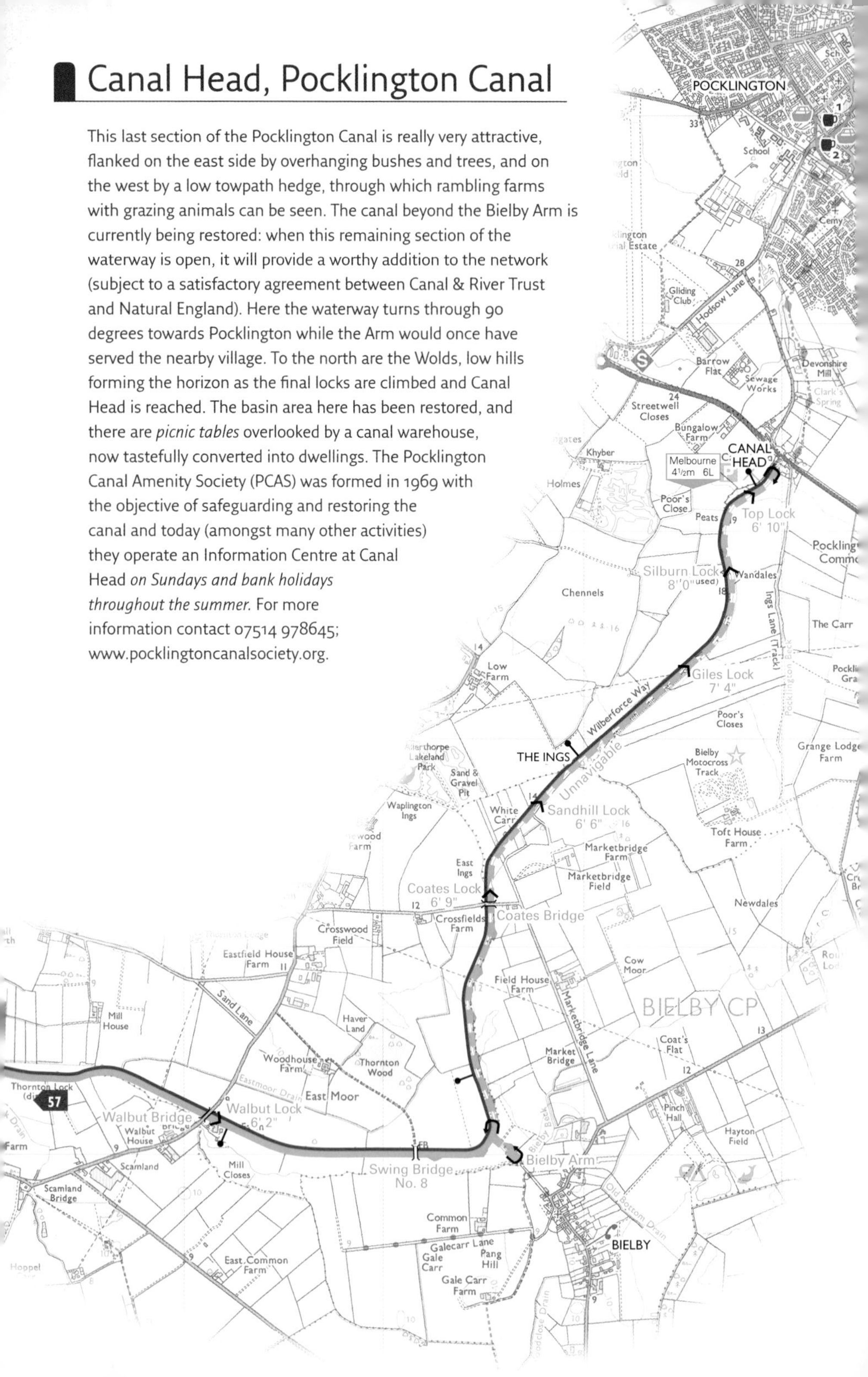

WALKING AND CYCLING

There is a footpath from the east side of the Wellington Oak pub, Canal Head, which can be followed into Pocklington.

- **Bielby**
  E. Riding. Tel. Quiet and attractive. The little church of St Giles dates from 1792, but has some far more ancient features. The Wesleyan chapel on the other side of the road dates from 1837, and is now a house, with an attractive sundial on the wall.
- **Pocklington**
  E. Riding. PO, tel, stores, off-licence, butcher, baker, delicatessen, greengrocer, chemist, takeaways, banks, hardware, fish & chips, garage. A quaint, traditional, rambling market town lying a mile to the north of Canal Head. It is, however, well worth a walk to explore this delightful East Riding settlement with its plethora of enticing pubs and charming cafés. Prominent is the tall battlemented tower of All Saints Church, an endearing mixture of Early English and Perpendicular styles, with Norman fragments. By the pulpit is an engraved slab dating from the 13th C, but re-used to record the death of Margaret Easingwold, Prioress of Wilberfoss Priory in 1512. Kept inside is a churchyard cross dating from the 14th C: the crucifixion is depicted on one side, with the Virgin on the reverse. Readers of the inscription are asked to pray for John Sotheby. The Grammar School was founded in 1514 and proudly records the attendance of the philanthropist William Wilberforce (1759-1833), who was born in Hull. He led the parliamentary campaign against the slave trade, which was finally abolished in 1807.
  Stewart's Burnby Hall Gardens and Museum Trust 33 The Balk, Pocklington, York YO42 2QF (01759 307125; www.burnbyhallgardens.com). On the way into Pocklington from Canal Head. The gardens contain the finest collection of water lilies in Europe, with 80 varieties to be seen. The gardens and museum are open *Apr-Oct, daily 10.00-17.30.* There is a café on site and good facilities, particularly for children, disabled and the elderly. Admission charge (parties of over 20 people *should telephone to book* and will get a discount).

Pubs and Restaurants

1 The Market Tap 11-13 Market Place, Pocklington YO42 2AS (01759 307783; www.facebook.com/pocktap). Town-centre pub with a light, spacious and airy feeling, set over two floors, serving up to nine real ales and food *daily 12.00-21.00 (Mon 16.00).* Dog- and family-friendly. Wi-Fi. *Open Mon 16.00-23.00; Tue-Sat 12.00-23.00 (Fri-Sat 00.00) & Sun 12.00-22.00.*

1 The Station 1 Pavement, Pocklington YO42 2AU (01759 307916; www.facebook.com/stationhotelpocklington). Welcoming, family-friendly pub and restaurant in the centre of this delightful old town. Real ale. Excellent value, home-cooked food available *Thu-Tue 12.00-21.00 (Sun 19.00). Open Thu-Tue 12.00-23.00.*

MISSING THE BOAT

What is now called the canal age was the short period from 1760 to 1840 - 80 years during which the population of England and Wales rose from 6½ million to 16 million. In 1760 Josiah Wedgwood founded his pottery works at Etruria, Stoke-on-Trent, and Clive left India. In 1840 the penny post was established.

Ideas for building the Pocklington Canal were first mooted in the 1770s: a public meeting was called, and agreed the canal would be a 'great utility'. In 1813 Lord Fitzwilliam, owner of the River Derwent Navigation, asked George Leather to make a survey, and this finally appeared in 1814. Subscriptions were opened and an Act of Parliament to enable the selling of shares was passed in 1815. Construction work began in August 1816, when it was agreed to 'let by ticket the cutting of the canal', and the 9½ mile route was finally completed in 1818, remarkably at less than the estimated cost. A mere 29 years after the initial celebrations it began its inevitable decline in the face of railway competition, slowly falling into disuse. The last commercial traffic used the canal in 1932.

Boston and the River Witham (see *page 82*)

FOSSDYKE & WITHAM NAVIGATIONS

MAXIMUM DIMENSIONS

Fossdyke Navigation (Torksey to Lincoln)
Length: 75'
Beam: 15' 3"
Headroom: 11' 3"
Draught: 5'

Witham Navigation (Lincoln to Boston)
Length: 75'
Beam: 15' 3"
Headroom: 9' 2" (Kyme Eau: 6' 0")
Draught: 5'

MANAGER

0303 040 4040
enquiries.eastmidlands@canalrivertrust.org.uk

MILEAGE

TORKSEY to:
Saxilby: 5½ miles
Brayford Pool, Lincoln: 11 miles
Bardney: 20½ miles
Southrey: 23½ miles
Kirkstead: 26¾ miles
Dogdyke: 31¾ miles
Anton's Gowt: 40¼ miles

BOSTON Grand Sluice: 42¾ miles

Locks: 3

The numbered red markers on the mapping represent the CRT kilometre posts visible along the bank of the navigation.

The Fossdyke Navigation was built about AD120 by the Romans, and is the oldest artificially constructed waterway in the country which is still navigable. It was designed to connect the River Witham (made navigable by the Romans) to the Trent and the Humber. The two navigations were used by the Danes when they invaded England, and later by the Normans to carry stone to build Lincoln Cathedral. Subsequently the Fossdyke and the Witham navigations became the responsibility of various riparian landowners, and of the church. The navigations gradually deteriorated and by the beginning of the 17th C were virtually impassable. King James I then transferred the Fossdyke to the Corporation of Lincoln, and from that time conditions improved. Acts of Parliament were passed in 1753 and 1762 for straightening and dredging both navigations, and in 1766 the Grand Sluice at Boston was built, to protect the Witham from the damaging effects of tides and floods. In the 18th and 19th C further improvements were made, many related to the extensive drainage systems carried out throughout the Fenlands. Thus over a period of centuries the two navigations came to assume the wide, straight course that is so characteristic of them today.

In 1846 the navigations were leased to the Great Northern Railway Company, and immediately their revenue began to fall. Railway competition continued, and by the end of the 19th C both navigations were running at a loss. After a period of dormancy the Witham & Fossdyke navigations became established cruising waterways, as pleasure boats replaced the last surviving commercial operators.

Today their isolation and total lack of development attracts many, while their survival preserves the pleasures of visiting Lincoln by boat; and Boston is one of the vital links between the inland waterways system and the open sea.

The newly constructed first stage of the Fens Waterways Link, connecting the South Forty Foot Drain with the Haven in Boston, has the potential to open up 150 miles of new and little used waterway, linking the cathedral cities of Lincoln, Ely and Peterborough with the towns of Spalding, Boston, Crowland and Ramsey. However, driven by the more pertinent need for strategic water management, it looks now as if the concept has been overtaken by the Boston to Peterborough Wetland Corridor (www.waterways.org.uk/news_campaigns/campaigns/regional_campaigns/boston_peterborough/wetland_corridor).

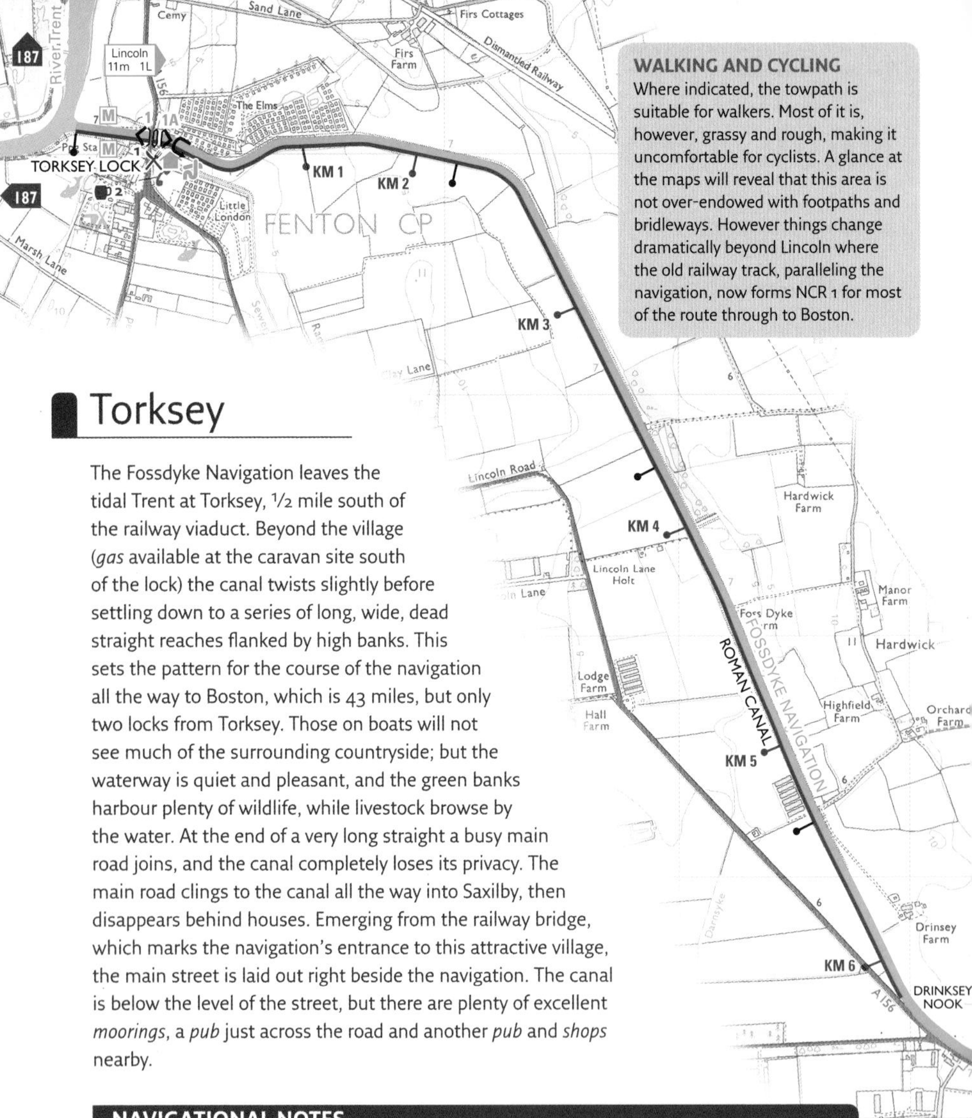

WALKING AND CYCLING

Where indicated, the towpath is suitable for walkers. Most of it is, however, grassy and rough, making it uncomfortable for cyclists. A glance at the maps will reveal that this area is not over-endowed with footpaths and bridleways. However things change dramatically beyond Lincoln where the old railway track, paralleling the navigation, now forms NCR 1 for most of the route through to Boston.

Torksey

The Fossdyke Navigation leaves the tidal Trent at Torksey, 1/2 mile south of the railway viaduct. Beyond the village (*gas* available at the caravan site south of the lock) the canal twists slightly before settling down to a series of long, wide, dead straight reaches flanked by high banks. This sets the pattern for the course of the navigation all the way to Boston, which is 43 miles, but only two locks from Torksey. Those on boats will not see much of the surrounding countryside; but the waterway is quiet and pleasant, and the green banks harbour plenty of wildlife, while livestock browse by the water. At the end of a very long straight a busy main road joins, and the canal completely loses its privacy. The main road clings to the canal all the way into Saxilby, then disappears behind houses. Emerging from the railway bridge, which marks the navigation's entrance to this attractive village, the main street is laid out right beside the navigation. The canal is below the level of the street, but there are plenty of excellent *moorings*, a *pub* just across the road and another *pub* and *shops* nearby.

NAVIGATIONAL NOTES

1 Torksey Lock is operated by a lock keeper and is manned for all serviceable daylight tides. The period of access to the lock is determined by the height of the tide and the amount of fresh water in the river. Contact the lock keeper on 01427 718202 or 07884 238781 – VHF Channel 74 – for further details.

2 There is no overnight mooring in the basin unless penning out the next morning.

3 *See* Navigational Notes, page 186. This also applies to Torksey Lock. Also notes 4 and 5 on page 190.

4 During the winter months these navigations perform a vital drainage function. Bear in mind that *water levels can change rapidly*.

5 Commercial river traffic operates on VHF Channel 6 upstream of Keadby Bridge on the River Trent. It is useful for VHF users to monitor this channel to establish the whereabouts of large craft on the river.

6 Boaters should be aware of grounding on the river and take extreme care when the Trent is low and on neap tides above Gainsborough.

Pubs and Restaurants (pages 66-68)

✕ 1 **Torksey Tearoom** The Lock House, Torksey LN1 2EH (01427 717923). Beside the lock, this establishment is rightly famed for its sausage rolls, homemade cakes and pastries, superb teas and coffees and for its jams and pickles. Also snacks, ices and a Civil Ceremony Licence! *Open 5 days a week 11.00-16.00 (closed Mon & Fri).*

2 **The White Swan** Newark Road, Torksey LN1 2EJ (01427 718653; www.facebook.com/whiteswantorkseylock). Near the lock. A local village pub, popular with boaters and fishermen. Real ale is served, along with food *Mon-Sat L and E (not Mon & Thu L) and Sun 12.00-16.00.* Children welcome, and there is a play area and garden. Traditional pub games, real fires and sports TV. Basic provisions available. Dog-friendly. *Open 12.00-23.00 (Mon, Tue & Thu 16.00).*

3 **The Anglers** 65 High Street, Saxilby, Lincoln LN1 2HA (01522 702200; www.anglerspublichouse.com). Real ale in a friendly local, with plenty of pub games each night. Stores nearby. *Occasional* live music. Dog-friendly and Wi-Fi. *Open Mon-Sat 11.30-23.30 (Fri-Sat 00.30) & Sun 12.00-23.00.*

✕ 4 **Scrummies** 21-23 High Street, Saxilby, Lincoln LN1 2LN (01522 703528; www.facebook.com/ScrummiesSaxilby). Welcoming coffee shop and café in the centre of Saxilby. *Open Mon-Sat 09.00-17.00 & Sun 10.00-16.00.*

5 **The Sun Inn** Bridge Street, Saxilby, Lincoln LN1 2PZ (01522 702326). Canalside hostelry dating from the early 19th C, dispensing real ale. Dog- and child-friendly. Traditional pub games, real fires and sports TV. Mooring. *Open 15.00-23.00 (Fri-Sun 12.00).*

6 **The Woodcocks** Burton Lane End, Saxilby Road, Burton Waters, Lincoln LN1 2BE (01522 703460; www.woodcockspub.co.uk). Large modern pub beside the marina serving real ale and food available *all day.* Garden and children's play area. Wi-Fi. B&B. Moorings nearby in the marina. *Open daily 07.00-23.00 (Sat-Sun 08.00).*

✕ 7 **The Pyewipe Inn** Fossebank, Saxilby Road. Lincoln LN1 2BG (01522 528708; www.pyewipe.co.uk). Two miles west of Lincoln. A comfortable, isolated and traditionally furnished pub first licensed in 1788 as an inn for the bargees. It has panoramic views over Lincoln, the cathedral and the Fossdyke as well as a helicopter landing pad in the grounds. Real ale, plus an extensive home-cooked menu with fresh vegetables and à la carte restaurant *open daily 12.00-21.00.* Dogs and children welcome, four-acre garden. Look out for the ghost floating along the navigation. Moorings. B&B. *Open 11.00-23.00.*

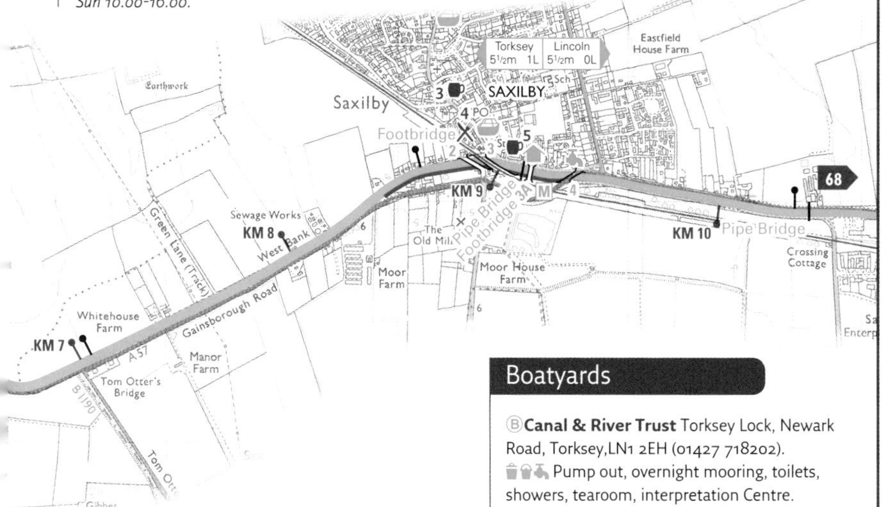

Boatyards

Ⓑ **Canal & River Trust** Torksey Lock, Newark Road, Torksey,LN1 2EH (01427 718202). Pump out, overnight mooring, toilets, showers, tearoom, interpretation Centre. Tea room.

● **Torksey**
Lincs. tel. Once an important Roman port, this was also a thriving settlement in the Middle Ages. It is now a small riverside village, a short walk north of the settlement centred upon the lock.

● **Saxilby**
Lincs. PO, tel, stores, chemist, butcher, off-licence, takeaways, library, station. The presence of the Fossdyke has clearly determined much of the layout of the village, although the siting of the church over half-a-mile to the north has obviously provided another focal point, and as a result Saxilby extends between the two. Some of the buildings in the main street actually face the waterway, and a line of attractive cherry trees completes the scene. The church of St Boltolph is pretty, having an interesting mélange of building styles that may be the result of the west tower being at one time freestanding. There are excellent *moorings* on both sides of the waterway in the village and a *barbecue* for boaters' use west of the footbridge.

Lincoln

As the road finally moves away from the navigation, the Gainsborough–Lincoln railway line strikes in to take its place on the other bank, although separated from the canal for much of the way by a low hedge. After a few industrial works on the way out of Saxilby, the canal is entirely in countryside, green and flat. There then follows a fascinating stretch of waterway. The approach of Lincoln is marked by the magnificent towers of the cathedral on the hill. Passing the isolated Pyewipe Inn (old English for Lapwing) on the canal bank, the Fossdyke bends briefly as it makes its final

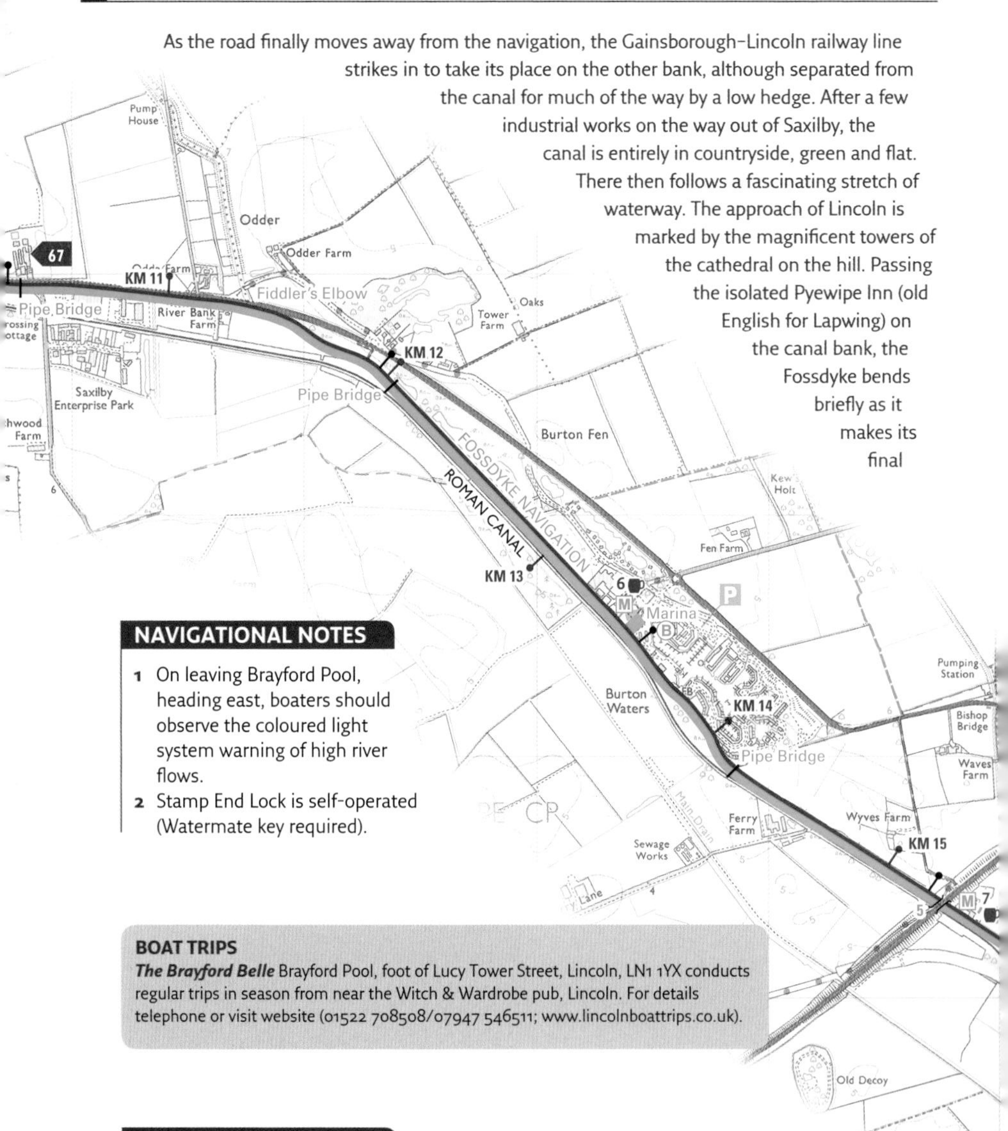

NAVIGATIONAL NOTES

1. On leaving Brayford Pool, heading east, boaters should observe the coloured light system warning of high river flows.
2. Stamp End Lock is self-operated (Watermate key required).

BOAT TRIPS

The Brayford Belle Brayford Pool, foot of Lucy Tower Street, Lincoln, LN1 1YX conducts regular trips in season from near the Witch & Wardrobe pub, Lincoln. For details telephone or visit website (01522 708508/07947 546511; www.lincolnboattrips.co.uk).

Boatyards

Ⓑ**Burton Waters Marina** Burton Lane End, Burton Waters LN1 2WN (01522 567404; www.burtonwaters. co.uk). P D Pump out, short- and long-term moorings, slipway, servicing, repairs, chandlery, toilets, showers, laundry, Wi-Fi.

Ⓑ**Canal & River Trust** The Boatyard, Campus Way, Lincoln LN6 7WW (0303 040 4040; www.canalrivertrust.org.uk). Pump out, toilets, showers, laundry.

Ⓑ**Lincoln Marina** Campus Way, Lincoln LN6 7GA (01522 521452/07751 271786; www.lincolnbig.co.uk/who-we-are/about-lincoln/moorings-in-lincoln). Overnight and long-term mooring, small slipway, toilets, showers, café.

approach to Lincoln. Then a long line of moored pleasure boats, with new buildings behind, leads to a substantial road bridge. Beyond this the navigation widens out dramatically into the vast expanse of water known as Brayford Pool, overlooked by the university. There is a *boatyard* here, *boat clubs* and a floating *pub/restaurant*. The Brayford Trust (01522 521452) has 8 *visitor moorings* in the Pool for which there is a charge. Continuing through the pool, the River Witham can be seen flowing in as an unnavigable stream at the southern corner, and from here onwards (eastward) the Fossdyke Canal is replaced by the Witham Navigation. Leaving Brayford Pool, the channel becomes extremely narrow and goes straight through the heart of old Lincoln, passing through the famous and well-named Glory Hole, with an ancient half-timbered building concealing a busy street of shops astride the navigation. The arch dates from c.1160, and was once called the Murder Hole. In 1235 a chapel dedicated to St Thomas â Becket was built on the eastern side of the bridge, but it was destroyed during the Reformation. Houses on the bridge date from c.1540. East of the Glory Hole the navigation ducks under a striking new steel millennium sculpture and threads its way between a lively mélange of *shops, pubs and cafés*, where the waterway is overhung with trees, and a very large flock of swans lends an air of grace. The channel then once again widens and passes old flour mills which once used barges for shipping the grain, but have now found a new commercial life. Further on are Stamp End Lock and sluices. The top gate has no paddles, being simply raised *à la guillotine* into a steel framework to let the water in and boats pass underneath. Beyond the next railway bridge is another, larger bridge (with *moorings*): you are then back in an uncluttered, flat landscape, little different from that surrounding the Fossdyke Canal. To the west is Lincoln Cathedral, standing proudly on the hill above the town.

WALKING AND CYCLING

The Tourist Information Centre is the place to buy a ticket for Lincoln's guided walking tours, including the ghost walks. Many of these tours are seasonal, so please check the dates and times.

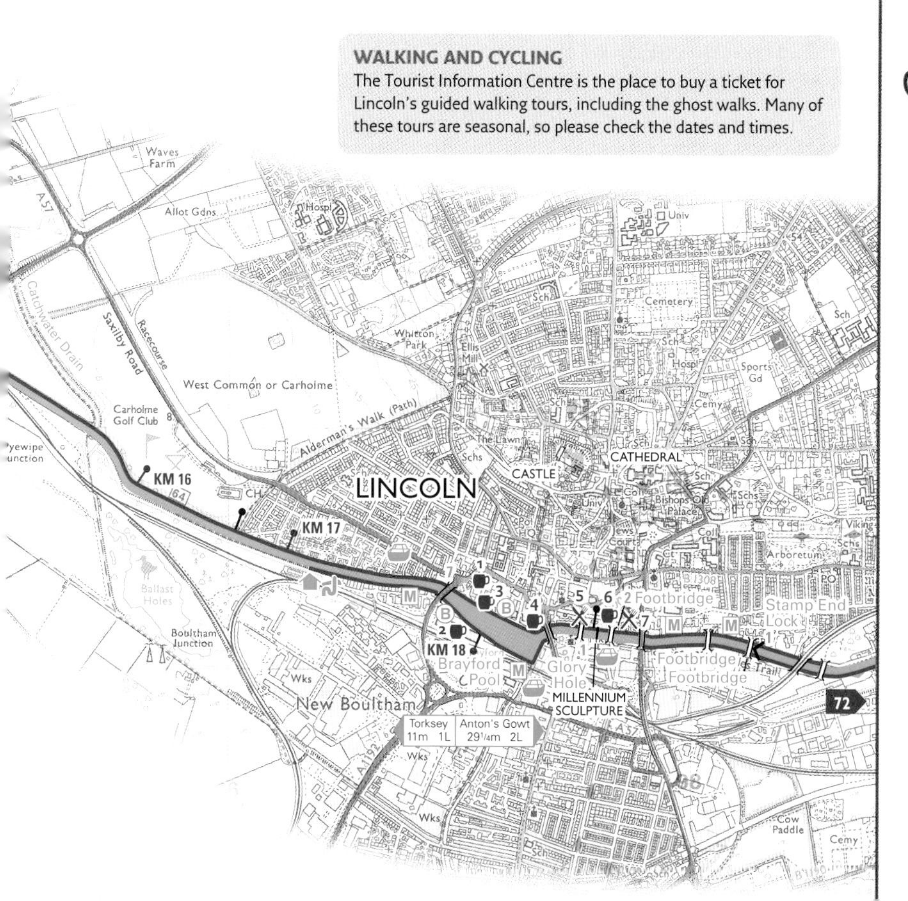

Brayford Pool
This expanse of water separates old Lincoln from industrial Victorian Lincoln. It joins the Fossdyke Canal to the Witham Navigation, and provides the navigator with a welcome relief from the long straight stretches of water either side of Lincoln. The modern building on the south bank is the campus of the University of Lincolnshire, opened by H M Queen on 11 October 1996. The annual Mayor's Regatta, held on Brayford Pool in *June*, is becoming a major event.

Lincoln
All services. Lincoln is a fine city, with a vast amount for the visitor to see. Once the Celtic settlement of Lindon, it became Lindum Colonia, a Roman town; many Roman remains have been discovered. Plenty of these traces can be seen around the town. The old part of Lincoln is of course grouped around the cathedral, which sits on a hill to the north of the river, overawing the city and the surrounding countryside for miles. There are some splendid rows of houses in the Close and just outside it, where the steep and narrow cobbled streets have remained unchanged for centuries, and motor traffic can hardly penetrate. The Christmas market, held in the square in front of the cathedral in early December, is particularly atmospheric.

Lincoln Cathedral 4 Priorygate, Lincoln LN2 1PX (01522 561600; www.lincolncathedral.com). This splendid building dominates the city and visitors to Lincoln should certainly find time for a visit. The original Norman cathedral was begun c.1074, but a fire and an earth tremor in the next century made two extensive restorations necessary. The present triple-towered building is the result of rebuilding in Early English style begun in 1192 by St Hugh of Avalon after the second disaster, although the magnificent central tower (271ft high) was not finished until 1311. The vast interior contains an abundance of fine stone monuments and wood carvings. In the Cathedral Treasury is one of the original copies of the Magna Carta. *Open Jul-Aug, Mon-Fri 07.15-20.00 and Sat, Sun 07.15-18.00; Sep-Jun, daily 07.15-18.00 (Sun 17.00).* Café, shop and library on site. Charge.

Lincoln Medieval Bishops Palace Minster Yard, Lincoln LN2 1PU (01522 527468/0370 333 1181; www.english-heritage.org.uk/visit/places/lincoln-medieval-bishops-palace). Once the domain of the wealthy bishops of Lincoln, standing in the shadow of the cathedral. Banqueting halls, apartments and offices. Vineyard. *Open Apr-Oct, Wed-Sun 10.00-18.00 (Oct 17.00) and Nov-Mar, Sat-Sun 10.00-16.00 and B Hols.* Charge.

Lincoln Castle Castle Hill, Lincoln LN1 3AA (01522 782040; www.lincolnshire.gov.uk/visiting/historic-buildings/lincoln-castle). Built as a stronghold for William the Conqueror in 1068, it stands on the crest of the hill close to the cathedral, where 166 houses were demolished to make the necessary space. Over 6 acres of lawns and trees are enclosed by the thick walls, the two towers and the Cobb Hall - a 14th-C addition. The Observatory Tower and the old keep were built on separate mounds on the south side of the castle. The keep is now a mere shell, but the Observatory Tower is in good repair and there is an excellent view of the surrounding area from the top. Cobb Hall, a lower battlemented tower, was built in the north east corner of the castle and was a place of imprisonment and execution. *Open daily 10.00-16.00.* Café. Charge.

The Collection Museum 1 Danes Terrace, Lincoln, LN2 1LP (01522 550965; www.thecollectionmuseum.com). A permanent exhibition of Lincolnshire's rich archaeological heritage and a changing programme of exhibitions, events and education workshops. Shop and Café. *Open daily 10.00-16.00.* Free.

Tourist Information Centre 9 Castle Hill, Lincoln LN1 3AA (01522 545458; www.visitlincoln.com). Friendly and helpful. Guided walks and ghost walks are run *Easter, Whitsun, Spring and Aug B Hols; daily Jul-Aug; weekends Sep-Oct.* You can also obtain information on river trips and horse and carriage rides. Telephone for details of the City Cycle Race. *Open daily 10.00-18.00 (Sun 17.00).*

FLYING AROUND LINCOLNSHIRE

Finding yourself with some time to spare on the Fossdyke & Witham, you might like to make an excursion to see some of the county's RAF airfields. East of Tattershall Bridge is the Battle of Britain Memorial Flight Centre, where a Lancaster bomber, five Spitfires, a Hurricane and a Dakota are maintained at RAF Coningsby. These aircraft are not empty airframes filling a museum, but are fully maintained airworthy examples. You can visit *10.00-17.00 on weekdays* (01522 782040; www.lincolnshire.gov.uk/history-heritage/battle-britain-memorial-flight-visitor-centre). Charge.

South of Lincoln is RAF Waddington, and here you can watch the activity from a public viewing area alongside the A15 road. This airfield came into service in 1916 as a training station for the Royal Flying Corps. It closed down in 1918 but re-opened in 1926, becoming a base for Hampdens, which attacked enemy shipping in the channel during the early part of World War II. The indomitable Lancaster first entered service at this base, on Christmas Eve 1941, flown by 44 Squadron. The long runway was built in 1953, assuring the airfield's future, and today AWACs (airborne early warning and control aircraft), with their prominent radar dishes mounted in front of the tail fin, fly from here. There is a Heritage Centre for aviation enthusiasts which can be visited by appointment only - contact 01522 728595.

Waterside, Lincoln

Pubs and Restaurants (pages 69)

1 The Horse & Groom 31 Carholm Road, Lincoln LN1 1RH (01522 548866; www.horseandgroomlincoln.com). At the western end of Brayford Pool. Real ale and highly regarded, home-made food including takeaways is served *daily 12.00-21.00*. Children welcome and there is outside seating in the large beer garden. *Open 11.00-23.00.*

2 The Swan Campus Way, Lincoln LN6 7TS (01522 837611; www.facebook.com/theswanULSU). Well situated, with a terrace, this fine warm and friendly pub offers real ale and food *L and E daily*. Wi-Fi. *Open 11.00-00.00 (Sat-Sun 12.00).*

3 The Barge Brayford Wharf North, Lincoln LN1 1YW (01522 255794; www.thebargelincoln.co.uk). A fine floating restaurant specialising in fresh fish and continental cuisine. Meals are available *daily 17.00-21.00 & Sat-Sun 12.00-15.00. Open Mon-Fri 15.00-23.00 (Fri 00.00) & Sat-Sun 12.00-00.00 (Sun 23.00).*

4 The Royal William IV 1 Brayford Wharf North, Lincoln LN1 1YX (01522 528159; www.royalwilliamlincoln.com). A stylish old pub which is *open 12.00-23.00* serving food *12.00-21.00*. Dog- and child-friendly. Extensive outside seating.

5 The Moonraker Tearooms Waterside, Lincoln LN2 1AP (07551 876758; www.facebook.com/pages/category/Tea-Room/Moonraker-floating-tearoom-511085305594652). Floating tearoom and coffee shop in the centre of the city serving scones, cakes and light meals. Vegan and vegetarian options. Tea cruises. *Open daily (weather permitting) 09.30-16.00.* Also home to **Oliver's Tugboat Trips** and a venue for special *seasonal activities at Christmas, Easter and the like.*

6 The Witch and Wardrobe 21 Waterside North, Lincoln LN2 5DQ (01522 244385; www.witchwardrobelincoln.co.uk). Smart pub serving real ale and food *L daily*. Children welcome at meals *L daily*. Traditional pub games and Wi-Fi. *Open Mon-Sat 11.00-00.00 & Sun 12.00-22.30.*

7 Stokes High Bridge Café 207 High Street, Lincoln LN5 7AU (0522 513825; www.stokescoffee.com/pages/cafe-lincoln-high-bridge). Above the Glory Hole. Established in 1902, they serve fine tea and freshly roasted coffee; breakfast; lunch and afternoon tea. Excellent ice-cream. *Open daily 08.00-15.00 (Sun 10.00).*

Washingborough

Leaving Lincoln, the River Witham heads due east in a series of straight, wide reaches through landscape little different to that seen from the Fossdyke, following the bottom of a wide valley. To the west, the towers of Lincoln Cathedral remain visible from the river for about 10 miles to the east. Overhead ISTAR (Intelligence, Surveillance, Target Acquisition and Reconnaissance – the RAF's eyes and ears in the sky) aircraft fly lazily away on their missions, having taken off from nearby Waddington Airfield (www.raf.mod.uk/our-organisation/stations/raf-waddington) where some 3,500 service personnel, civil servants and contractors are employed. There are several villages on the hills overlooking the Witham; to the south is Washingborough, all trees and chimneys, while opposite is Greetwell Hall and its little stone church. Further east is the unappealing sprawl of Cherry Willingham, and then Fiskerton. There is an *overnight stay jetty* at Washingborough.

Greetwell
Lincs. About ½ mile west of Cherry Willingham is All Saints, a beautiful church of Norman origin, next to Greetwell Hall Farm. This was the site of a medieval village, with cultivation and post-medieval garden remains.

Washingborough
Lincs. PO, tel, stores, chemist, off-licence, fish & chips, takeaways, library. The centre of this village on the south side of the Witham valley is quite pretty. There are some attractive stone terraced cottages, and many trees around the church of St John Evangelist, which contains an ornate Georgian chandelier, thought to have originated in Brighton. Stores *open daily 07.00-22.00.*

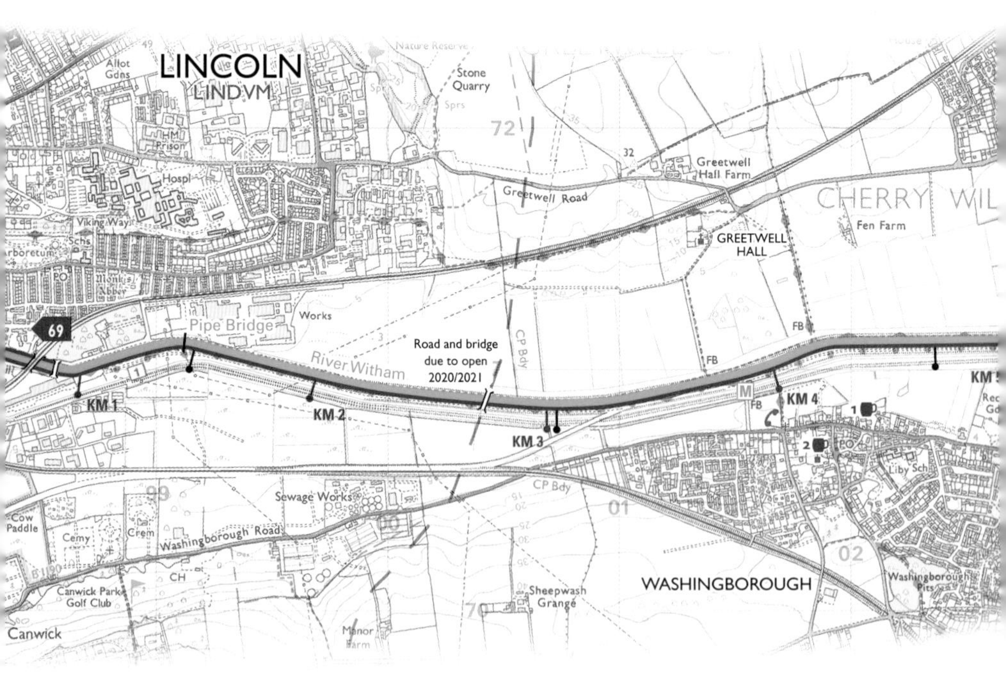

Fiskerton

Lincs. PO box. The name of this village comes from 'fisher's town', since in the old days it was a fishing village, where boats could sail right up to the church on the tide. Later, the Fens here were drained and the river diverted into its present straight course. Since then Fiskerton has stood back from the water. When the river breached its banks in 1962 however, the water once again reached the church. St Clement's itself is curious, as its Perpendicular west tower was built around the only circular tower in Lincolnshire. The rest of the building is a rich mélange of styles and parts, perhaps from the monastic houses at Bardney or Tupholme. The village itself is now full of new housing.

Pubs and Restaurants

1 **The Ferry Boat** High Street, Washingborough LN4 1AZ (01522 790794; www.ferryboatwashingborough.co.uk). Friendly, low-beamed hostelry serving real ales and food. This 16th-C building is listed and there has been a pub on the site since 1547 when the Witham was very much wider. Dogs and children welcome. Food available *daily 12.00-21.00. Open 12.00-23.00 (Fri-Sat 00.00).*

2 **The Hunters Leap Inn** Oak Hill, Washingborough LN4 1BA (01522 790458; www.huntersleapwashingboroughpub.co.uk). Welcoming local serving real ales and dispensing good cheer. Dog-friendly. Traditional pub games, sports TV and Wi-Fi. *Open Mon-Sat 12.00-23.00 (Tue 19.00) & Sun 12.00-22.30.*

3 **The Carpenter's Arms** High Street, Fiskerton, Lincoln LN3 4HF (01522 751806; www.thecarpentersfiskerton.co.uk). A black and white village pub serving real ale, and food *Mon E; Thu-Sat L and E & Sun 12.00-20.00.* Garden and traditional pub games. *Open Mon-Thu L and E & Fri-Sun 12.00-17.00.* Garden and traditional pub games. *Open 12.00-23.00 (Mon 18.00).*

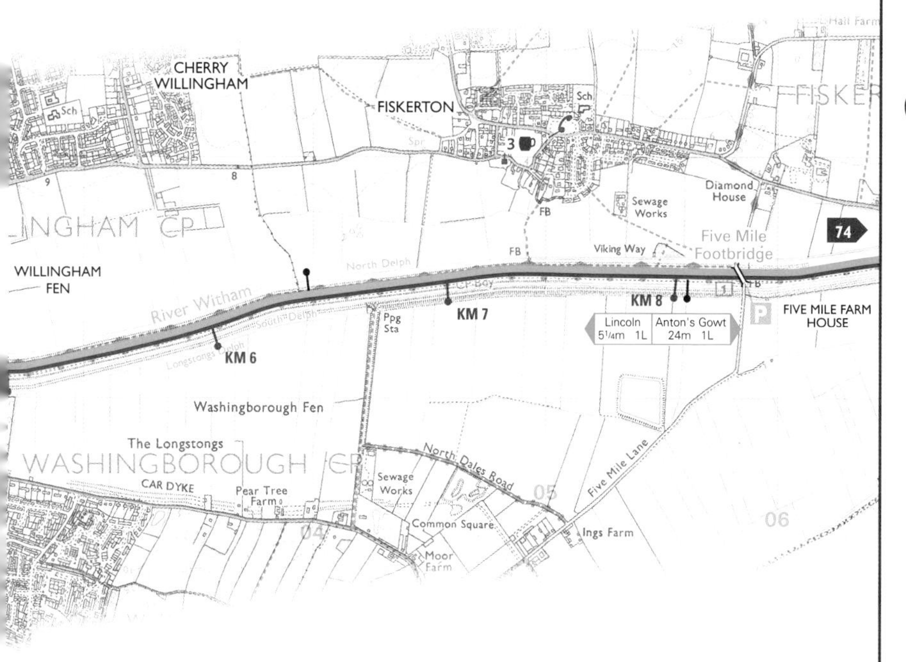

WALKING AND CYCLING

There are footpaths down to the river from Greetwell, Fiskerton and the western end of Washingborough. You can walk from Fiskerton to Washingborough, crossing Five Mile Footbridge. National Cycle Route 1 uses the dismantled railway track alongside the navigation between Lincoln and Woodhall Spa and follows the waterway closely for the remainder of the journey into Boston.

Branston Island

Leaving Five Mile House, the river continues eastwards for nearly two miles through the unchanging flat and empty landscape. Then it turns south east and maintains this general course all the way to Boston. There is a small pumping station at the point where the old course of the river branches off round a loop to the north, forming a large island known as Branston Island. Meanwhile the navigation runs in a straight line to Bardney Lock (*showers and toilets*), the only lock between Lincoln and Boston. Below the lock, the old course of the river, navigable to Short Ferry, flows in again from the north, and a river-sized drain enters from the north west. The village of Bardney is near the next bridge; a *pub* and *fish & chips* are close here, with more choice up the road, and there is an *overnight stay jetty*. The large, ungainly buildings, once the Bardney sugar-beet factory, and now employed in the manufacture of golden syrup (and other sugar-based products) are conspicuous in the flat landscape and continue to dominate the countryside for several miles. The river flows between high banks to Southrey, passing the drain (or field dyke) called Nocton Delph. At the village there is another brief flurry of buildings, including a converted station complete with name board. There are occasional farms on the south bank; the closed railway continues to hug the other side of the navigation all the way to Boston. Southrey has an *overnight stay jetty*.

Pubs and Restaurants

1 Black Horse Restaurant 16 Wragby Road, Bardney, Lincoln LN3 5XL (01526 398900; www.bardneyblackhorse.co.uk). A fully licensed guest house and restaurant in a 16th-C building with beams and low ceilings, serving home-cooked food. Garden. B&B. Restaurant *open Wed-Sat 11.30-14.00 & Sun 12.00-14.00.* Booking advisable.

2 The Bardney Fryer Station Road, Bardney LN3 5UF (01526 397299; www.bardneyheritage.com). Housed in an original 1957 BR brake ballast van on Platform 1 of the old village station, this unusual establishment now dispenses fish and chips *Fri-Sat 12.00-14.00 & Fri 17.00-19.30.* B&B (see Bardney Heritage Centre page 75).

3 The Riverside Inn Ferry Road, Southrey, Lincoln LN3 5TA (01526 398374; www.theriversideinnsouthrey.wordpress.com). Spacious and pretty pub serving real ale. Restaurant and bar meals are served *during opening hours.* Dog- and family-friendly, garden. Moorings. Hidden on the roof is a message to low flying pilots: 'If you can read this, you are too b****y low'. *Open Mon-Thu 10.00-23.00 & Fri-Sun 10.00-23.30 in summer and Mon-Thu 16.00-23.00 & Fri-Sun 12.00-23.30 in winter.*

NAVIGATIONAL NOTES

At Bardney Lock boats heading upstream towards Lincoln must turn right to pass under the railway bridge and then turn immediately left into the lock chamber.

Bardney

Lincs. PO, tel, stores, chemist, off-licence, butcher, takeaway, fish & chips. A small village to the east of the river, on a slight rise, Bardney is attractive, with the mellow 15th-C church of St Lawrence and a pleasant village green. Inside the church is an incised slab to Abbot Richard Horncastle, 1508, taken from the abbey, together with many minor architectural features from the same source. The parish almshouses by the green were built in 1712. The remains of the Benedictine abbey lie to the north of the village. It was founded late in the 7th C and subsequently over-run by the Danes. Re-established in 1087 by Gilbert of Ghent as a cell of Charroux, the abbey buildings were begun again in 1115. The whole site was excavated 1909-14 and reported on by Sir Harold Brakspear in 1922, but much of what was found then has once again disappeared. Bardney has become well known in recent years as the scene of music festivals; in fact the site is to the south east of the village, towards Southrey. The shop is *open daily 07.00-22.00.*

Bardney Heritage Centre 123 Station Road, Bardney LN3 5UF (01526 397299; www.bardneyheritage.com). Offering a cordial welcome and a gateway to Lincolnshire's lime woods. Bardney has a diverse Industrial Heritage - from the canning factory of Morrells to the beet factory of British Sugar, plus the workings of the railways, the navigation and local agriculture. The Heritage Centre seeks to combine this with local parish history, creating an interpretation centre for all ages. Cycle hire and tearoom. *Open Thu-Sun 10.00-16.00 (not Thu Nov-Mar) and B Hols.* Charge. B&B in the unusual accommodation provided by two converted railway wagons - *Southrey* and *Stixwould*

Southrey

Lincs. PO box, tel. A small village of little intrinsic interest, but with reasonable river access. The little white wooden church of St John the Divine, with its belfry, is delightful. It was built by the villagers in 1898 and is clearly cherished. A mile to the north, in undulating countryside, are the ruins of Tupholme Abbey, founded in 1160. The station platforms and name board survive - the track has long since disappeared.

9½m 2L Lincoln
Anton's Gowt 19¾m 0L

76

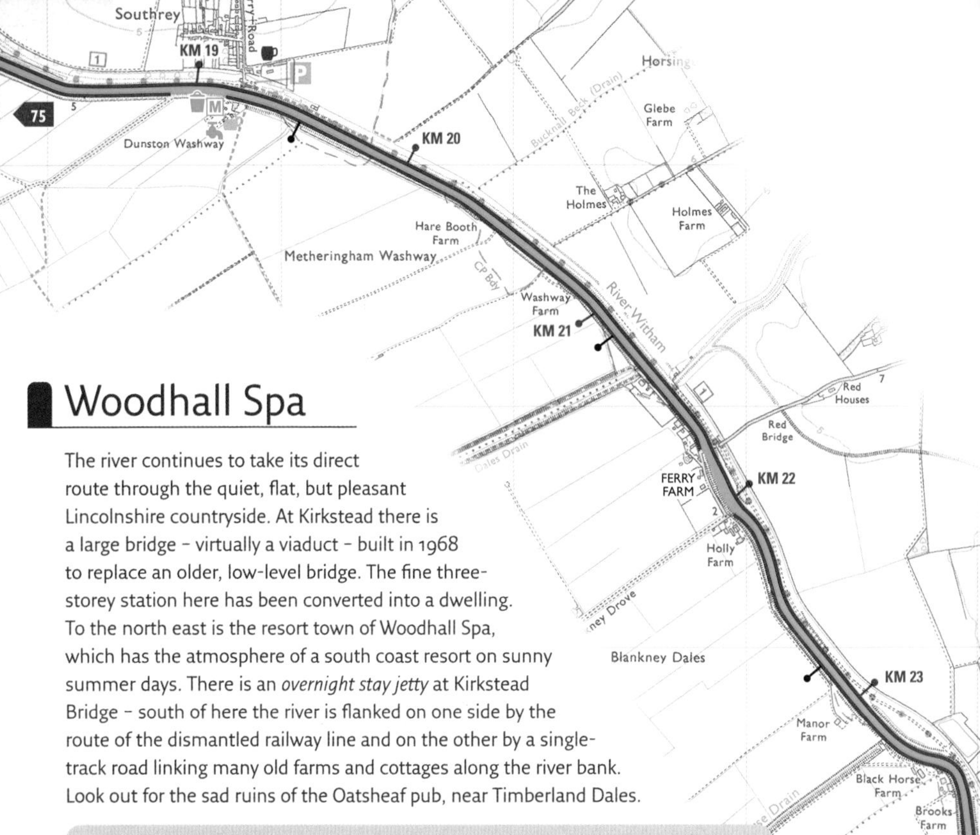

Woodhall Spa

The river continues to take its direct route through the quiet, flat, but pleasant Lincolnshire countryside. At Kirkstead there is a large bridge – virtually a viaduct – built in 1968 to replace an older, low-level bridge. The fine three-storey station here has been converted into a dwelling. To the north east is the resort town of Woodhall Spa, which has the atmosphere of a south coast resort on sunny summer days. There is an *overnight stay jetty* at Kirkstead Bridge – south of here the river is flanked on one side by the route of the dismantled railway line and on the other by a single-track road linking many old farms and cottages along the river bank. Look out for the sad ruins of the Oatsheaf pub, near Timberland Dales.

WALKING AND CYCLING

There is a 5-mile circular cycle route through Ostler's Plantation, to the east of Woodhall Spa. Start from the car park off Kirkby Lane (B1191). It is an easy ride through a managed woodland established on the site of a World War II airfield which was the base of 617 Squadron, the famous 'Dambusters'. One of the old buildings is now a hibernaculum for long-eared bats. The Spa Trail is a traffic-free route for walkers and cyclists which starts just off the B1191 at Martin Moor, to the east of Woodhall Spa, and extends to Thornton Lodge Farm, near Horncastle. For more walking and cycle trails, visit www.poacherguide.co.uk.

Martin Dales

Sim Booth Grange

Dales Head Bank

Dales Head Bridge

Pubs and Restaurants

1 The Railway Inn 195 Witham Road, Woodhall Spa LN10 6QX (01526 352580). On the east bank near the station, this is a traditional pub with open fires, in a railway house. Real ale. Food is served *Mon-Thu E & Fri-Sun L and E (not Sun E).* Dog- and family-friendly, garden and children's playground. Traditional pub games, real fires and Wi-Fi. B&B. *Open Mon-Thu 17.00-21.00 & Fri-Sun 12.00-00.00 (Sun 21.00).*

2 Janet's Tea Room 18 Station Road, Woodhall Spa LN10 6QL. Homely, welcoming teashop – opposite the Dambusters Memorial-serving teas, coffees, cake and pastries, snacks and light meals in surroundings decorated with Lancaster Bomber memorabilia. *Open daily 08.30-15.30.*

3 Zucci 1 Station Road, Woodhall Spa LN10 6QL (01526 354466; www.zucci.co; www.zucci.org). Popular Mediterranean bistro, with an open kitchen, where the 'off-stage' activity and aromas percolate into the cosy, rustic and relaxed atmosphere of the restaurant. *Open daily 17.00-21.00.*

4 The Mall Hotel Station Road, Woodhall Spa LN10 6QL (01526 352342; www.themallpubwoodhallspa.co.uk). The only pub in the town, and thankfully it serves real ale. Bar and restaurant meals available *Mon-Sat 12.00-19.30 (Wed 18.00) & Sun L and E.* Dog- and family-friendly, garden. Real fires, sports TV and Wi-Fi. *Open daily 12.00-23.00 (Sun 22.30).*

5 The King's Arms Church Road, Martin Dales, Woodhall Spa N10 6XZ (01526 352633; www.kingsarmsmartindales.co.uk). On the west bank of the river. A sociable and comfortable pub serving real ale. Bar meals available *Tue-Sun L and E (not Sun E).* Family-friendly. Traditional pub games, real fires, sports TV and Wi-Fi. *Open Tue-Sun 12.00-23.00.*

Kirkstead Abbey Abbey Lane, Kirkstead, Woodhall Spa LN10 6QZ. 3/4 mile east of Kirkstead Bridge. A solitary finger of masonry about 30ft high is all that remains of the enormous Cistercian monastery founded in 1139, and moved here in 1187. A trained eye can recognise the former fishponds attached to the monastery grounds.

St Leonard's Church Abbey Lane, Kirkstead, Woodhall Spa LN10 6QZ. Originally an extramural chapel of the abbey, it was built in the mid 13th C and survives largely intact as one of the finest examples of its kind. Beautifully decorated, it was sensitively restored in 1913–14. The 13th-C wooden screen is one of the oldest in the country, and an effigy of a knight, dating from c.1250, must also be one of the earliest in the country. The church is just a few hundred yards north east of the bridge.

Woodhall Spa

Lincs. PO, tel, stores, takeaways, library, butcher, hardware, chemist, fish & chips, off-licence, cinema, garage. A resort town in the woods a mile north east of Kirkstead Bridge, and which would not look out of place on the south coast of England. Perhaps you will notice also that the town sign features a fine railway engine, although regrettably the line to Woodhall Spa is no more. In 1811, while drilling for coal, iodine mineral water was found at a depth of 511ft. An inn was built beside the shaft, and a new well was sunk in 1824. The town then grew and it still has the characteristic Victorian atmosphere of many English spa towns. Jubilee Park has a heated outdoor swimming pool, open in the *summer*. There is a very popular and curious Kinema, complete with Compton organ, tucked away in the woods near to the spa building. It was built in the 1920s, and is unusual in that it uses back-projection (01526 352166; www.thekinemainthewoods.co.uk). Petworth House, now a hotel, served as the officers' mess for 617 Squadron, the 'Dambusters', stationed nearby. One-and-a-half miles north east of the town is the Wellington Monument, by Waterloo Wood, which was planted from acorns 'sown immediately after the memorable Battle of Waterloo'. The stores are *open daily 07.00-22.00.*

The Cottage Museum Iddesleigh Road, Woodhall Spa LN10 6SH (*see* below) (01526 352456; www.cottagemuseum.co.uk). Contains a variety of historical information about the village and a changing display of local history. *Open Easter to end Oct, daily, 10.30-16.30.* Charge.

Tourist Information Centre Seasonal at the Cottage Museum, Iddesleigh Road, Woodhall Spa LN10 6SH (01526 353775; www.cottagemuseum.co.uk/tourist-information). Friendly and helpful. *Open daily Easter-Oct 10.30-16.30.* There are a series of 10 walks based on the TIC.

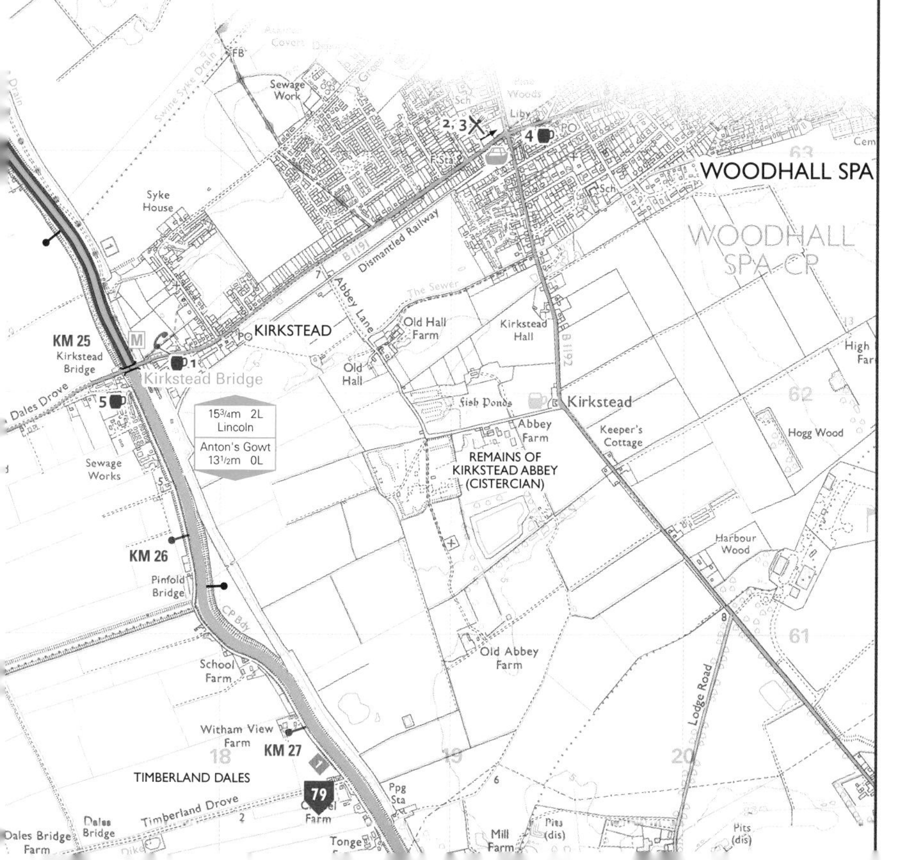

Dogdyke

The river continues southward, now on a pretty and winding course which provides a pleasant contrast to the former straight navigation. Along the Kesteven bank are a number of farm cottages served by a minor road. The old junction with the Horncastle Canal can still just be seen as a slight dent in the east bank. Less than a mile from Tattershall Bridge is Dogdyke, just a short way beyond the old steam pump. It is an attractive place with a *marina* and a riverside *pub*. Coningsby Airfield is close by: one end of the runway is near the river, so navigators may find aircraft screaming over them at a height of perhaps 100ft. This can be disconcerting on an otherwise quiet summer's afternoon. South of Dogdyke there is a small *landing stage* (charge) on the west bank; this marks a caravan site with *facilities* useful to those on boats (*shop, shower, gas,* *etc*). Beyond it are the houses of Chapel Hill, where the Kyme Eau or Sleaford Navigation joins *(see below)*. Beyond here the river becomes straight and wide once again, with piling to protect and strengthen the bank on one side, and reeds on the other. Boston Stump, the tower of the church, can be seen from here some nine miles away beneath breezy open skies. There is an *overnight stay jetty* at Tattershall Bridge.

Tales of the River Bank Visitor Centre Telephone Horncastle TIC for opening times (*see* below). An exhibition explaining how the fen was formed, and is now drained and used.

Timberland Pumping Station Telephone Horncastle TIC for opening times (*see* below). This pumping station was built in 1839 to drain 2500 acres of Timberland and Thorpe Tilney fens It is a splendid working example, and once featured a scoop wheel over 26ft in diameter, lifting water from Walton Delph into the River Witham. The present pump was installed by Gwynnes of London in 1924.

Tattershall Castle Tattershall, Lincoln LN4 4LR (01526 342543; www.nationaltrust.org.uk). *NT*. 1 mile north east of Tattershall Bridge. The original castle was built by Sir Robert de Tateshall in 1231, and rebuilt in brick in the 15th C for Ralph Cromwell, Treasurer of England 1434–5. Rescued by Lord Curzon between 1911 and 1914, only the keep of this superb building remains. It is 110ft high, and the bricks, 322,000 of them, were supplied from Edlington Moor, 9 miles to the north. *Open Mar–Oct, Sat–Wed 11.00–17.00; Nov–Dec, weekends only 11.00–16.00; closed Jan–Feb*. Shop, teas. Charge

Horncastle Canal This navigation, 10 miles long, was built 1792–1802 to serve the small country town of Horncastle. The remains of the first lock are about 300yds from the river. Nearer Horncastle parts of the canal are still in water, and the town basin survives. It was abandoned in 1885.

Tourist Information Centre Sir Joseph Banks Centre, Bridge Street, Horncastle LN9 5HZ (01507 526065; www.explorelincolnshire.co.uk/horncastle/tourist-information-centres/horncastle-tourist-information-centre-36839.html). Out of season, contact Louth TIC (01507 609289; louthinfo@e-lindsey.gov.uk).

● **Dogdyke**

Lincs. PO box, tel. 'A ditch where docks grow', and now a riverside settlement close to a signpost which indicates 2½ miles to New York and 12 miles to Boston – nice for a photograph.

Dogdyke Pumping Station Bridge Farm, Tattershall Bridge LN4 4JG (01522 683755; www.dogdyke.com). Between Tattershall Bridge and Dogdyke, off A153 at Bridge Farm. Home of the two remaining land drainage engines: a 1856 beam engine, driving a land drainage scoop wheel (the last example still steaming in Britain) and the 1940 Ruston and Hornsby 7 XHR oil engine powering a Gwynne's pump that superseded it. There is a small museum of land drainage, a plant and gift stall together with a tea room serving homemade cakes. Steaming *May–Oct, 1st Sun of month and on occasional, additional days* – see website. Free, but donations welcome.

● **Chapel Hill**

Lincs. PO box, tel. A pleasantly compact and tiny village.

Kyme Eau (01522 689460; www.sleafordnavigation.co.uk). Navigable through Kyme Lock (Watermate key required) for over 7½ miles to Cobblers Lock, where it is possible to wind. Maximum dimensions are 70' 0" x 14' 0" with a headroom of 5' 6" and a draught of 2' 0". Progress can be slow on this navigation. From *Oct–Mar* the gates at Lower Kyme Lock are chained back for flood prevention reasons, and navigation is difficult in winter. Full restoration to Sleaford is planned. See pages 86–87 for further details.

Boatyards

Ⓑ **Belle Isle Marina** Dogdyke, Coningsby LN4 4UU (01526 342124/07768 292100; www.belleislemarina.co.uk). Gas, overnight and long-term mooring, winter storage, slipway, crane, boat and engine sales and repairs, toilets, showers, holiday accommodation.

Ⓑ **Orchard Caravan Park** Witham Bank, Chapel Hill, Lincoln LN4 4PZ (01526 342414). Overnight mooring, swimming pool, toilets, showers, laundrette, children's playground, games room, café and bar.

Ⓑ **Chapel Hill Marina & Holiday Park** Chapel Hill, Lincoln LN4 4QB (01526 342750; www.holidaycaravansdirect.com/lincolnshire/lincoln/chapel-hill-marina-and-caravan-park). At the entrance to the Kyme Eau. D Gas, overnight and long-term mooring, boat sales, restaurant nearby.

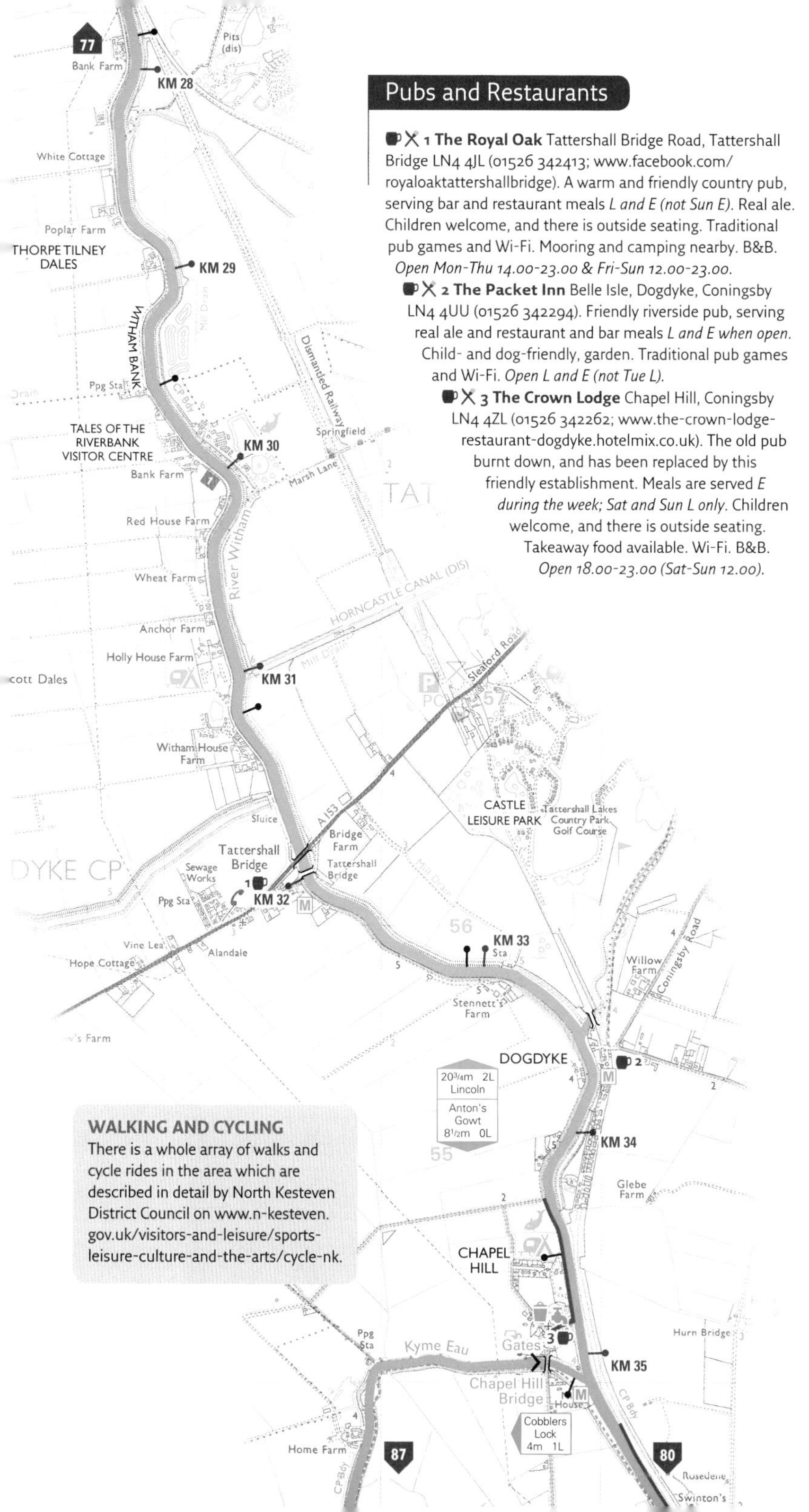

Pubs and Restaurants

1 The Royal Oak Tattershall Bridge Road, Tattershall Bridge LN4 4JL (01526 342413; www.facebook.com/royaloaktattershallbridge). A warm and friendly country pub, serving bar and restaurant meals *L and E (not Sun E)*. Real ale. Children welcome, and there is outside seating. Traditional pub games and Wi-Fi. Mooring and camping nearby. B&B. *Open Mon-Thu 14.00-23.00 & Fri-Sun 12.00-23.00.*

2 The Packet Inn Belle Isle, Dogdyke, Coningsby LN4 4UU (01526 342294). Friendly riverside pub, serving real ale and restaurant and bar meals *L and E when open*. Child- and dog-friendly, garden. Traditional pub games and Wi-Fi. *Open L and E (not Tue L).*

3 The Crown Lodge Chapel Hill, Coningsby LN4 4ZL (01526 342262; www.the-crown-lodge-restaurant-dogdyke.hotelmix.co.uk). The old pub burnt down, and has been replaced by this friendly establishment. Meals are served *E during the week; Sat and Sun L only*. Children welcome, and there is outside seating. Takeaway food available. Wi-Fi. B&B. *Open 18.00-23.00 (Sat-Sun 12.00).*

WALKING AND CYCLING

There is a whole array of walks and cycle rides in the area which are described in detail by North Kesteven District Council on www.n-kesteven.gov.uk/visitors-and-leisure/sports-leisure-culture-and-the-arts/cycle-nk.

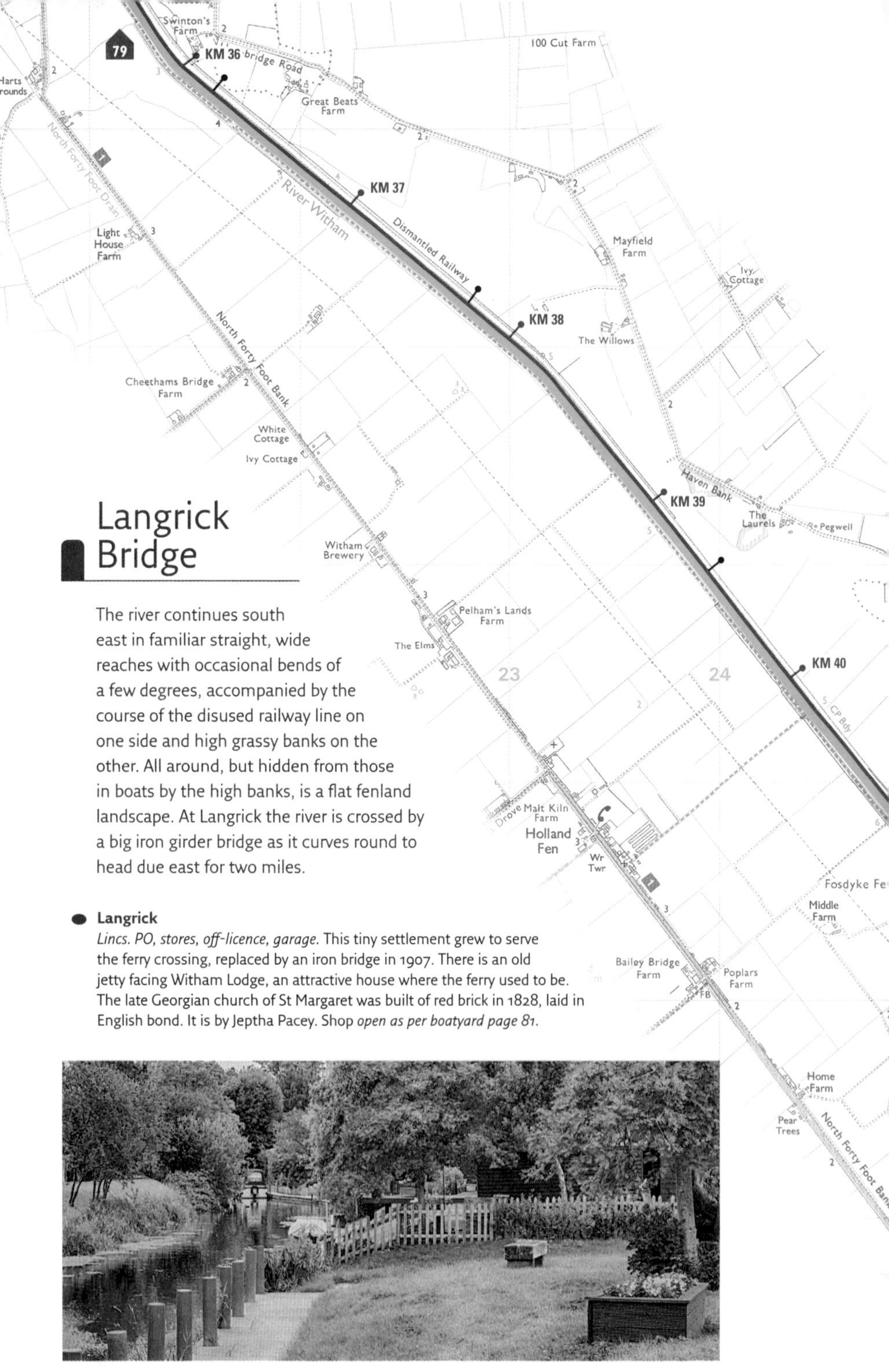

Langrick Bridge

The river continues south east in familiar straight, wide reaches with occasional bends of a few degrees, accompanied by the course of the disused railway line on one side and high grassy banks on the other. All around, but hidden from those in boats by the high banks, is a flat fenland landscape. At Langrick the river is crossed by a big iron girder bridge as it curves round to head due east for two miles.

Langrick
Lincs. PO, stores, off-licence, garage. This tiny settlement grew to serve the ferry crossing, replaced by an iron bridge in 1907. There is an old jetty facing Witham Lodge, an attractive house where the ferry used to be. The late Georgian church of St Margaret was built of red brick in 1828, laid in English bond. It is by Jeptha Pacey. Shop *open as per boatyard page 81*.

Kyme Eau, South Kyme

Boatyards

Ⓑ **Langrick Bridge Stores** (Geordie's Boat Sales) Main Road Garage, Brothertoft, Boston PE20 3SW (01205 280311; www.langrick-bridge-stores.co.uk). D Pump-out, gas, solid fuel, overnight and long-term mooring, boat sales, Gas Safe engineering service, boat safety examinations, new and second-hand chandlery,well-stocked grocery shop, hot and cold snacks, ice creams, newspapers, stamps, off-licence. Open Mon-Fri 08.00-17.30 & Sat 09.00-13.00. **Note that this is the last source of diesel before the Wash.**

Pubs and Restaurants

1 **Witham & Blues** Main Road, Langrick, Boston PE22 7AJ (01205 280546; www.withamandblues.com). A licensed New York style bar and grill, with separate café, serving light refreshments and meals *Thu-Sat 17.00-23.30 (Thu 22.00)*. Children and dogs welcome. Large garden with play area.

2 **Langrick Station Café** Main Road, Langrick, Boston PE22 7AH (01205 280023; www.facebook.com/pages/category/Advertising-Marketing/Langrick-Cafe-108392890493556). Lively, welcoming establishment serving appetising food *Mon-Fri 06.30-14.45 & Sat-Sun 08.00-13.30. Sun* roasts a speciality. Fully licensed. Built on the site of the old station, this is the place where, on 8th March 1937, the London express derailed at speed. The engine remained upright on the tracks but the tender and six carriages completely left the rails. There were no serious injuries.

HE WHO LAUGHS LAST . . .

The line of a dismantled railway closely follows the north bank of the River Witham – it was opened on 17 October 1848 following an agreement between the proprietors of the navigation and the Great Northern Railway company, which leased the river for 999 years at £10,545 per annum. The competition between steam packet boats and railway trains was intense, with the railway ultimately providing *fourth-class* carriages at the fare of a halfpenny per mile, undercutting anything the boats could do, and finally putting them out of business in 1863. Railway trains also took freight from the river – 19,535 tons of coal passed through the Grand Sluice at Boston in 1847 but, after the railway opened, this had fallen to 3,780 tons in 1854. A large railway warehouse was built in 1897 alongside Brayford Pool in Lincoln, with a branch dock to provide shipment facilities. But swans now occupy what was the dock, and the railway is no more. The River Witham, made navigable by the Romans, flows quietly on.

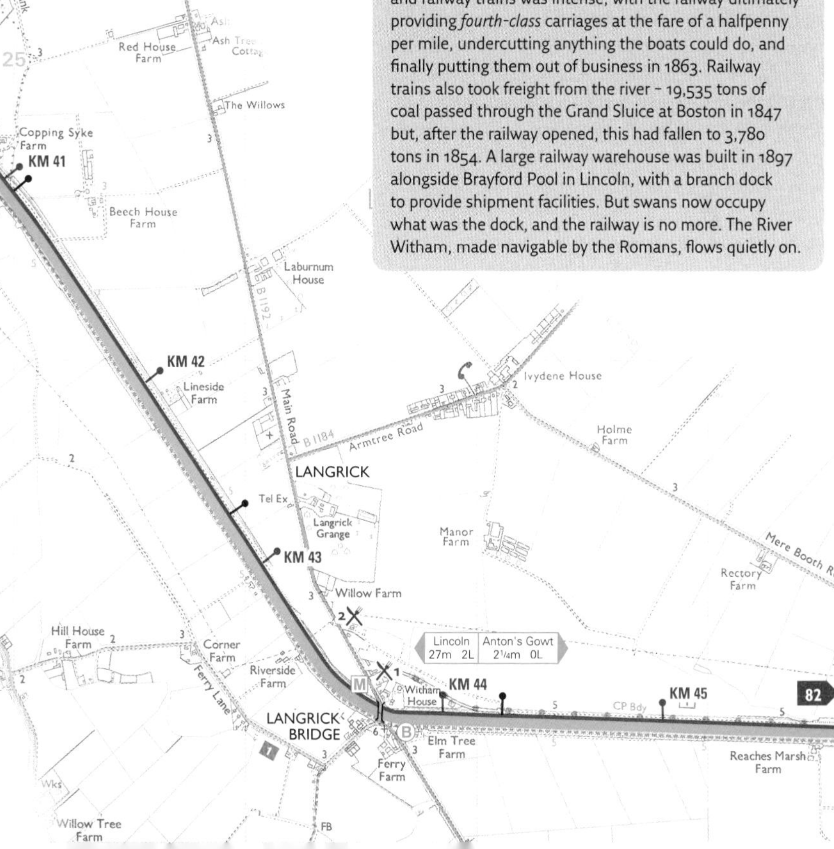

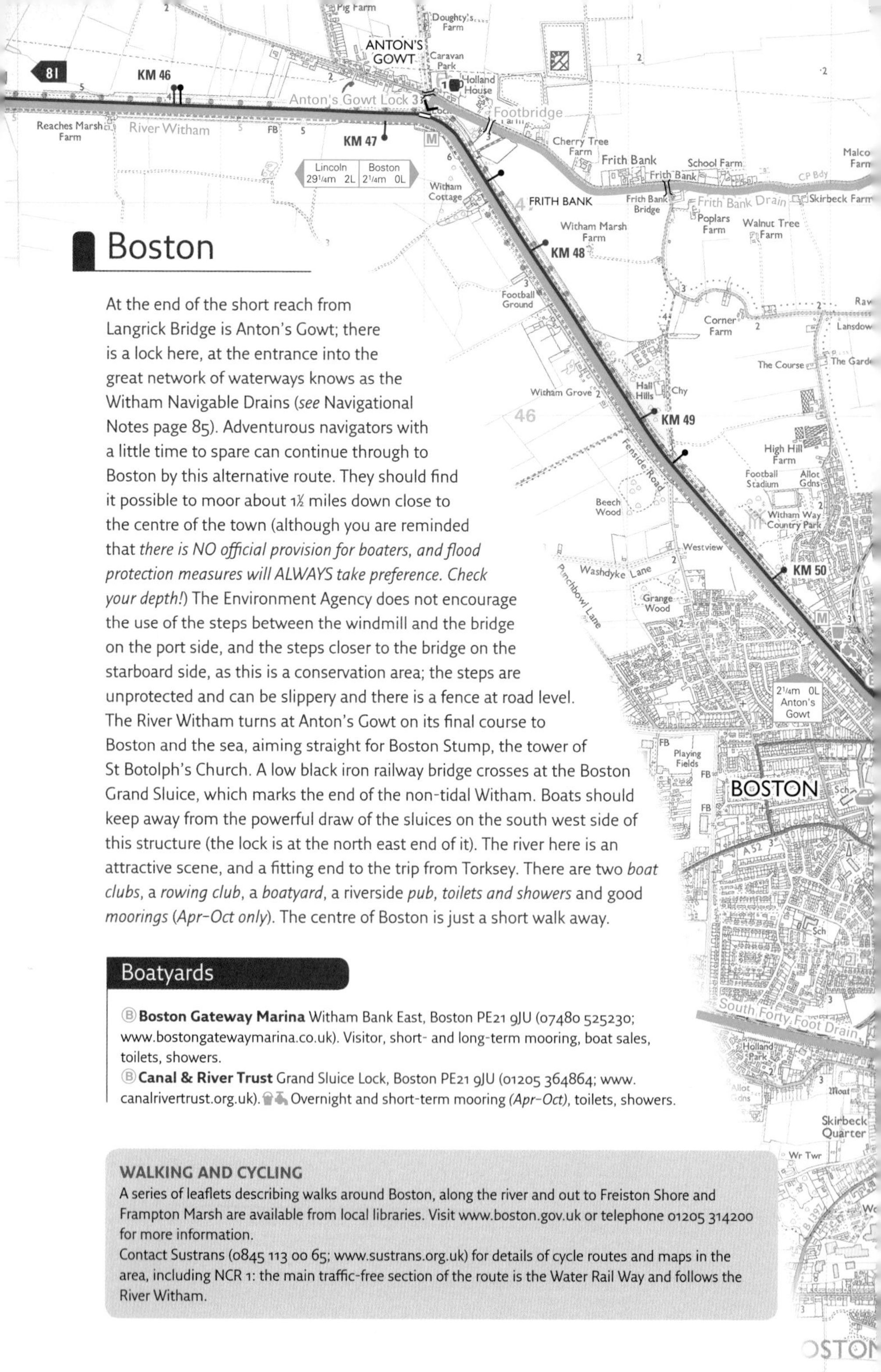

Boston

At the end of the short reach from Langrick Bridge is Anton's Gowt; there is a lock here, at the entrance into the great network of waterways knows as the Witham Navigable Drains (*see* Navigational Notes page 85). Adventurous navigators with a little time to spare can continue through to Boston by this alternative route. They should find it possible to moor about 1½ miles down close to the centre of the town (although you are reminded that *there is NO official provision for boaters, and flood protection measures will ALWAYS take preference. Check your depth!*) The Environment Agency does not encourage the use of the steps between the windmill and the bridge on the port side, and the steps closer to the bridge on the starboard side, as this is a conservation area; the steps are unprotected and can be slippery and there is a fence at road level. The River Witham turns at Anton's Gowt on its final course to Boston and the sea, aiming straight for Boston Stump, the tower of St Botolph's Church. A low black iron railway bridge crosses at the Boston Grand Sluice, which marks the end of the non-tidal Witham. Boats should keep away from the powerful draw of the sluices on the south west side of this structure (the lock is at the north east end of it). The river here is an attractive scene, and a fitting end to the trip from Torksey. There are two *boat clubs*, a *rowing club*, a *boatyard*, a riverside *pub, toilets and showers* and good *moorings* (*Apr–Oct only*). The centre of Boston is just a short walk away.

Boatyards

Ⓑ **Boston Gateway Marina** Witham Bank East, Boston PE21 9JU (07480 525230; www.bostongatewaymarina.co.uk). Visitor, short- and long-term mooring, boat sales, toilets, showers.

Ⓑ **Canal & River Trust** Grand Sluice Lock, Boston PE21 9JU (01205 364864; www.canalrivertrust.org.uk). Overnight and short-term mooring *(Apr–Oct)*, toilets, showers.

WALKING AND CYCLING

A series of leaflets describing walks around Boston, along the river and out to Freiston Shore and Frampton Marsh are available from local libraries. Visit www.boston.gov.uk or telephone 01205 314200 for more information.

Contact Sustrans (0845 113 00 65; www.sustrans.org.uk) for details of cycle routes and maps in the area, including NCR 1: the main traffic-free section of the route is the Water Rail Way and follows the River Witham.

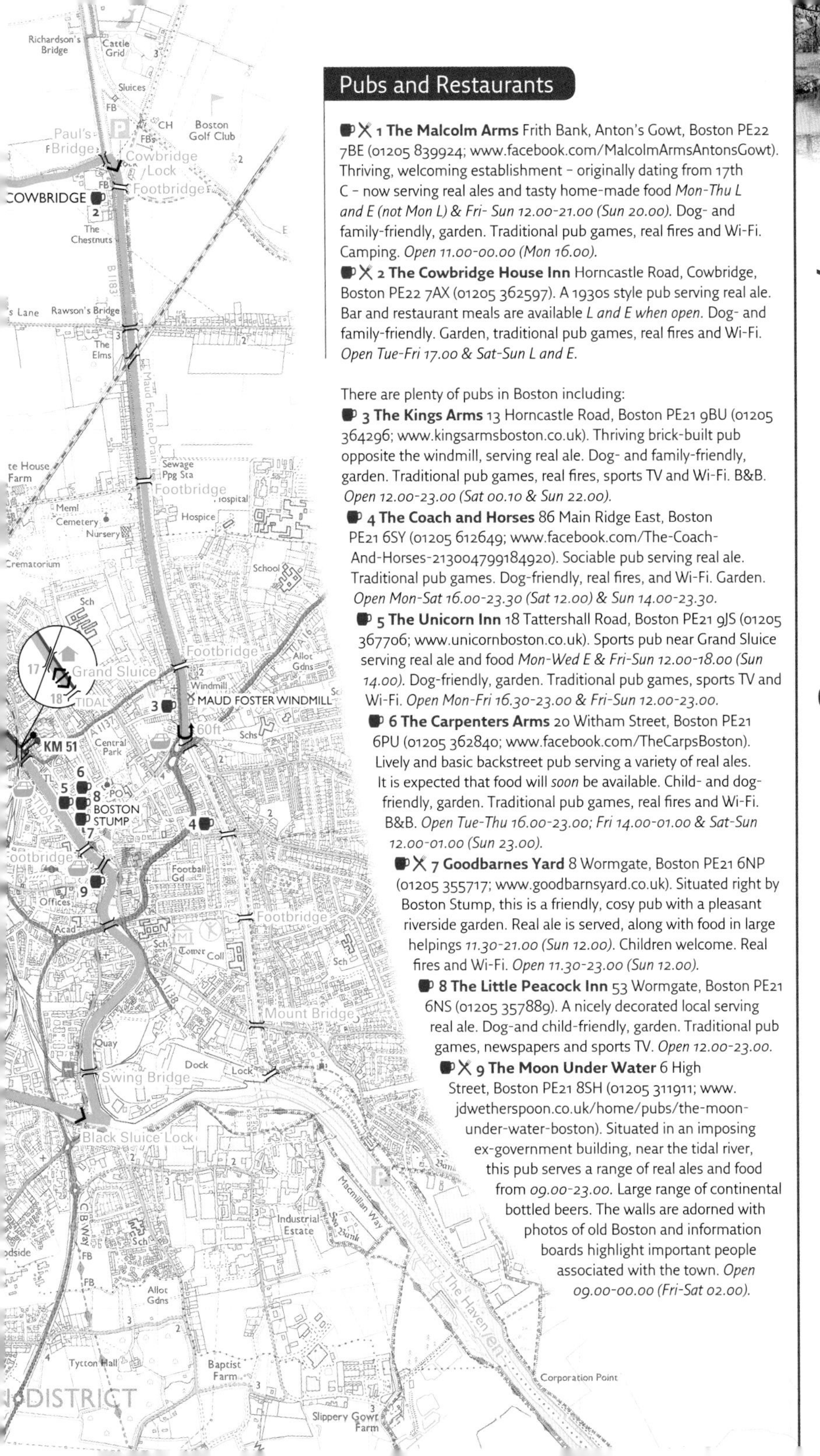

Pubs and Restaurants

1 The Malcolm Arms Frith Bank, Anton's Gowt, Boston PE22 7BE (01205 839924; www.facebook.com/MalcolmArmsAntonsGowt). Thriving, welcoming establishment – originally dating from 17th C – now serving real ales and tasty home-made food *Mon-Thu L and E (not Mon L) & Fri- Sun 12.00-21.00 (Sun 20.00)*. Dog- and family-friendly, garden. Traditional pub games, real fires and Wi-Fi. Camping. *Open 11.00-00.00 (Mon 16.00).*

2 The Cowbridge House Inn Horncastle Road, Cowbridge, Boston PE22 7AX (01205 362597). A 1930s style pub serving real ale. Bar and restaurant meals are available *L and E when open*. Dog- and family-friendly. Garden, traditional pub games, real fires and Wi-Fi. *Open Tue-Fri 17.00 & Sat-Sun L and E.*

There are plenty of pubs in Boston including:

3 The Kings Arms 13 Horncastle Road, Boston PE21 9BU (01205 364296; www.kingsarmsboston.co.uk). Thriving brick-built pub opposite the windmill, serving real ale. Dog- and family-friendly, garden. Traditional pub games, real fires, sports TV and Wi-Fi. B&B. *Open 12.00-23.00 (Sat 00.10 & Sun 22.00).*

4 The Coach and Horses 86 Main Ridge East, Boston PE21 6SY (01205 612649; www.facebook.com/The-Coach-And-Horses-213004799184920). Sociable pub serving real ale. Traditional pub games. Dog-friendly, real fires, and Wi-Fi. Garden. *Open Mon-Sat 16.00-23.30 (Sat 12.00) & Sun 14.00-23.30.*

5 The Unicorn Inn 18 Tattershall Road, Boston PE21 9JS (01205 367706; www.unicornboston.co.uk). Sports pub near Grand Sluice serving real ale and food *Mon-Wed E & Fri-Sun 12.00-18.00 (Sun 14.00)*. Dog-friendly, garden. Traditional pub games, sports TV and Wi-Fi. *Open Mon-Fri 16.30-23.00 & Fri-Sun 12.00-23.00.*

6 The Carpenters Arms 20 Witham Street, Boston PE21 6PU (01205 362840; www.facebook.com/TheCarpsBoston). Lively and basic backstreet pub serving a variety of real ales. It is expected that food will *soon* be available. Child- and dog-friendly, garden. Traditional pub games, real fires and Wi-Fi. B&B. *Open Tue-Thu 16.00-23.00; Fri 14.00-01.00 & Sat-Sun 12.00-01.00 (Sun 23.00).*

7 Goodbarnes Yard 8 Wormgate, Boston PE21 6NP (01205 355717; www.goodbarnsyard.co.uk). Situated right by Boston Stump, this is a friendly, cosy pub with a pleasant riverside garden. Real ale is served, along with food in large helpings *11.30-21.00 (Sun 12.00)*. Children welcome. Real fires and Wi-Fi. *Open 11.30-23.00 (Sun 12.00).*

8 The Little Peacock Inn 53 Wormgate, Boston PE21 6NS (01205 357889). A nicely decorated local serving real ale. Dog-and child-friendly, garden. Traditional pub games, newspapers and sports TV. *Open 12.00-23.00.*

9 The Moon Under Water 6 High Street, Boston PE21 8SH (01205 311911; www.jdwetherspoon.co.uk/home/pubs/the-moon-under-water-boston). Situated in an imposing ex-government building, near the tidal river, this pub serves a range of real ales and food from *09.00-23.00*. Large range of continental bottled beers. The walls are adorned with photos of old Boston and information boards highlight important people associated with the town. *Open 09.00-00.00 (Fri-Sat 02.00).*

Witham Navigable Drains

This remarkable network of waterways north of Boston exists to drain and irrigate a flat and highly vulnerable tract of fenland. The network is a vital part of the local economy and of the defence of the area against the encroachment of the North Sea. Castle Dyke Drain, Houghbridge Drain, Newham Drain, Frith Bank Drain, Medlam Drain, Stonebridge Drain, West Fen Catchwater Drain, East Fen Catchwater Drain, Maud Foster Drain (these last three are classified as 'main river'), are only navigable *May–Sep*. Craft of 75' x 18' can pass through Anton's Gowt Lock, and the limiting size at Cowbridge is 70' x 10', but note there are no formal turning points on the Maud Foster Drain. *Information regarding water levels* can be obtained from the gauging board fitted to the tail wing of Anton's Gowt Lock (a zero reading indicates sufficient water for navigation). Access to Cowbridge Lock is by CRT Watermate key or by telephoning 01205 310099 *during office hours*. However, it should always be remembered that navigation is NOT the top priority of the drainage authority, and sometimes a navigator is brought up sharply by a low bridge, often in a place where the channel is no wider than 30ft for several miles. Anton's Gowt Lock is the only entrance to these waterways. The best (widest) course is to head east from this lock, along Frith Bank Drain for 2 miles, to the great junction of waterways at Cowbridge Lock. From here you can go north towards the Lincolnshire Wolds, or south for about 1½ miles to the outskirts of Boston along the Maud Foster Drain. You can visit the centre of Boston via this non-tidal route. Such a visit should only be made between *May–Sep*, and be prepared to be flexible regarding your mooring. BE WARNED that levels on ALL the drains can rise or fall rapidly – moor cautiously, allowing plenty of slack in your warps. NOTE: THERE IS NO CONNECTION WITH THE TIDAL WITHAM VIA THE MAUD FOSTER DRAIN.

Boston

Lincs. All services. An immensely attractive town at the mouth of the Witham, Boston has been an important seaport for over 800 years – indeed in 1205 it was second only to London. There are many splendid buildings in the town, but of course the most conspicuous among them is the famous Boston Stump – the 272ft tower of the parish church. There are two large market places, virtually contiguous. This area is the scene of much revelry in the spring, when the May Fair takes place. Under a charter of Elizabeth I dated 1573, the fair is held *3–10 May*.

St Botolph's Church beside the Witham. This enormous building, the largest parish church in England, is a magnificent example of the late Decorated architecture, and reflects the prosperity of Boston following the rise of its wool trade in the 13th C. The thriving guilds paid for the church, into which were built their respective chapels. Inside, the church is immensely spacious, the tall roof carried by slender quatrefoil columns. There are plenty of interesting things to look at here. The main south door is a remarkable piece of dovetailing, the pulpit is an elaborate Jacobean affair and the choir stalls are an excellent example of 14th-C carving. There are some good brasses and other monuments. The 272ft tower may be ascended, at a small charge; with 365 steps up a claustrophobic narrow turret, this can be hard going, but one may walk right around a balcony near the top and of course the view over the fenland is unbeatable – on a clear day Lincoln, 32 miles away, is visible. The openness of the work at the top of the tower has led to speculation that it perhaps at one time carried a light for the benefit of shipping; speculation also suggests that it was intended to carry a tall spire – otherwise why call it the stump? Whatever plans there may have been, the church is much loved by the inhabitants of Boston, Massachusetts, who have largely financed its structural repairs this century.

Boston Guildhall Museum South Street, Boston PE21 6HT (01205 365954; www.bostonguildhall.co.uk). Near the river, south of the Market Place. An ancient and fascinating building constructed in 1450 for the Guild of St Mary, and now a museum illustrating Boston's history. It contains the cells that in 1607 held William Brewster and his friends after their unsuccessful attempt to leave the country. They were tried in the courtroom above. On the ground floor of this dark but historic building is the original kitchen. The roasting spit is self-propelled; the heat rising from the fire drives simple fans connected to a chain that operates the turning gear. This remarkably useful device is over 500 years old. There is also a Banqueting Hall, a Council Chamber and a Maritime Room to be visited. *Open Wed–Sat 10.30–15.30. Last admission 15.00.* Free.

Maud Foster Mill 16 Willoughby Road, Boston PE21 9EG (01205 352188; www.maudfoster.co.uk). A beautifully preserved windmill, built in 1819. Organic stoneground flour is sold here. *Open throughout the year Wed & Sat 10.00–17.00.* Shop and a holiday let in the mill. Excellent views out over Boston. Charge.

Tourist Information Centre Boston Guildhall Museum, South Street, Boston PE21 6HT (01205 365954; www.boston.gov.uk). The usual friendly and helpful service. *Open as per the Guildhall Museum.*

NAVIGATIONAL NOTES

1 At Boston Grand Sluice the River Witham becomes tidal, leading down through Boston past the docks and into the Wash. It is most inadvisable to venture along the tideway unless you have a suitable, seagoing boat and are familiar with the currents and shallows in the Wash. The Grand Sluice is of course a sea lock, operated and manned at tide times by Canal & River Trust, with gates facing both ways, but what is particularly interesting about it is that, unlike most tidal locks, the sea gates (referred to locally as doors) here are actually used at every tide. In other words the North Sea at high water is always above the level of the non-tidal Witham, and the sea gates close automatically twice a day to keep out the tide. This makes locking through the Grand Sluice somewhat complicated as far as times are concerned. It is not possible to lock up into the tide, since there is only one pair of outward facing gates, but on the other hand the tidal river practically dries out at low water. The only time to lock through is *2½ hrs prior to high water and 2½ hrs after high water.* The lock will take boats up to 41' long by 14' wide by 14' height - below 12' height beam increases to 20', and larger craft can pass straight through when the tidal and non-tidal Witham 'make a level'. Draft to Bardney is 5'. A lock keeper is on duty in the nearby office: telephone 01205 364864/07387 050967 (or VHF Channel 74 - *only manned during tidal operations*) and you should *give as much notice as possible (minimum 24 hrs for craft wishing to use the lock 06.00-21.00 & 5 days for night passage 21.00-06.00).* There is an answerphone for messages. The sluice is not automatically manned during the night. Telephone CRT Emergency Helpline (0800 47 999 47) in an emergency.

2 There are also visitor moorings here for up to 50 boats *Apr-Oct* with and access ramps for the disabled. You may stay *for up to 5 days* free and then you must move away for a period of at least *14 days before returning*. For access to Boston via the Maud Foster Drain, *see* Witham Navigable Drains opposite.

3 Passage across The Wash (which is classified as 'Tidal - Rough' for insurance purposes) is not deemed suitable for most inland craft and you may well not be able to obtain cover for the voyage. However, employing the services of a qualified pilot is all but essential. The main pilot covering private leisure boat passage is Daryl Hill (07909 880071; ongarhillbillies@hotmail.com). To book a berth in Kings Lynn contact the Tourist Information Centre on 01553 763044.

4 The first point of contact for passage through Black Sluice Lock should be CRT at Grand Sluice giving at least 48 hours notice - see contact details at 1) above. Direct contact, during passage between Grand Sluice and Black Sluice, can be maintained with Environment Agency staff on either 07721 390128 or 07714 064043. The Black Sluice locking will effectively mirror your Grand Sluice locking.

5 There is no manned radio or telephone at Black Sluice except during the actual locking operation. However, during your passage from Grand Sluice to Black Sluice the lock keeper can be contacted on one of the mobile numbers in Note 4 above or on VHF channel 74.

6 At Grand Sluice, if your craft is over 41' in length, you will normally be let out on the second occasion that the tide makes a level, giving you a 'window' of approximately 3 minutes. The journey to Black Sluice takes 10-15 minutes on the falling tide.

7 To prevent damage to the lock or boats, sending craft through on level water will not be possible when the incoming tide exceeds 7.3m or an outgoing tide exceeds 7.7m. Under these circumstances, any boats will need to be penned up or penned down. This will inevitably slow down the movement of boats.

8 When you have cleared the railway swing bridge, on the tidal side of the Witham, you should switch to VHF Channel 12, Boston Port information to monitor the possibility of conflicting shipping movements.

9 For access to Boston via the Maud Foster Drain, *see* Witham Navigable Drains opposite.

10 The footbridge on the Maud Foster Drain, close to the cemetery, is very low.

11 Mooring at Grand Sluice and on the Witham Navigable Drains is not allowed *Nov-Mar*.

12 No attempt should be made to navigate beyond Bargate Bridge, which is immediately south of the Maud Foster Mill.

13 Once the new Boston Barrier is completed operational details at Grand Sluice may change so check with the lock keeper.

Kyme Eau

This remarkable navigation leaves the Fossdyke & Witham at Chapel Hill (*see* page 79), slipping through flood gates and beginning its journey across the flat fenlands, hemmed in by high banks and seeming at times to be impossibly narrow. Turning sharply south the nicely restored Bottom Lock is soon reached, opened in November 1986, standing alone amidst the fields. After passing Terry Booth Farm the navigation turns to the west and makes a pretty passage through South Kyme, where there is a *pub*, Kyme Tower and the remains of a priory. Once again the waterway enters open farmland, although those in boats will see only the high grassy banks. There is a brief flurry of interest at Ferry Bridge, where the navigation makes a sharp turn to head towards the present limit of navigation at Cobblers Lock. Those who fancy a challenge can then undertake to walk the remaining five miles of unrestored section into Sleaford (beware, the towpath is, in places, blocked), passing what appear to be the disproportionately large and, as yet, unrestored locks.

● **Kyme Eau** (01522 689460; sleaford.navigation@ntlworld.com; www.sleafordnavigation.co.uk). This 13-mile-long navigation leaves the Witham at Chapel Hill to reach Sleaford to the south west, through seven locks. Slea is taken from the old English sleow, meaning a slimy, muddy stream. Plans for a commercially viable waterway were mooted as early as 1343, and Gilbert d'Umfraville, one of the Lords of Kyme, received royal assent for charging tolls on a part of the river. It was not until 1773, however, that local businessmen initiated plans to make the river navigable. Their scheme was not accepted, and it was not until 1792 that a new plan by Creasey and Jessop was put forward and accepted. The Sleaford Navigation Company was formed, supported by local people and the City of Boston. William Jessop was appointed as engineer, and local funds were made available. The navigation opened in 1794 amidst great celebration, and the eagerly anticipated boom in local prosperity duly followed. At one point plans were even mooted to extend the navigation westwards to Grantham thereby connecting back into the main waterways system. A builders, a coach-makers, a brickworks, an iron foundry, a mill and a brewery were all founded near Navigation Wharf in Sleaford. Navigation House, in Carre Street, still stands as a testimony to the waterway's early prosperity. However, as with all such local navigations, the coming of the railways brought about a rapid decline in prosperity. Tolls were lowered but to no avail, and navigation finally ceased around 1880. The opening in 1857 of the Boston, Sleaford and Midland Counties Railway had reduced the importance of the town of Sleaford, since it now became a mere stop on the line between Boston and Grantham. The Navigation Society was formed in 1976 and their restoration achievements have been considerable. Kyme Eau is now navigable through Kyme Eau Lower Lock (CRT Watermate key needed) for over 7½ miles to Cobblers Lock, where it is possible to wind. Maximum dimensions are 70' 0" x 14' 0" with a headroom of 5' 6" and a draught of 2' 0". Progress can be slow on this navigation. From *Oct–Mar* the gates at Lower Kyme Lock are chained back for flood prevention reasons, and navigation is difficult in winter. Full restoration to Sleaford is planned.

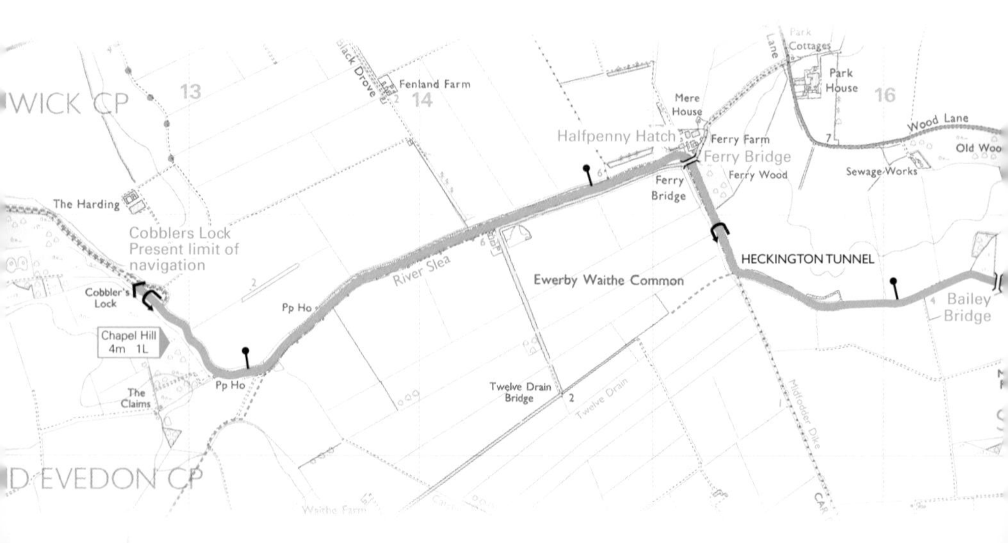

● **South Kyme**

Lincs. PO box, tel. A quiet, remote and inauspicious fenland settlement, enlivened by the fine wooden sculpture of a kingfisher made by Simon Todd in 1990, and a handsome schoolhouse dated 1843. However, just to the west, and enclosed by the road and the navigation, are the timeless remains of a tower and priory, standing starkly amidst the fields. South Kyme Tower is a very impressive four-storey battlemented turret which dominates the surrounding flat landscape. It was built sometime between 1338 and 1381 by Sir Gilbert d'Umfraville, and was probably at one time part of a larger house, dismantled around 1720. It now stands desolate and empty, with no floors above the second which, due to its pattern, was known as the Chequer Chamber. The nearby church was built in 1890 onto the surviving fragments of a grand priory of Augustinian Canons, founded in 1169. A handsome Norman doorway survives, decorated with lions and other beasts, together with some fine Anglo-Saxon carving dating from the 7th or 8th C, at the east end of the north wall. It depicts trumpet spirals and foliage, and is reminiscent of early manuscripts.

NAVIGATIONAL NOTES

1 The maximum length of boat able to use the new winding hole is 72ft. It is suggested that craft reverse in and let the current take the bows round.
2 It is possible to wind a 72ft boat below Cobblers Lock which is still the Head of Navigation. Please note that boats that should wind by reversing into the bywash, on the right-hand side going upstream.
3 Halfpenny Hatch Bridge (aka Ferry Bridge) which is just upstream of the winding hole, has a nominal air draft of 6ft.
4 Boats mooring in South Kyme should note that the landing stages are built on land owned by the Parish Council who have stipulated a 72-hour mooring limit. After that time a charge will be levied.

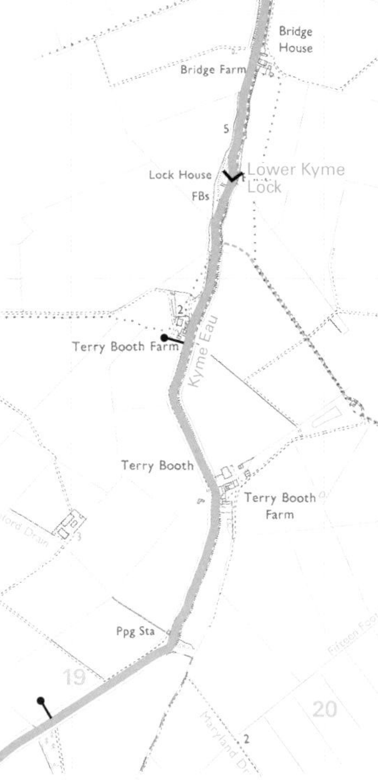

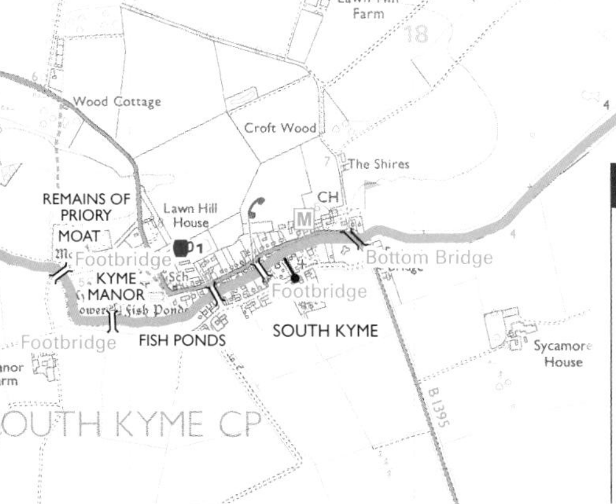

Pubs and Restaurants

1 The Hume Arms High Street, South Kyme, Lincoln LN4 4AD (01526 869143; www.south-kyme.co.uk/the_hume.html). Friendly village hostelry serving highly regarded, good value, home-made food - including authentic Indian cuisine - together with a takeaway menu *L and E.* Popular *Sun* roasts and a good selection of real ales. Dog- and child-friendly, garden. Real fires and Wi-Fi. B&B. *Open 18.00-00.00 (Sat-Sun 11.00).*

GRANTHAM CANAL

MAXIMUM DIMENSIONS

Length: 75' 0"
Beam: 14' 0"
Draught: 4' 0" (as built)
Headroom: 8' 0" (as built)

MANAGER

0303 040 4040
enquiries.eastmidlands@canalrivertrust.org.uk

MILEAGE

NOTTINGHAM to:
Tollerton Bridge 7: 3 miles
Fosse Bridge 18: 6¾ miles
Mackley's Bridge 25: 9¾ miles
HICKLING: 13¼ miles
Hose Bridge 39: 16½ miles
Plungar Bridge 49: 20¼ miles
REDMILE: 22¾ miles
Woolsthorpe Bridge 61: 28¼ miles
Denton Wharf: 29½ miles
GRANTHAM: 32½ miles

Locks: 18

There is somewhere close at hand to park at all the above locations and, in many cases, a picnic site.

NOTE

Apart from a dry section between Bridges 17-23, the canal is nominally in water - albeit heavily choked with weed and rushes in many sections - with only Locks 1, 6, 7, 14, 15, 16, 17 & 18 currently operational. See individual Navigational Notes for further details.

An item in the *Nottingham Journal*, dated 27 August 1791, announced a proposal by a group of 'Grantham men' to build a canal from Grantham to Radcliffe, a scheme provoked largely as a response to plans for neighbouring waterways to Sleaford and Melton Mowbray. This coincided with the completion of William Jessop's survey and estimate for the Nottingham Canal, thereby opening up potential links to plentiful and cheap coal from the north Nottingham coalfield.

The initial bill was opposed by Newark merchants, who had traditionally supplied coal to the Grantham district and those fearful that it would deplete the water level of the River Witham, which flows north through Grantham on its way to Lincoln and the Wash.

Subscribers to the bill succeeded on their second attempt having agreed to move the navigation's junction with the Trent 3½ miles upstream to West Bridgford, together with the addition of a 3¾-mile branch to Bingham - never built. The Act was passed on 30 April 1793, a year after the Bill for the Nottingham Canal was enacted. Construction commenced shortly afterwards, overseen by James Green of Wollaton - covering the Trent to Leicestershire border section - and William King (the Duke of Rutland's agent) for the remainder, including reservoirs at Knipton and Denton. William Jessop was retained to oversee progress.

On 1 February 1797 King reported that the eastern section was complete and this opened in April, the first cargo being a 'boat load of coals' carried by Thos Lockwood of Hickling. The canal opened during the summer of that year, having been completed at a relatively modest cost of £118,500, the most demanding engineering being the one and a half mile long cutting at Harlaxton, initially constructed to take a single wide beam boat. The finished navigation was 33 miles long, with 18 wide locks - each measuring 75' x 14' - lifting the canal a total of 139' 9".

Traffic was predominantly from the Trent heading towards Grantham, boats being worked into the canal from the river's flow by a rope and capstan - hence the name given to the now demolished horse bridge across the river: the Trent Hauling Bridge. Cargoes consisted of coke, coal, lime, building materials and general groceries, dropped off at villages along the relatively remote line of the waterway.

On return journeys boats carried corn, wool, beans, malt, together with other agricultural produce and, in 1798, a passenger boat service was implemented between Cotgrave and Nottingham on Saturdays.

For a while the canal prospered, soon paying off its debts, with dividends paid to its shareholders ranging from 5-8.7%, although in its first 25 years of operation receipts from tolls never exceeded £9,000 in any one year. However, they later went on to peak at £13,079 in 1841. A comfortable relationship existed between the boards of the Grantham and Nottingham Canals (they shared two board members in 1833) ensuring that most of the coal carried to Grantham originated from the coalfields north west of the city.

Generally the Grantham Canal proprietors were conservative in their approach and slow to adapt to the changing patterns of trade locally in which, for instance, there was a progressive increase in coal and groceries being carried to Sleaford and its environs from Boston, via the Witham and South Forty Foot Drain. Similarly, the Oakham & Melton Mowbray Navigations, by reducing their tolls, managed to capture the carriage of most of the corn grown between Stamford and Colsterworth. Charges for grain traded to Manchester, via an overland route to Newark and thence to Selby and a connecting railway journey, worked out at 18s 6d as opposed to 21s 9d when despatched down the Grantham Canal and over the Cromford & High Peak Railway.

In the face of these irrefutably damning statistics, marshalled by their traders, the canal company could do little but acquiesce to a one-third reduction in tolls for all but coal, coke and lime traffic.

Had a proposal, mooted in 1833, to build a 16-mile canal joining Grantham with Sleaford come to fruition, things could have been very different. The Midlands would have been given a direct link to the east coast and the port of Boston, without the need of a double transhipment at Shardlow and Torksey.

By now railways were making their presence felt and, after much shilly shallying, the grandly named Ambergate, Nottingham and Boston & Eastern Junction Railway & Canal Co. took over the Grantham Canal. This small railway company, having enjoyed a brief flirtation in 1850 with the mighty Great Northern (GNR) - a company renown for its antipathy towards canals - then went on to append itself to the GNR on a 999 year lease, commencing on 1 August 1861.

Traffic on the waterway, under an antagonistic owner, steadily dwindled and by 1905 was down to an annual tonnage below 19,000 - principally night soil from the middens of Nottingham - earning tolls of just £242.

The Grantham Canal was finally abandoned in 1937, by Act of Parliament, on the grounds that the lock gates were unsafe; all commercial traffic having ceased in 1929 due, largely, to heavy silting. However, the Act required the LNER to maintain 2ft of water in the canal for agricultural purposes.

In 1947 the fledgling Docks and Transport Executive was given the brief of doing away with the navigation altogether and, although thwarted by vociferous local opposition, 1950s housing and road development has subsequently gone some way in preventing full restoration in the Nottingham area.

Faced with the threat of complete infilling of the waterway in 1969, the Grantham Canal Restoration Society was formed and, together with the Inland Waterways Association and the local MP, took up the cudgels, steering an intact - though largely derelict - waterway into more enlightened times. Their objective now is complete restoration, with a projected completion date of 2035, and to this end the society has identified at least two possible routes for a new connection with the Trent.

Gamston

The canal leaves the River Trent just downstream from the junction between the river and the Nottingham Canal at Meadow Lane Lock. The initial section is owned by the Environment Agency and although the river lock is remarkably intact, there is a concrete dam immediately above the top gates. A quarter of a mile further on the waterway meets its first (and indeed the most) major obstruction in the form of a complex junction on the A6011, constructed virtually at water level. Liberally laced with fibre optic communication cables, figures upwards of £25 million have been set on negotiating this current impasse and an alternative connection with the river is seen as the most cost effective solution to the problem. Beyond, the canal runs in tandem with the road, which although at times intrusive and noisy, does not ultimately detract from its typical, suburban waterway ambience, running as it does along the bottom of leafy, well-tended gardens. Now promoted to dual-carriageway status, the road soon departs northwards, while the waterway heads via the de-gated Bridgford and Gamston Locks into open countryside, although negotiating the lowered A52 bypass culvert presents something of a challenge to the less than fleet of foot. The Canal-side fields of nearby Tollerton would have been the first to benefit from the nocturnal ministrations of Nottingham 'Sani-boats', carrying their regular cargoes of night soil. There is a useful *cycle repair shop* (0115 982 2459) immediately to the south of Bridgford Swing Bridge 3 and a *supermarket* beside the towpath at Elmors Bridge 6.

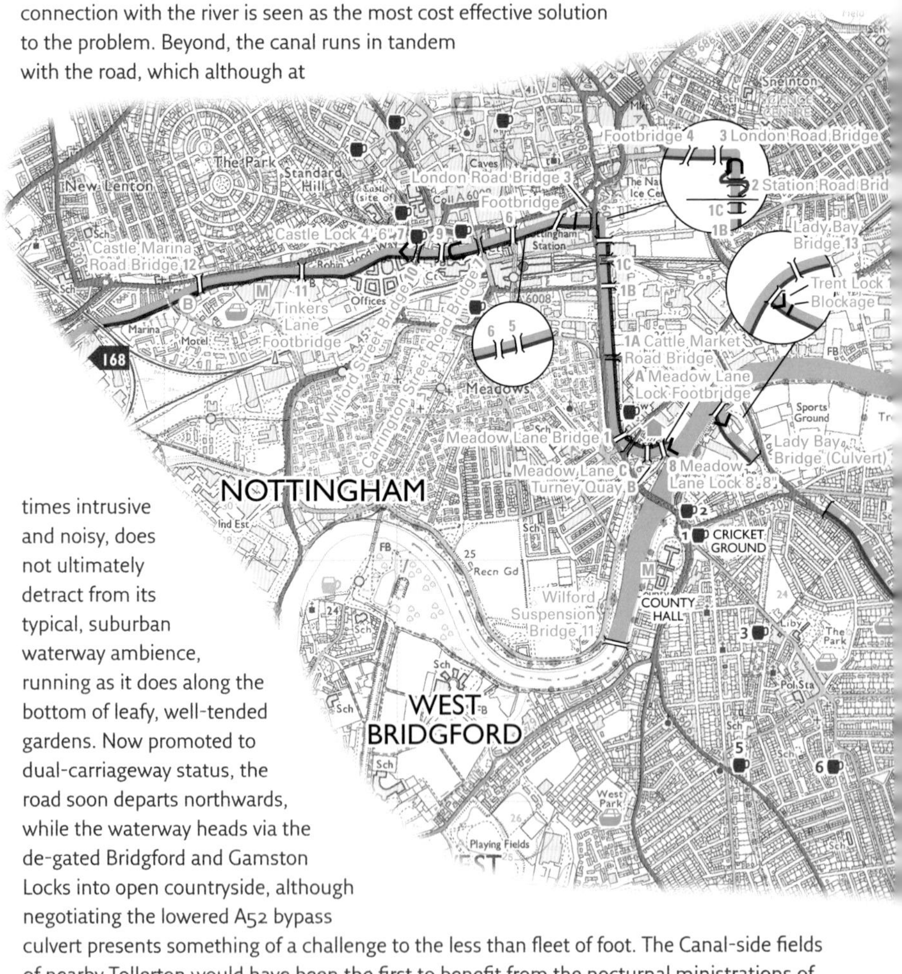

- **Nottingham**
  Notts. All services. See River Trent, page 170 for full details of the city north of the River Trent.
- **West Bridgford**
  Notts. Tel, stores, PO, chemist, bakery, butchers, takeaways, off-licence, banks, hardware, garage. This is an intriguing settlement, growing up largely in the latter part of the Victorian period. It is built upon land once owned by the Musters family who, finally bowing to pressure, sold off part of their estate but insisted on applying strict controls over the type of housing built thereon. It was constructed on a grid of tree-lined roads, with both the size and density of the properties stipulated, as were the number of bedrooms each one contained. Terraces and smaller dwellings were only permitted on side streets, predominantly for the occupation of servants. There were to be no 'Streets' (too urban) and therefore today the addresses only feature 'Roads'. Amongst inhabitants of Nottingham, separated by the Trent, West Bridgford became known as 'Bread and Lard Island' based on the belief that the owners of the large houses, wearing fur coats, were reduced to eating bread and lard behind closed doors, having spent all their money on their property and fine apparel!
- **Gamston**
  Notts. Tel, stores, chemist, takeaways, garage. Known as Gamelestune in Domesday: Gamal being an old Scandinavian name commonly found in this part of England, known as the Danelaw. Now a large dormitory village for Nottingham (dating from the 1980s) Gamston had for centuries remained a tiny rural community, little affected by the arrival of the Grantham Canal. However, upon the end of First World War, Nottingham County Council purchased much of the land to settle returning soldiers on farms and smallholdings.
- **Tollerton**
  Notts. Tel, stores, PO, takeaway, off-licence, garage. Best known for its eponymous airfield, now regarded as Nottingham's airport. The present Church of St Peter is of early medieval origins, its interior decorated by eight hatchments dating from between 1770 and 1875, relating to deaths at the hall and rectory. These were funeral memorials, bearing the coat of arms of the deceased, hung on the house front or gate during the period of mourning and then removed to the church. The word is thought to derive from the 16th-C French *hachement*, meaning adornment. The medieval font was thrown out during an 1812 restoration and served time at the village pump before its eventual return in 1918. The equally valuable (and extremely rare) 12th-C piscine met a similar fate, carrying out a tour of duty adorning the local squire's grounds, before its timely return.
- **Bassingfield**
  Notts. Tel. Recorded as Basingfelt in 1086, meaning 'Open Country of Bassa's People', Bassa being probably of Saxon origin although there is archaeological evidence of human habitation going back some 3000 years. This is a long village, running parallel with the canal 200 yards to the north, strung out along Nathan's Lane. The 1851 census recorded one Nathan Peters, a two year old child living in the hamlet with his grandfather John Clator, who went on to inhabit that same dwelling for well over 80 years.

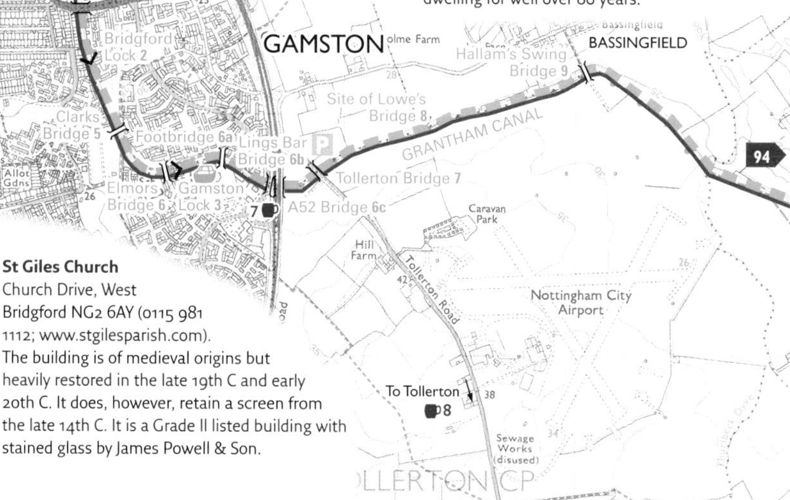

St Giles Church
Church Drive, West Bridgford NG2 6AY (0115 981 1112; www.stgilesparish.com).
The building is of medieval origins but heavily restored in the late 19th C and early 20th C. It does, however, retain a screen from the late 14th C. It is a Grade II listed building with stained glass by James Powell & Son.

Pubs and Restaurants (pages 90-91)

See page 171 for pubs in Nottingham north of the River Trent.

1 **The Trent Bridge Inn** 2 Radcliffe Road, West Bridgford, Nottingham NG2 6AA (0115 977 8940; www.jdwetherspoon.com/pubs/all-pubs/england/nottingham/the-trent-bridge-inn-nottingham). Close to the cricket ground, walls adorned by cricket-themed photos and paintings, this large pub serves a changing (and wide) selection of reasonably priced real ales and real cider from five separate bars, together with inexpensive food *from 08.00-23.00*. Children welcome *until 20.00*. Newspapers, real fires, sports TV and Wi-Fi. Charge for car parking. *Open daily 08.00-00.00.*

2 **The Waterside Bar & Kitchen** 1 Bridgford House, Trent Bridge, Nottingham NG2 5GJ (0115 945 5541; www.waterside.bar). Another establishment close to the sporting action, this pub, nevertheless, offers a total of three wide and plasma screen sports TVs! In addition there is variety of inexpensive food available *Mon-Sat 12.00-21.00 (Sat 10.00) & Sun 10.00-17.00*. Also real ale, outside seating overlooking the River Trent, newspapers and Wi-Fi. *Open Mon-Fri 12.00-23.00 (Fri 01.00) & Sat-Sun 10.00-02.00 (Sun 23.00).*

3 **The Stratford Haven** 2 Stratford Road, Nottingham NG2 6BA (0115 982 5981; www.castlerockbrewery.co.uk/pubs/stratford-haven). Popular local brewery pub serving a wide range of real ales and real cider. Food available *11.00-21.00 (Sat-Sun 10.00)*. Children welcome during the day. Quiz *Sun*. Garden, dog-friendly, traditional pub games, newspapers and Wi-Fi. Live music *Wed. Open Mon-Fri 11.00-23.00 (Thu-Fri 00.00) & Sat-Sun 10.00-00.00 (Sun 23.00).*

4 **The Poppy and Pint** Pierrepont Road, Lady Bay, Nottingham NG2 5DX (0115 981 9995; www.castlerockbrewery.co.uk/pubs/poppy-pint). Another popular pub from the local Castle Rock Brewery stable, well known for its welcoming staff, excellent range of real ales and appetising pub food. *Sunday* roasts a speciality. Dog- and child-friendly. Quiz and curry night *Tue*. Food available *Mon-Sat 09.30-21.00 & Sun 10.00-20.00*. Outside seating. Folk club, newspapers, sports TV and Wi-Fi. *Open 09.30-23.00 (Sun 10.00).*

5 **The Refinery** 100 Melton Road, West Bridgford NG2 6EP (0115 982 5681; www.refinerywb.co.uk). Large open-plan café/bar serving a tapas-type menu *(daily 09.00-21.00)* and real ale. Family-friendly, patio seating. Wi-Fi. *Open 09.00-23.00 (Fri-Sat 00.00).*

6 **The Test Match Hotel** Gordon Square, West Bridgford, Nottingham NG2 5LP (0115 981 1481; www.testmatchhotel-westbridgford.co.uk). Trading on the prevailing 'sportiness' of the area, this pub serves real ales and food (including breakfast) *11.00-21.00 daily*. Family-friendly, garden. Traditional pub games, newspapers, sports TV and Wi-Fi. Live music *Sat. Open Mon-Sat 10.30-23.30 & Sun 11.30-23.00.*

7 **The Goose at Gamston** Ambleside, West Bridgford, Nottingham NG2 6NA (0115 982 1041; www.eating-inn.co.uk/house/goose-gamston). Child-friendly establishment with both indoor and outdoor play areas renown for its pleasant, friendly and efficient staff. Real ale and a wide variety of inexpensive food available *09.00-22.00*. Breakfast from *09.00*. Dog- and family-friendly, garden. Traditional pub games, sports TV and Wi-Fi. *Open 11.00-23.00.*

8 **The Air Hostess** Stanstead Avenue, Tollerton, Nottingham NG12 4EA (0115 648 0439; www.airhostesspub.co.uk). Community pub, close to the airfield, with a sign representing the archetypal 'tart with a cart,' serving real ale and good value, home-cooked food *12.00-21.30 (Sun 16.30)*. Children and dogs welcome, garden. Traditional pub games (including petanque) sports TV and Wi-Fi. *Open Mon-Sat 11.00-23.00 & Sun 12.00-22.00.*

WALKING AND CYCLING

Nottingham can rightfully be regarded as the home of the bicycle as it plays host to Raleigh Cycles, founded in 1887 in Raleigh Street, and once the largest cycle manufacturer in the world. Today dedicated cycle routes abound throughout the city, intersecting in various places with the canal towpath. For details of both urban and rural cycle routes, together with long distance trails in the area, telephone 0300 500 8080 or visit www.nottinghamshire.gov.uk/planning-and-environment/walking-cycling-and-rights-of-way/cycling.

NAVIGATIONAL NOTES

No part of this section is currently open for navigation. Although Trent Lock 1 is fully gated there is a concrete barrier immediately above it, followed by an infilled section accommodating a complex junction on the A6011. Locks between here and the culverted A52 Lings Bar Road at Gamston are de-gated and there are several lowered bridges.

Belvoir Castle, looking out over the Vale and visible from many points on the canal

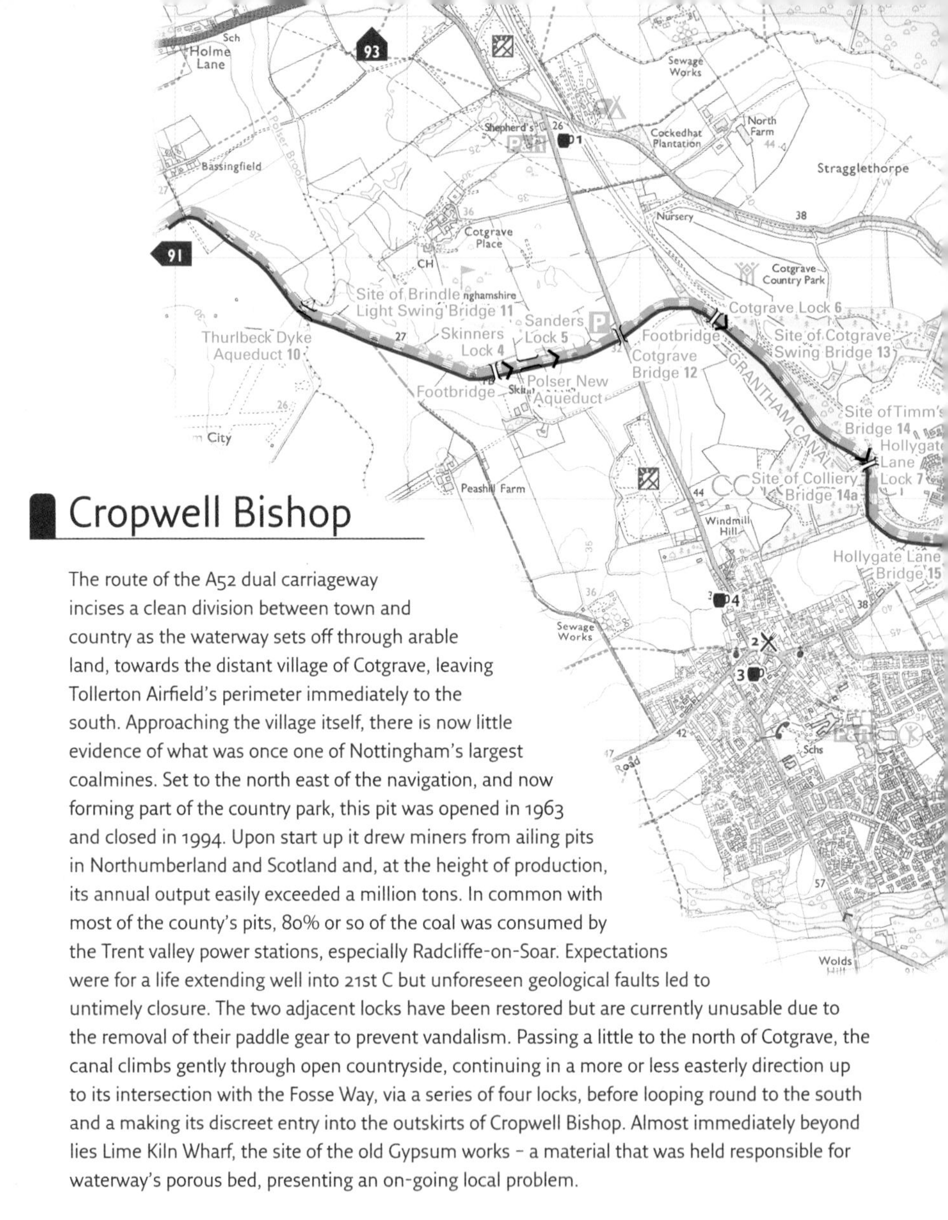

Cropwell Bishop

The route of the A52 dual carriageway incises a clean division between town and country as the waterway sets off through arable land, towards the distant village of Cotgrave, leaving Tollerton Airfield's perimeter immediately to the south. Approaching the village itself, there is now little evidence of what was once one of Nottingham's largest coalmines. Set to the north east of the navigation, and now forming part of the country park, this pit was opened in 1963 and closed in 1994. Upon start up it drew miners from ailing pits in Northumberland and Scotland and, at the height of production, its annual output easily exceeded a million tons. In common with most of the county's pits, 80% or so of the coal was consumed by the Trent valley power stations, especially Radcliffe-on-Soar. Expectations were for a life extending well into 21st C but unforeseen geological faults led to untimely closure. The two adjacent locks have been restored but are currently unusable due to the removal of their paddle gear to prevent vandalism. Passing a little to the north of Cotgrave, the canal climbs gently through open countryside, continuing in a more or less easterly direction up to its intersection with the Fosse Way, via a series of four locks, before looping round to the south and a making its discreet entry into the outskirts of Cropwell Bishop. Almost immediately beyond lies Lime Kiln Wharf, the site of the old Gypsum works – a material that was held responsible for waterway's porous bed, presenting an on-going local problem.

NAVIGATIONAL NOTES

Apart from the notoriously porous bed of the canal in the area of the Cropwell Bishop gypsum mines, a leaking culvert has also been identified near the village. Repair, and ultimate re-watering of this section of the navigation, is high up the Canal Society's 'to do' list.

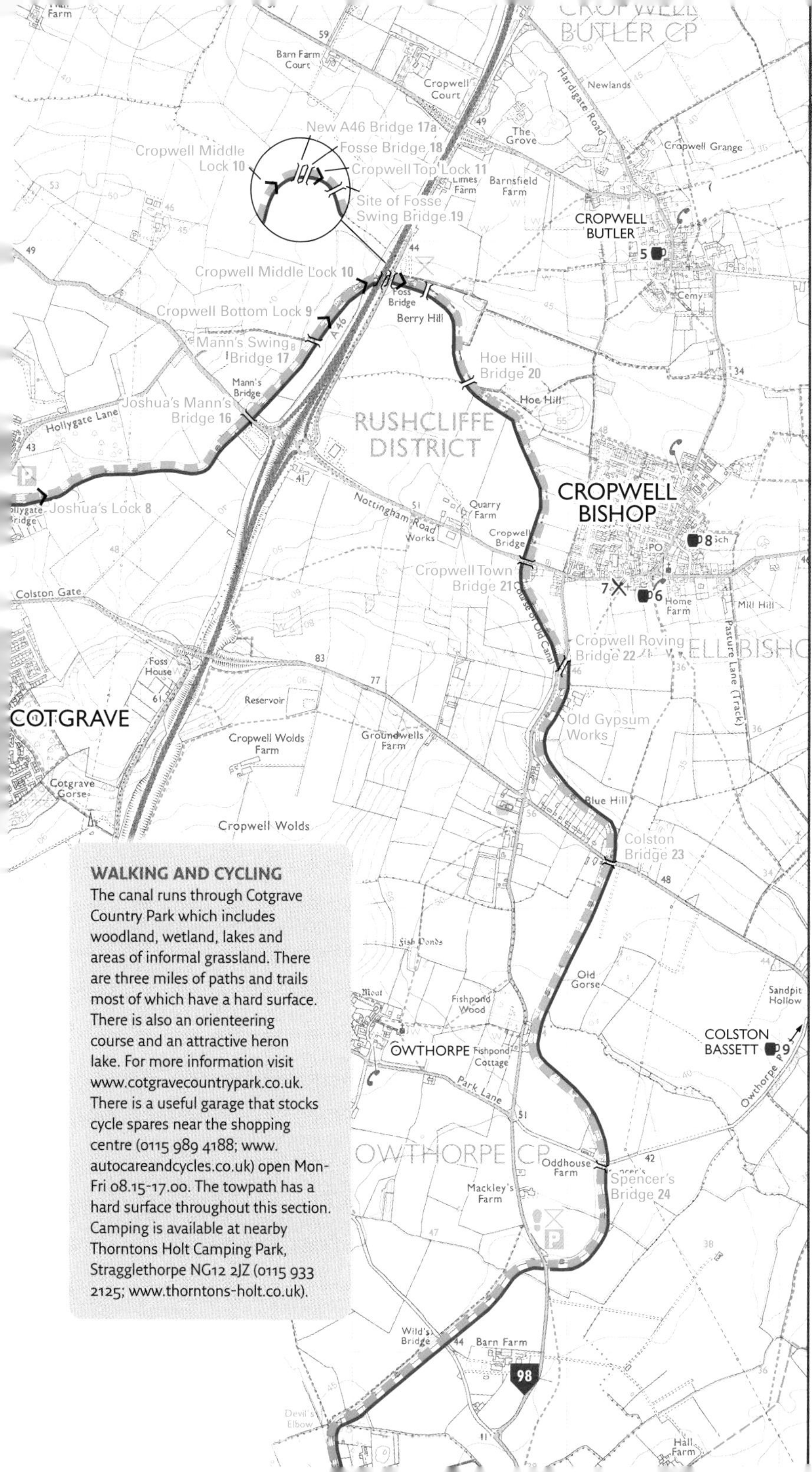

WALKING AND CYCLING

The canal runs through Cotgrave Country Park which includes woodland, wetland, lakes and areas of informal grassland. There are three miles of paths and trails most of which have a hard surface. There is also an orienteering course and an attractive heron lake. For more information visit www.cotgravecountrypark.co.uk. There is a useful garage that stocks cycle spares near the shopping centre (0115 989 4188; www.autocareandcycles.co.uk) open Mon-Fri 08.15-17.00. The towpath has a hard surface throughout this section. Camping is available at nearby Thorntons Holt Camping Park, Stragglethorpe NG12 2JZ (0115 933 2125; www.thorntons-holt.co.uk).

98

Cotgrave

Notts. PO, tel, stores, chemist, off-licence, bakery, fish & chips, takeaways, hardware, butcher, delicatessen, library, garage. Despite a population in excess of 7,000, and its proximity to Nottingham, Cotgrave retains a village atmosphere. Its origins may well lie in the Iron Age while, just to the north of the village, a 6th C- Saxon burial ground at Mill Hill has been excavated. More recently, in the early 1960s, the opening of a large modern coal mine soon swelled the population from 700 to 5,000 with the influx of miners from the nearby, worked out Radford mine, and later from closed pits in the north east. To accommodate the miners and their families, large purpose-built housing estates were established on the periphery of the village. As a further incentive to encourage miners to 'up sticks', these dwellings were often completely furnished, although special meetings were necessary so that incoming miners could understand the local dialect for reasons of pit safety. (And, of equal importance, be understood themselves!). Stores *open daily 07.00-22.00 (Sun 08.00).*

All Saints Church Lane, Cotgrave NG12 3HR (0115 989 2667; www.allsaintscotgrave.co.uk). Dating from the 12th C, this building underwent alteration in the three subsequent centuries. In 1996 it was severely damaged in an arson attack and was repaired at considerable expense.

Cropwell Butler

Notts. PO box. This was a wartime *Starfish* site: an area of land upon which strategically placed fires were set alight to simulate a burning city during a night air attack. On 9th May 1940, 95 bombers mounted a blitz on Nottingham. However, a significant number of the Luftwaffe crew were deflected from their real target, and their ordnance fell relatively harmlessly on the Vale of Belvoir, with cows the sole casualties.

Cropwell Bishop

Notts. PO, tel, stores, butcher, off-licence. It would not, perhaps, be stretching the imagination too far to suggest that the expression 'to tell chalk from cheese' originated in this very village, with its Stilton cheese manufacture and nearby worked-out gypsum seams! Otherwise, this is a habitation built largely from mellow brick and tile and, for the most part, with sensitively designed infill. It is one of only five villages licensed to produce Blue Stilton cheese, the creamery using milk bought in largely from family farms in the Peak District. The stores are *open daily 07.00-22.00.*

Cropwell Bishop Creamery Limited Cropwell Bishop NG12 3BQ (0115 989 2350; www.cropwellbishopstilton.com). Members of the Stilton Cheesemakers Association, and passionate about their handmade products, this family business welcomes visitors to their creamery shop (0115 989 1788) *Mon-Fri 10.00-14.30 & Sat 09.00-13.00.*

Owthorpe

Notts. PO box. There is an enticing view of the diminutive, Grade II* listed St Margaret's Church - appearing to be set amid farm buildings - visible down a grassy track from the centre of this tiny, sleepy village. Erected in 1705 by Colonel Robert Hutchinson, and constructed from materials from an earlier church on the site, it has a simple rectangular nave plan with a square west tower. The screen is reputed to have come from Owthorpe Hall – owned for many generations by the Hutchinson family – and there is also a decorative, octagonal 15th-C font. Various memorials adorn the walls dating back to 1664. Although locked, key holders can be contacted on 01949 837346/823743 or the vicar on 0115 989 2223.

GYPSUM

The solid geology of much of the eastern part of Nottinghamshire is dominated by the mudstones of the Triassic Mercia Mudstone Group, which give rise to the relatively flat, undulating landscape of the Vale of Belvoir. Composed largely of clay soils, this tract of fertile land supports rich farmland and scattered woods. The mudstones probably represent wind-blown dust that settled in shallow salt-lakes and sun-baked mudflats on what would have been an extensive alluvial plain. They are up to 1,000ft thick, outcrop over much of the eastern and southern areas of the county, and contain nationally important deposits of gypsum. Evidence that the ocean was never far away from the edge of the desert plain at this time, is provided by muds and silts in the Mercia Mudstone (as exposed at Colwick) which preserve fossil intertidal ripple marks, together with the fossils of burrowing shallow marine shells.

In Nottinghamshire gypsum is present throughout the Mercia Mudstone, but extraction has been limited to two distinct deposits found in the upper 130ft of the sequence, known as the Newark and Tutbury gypsum deposits. The Newark gypsum has a long narrow outcrop, rarely more than 1½ miles wide, extending from Newark to Cropwell Bishop and is the source of high purity gypsum, much prized by the pharmaceutical industry. This outcrop is no more than 3ft thick and thus opencast extraction was the only feasible method of working.

Pubs and Restaurants (pages 94-95)

1 The Shepherds Stragglethorpe, Radcliffe-on-Trent NG12 2JZ 0115 933 3337; www.crowncarveries.co.uk/nationalsearch/eastandwestmidlands/theshepherdsradcliffeontrent). Open for breakfast *daily 09.00-11.00 (Sat & Sun 11.30)*; bar *open 11.00-22.00*; food *served 09.00-21.00 (Fri-Sun 08.00)*. Family-friendly establishment, majoring on all day carvery food, including a takeaway service. Garden, sports TV and Wi-Fi. Close to Thorntons Holt Camping Park (0115 993 2125; www.thorntons-holt.co.uk).

2 Grannies Tearoom 3 Bingham Road, Cotgrave NG12 3JS (0115 989 4461). Friendly, bustling village meeting place serving teas, coffee and homemade snacks. Also cards, flowers and gifts. *Open Mon-Sat 09.00-17.00.*

3 Manvers Arms The Cross, Cotgrave NG12 3HS (0115 989 3049; www.facebook.com/themanversarmsatcotgrave). Friendly, village local serving real ale and food *Mon-Fri L and E; Sat 12.00-21.00 & Sun 12.00-16.00*. Dog- and family-friendly, garden. Traditional pub games, newspapers, real fires, sports TV and Wi-Fi. *Open 12.00-23.00 (Fri-Sat 00.00).*

4 The Rose & Crown Main Road, Cotgrave NG12 3HQ (0115 989 2245; www.roseandcrowncotgrave.co.uk). Comfortably furnished village pub, with a warm atmosphere, serving home-cooked food - *Mon-Fri L and E; Sat 12.00-22.00 & Sun 12.00-20.00* - real cider and real ales. Dog- and child-friendly, garden. Traditional pub games, newspapers, real fires and Wi-Fi. *Open 12.00-23.00 (Sun 22.30).*

5 The Plough Inn Main Street, Cropwell Butler NG12 3AB (0115 933 3124; www.theplough-cropwellbutler.co.uk). A real ale haven that welcomes families. Log fires, pool, a patio and a beer garden make this a good place to relax. Appetising homemade food is available *Mon E; Tue-Thu L and E; all day Fri & Sat and Sun L.* Takeaway service. Traditional pub games, newspapers and Wi-Fi. *Open Mon-Thu L and E & Fri-Sat 12.00-00.00 (Sun 22.30).*

6 The Wheatsheaf 11 Nottingham Road, Cropwell Bishop NG12 3BP (0115 989 2247). Country pub serving real ale. Children and dogs welcome. Traditional pub games and real fires. *Open Mon-Fri 16.00-23.00 (Fri 00.00) & Sat-Sun 12.00-00.00 (Sun 23.00).*

7 Nyce 11 Nottingham Road, Cropwell Bishop NG12 3BP (0115 989 0093). Purveyors of freshly made hot and cold food. *Open Mon-Fri 07.30-15.30.*

8 The Chequers Inn Church Street, Cropwell Bishop NG12 3DB (0115 989 4739; www.starpubs.co.uk/pubs/chequers-inn-cropwell-bishop). Village local serving real ale and food *daily 12.00-21.00 (Sun 20.00)*. Dog- and Child-friendly, garden. Sports TV and Wi-Fi. *Open 12.00-23.00.*

9 Martin's Arms School Lane, Colston Bassett NG12 3FD (01949 81361; www.themartinsarms.co.uk). Nottinghamshire's dining pub of the year and a regular CAMRA award-winner, this idyllic country pub serves a variety of real ales and appetising, home-cooked food *L and E (not Sun E)*. Children welcome, delightful garden and real fires. *Open daily L and E.*

The Carpenter's Shop Canal Depot, Lock 16

Hickling

Narrow country roads prescribe long sweeping bends across the open countryside, seemingly more intent on keeping to ancient field boundaries than in getting from A to B. The course of the waterway shares a similar philosophy. Closer to Nottingham an occasional glasshouse could be glimpsed but now the farmland is predominantly arable, although from time to time cattle can be seen fattening contentedly on pasture. Small settlements punctuate the countryside in a delightfully random patterning, while antiquity, in many varied guises, appears around almost every bend: a reminder that in this landscape the past is but a hop, skip and jump away. Gated roads and ancient hedge-lines both connect with a more leisurely age where the rhythms of nature, rather than the pressures of agri-business, dictated the shape and pace of life.

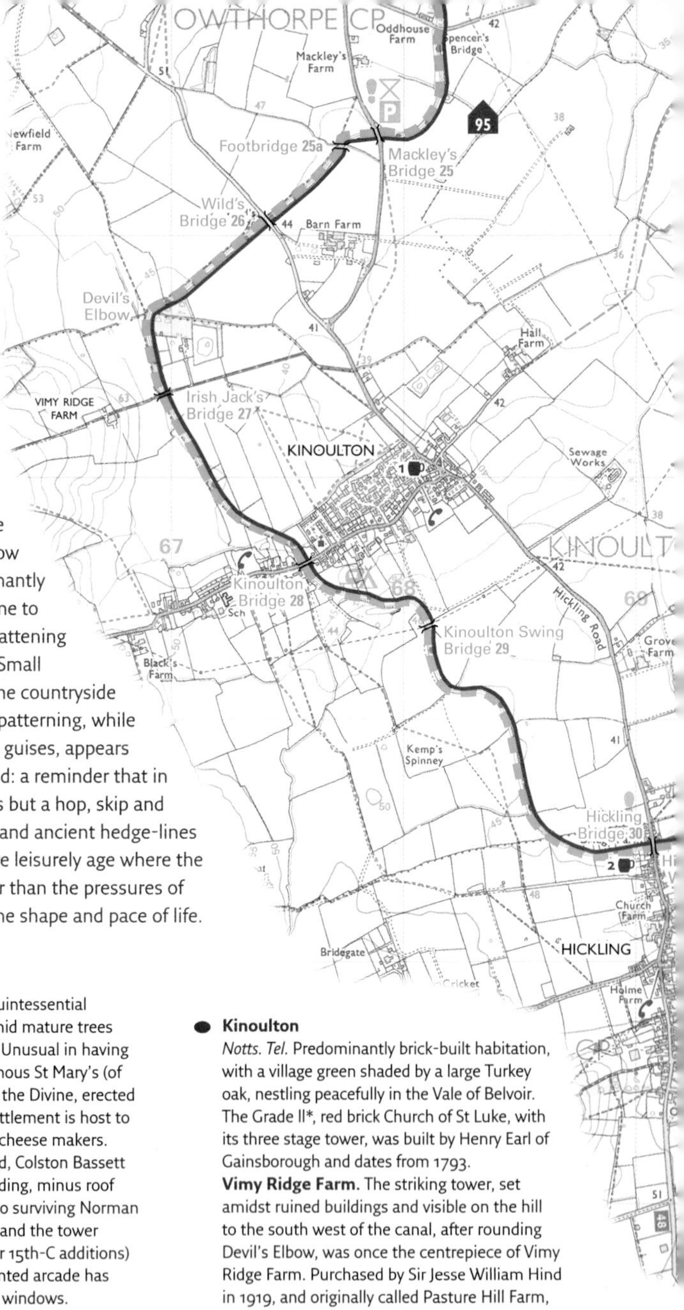

Colston Bassett
Notts. Tel. An intimate and quintessential estate village, slumbering amid mature trees and uninterrupted birdsong. Unusual in having two parish churches, the ruinous St Mary's (of Norman origins) and St John the Divine, erected by the squire in 1892, this settlement is host to another of the area's Stilton cheese makers.
St Mary's Church New Road, Colston Bassett NG12 3FX. Grade I listed building, minus roof and north aisle. There are two surviving Norman circular piers, 12th-C arcade and the tower dating from 14th C (with later 15th-C additions) is in good condition. The pointed arcade has inserted round arched Gibbs windows.
Colston Bassett Dairy Ltd Harby Lane, Colston Bassett NG12 3FN (01949 81322; www.colstonbassettdairy.co.uk). This is a farmers Cooperative, made up of local milk producers - founded in 1913 - and in continuous production since then, apart from breaks during the two World Wars when a little Cheddar was made. Shop *open Mon–Fri 09.00–12.30 & 13.30–16.00; Sat 09.30-12.00.*

Kinoulton
Notts. Tel. Predominantly brick-built habitation, with a village green shaded by a large Turkey oak, nestling peacefully in the Vale of Belvoir. The Grade II*, red brick Church of St Luke, with its three stage tower, was built by Henry Earl of Gainsborough and dates from 1793.
Vimy Ridge Farm. The striking tower, set amidst ruined buildings and visible on the hill to the south west of the canal, after rounding Devil's Elbow, was once the centrepiece of Vimy Ridge Farm. Purchased by Sir Jesse William Hind in 1919, and originally called Pasture Hill Farm, it was used to train ex-servicemen returning from the 1st World War and, later, orphan boys to help them find employment. The access driveway was planted with 184 Lombardy poplars, reminiscent of those found in northern France, to commemorate Lt. Francis Montagu Hind, killed in action at the Battle of the Somme on 27th September 1916. Sir Jesse Hind planted the avenue in memory of his son and the 183

other officers and men, of The Sherwood Foresters Regiment, killed between 7th July and 30th November – the official end of the battle. Now well past their natural life, the trees are being felled and re-planted by Kinoulton Parish Council.

- **Hickling**

Notts. Tel. A small, thriving community with a very active fund raising focus, via an annual September show and scarecrow competition. The attractive wharf, opposite the pub, is a magnet for fishermen and visitors alike. A 2¼-mile section of the canal, heading east towards Hose, was dredged in 1994, funded by a Derelict Land Grant and three low-level, occupation crossings were replaced by new swing bridges. An original warehouse, built in 1797 when the waterway opened, lies on the south side of the wharf, while beyond stands the squat, square tower of St Luke's Church. The former Wesleyan Chapel, dating from 1848, has been converted into a private dwelling.

- **Long Clawson**

Leics. Tel. Reckoned to be over a mile long, and harbouring 14 sharp bends, this village is reputed to be composed of the two previous habitations of Clawson and Claxton. Standing imposingly beside Mill Farm there is a windmill with a characteristic Lincolnshire-style cap and a Grade II listing. 40 local dairy farms supply milk for the 6,500 tons of Stilton cheese produced in the village, an industry that employs over 200 people.

Long Clawson Dairy Limited Long Clawson LE14 4PJ (01664 822332; www.clawson.co.uk). Possibly the oldest Stilton producer in the area, and with an enviable range of over 30 different cheeses in its stable, this creamery also has a presence in nearby Harby and Bottesford. For further details visit their website.

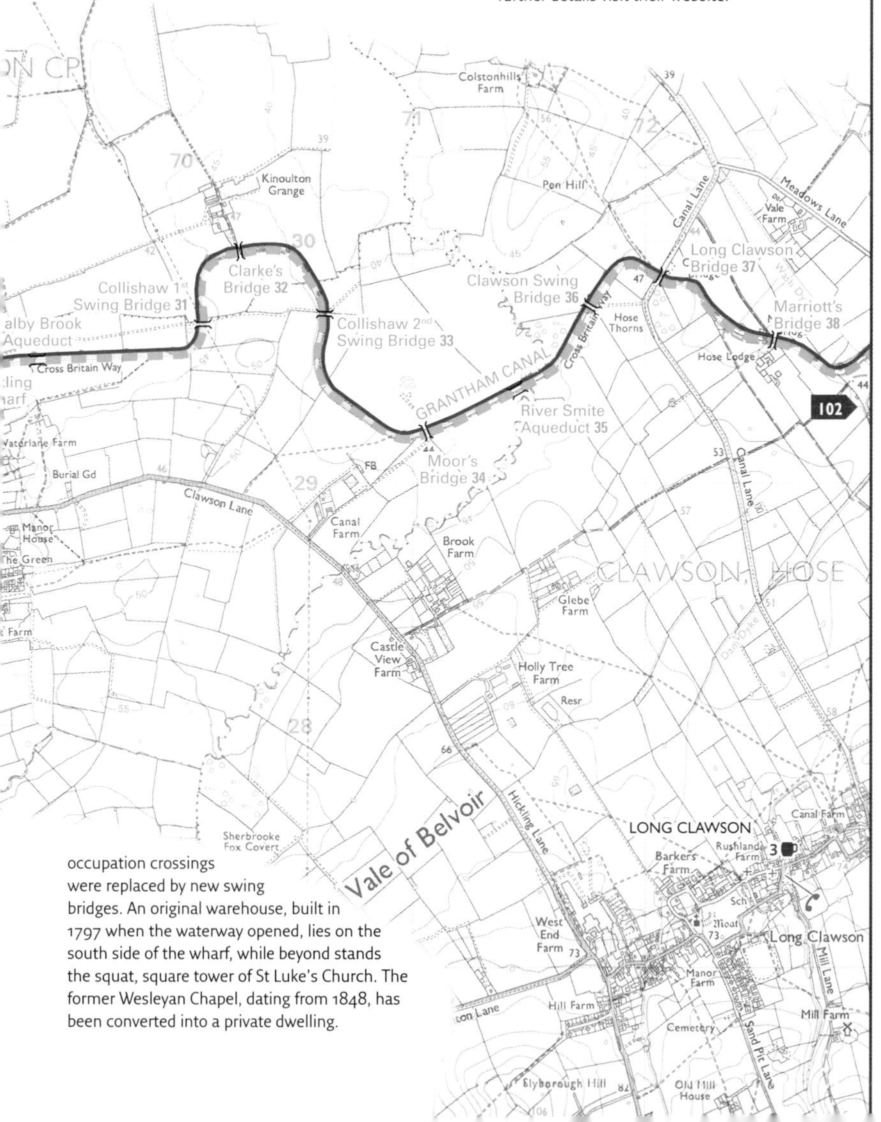

Pubs and Restaurants (pages 98-99)

1 **The Neville Arms** Owthorpe Lane, Kinoulton NG12 3EH (01949 81751). Many eulogise about this popular village hostelry with the consensus being top restaurant food at pub prices. The staff are welcoming, friendly and helpful - without being intrusive - and all dietary requirements are cheerfully accommodated. Real ale, a large garden and children's play area. Food available *Tue-Sun L and E (not Sun E)*. Booking advisable. Child- and dog-friendly, garden. Newspapers, real fires and Wi-Fi. *Open Tue-Sun 12.00-23.00 (Sun 18.00).*

2 **The Plough Inn** Main Street, Hickling LE14 3AH (01664 822225; www.facebook.com/ThePloughInnHickling). Very much the focus of the village, this welcoming hostelry dispenses real ale and appetising, home-cooked food *daily 12.00-21.00 (Sun 17.00)*. Children and dogs welcome; garden. Traditional pub games and *regular* live music. Newspapers, real fires and Wi-Fi. *Open 12.00-23.00 (Sun 22.30).*

3 **The Crown & Plough** 3 East End, Long Clawson LE14 4NG (01664 822322; www.thecrownandplough.co.uk). Comfortable village pub serving real ales and homemade food *Thu-Sun*. Child- and dog-friendly, garden. Traditional pub games, real fires and Wi-Fi. B&B. *Open Tue-Fri 17.00-00.00 (Fri 16.00) & Sat-Sun 09.00-00.00.*

WALKING AND CYCLING

Rectory Bridge 44 is the start of a Site of Special Scientific Interest (SSSI), which includes the towpath for some four miles to Redmile Mill Bridge 54. The site is of importance for its exceptional range of aquatic and marginal plants, all of which are adapted for slow moving water. The towpath is lined with abundant horsetails - members of the Equisetaceae family of non-flowering plants - and one of our most ancient plant species. The notification also takes account of the associated habitats such as the emergent vegetation, trees and hedgerows. As a consequence it is highly unlikely that this section of the towpath will ever be treated to a hard surface.

The Kinoulton Marshes SSSI - further to the west - was designated in 1983, the special interest of the site relating to the grazing marshland and neutral grassland of the land adjacent to the navigation. However, the canal channel has been included in the designation as associated, valuable habitat.

NAVIGATIONAL NOTES

For the most part this section is in water but in many areas very overgrown by rushes and other marginal plants. However, some stretches are kept clear by members of the very active angling clubs based on the canal.

STILTON CHEESE

With origins seemingly as old as the surrounding countryside itself, production of Stilton cheese can easily be traced back to the early 18th C. Although many changes have subsequently taken place, this quintessentially English cheese has its own Certification Trade Mark and is an EU Protected Food Name. This means that it can only be produced in the three Counties of Derbyshire, Nottinghamshire and Leicestershire; that it must be made from locally produced milk that has been pasteurised before use; it can only be made in a cylindrical shape and must be allowed to form its own coat or crust; it must never be pressed and must have the magical blue veins radiating from its centre.

The somewhat tenuous link between present day cheese production in Leicestershire, and the village of Stilton in Cambridgeshire, seems to be connected to a cheese-making farmer's wife living near Melton Mowbray, who procured cheese for her brother-in-law - one, Cooper Thornhill - then the landlord of the Bell Inn, Stilton.

Today there are just six dairies licensed to produce the blue (and lesser known white) Stilton cheese - three in Leicestershire, two in Nottinghamshire and one in Derbyshire: the last one coming late to the party, started by two former employees from the old Dairy Crest Hartington Creamery and granted a licence in 2014.

Recently restored Middle Lock 15 on the Woolsthorpe Flight

Harby

The navigation continues to prescribe an erratic course, meandering its way across the giant bowl that is the Vale of Belvoir, its south eastern perimeter ringed by the Jurassic escarpment of the Nottinghamshire Wolds. Perched on their most easterly outcrop stands the fairy-tale structure of Belvoir Castle, looking out over the Vale, commanding stunning views and overseeing all its activity. Had this edifice been there in the pre-Ice Age era, its inhabitants would have surveyed the old course of the Trent. In those days the river headed almost due east, on departure from present-day Nottingham, joining the North Sea via The Wash. Debris, in the form of lateral moraine left by a melting glacier, blocked its eastward passage at Ancaster – just to the north east of Grantham – forcing the river to find a new outlet to the north, courtesy of the remodelled Humber Estuary. When the weather is fine parachutists can be seen drifting languidly down from the sky, preceded by the angry buzz of an aircraft scrabbling for altitude, followed by their brightly hued canopy. Their descent marks the location of the British Parachute School's base at Langar Airfield, which is the busiest civilian skydiving centre in the UK. Recently, the lowered Bridge 43 has been replaced with a structure designed to form a lift bridge when navigation is restored.

Hose
Leics. PO, tel, stores, garage. The archetypal English village, complete with blacksmith at work under the shade of a massive, spreading chestnut tree. The delightful Church of Michael and All Angels is buttressed by a mellow, honey-coloured, limestone tower – albeit badly eroded. There is an hourly bus service to Melton Mowbray and Bottesford. The stores are *open Mon-Fri 08.00-13.00 (Tue 12.00) & Sat 09.00-12.00.*

Langar cum Barnstone
Leics. Tel. The combined communities of Langar and Barnstone sprawl over a large area, embracing both the ex-World War II Bomber Command airfield and the old Blue Circle cement quarries, now owned and operated by Lafarge as a packing plant for a range of specialist cementitious products. It employs approximately 60 people. Having served as a base for the Royal Canadian Air Force after the War, the airfield became home to the British Parachute School in 1977 and, more recently, to Langar Karting and Quad Centre.
St Andrew's Church, known as the Cathedral of the Vale due to its size, has been a place of pilgrimage since Saxon times and is now a Grade I listed building. It was heavily restored by Thomas Rutter in 1860.
Langar Karting and Quad Centre Langar Airfield, Langar NG13 9HY (01949 861155; www.lkqc.com). Much as 'it says on the tin' and a good deal more besides.

Harby
Leics. PO, tel, stores, takeaway, garage. This village has been at the hub of much of the activity – be it agricultural or industrial – centred in the Vale of Belvoir over the past few centuries. Iron ore was quarried in the Harby Hills and brought down an inclined plane railway to the main line and dairy herds, supplying the local Stilton Cheese industry, were once the backbone of the traditional mixed farming system. In the early 19th C there are records of Chalybeate springs being visited for their health-giving properties thought to reside in the water's high iron and manganese content.
The Church of St Mary the Virgin is constructed from a delightful mix of brick and honey-coloured limestone. For further details of the history of this area visit the excellent village website at www.harby.co.uk/history.htm

Stathern
Leics. PO, tel, stores, off-licence, greengrocer. The village occupies a natural terrace, 330 feet above sea level, on the steep escarpment forming part of the Belvoir Ridge that terminates at the Castle three miles to the northeast. It is famed in the Vale for its 10 day, summer fund-raising festival. Two Iron Age sites are recorded locally, which are confirmed by the recovery of a loom weight and a group of skeletons complete with Neolithic axes. There is also evidence of Romano-British occupation, most notably in the form of a coin hoard and, more recently, of Anglo Saxon activity supported by the find – in 1982 – of a trefoil-headed broach. Recognised as being of the 'small-long variety', it supports late 5th or early 6th-C settlement. The post office is in the Plough and is *open Mon & Fri 09.00-13.00 and Thu 08.30-10.30.*

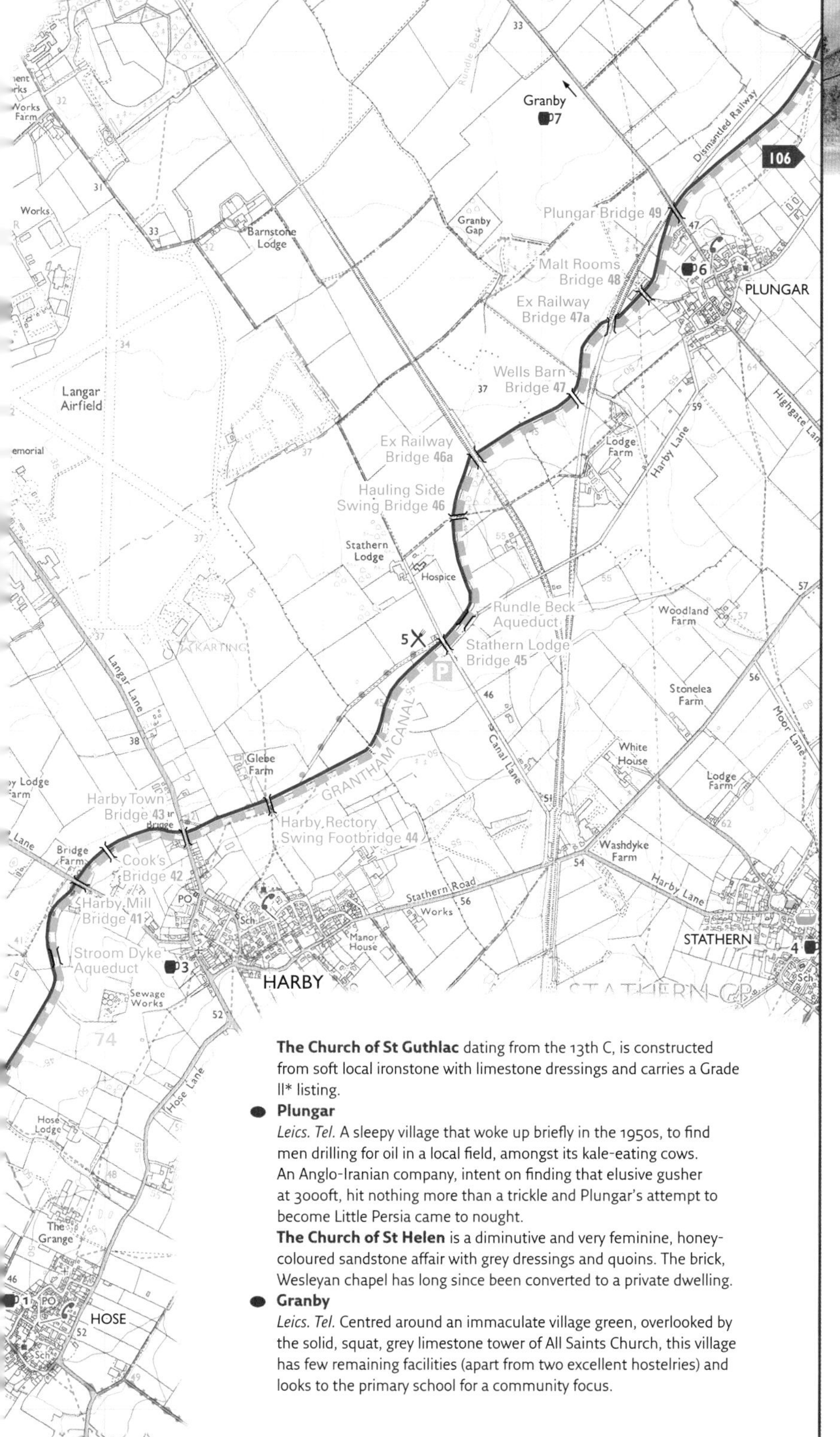

The Church of St Guthlac dating from the 13th C, is constructed from soft local ironstone with limestone dressings and carries a Grade II* listing.

● **Plungar**

Leics. Tel. A sleepy village that woke up briefly in the 1950s, to find men drilling for oil in a local field, amongst its kale-eating cows. An Anglo-Iranian company, intent on finding that elusive gusher at 3000ft, hit nothing more than a trickle and Plungar's attempt to become Little Persia came to nought.

The Church of St Helen is a diminutive and very feminine, honey-coloured sandstone affair with grey dressings and quoins. The brick, Wesleyan chapel has long since been converted to a private dwelling.

● **Granby**

Leics. Tel. Centred around an immaculate village green, overlooked by the solid, squat, grey limestone tower of All Saints Church, this village has few remaining facilities (apart from two excellent hostelries) and looks to the primary school for a community focus.

Pubs and Restaurants (page 103)

1 The Rose & Crown Inn 43 Bolton Lane, Hose, LE14 4JE (01949 358913; www.roseandcrownhose.com). Welcoming pub serving real ale and food *Tue-Fri E & Sat-Sun 12.00-21.30 (Sun 16.30)*. Dog- and family-friendly, garden. Traditional pub games, real fires and Wi-Fi. Camping nearby. *Open Mon-Thu 17.00-23.00; Fri-Sat 12.00-00.00 (Sat 01.00) & Sun 12.00-22.30.*

2 The Unicorn's Head Main Street, Langar NG13 9HE (01949 861604; www.unicornshead.co.uk). Built in 1717, originally with its own brewhouse, this pub now serves real ales and classic homemade pub food *Wed-Fri 16.00-21.00 & Sat-Sun 12.00-21.00 (Sun 20.00)*. Dog- and family-friendly, garden. Traditional pub games, real fires and Wi-Fi. *Open Wed-Fri 16.00-22.00 & Sat-Sun 12.00-22.00 (Sun 20.00).*

3 The Nags Head 20 Main Street, Harby LE14 4BN (01949 869629; www.nagsheadharby.com). A traditional traditional local serving real ale and bar meals *Mon-Fri L and E (not Mon L); Sat 12.00-21.30 & 12.00-16.00*. Dog- and family-friendly, outside seating. *Regular* live music, real fires and Wi-Fi. *Open Mon-Thu L and E (not Mon L) & Fri-Sun 12.00-23.00.*

4 The Plough Inn 12A Main Street, Stathern LE14 4HW (01949 860411; www.theploughstathern.com). Friendly village hostelry serving real ale and home-cooked, traditional pub food *daily L and E (not Sun E)*. Children and dogs welcome. Beer garden, pool and skittle alley. Newspapers, sports TV and Wi-Fi. *Open Mon-Sat 12.00-23.00 (Mon-Tue 22.00) & Sun 12.00-18.00.*

5 Dove Cottage Tearoom and Charity Shop Bridge Cottage, Canal Lane, Stathern LE14 4EX (01949 861950; www.dovecottage.org). Beside Bridge 45. Serving light lunches, afternoon tea and cake, this establishment welcomes muddy walkers, cyclists and horse riders. Children's playground. *Open daily 10.30-15.30 (Sat-Sun 16.00)*. Wheelchair and pushchair friendly. The Charity Shop is *closed Sun.*

6 The Anchor 1 Granby Lane, Plungar NG13 0JJ (01949 860589; www.plungar.org/the-anchor-pub). Inhabiting what were once a row of cottages (and subsequently the local courtroom) this welcoming establishment serves local real ales and highly-regarded, home-cooked food *Tue-Thu E; Fri-Sat L and E & Sun 12.00-14.00*. Dog- and child-friendly, garden. Traditional pub games, real fires, sports TV and Wi-Fi. *Open Mon-Thu 17.00-23.00; Fri L and E & Sat-Sun 12.00-23.00 (Sun 22.30).*

8 The Marquis of Granby Dragon Street, Granby NG13 9PN (01949 859517). Reputed to date from 1565 and, in 1744, gifted to a general as a post-war pension, this delightful hostelry serves local real ales and is a regular CAMRA award winner. Children and dogs welcome. Open fires in winter and outside seating. Traditional pub games, newspapers and Wi-Fi. *Open Mon-Fri 16.00-23.00 (Fri 00.00) & Sat-Sun 12.00-00.00 (Sun 23.00).*

WALKING AND CYCLING

For a list of walks in the Hose area visit the village website at walk4life.info/walksearchadv?searchType=typeAll&walksearch=le144jr&op=Search. There are also several undemanding walks, starting from Dove Cottage tearooms, that can be downloaded at my.viewranger.com/route/details/MjAzMDY3Mw.

Grantham Guildhall (built 1869)

Redmile

Beyond Plungar the trackbed of the Great Northern Railway and London & North Western Railway Joint Line (running from Market Harborough to Bottesford, via Melton Mowbray) abuts the towpath, continuing almost as far as Redmile. Together with the Barnestone Branch - which once served the cement works north of Langar Airfield - this casualty of the pre-Beeching era serves as a poignant reminder that the Vale of Belvoir (and its environs) did not always proclaim a story of fairy tale enchantment. In the 19th C, ironstone was discovered in the hills running from Caythorpe in Lincolnshire all the way through to Oxford, surfacing in the rim of the bowl forming the Vale of Belvoir. The Wolds to the south and west of Belvoir Castle were extensively quarried from the 1870s through to the closure of the final workings in 1964. Much of the ore was transported over these lines to steelworks in Stanton on the Erewash Canal and to Staveley and Renishaw, close to the Chesterfield Canal near its western terminus. Muston Gorse Bridge 57 marks the site of the former Muston Gorse Wharf, which opened in 1815 and, for more than 100 years, serviced the needs of the castle via a horse-drawn tramway. With an elevation of 370ft above the waterway, the then Duke's initial plans for a connection using a branch canal were totally impractical. A mile or so further east the 20-mile pound comes to an abrupt end as the navigation swings south and, crossing the infant River Devon, is confronted with the currently, very derelict, Woolsthorpe Bottom Lock 12.

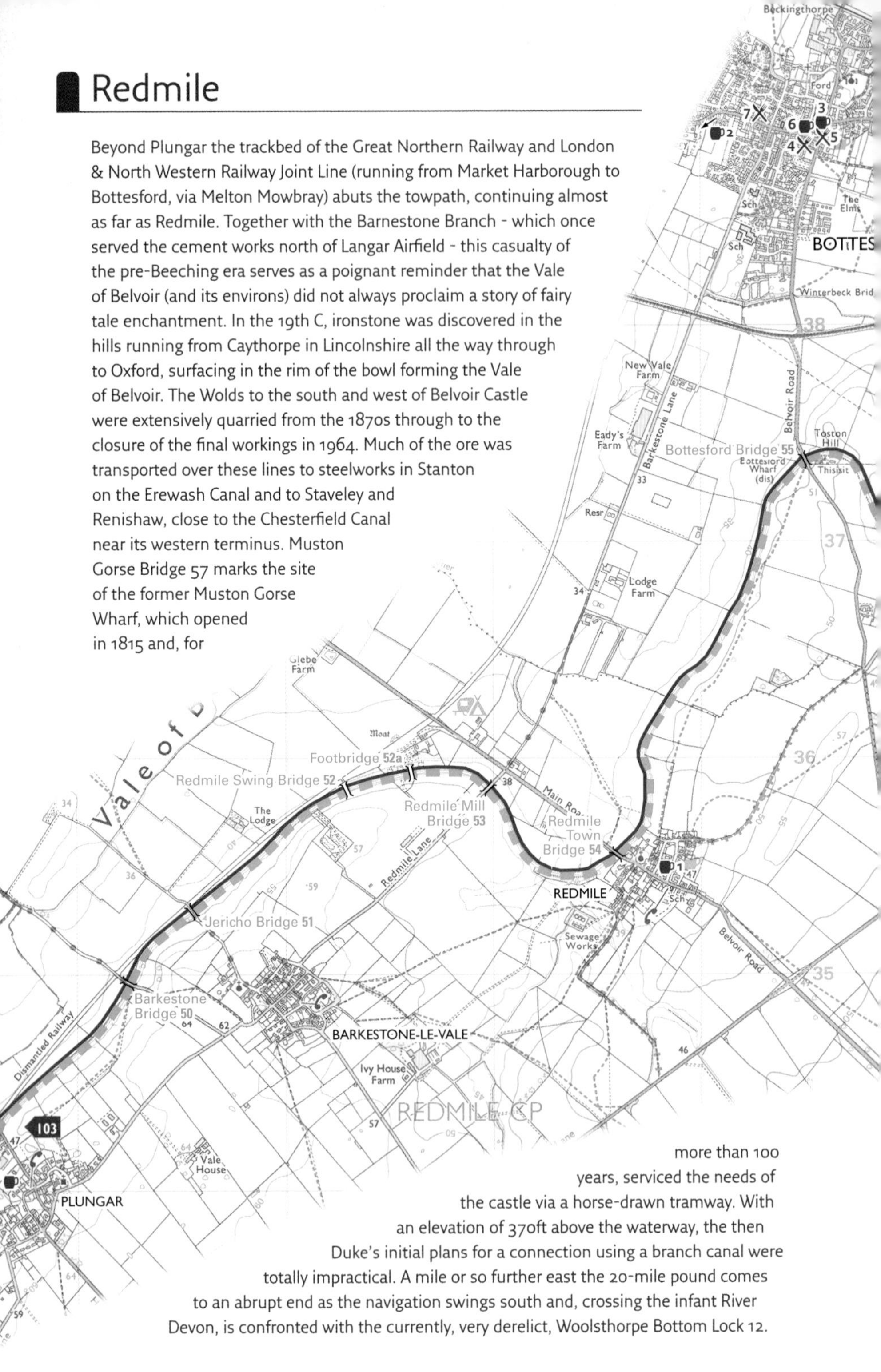

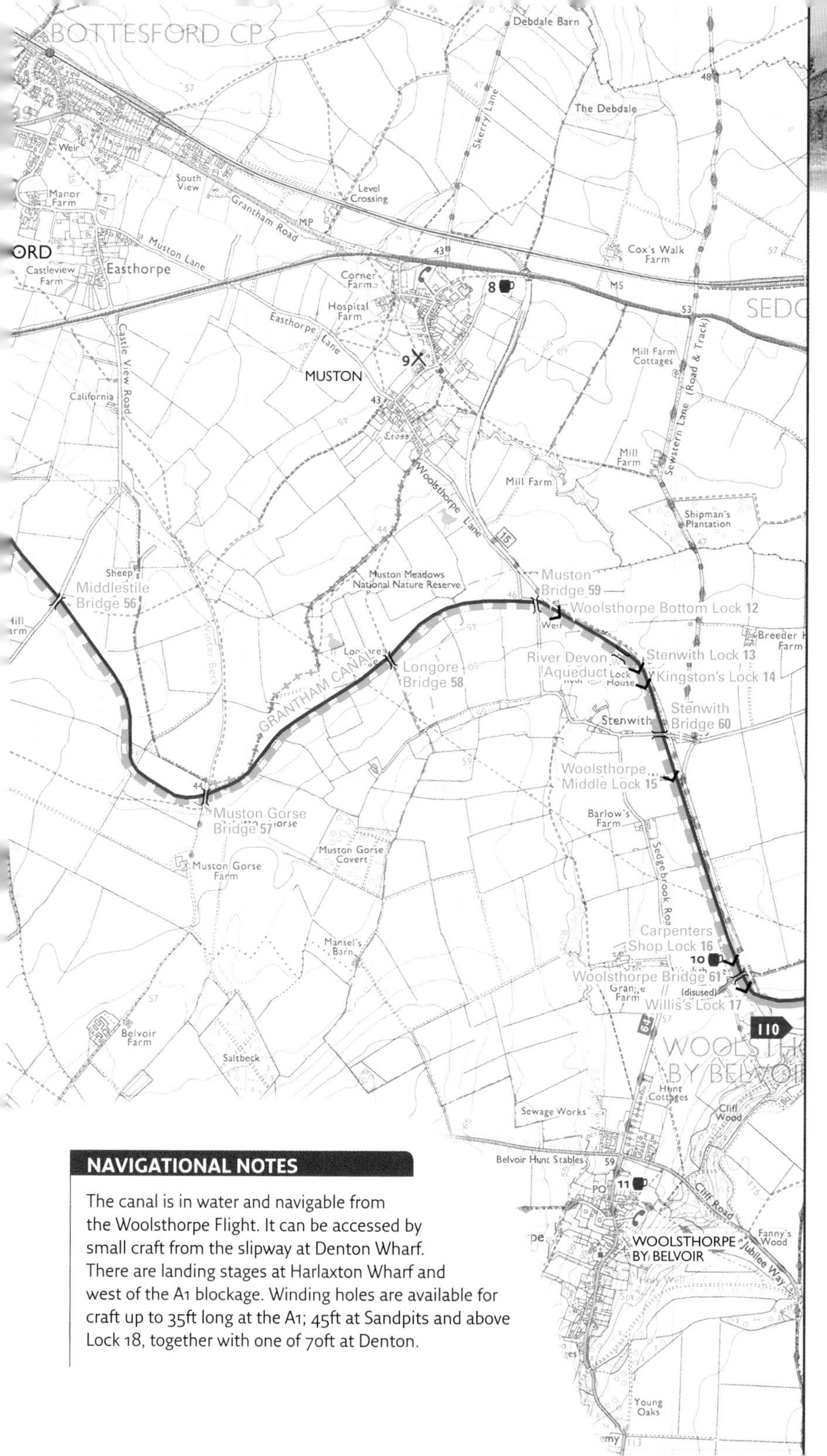

NAVIGATIONAL NOTES

The canal is in water and navigable from the Woolsthorpe Flight. It can be accessed by small craft from the slipway at Denton Wharf. There are landing stages at Harlaxton Wharf and west of the A1 blockage. Winding holes are available for craft up to 35ft long at the A1; 45ft at Sandpits and above Lock 18, together with one of 70ft at Denton.

Barkestone-le-Vale

Leics. Tel. Once a small, compact village but now somewhat overwhelmed by modern development. Recent excavation of a medieval, rural dwelling revealed rare imported European ceramics and what was thought to be re-used Romano-British pottery. In the early hours of 27th February 2008 an earthquake, measuring 5.3 magnitude on the Richter Scale, hit the village, leaving 16ft of the spire of St Peter & St Pauls Church to be dismantled and re-built.

Redmile

Leics. Tel. A cacophony of colours – mainly reds, pinks and ochres – reside in the materials from which this village is constructed. The name does nothing to lessen the impact, although there is a choice when it comes to deciding on the origins of its appellation. Some say that following a particularly gory battle, at nearby Belvoir Castle, the blood ran downhill for a mile, coating the village street. Those of a more serene disposition attribute the name to the abundance of red clay, extending for a mile, to be found in the surrounding fields. Either way no one disputes the fact that the village was used for much of the filming of the second series the popular television comedy Auf Wiedersehen Pet, featuring seven migrant British construction workers.

Bottesford

Leics. PO, tel, stores, chemist, off-licence, greengrocer, takeaway, fish & chips, butcher, library, station. Although lying a mile or so north of the canal, this is by far the largest habitation between Nottingham and Grantham, providing all the services a visitor to the waterway could require. St Mary's Church is of medieval origins, dating from 15th C, and its remarkably tall, slender, sprocketed spire – at 212ft – is the tallest in Leicestershire. The chancel was re-built in 17th C to accommodate the tombs of the Dukes of Rutland who have all been buried here over the ages. The churchyard is circled in part by the infant River Devon: the siting of the village may well originate from an early fording point of this watercourse. There is growing evidence of occupation during Roman times and beyond.

Muston

Leics. Tel. Pronounced 'Musson', this peaceful and secluded village slumbers around the Church of St John the Baptist with its interesting, rocket-shaped tower attired in the ubiquitous honey-coloured stone with grey dressings of these parts.

Muston Meadows National Nature Reserve

Between Muston village and the canal (at Longore Bridge 58) lies Muston Meadows National Nature Reserve. This SSSI is home to over 10,000 May-flowering, green winged orchids and also contains a wealth of wildlife, including invertebrates, amphibians and birds. The site supports a variety of insects, including many butterflies and moths. Ponds - originally dug to provide water for grazing animals - are now home to dragonflies, frogs and the rare great-crested newt. Skylarks and meadow pipits build their nests in the long grass, while yellowhammers, linnets and whitethroats nest in hedgerows. There are large numbers of small mammals such as bank and field voles, and on summer evenings bats can be seen hunting for insects over the site.

Woolsthorpe by Belvoir

Lincs. PO, tel. Set a little way to the south of the canal and immediately beneath the castle's lofty perch, the village sprawls snug and secure under the watchful eye of the Duke of Rutland – willing to do his bidding, yet safe in his patronage. The buildings are, for the most part, constructed from a mix of brick and warm, honey-hued limestone, with a dappling of bright colour-washed examples here and there. The Church of St James was completed in 1846, built in the Decorated style as a replacement for the original edifice destroyed by Parliamentary forces in 1643. There is evidence of two abandoned villages in the area, together with earlier Roman and Bronze Age occupation. The 'Dirty Duck' pub, cottages and old BW workshop form a pleasant grouping of buildings, somewhat apart from the village itself, adjoining the three Woolsthorpe Locks. The post office is *open Thu 14.00-16.30* in the village hall.

IRON IN THEIR SOLE

It is said that, in days of yore, members of the peasantry trudging through Wold country, south of the canal - giving the castle a wide birth to avoid any cap-doffing encounters with a wandering Duke - were more than likely to stumble over rocks of a rusty brown hue. In the light of more recent knowledge, this was readily identified as iron ore and, in its celebration, a huge industry sprang up in the later part of the 19th C, to extract this mineral for gain. Small hamlets such as Branston, Eaton, Eastwell and Goadby Marwood, lying to the south and west of Belvoir Castle, were soon established as centres for iron ore quarrying, where activity moved, ant-like, across the surrounding countryside, pursued by an ever-expanding network of narrow-gauge railways. Most of their track beds were too steep for steam traction and employed rope haulage, sitting up to 250ft above the permanent way of their standard gauge, Great Northern and North Western Railway counterparts. Tippler trucks were the stock-in-trade and these deposited their spoils into waiting wagons on mainline, ironstone sidings - like the ones just south of Harby & Southern Station. At the height of production three loaded trains a day left this siding alone, bound largely for steelworks near Chesterfield. Quarrying was active in the area from 1876–1964 when it finally fell foul of cheaper, foreign imports. While most extraction was from opencast workings, two mines - at Thistleton and Irthlingborough, some way south of Melton Mowbray – were excavated and employed battery-driven locomotives to haul the ore to the surface.

Pubs and Restaurants (pages 106-107)

1 The Windmill Inn 4 Main Street, Redmile NG13 0GA (01949 842281; www.windmillinn-redmile.co.uk). A gastro pub with a friendly, relaxed atmosphere, serving real ales and reasonably priced food *Tue-Sun L and E (Not Tue L or Sun E)*. Famed for its rôle as the Barley Mow in the TV cult series Auf Wiedersehen, Pet - to which framed photos on the walls attest. Dog- and family-friendly, garden. Real fires and Wi-Fi. Camping nearby. *Open Tue-Thu L and E (not Tue L) & Fri-Sun 12.00-23.00 (Sun 18.30).*

2 The Durham Ox Church Street, Orston NG13 9NS (01949 850059; www.thedurhamoxorston.co.uk). A traditional - and very attractive - country pub dispensing real ales and highly-though of food *Tue-Thu L and E & Fri-Sun 12.00-20.30 (Sun 16.00)*. Dog- and child-friendly, garden. Newspapers, real fires, sports TV and Wi-Fi. *Open Mon-Thu L and E & Fri-Sun 12.00-23.00 (Sun 22.30).*

3 The Bull Inn 5 Market Street, Bottesford NG13 0BW (01949 842288). An 18th-C hostelry in the centre of the village that can claim Laurel and Hardy as one-time visitors. It now serves real ale and offers traditional pub games, newspapers, real fires, sports TV and Wi-Fi. Garden. *Open Mon-Fri 16.00-23.00 (Fri 00.30) & Sat-Sun 12.00-00.30 (Sun 22.30).*

4 Coffee Shop & Pizzini 5 High St, Bottesford NG13 0AA (01949 844533; www.pizzinicoffeeshop.co.uk). Coffee shop and takeaway service - majoring on breakfasts, pizzas, kebabs and burgers - in the centre of the village. *Open Thu-Sat 10.00-23.00.*

5 Paul's Restaurant & Wine Lodge 1 Market Street, Bottesford NG13 0BW (01949 842375; www.pauls-restaurant.co.uk). A lively restaurant serving value for money, contemporary cuisine combining excellent service with a friendly relaxed atmosphere. *Open Tue-Sun L and E (not Sun E).* Children welcome (high chairs available). Takeaway service. Booking advisable (essential *Fri & Sat*).

6 The Rutland Arms 2 High Street, Bottesford NG13 0AA (01949 843031; www.rutlandarmsbottesford.com). *Open 12.00-23.00 (Sun 22.30)* serving real ale and traditional pub food *Mon-Fri 12.00-14.00*. Dog- and family-friendly, outside seating. Pool table, real fires, sports TV and Wi-Fi.

7 The Thatch 26 High Street, Bottesford NG13 0AA (01949 842330; www.thethatchbottesford.co.uk). One of the earlier practitioners of 'slow food', this restaurant with rooms values its customers and offers a menu based on fresh local produce, in season, wherever possible. Children are welcome to share the same food with portions scaled down in size and price. The Grade II listed building adds charm to an unhurried dining experience, complete with log fires *in winter*. There is an outdoor terrace for the summer months. *Open Wed-Sun L and E (not Sun E).*

8 The Gap Inn Church Lane, Muston NG13 0FD (01949 842374; www.sizzlingpubs.co.uk/findapub/eastandwestmidlands/thegapinnnottingham). One of the Sizzling pubs chain designed to accommodate inexpensive family eating. *Open daily 09.00-21.00 (Sun 08.00).*

9 The Old Forge Tearooms 1 Main Street, Muston NG13 0FB (01949 842265; www.facebook.com/thisbritain/posts/1127635467373691). Old fashioned tearooms, in a charming setting in the centre of the village, serving teas, locally produced fruit cordials and home-made cakes and scones. *Open Sat-Sun 10.00-16.00.*

10 The Dirty Duck Duck Lane, Woolsthorpe Wharf, Woolsthorpe, Grantham NG32 1NY (01476 870111; www.thedirtyduckpub.co.uk). Formerly known as the Rutland Arms, this hostelry has adopted its nickname by way of its main appellation, but still dispenses real ale and homemade pub grub *Tue-Sun L and E (not Sun E)*. Live music and barbeques *in summer*. Dog- and child-friendly, garden. Real fires, sports TV and Wi-Fi. Camping. *Open Tue-Thu L and E & Fri-Sun 11.00-00.00 (Sun 19.00).*

11 The Chequers Main Street Woolsthorpe, Grantham NG32 1LU (01476 870701; www.chequersinn.net). Popular pub in the centre of the village that attracts a clientele from a wide area. Real ales and cider, over 30 gins and a wide range of wines and cocktails (including champagne) by the glass are certainly one draw. The generous portions of home-cooked food available *Mon-Sat L and E & Sun 12.00-20.30* are clearly another. Dog- and family-friendly, garden. Real fires and Wi-Fi. B&B. *Open daily 12.00-23.00 (Sun 22.30).*

WALKING AND CYCLING

The Viking Way joins the towpath just south of Stainwith Bridge 60, leaving a mile or so later at Longmoor Bridge 62. This long distance path links the Humber Bridge to the shores of Rutland Water, a total distance of 147 miles.

The cycle routes numbers 15 & 64 - of the National Cycle Network (NCN) - both make use of the ccanal towpath. NCN 15 links Castle Donnington to Tattershall in Lincolnshire, via Nottingham. NCN 64 runs from Market Harborough to Lincoln via Melton Mowbray and Newark-on-Trent.

Grantham

From the pound separating the newly restored Woolsthorpe Middle Locks 14 and 15, and Carpenter's Shop Lock 16, Cliff Wood looms almost menacingly, posing an as yet unanswered challenge to the current direction of the navigation. Once at the 'Dirty Duck' pub all suddenly becomes clear as, climbing the final two locks to its summit pound, it becomes apparent that the canal swings smartly through 90 degrees, to skirt the foot of this affronting Wold spur. Similar challenges have still to be met by the Canal Society, tasked with the job of this waterway's full restoration. In an attempt to stretch what few funds are currently available, in as many directions as possible, they have come up with the 'win, win' concept of re-building Locks 14 & 15 as part of a grant-aided, on-the-job training exercise. Restoration now complete, members of the local community have gained expertise that has increased their employability, whilst at the same time adding to the overall 'skill bank' of the Society: currency that can be employed

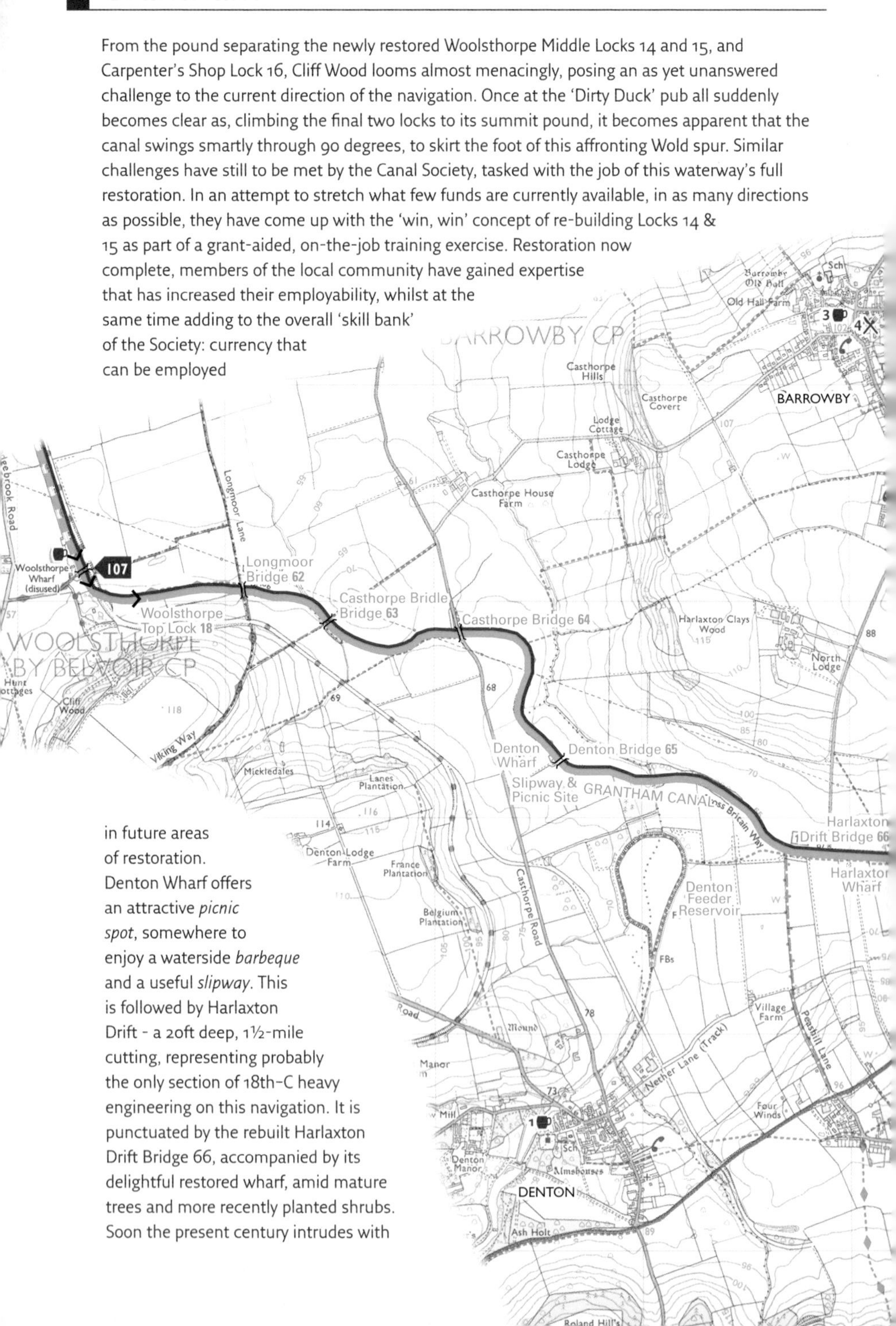

in future areas of restoration. Denton Wharf offers an attractive *picnic spot*, somewhere to enjoy a waterside *barbeque* and a useful *slipway*. This is followed by Harlaxton Drift - a 20ft deep, 1½-mile cutting, representing probably the only section of 18th-C heavy engineering on this navigation. It is punctuated by the rebuilt Harlaxton Drift Bridge 66, accompanied by its delightful restored wharf, amid mature trees and more recently planted shrubs. Soon the present century intrudes with a vengeance in the form of the A1 dual-carriageway that severs the line of the canal, breaking the spell that ensnares any boater, walker or cyclist following the line of this time-warp waterway. Although half a mile of the navigation is still in water beyond this trunk road, opinion is divided as to whether a new terminal basin should be formed here, or efforts made to re-instate the original almost a mile away. Currently under an industrial estate, restoration of the original terminus would bring the canal closer to the centre of Grantham, together with a much needed boost to the town's economy. The potential benefits are perceived to be so great that moves are already afoot to purchase and demolish the offending infrastructure.

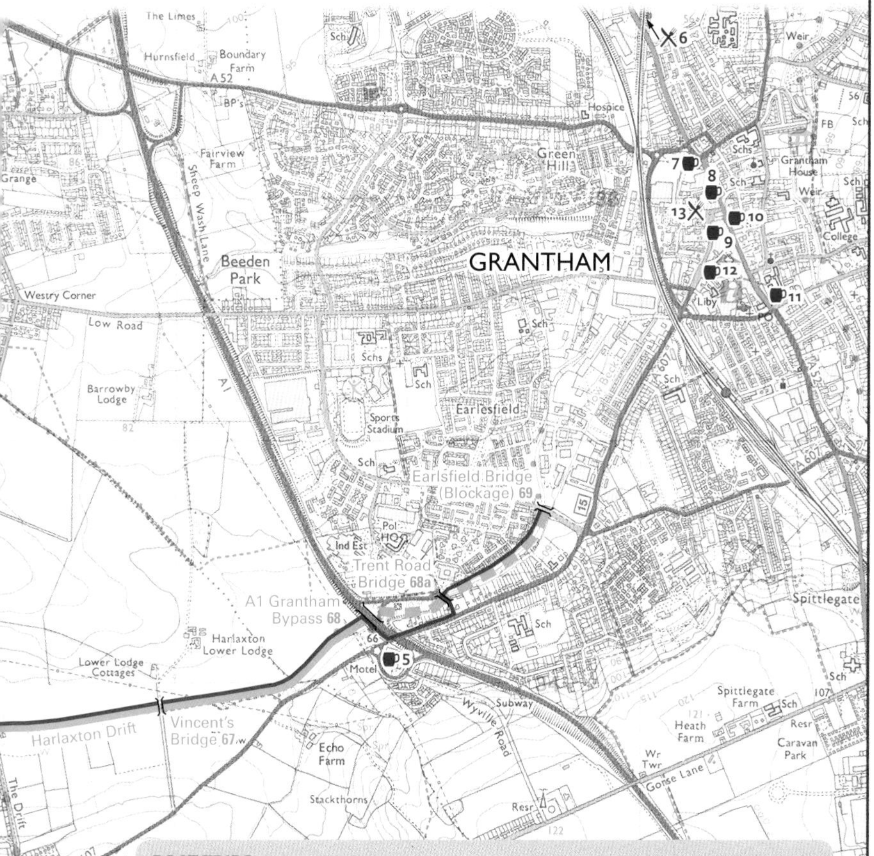

BOAT TRIPS

The Three Shires is the Grantham Canal Society's new trip boat and offers luxury cruises along the 4-mile navigable length of the Grantham Canal between Woolsthorpe and the A1 near Grantham. The boat has comfortable seating in the cabin for 10 people and space to enjoy the outdoors with a couple of seats on the fore-deck. It is equipped with a small kitchen. You may book cruises of 2, 3 or 4 hours duration, starting any time from 10am but the latest finishing time must always be at sunset. Of course the length of time determines how far you can go. Travel along the canal is not fast and a 2 hour cruise reaches Denton Wharf; a 3 hour cruise reaches the A1 near Grantham and, if you wish to pop into the nearby Farrier pub for a drink, please select a 4 hour cruise.

Ticketed timetabled services only operate *on selected B Hols* and on *special days* – see Society website for details.

To book telephone 01949 850999 or visit www.granthamcanal.org/the-three-shires-trip-boat.

Denton
Lincs. Tel. The name derives from the old English words 'dene' and 'tun' meaning village in a valley. The Grade I listed Church of St Andrew is built largely in the Perpendicular style and was heavily restored in 1888. In 1727 a mosaic pavement, together with several large pieces of Roman brick comprising part of a foundation, were discovered in local fields.
Belvoir Castle Grantham NG32 1PE (01476 871002; www.belvoircastle.com). This is the fourth building to have occupied the site since the Norman Conquest, replacing structures destroyed during the Wars of the Roses, the Civil War and a disastrous fire in 1816. The present castle houses paintings by Gainsborough, Holbein, Poussin and Reynolds; has a fine collection of porcelain, tapestries, furniture and silks as well as Italian sculptures. Contrasting rooms on show range from the grandeur of the State Rooms and the elegance of the Elizabethan Saloon, through to the 'below stairs' life lived in the old kitchen and bakery, or the military splendour of the guardroom.
In designing and landscaping the gardens of James Wyatt's 1799 commission to rebuild the castle, Elizabeth (the 5th Duchess) merely framed what she saw as her garden - the entire Vale of Belvoir - as vistas stretching beyond her valley gardens. Entry to the castle by guided tours only on selected dates (usually *Sun & Mon*) from *Easter–Aug*, commencing *11.15; 13.15 & 15.15*. Allow at least *15 mins* to walk from the ticket office to the castle. Gardens open *11.00-17.00* when castle is open for tours. Charge.

Barrowby
Lincs. PO, tel, stores, butcher. Now situated close to the intersection of two trunk roads - the A52 and the A1 - the village is reputed to have been founded by the Vikings: 'berg - by' being the Norse for village by the hill. The Church, constructed from local ironstone and limestone, dates from the late 13th C and carried an All Hallows dedication until the mid-16th C. Lying 300ft above sea level, northerly views from the village range from the divine to the mundane: Lincoln Cathedral and the Trent Valley power stations. The post office is *open Mon-Fri 09.00-15.00 (Wed 13.00) & Sat 09.00-12.30.*

Harlaxton
Lincs. PO, stores. A delightful ensemble of buildings, both great and small, flock this village many owing part, or all, their origin to the manor house that was pulled down in 1857 and assiduously re-recycled. In all there are 36 Grade II listed structures in Harlaxton, which was listed in the Domesday Book as 'Herlavestune' - from the old English meaning 'farm of Herelaf'. The Grade I listed Church of St Mary and St Peter, built in the Perpendicular style from ironstone and limestone ashlar, dates from 12th C. The tower is a later, 14th-C addition.

Grantham
Lincs. All services. This is a solid and comfortable market town, home to a veritable hotch potch of building styles - very few without a degree of charm - many reflecting its past, agricultural and industrial prosperity. Within the generous proportions of the town centre, mellow brick buildings, some with elegant Dutch gables, jostle with timber-frame black and white, while grey and honey-coloured ashlar share the streetscape with annotated classical façades. The Victorian Gothic Guildhall on St Peter Hill, designed by William Watkin in 1869, is particularly flamboyant with its pagoda-like clock tower. Grantham is the birthplace of Margaret Thatcher and the town where Sir Isaac Newton underwent his schooling. It is perhaps less well-known as the home of the first true compression ignition (Diesel) engine, developed in 1892, and of the first UK Tractor - dating from 1896: both from the local Richard Hornsby and Sons works. Nine years later Hornsby went on to develop the caterpillar track, which generated little interest, even from the army who eventually bought just four caterpillar tractors to tow artillery.
In 1914 Hornsby sold the patent to The Holt Manufacturing Co of California for $8,000 who, on the strength of that single patent, went on to become the highly successful Caterpillar Inc. of worldwide renown. In the same year it finally dawned on Colonel Ernest Swinton, of the British army, that here lay the basis for an attack vehicle. Other successful engineering firms have come and gone - notably Aveling-Barford - as have a diversity of manufacturers to the point where Grantham's economy is now based largely on the food processing industry. On a somewhat less prosaic level the town can boast the world's first women constables outside the Metropolitan force, while in 1740 a local baker, one William Egglestone, mistaking one ingredient for another, produced the first gingerbread biscuit, to become known as Grantham Whetstones.
Belton House Grantham NG32 2LS (01476 566116; www.nationaltrust.org.uk/belton-house). Three miles north of Grantham. A Restoration country house with 25 rooms open to the public. 1300 acre landscaped park, formal gardens, woodland adventure playground, wildlife discovery centre and much more. *Open early Mar-Nov including B Hols.* Telephone for further details or visit the website. Charge.
Easton Walled Gardens Easton, Nr Grantham NG33 5AP (01476 530063; www.eastonwalledgardens.co.uk). South of Grantham, just off the A1 on the B6403. Lincolnshire Visitor Attraction of the year. Set in a delightful 12-acre valley, this 400-year-old garden has walks, drifts of bulbs, sweet peas, roses, meadow and cottage gardens and a

stone bridge crossing the River Witham. Tea room and gift shop. *Open Mar-Oct, Wed-Fri; Sun & B Hol 11.00-16.00*. Charge.

The George Centre High Street, Grantham NG31 6LH (01476 592818; www.thegeorgecentre.com). Shopping and business centre located behind an impressive Georgian façade in the middle of the town. *Open Mon-Sat 09.00-17.30 & Sun 10.00-14.00*.

Grantham House Castlegate, Grantham NG31 6SS (01476 564705; www.nationaltrust.org.uk/grantham-house). Handsome town house dating from 1380 with architectural features from various eras and a walled riverside garden. Limited *opening Apr-Oct* largely by appointment - telephone for details. Charge.

Grantham Markets (01476 406153/07786 171379). There is a weekly *Sat* street market and a Farmers' Market on the *2nd Sat of each month*.

Grantham Museum Saint Peter's Hill, Grantham NG31 6PY (01476 568783; www.gramuseum.wordpress.com). *Open Thu-Sat 10.00-16.00*.

Guildhall Arts Centre Saint Peter's Hill, Grantham NG31 6PZ (01476 406158; www.guildhallartscentre.com). The original Guildhall was made up of three buildings- a ballroom and courtroom, the governor's residence and a jail. Now it houses a lively Arts Centre, the Tourist Information Centre and a Coffee Shop. Box office *open Mon-Fri 09.30-16.30 & Sat 09.30-14.00*.

St. Wulfram's Church Church Street, Grantham NG31 6RR (01476 561342; www.stwulframs.org.uk). Constructed from Ancaster limestone, this Grade I building is reputed to be the largest Medieval place of worship (700 seats) in the country, with the tallest spire of any English parish church. It stands at 282ft and was erected in the early part of the 14th C. There is a chained library and a crypt chapel, together with some fine Victorian and modern stained glass. The Visitor Centre features touch-screen interpretation and there is an audio Tour available. Coffee shop *open Apr-Sep, Wed-Sat 10.00-13.00 & Oct-Mar Sat 10.00-13.00*. Church *open Apr-Sep, Mon-Sat 10.00-16.00 & Oct-Mar, Mon-Sat 09.00-13.00 (Sat 09.30)*.

Woolsthorpe Manor Water Lane, Woolsthorpe by Colsterworth, Grantham (01476 860338; www.nationaltrust.org.uk/woolsthorpe-manor). 7 miles south of Grantham. The 17th-C birthplace and family home of Sir Isaac Newton who formulated some of his major works here. The interactive science discovery centre in the grounds explains his life and theories. For *opening times* of both attractions, telephone or visit the website. Charge.

Tourist Information Centre Guildhall Arts Centre St. Peter's Hill, Grantham NG31 6PZ (01476 406166/406158; www.guildhallartscentre.com/about-us/grantham-tourist-information-centre). *Open Mon-Sat 09.30-17.00 (Sat 14.00)*.

Pubs and Restaurants (pages 110-111)

1 **The Welby Arms** Church Street Denton NG32 1LG (01476 855099; www.welbyarms.com). Delightful early 19th-C, grade II listed building constructed from coursed ironstone with mellow, red brick gables. Today this hostelry dispenses real ale and offers en suite accommodation. Dog-friendly with a garden. Real fires and Wi-Fi. B&B. *Open Tue-Fri 17.00-23.00 & Sat-Sun 12.00-23.00 (Sun 22.30)*.

2 **The Gregory Arms** The Drift, Harlaxton NG32 1AD (01476 577076; www.thegregory.co.uk). Substantial, 19th-C pub whose landlord once doubled as the local coal merchant drawing his supplies from the canal at nearby Harlaxton Wharf. The weighbridge is reputed to be buried somewhere under the car park's tarmac. Today, however, there are open fires, Wi-Fi, real ales and a full à la carte menu served *Mon-Sat L and E & Sun 12.00-19.00*. Dog- and family-friendly, patio seating. B&B. *Open Mon-Sat 11.00-23.00 & Sun 12.00-22.00*.

3 **The White Swan** Main Street, Barrowby NG32 1BH (01476 562375; www.facebook.com/thewhiteswanbarrowby). Friendly local with its own football team serving real ale and bar food *Wed-Sat L and E (not Wed E)*. Dog- and family-friendly, garden. Traditional pub games, real fires and Wi-Fi. *Open daily 12.00-00.00 (Fri-Sat 01.00)*.

4 **Dougies Bistro** 1 Main Street, Barrowby NG32 1BZ (01476 564250; www.dougiesbistro.com). A modern bistro and wine bar in relaxing surroundings, offering a seasonally influenced menu which changes *monthly* with everything home-made. Also a wide choice of light lunches, soups, cakes and daily specials served *Wed-Sat 11.30-14.30* (telephone first). Afternoon tea is available *(24hr booking required)*. Evening meals *currently* served *Fri 19.30-23.30* but check for updates on www.facebook.com/dougiesbistro.

5 **The Farrier** Harlaxton Road, Grantham NG31 7JT (01476 542920; www.brewersfayre.co.uk/en-gb/locations/lincolnshire/the-farrier). Modern, family-friendly chain pub situated between the canal and A1 serving real ale and food *all day, every day*. Children's 'Play Zone'. Breakfast available *Mon-Fri 06.30-10.30; Sat & Sun 07.00-11.00*. Garden. Tea and coffee. *Open daily 12.00-23.00 (Sun 22.30)*.

WALKING AND CYCLING

There are a range of walks based on the Denton and Harlaxton area, one of which can be downloaded at www.lincolnshirewalks.co.uk/location/vales/denton. Details of other walks in the area are available at www.lincolnshire.gov.uk/coast-countryside/walks-lincolnshire and www.lincolnshireramblers.org.uk.

Pubs and Restaurants (page 111 cont.)

✕🍷 **6 Harry's Place** 17 High Street, Great Gonerby, Grantham NG31 8JS (01476 561780; www.guide.michelin.com/gb/en/lincolnshire/grantham/restaurant/harry-s-place). Reputed to be the smallest Michelin starred restaurant in the country, this 10-cover restaurant serves superb food 'with razor-sharp classical French technique and an unerring eye for balance in flavour and texture'. There are just two choices for each course and the wine list is an almost exact French/Spanish split. Only children over 5 years old. Booking essential. *Open Tue-Sat L and E.*

🍺 **7 Nobody Inn** 9 North Street, Grantham NG31 6NU (01476 562206). Situated on what is claimed to be the shortest street in the world, this pub serves real ales in a friendly and welcoming atmosphere. For many the somewhat bizarre interior will more than justify a visit. Real cider. Dog-friendly, traditional pub games, sports TV and Wi-Fi. *Open daily 12.00-23.00 (Sun 22.30).*

🍺 **8 The Black Dog** 19 Watergate, Grantham, NG31 6NS (01476 978507). Friendly town pub serving real ale and inexpensive bar meals available *daily 12.00-22.00 (Sun 19.00).* Beer garden, sports TV and quiz *Thu. Open Sun-Fri 11.00-23.00 & Sat 12.00-00.00.*

🍺 **9 The Chequers** 25 Market Place, Grantham NG31 6LR (01476 570149). Relaxed during the day, this vibrant pub really comes alive at *weekends and evenings.* Real ales from local breweries and real cider are served. Outside seating, dog-friendly. Newspapers, real fires and Wi-Fi. *Open daily 12.00-00.00 (Fri-Sat 02.00).*

🍺✕ **10 The Angel & Royal** High Street, Grantham NG31 6PN (01476 565816; www.angelandroyal.co.uk). It has been suggested that the old Angel has more historical interest than many of our stately homes. Reputed to be the oldest surviving Inn in England, the main façade is approximately 600 years old. The original building pre-dates this by a further 200 years and was built as a hostel for the Knights Templar. King John's visit in 1213, complete with Royal Court, dates from this era. Today this venerable hostelry serves real ale and boasts a collection of more than 200 single malt whiskies. An informal bistro menu is served *daily 06.30-21.00.* Afternoon tea is also available. The building's inherent character and quirky detail does nothing to detract from the friendly, welcoming service. Dogs and families welcome, garden. Real fires and Wi-Fi. B&B. *Open 11.00-23.00.*

🍺 **11 The Tollemache Inn** 17 Saint Peter's Hill, Grantham NG31 6PY (01476 594696; www.jdwetherspoon.com/pubs/all-pubs/england/lincolnshire/the-tollemache-inn-grantham). Named after the Honourable Frederick Tollemache - MP to the town for much of 19th C - whose statue stands outside the pub's doors, this family-friendly pub now serves real ale and food *08.00-23.00.* Outside seating and large screen TV. Wi-Fi. *Open 08.00-00.00 (Fri-Sat 01.00).*

🍺 **12 The Old Bank** 55 High Street, Grantham NG31 6NE (01476 574920; www.greatukpubs.co.uk/the-old-bank-grantham). A plethora of large screens cater for all sporting needs in this recently refurbished hostelry serving real ale, real cider and food *daily 10.00-22.00 (Sun 11.00).* Dog- and child-friendly, garden. Traditional pub games, sports TV and Wi-Fi. *Open Mon-Sat 10.00-00.00 (Fri-Sat 02.00) & Sun 11.00-00.00.*

✕🍷 **13 Eden Wine Bar** 6 Market Place, Grantham NG31 6LJ (01476 589401/589399; www.edenhq.co.uk). City-style wine bar offering a relaxed and friendly atmosphere in which to enjoy drinks and a 'new style' tapas menu. Pavement and courtyard seating together with a conservatory restaurant serving more substantial fayre. Crisp, contemporary décor. *Open Mon-Sat 09.00 & Sun 12.00.*

WALKING AND CYCLING

The Grantham Town Walk is available at northamptonshirewalks.co.uk/walks-outside-northamptonshire/walk-60-this-walks-not-for-turning-grantham while a whole series of walks in the vicinity of the canal can be downloaded at www.walkinginengland.co.uk/lincs/grantham.php. There is also 2½ miles of informal walkway - extending from north of Manthorpe Road to Dysart Park - beside the River Witham, passing through the town's three public parks and other areas of grassy open space.

NAVIGATIONAL NOTES

It is not feasible to launch a craft and navigate the short section of canal east of the A1 dual-carriageway that terminates abruptly at the blockage beneath Earlsfield Bridge 69.

THE GRANTHAM CANAL SOCIETY

In 1968 the canal was placed in the remaindered category, which purely involved maintenance of the water level, together with general upkeep. It is perhaps interesting to note that the Grantham fared better than many canals where, in some cases, the navigation was totally obliterated.

The waterway's future looked bleak. It was severed by a railway embankment at Woolsthorpe, locks had fallen derelict (with concrete weirs installed to control the water levels) and many hump-backed canal bridges were replaced by concrete pipe culverts under flattened decks.

The Grantham Canal Restoration Society was formed in the early seventies and, in collaboration with British Waterways, the Inland Waterways Association and the Waterways Recovery Group, it began the long road to full restoration. Early successes were the award-winning slipway at Denton, the removal of the railway embankment at Woolsthorpe and the rebuilding of the top three locks of the Woolsthorpe flight.

With renewal of the waterway gathering pace, it became clear that full restoration was going to involve many organisations – the Grantham Canal Restoration Society, British Waterways (now the Canal & River Trust) the Inland Waterways Association, local authorities and the newly formed Grantham Navigation Association. Understandably, there were a few organisational problems. These groups were all brought together with the formation of the Grantham Canal Partnership, an umbrella organisation that unites all the major stakeholders.

Ornate Waymark at Denton

RIVER OUSE, RIVER URE AND RIPON CANAL

MAXIMUM DIMENSIONS

River Ouse

Goole to tail of Naburn Locks:
Length: 134'
Beam: 24' 6"
Headroom: 59' 11"

Naburn to Scarborough Bridge, York:
Length: 134'
Beam: 24' 6"
Headroom: 21' 6"
Draught: 8'

Scarborough Bridge, York to Swale Nab:
Length: 57' 6"
Beam: 15' 3"
Headroom: 19' 6"
Draught: 3' 6"

River Ure

Length: 57' 6"
Beam: 15'
Headroom: 10'
Draught: 3' 6"

Ripon Canal

Length: 57'
Beam: 14' 3"
Headroom: 8' 6"
Draught: 3' 6"

MILEAGE

RIPON to:
Boroughbridge: 7½ miles
York: 28¼ miles
Selby: 47¼ miles
GOOLE: 63 miles

Locks: 7

MANAGER

0303 040 4040

enquiries.yorkshirenortheast@canalrivertrust.org.uk

Skippers of all craft planning passage on the River Ouse are reminded to book the locks 24hrs in advance of travel. All bookings should be made by contacting the lock keepers. Contact details for Naburn Lock are 01904 728500 and Selby Lock 01757 703182. Booking in advance ensures lock keepers will be ready to receive vessels avoiding any unnecessary delays. Pre-booking also improves safety on the river. Further details for planning safe passage on the River Ouse can be found at www.canalrivertrust.org.uk/about-us/our-regions/north-east-waterways/planning-a-safe-passage-on-river-tees-and-river-ouse. This includes contact details for all moveable bridges and manned locks.

The River Ouse, flowing as it does through the flat lands of north east England, has long been navigable to York, and has provided a natural transport artery for that city. Indeed, at one time, coal was brought in from Newcastle: a 200-mile journey involving a trip by keel down the Tyne, then by ship to the Humber and then on by barge up the Ouse, rather than undertake an overland journey of 20 miles from the coalfields of the West Riding. In 1766 it was decided to extend navigation along the River Ure and then by a short canal as far as Ripon. Proposals for this scheme were submitted by John Smeeton. Royal assent was granted in 1767 and work began. Milby Lock and Cut were completed in 1769 and a cast iron bridge, one of the first in the country, was built over the canalised section at Boroughbridge. This was replaced in 1946. This northerly section of the inland waterways network was immediately prosperous, with Boroughbridge serving as the port for Knaresborough, one of England's greatest linen manufacturing towns.

On the lower Ouse the Aire & Calder Navigation Company obtained an Act of Parliament in 1820 to extend to Goole, where a brand new port was to be created. When it opened in 1826, the population was 450: this increased to more than 20,000 over the following 100 years. The canal company built the grand and stately church of St John here in 1843–8.

The River Ouse escaped nationalisation in 1948, and until recently there was commercial traffic as far as Selby. Above York the river is quieter and more suited to pleasure boats.

Ripon

The demure, yet pretty Ripon Canal terminates in a fine basin overlooked by a handsomely restored warehouse, tasteful and sympathetically designed new dwellings, along with some fine older houses. The navigation, having lain derelict for years, now provides good moorings, excellent *facilities* including *showers* and *toilets* and easy access to Ripon. Leaving the city, the initial half-mile or so is closely accompanied by a main road. This is soon left behind, however, as the waterway swings to the south and descends Rhodesfield and Bell Furrows locks, passing to the west of Ripon Marina and the racecourse through quiet, open countryside. Ripon Boat Club's marina occupies a pretty spot near Littlethorpe, where the canal makes its approach to the River Ure, falling through Oxclose Lock. Entering the river, the character of the navigation is immediately less demure as it snakes towards Westwick Cut and Lock, set amidst flat farmland, with trees by the river. This unremarkable but pretty countryside makes Newby Hall and its attractively landscaped gardens stand out; its jetty beckons the passing boater, and its miniature railway makes quite a startling impression. At Cherry Island Wood there is another sharp turn as the handsome village of Roecliffe is approached.

Ripon
N Yorks. PO, tel stores, chemist, butcher, baker, hardware, off-licence, bank, takeaways, fish & chips, garage. The horn you will hear blown at 9 o'clock each evening is that of the City Wakeman, dressed in traditional clothes and fulfiling the 1000-year-old custom of setting the watch. This traditionally signified that the town was under the Wakeman's care for the night. If there was then a robbery, he was obliged to make good the loss! Alas this is no longer the case today. His two-storey 14th-C half-timbered house, standing in the square, was used as a museum but unfortunately the building became unsafe for visitors and the museum and Tourist Information Centre were moved to new premises. The centre of Ripon remains elegant and well preserved, with narrow winding streets enclosed by buildings of many periods, mostly brick built. The fine open square is dominated by a tall obelisk erected in 1781, which commemorates William Aislabie of Studley Royal's 60-year membership of Parliament. On the south side of the square is the imposing town hall, built in 1801 by James Wyatt.
Ripon Cathedral Minster Road, Ripon HG4 1QS (01765 603462; www.riponcathedral.org.uk). The central tower of this imposing building stands over a Saxon crypt, believed to have been built by St Wilfred c.670. Wilfred's original church was destroyed in 950 by King Edred of Northumberland, and rebuilding did not begin again until about 1180. It was Archbishop of York Roger de Pont l'Évêque who began the reconstruction, with the superb west front being completed around 1230. Further substantial work was carried out by Christopher Scune, who built the Gothic nave around 1520. The building was restored in 1832, with the re-creation of the diocese and elevation to cathedral status. Look out for the splendidly carved choir stalls 1489-94, the work of the Bromflets, a local family of wood carvers, and an interesting 1896 Arts & Crafts pulpit associated with William Morris. Admission by donation.
Yorkshire Law and Order Museums (01765 690799; www.riponmuseums.co.uk). Three award-winning museums. The **Prison & Police Museum** St Marygate, Ripon HG4 1LX is housed in part of the former House of Correction and Liberty Gaol which also housed the West Riding Constabulary for a while. The history of policing is traced through collections of police and prison memorabilia; visitors can also experience prison life as it was in Victorian times. The **Workhouse Museum** Sharon View, Allhallowgate, Ripon HG4 1LE, features the original Workhouse Kitchen Garden which has been restored and features vegetables and fruit from the 1890s. The museum itself provides an insight into the reality of life in a Victorian workhouse. The **Courthouse Museum** Minster Road, Ripon HG4 1QS, is housed the original, restored Georgian museum and includes a 19th-century court room scene. The museums are child-friendly and designed for all the family. Regular special events. *Open Mon-Sun 13.00-16.00, extended during school holidays.* Charge.
Tourist Information Centre Town Hall, Market Place South, Ripon HG4 1DD (01765 604625; www.visitharrogate.co.uk/things-to-do/ripon-tourist-information-centre-p1208361). *Open Apr-Oct daily 10.00-17.00 (Sun 13.00) & Nov-Mar Thur & Sat 10.00-16.00.* Closed for lunch. You can purchase head of canal plaques and walking trail leaflets from here.
Fountains Abbey & Studley Royal Water Garden Fountains, Ripon HG4 3DY (01765 608888; www.fountainsabbey.org.uk). Three miles south west of Ripon (bus service from the city). *NT.* The glorious ruins of a 12th-C Cistercian abbey and monastic waterwheel set amidst 100 acres of beautiful grounds. Founded in 1132, this was one of the most complete survivors of the dissolution. The superb water garden was designed by John Aislabie and his son William in the 1700s. Enjoy the Temple of Fame, the Octagon Tower and Serpentine Tunnel. Look out for the ghosts of a choir of monks. *Open Mar-Oct, daily 10.00-16.00, Nov-Feb, daily 10.00-16.00. Closed Nov-Jan, Fri.* St Mary's Church is *open Apr-Sep, daily 12.00-16.00.* Charge. Café and shop.

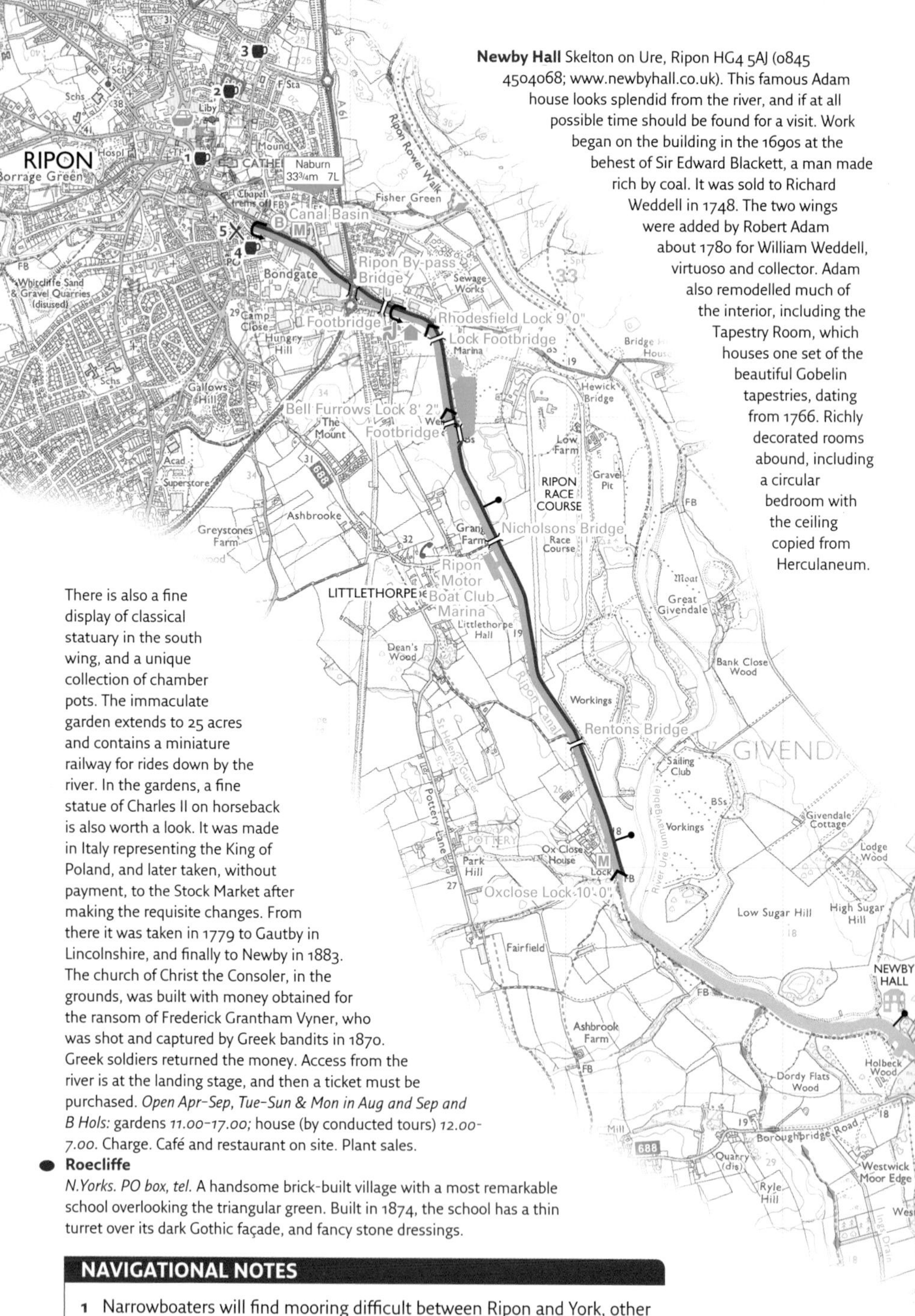

Newby Hall Skelton on Ure, Ripon HG4 5AJ (0845 4504068; www.newbyhall.co.uk). This famous Adam house looks splendid from the river, and if at all possible time should be found for a visit. Work began on the building in the 1690s at the behest of Sir Edward Blackett, a man made rich by coal. It was sold to Richard Weddell in 1748. The two wings were added by Robert Adam about 1780 for William Weddell, virtuoso and collector. Adam also remodelled much of the interior, including the Tapestry Room, which houses one set of the beautiful Gobelin tapestries, dating from 1766. Richly decorated rooms abound, including a circular bedroom with the ceiling copied from Herculaneum. There is also a fine display of classical statuary in the south wing, and a unique collection of chamber pots. The immaculate garden extends to 25 acres and contains a miniature railway for rides down by the river. In the gardens, a fine statue of Charles II on horseback is also worth a look. It was made in Italy representing the King of Poland, and later taken, without payment, to the Stock Market after making the requisite changes. From there it was taken in 1779 to Gautby in Lincolnshire, and finally to Newby in 1883. The church of Christ the Consoler, in the grounds, was built with money obtained for the ransom of Frederick Grantham Vyner, who was shot and captured by Greek bandits in 1870. Greek soldiers returned the money. Access from the river is at the landing stage, and then a ticket must be purchased. *Open Apr–Sep, Tue–Sun & Mon in Aug and Sep and B Hols:* gardens *11.00–17.00;* house (by conducted tours) *12.00–7.00*. Charge. Café and restaurant on site. Plant sales.

● **Roecliffe**

N.Yorks. PO box, tel. A handsome brick-built village with a most remarkable school overlooking the triangular green. Built in 1874, the school has a thin turret over its dark Gothic façade, and fancy stone dressings.

NAVIGATIONAL NOTES

1. Narrowboaters will find mooring difficult between Ripon and York, other than at the locks, or at Newton-on-Ouse and Boroughbridge.
2. Rhodesfield and Bell Furrows locks both require a CRT Watermate key. There are moorings above Rhodesfield and Oxclose Locks.

WALKING AND CYCLING

The towpath on the Ripon Canal is excellent, however cycling is not allowed. The towpath on the river is only approachable in parts.

Pubs and Restaurants (page 118)

1 The Royal Oak 36 Kirkgate, Ripon HG4 1PB (01765 602284; www.royaloakripon.co.uk). A historic coaching inn, close to the cathedral, serving real ales and food sourced from local ingredients *Mon-Fri L and E & all day Sat and Sun*. Breakfast from *08.00*. Real cider. Dog- and child-friendly, patio. Open fires and Wi-Fi. B&B. *Open 08.00-23.00 (Fri-Sat 00.00)*.

2 The One-Eyed Rat 51 Allhallowgate, Ripon HG4 1LQ (01765 607704; www.facebook.com/One-Eyed-Rat-104985532898059). It is easy to miss this highly regarded real ale pub, set in a terrace of 200-year-old houses. It more than makes up for its lack of food and music through its wealth of old fashioned charm and the friendly atmosphere. There is also a wide range of bottled continental beers, real cider and a large beer garden. Dogs and children welcome. Real fires and Wi-Fi. *Open Mon-Thu 17.00-23.00 & Fri-Sun 12.00-23.00*.

3 Magdalens 26 Princess Road, Ripon HG4 1HW (01765 604746; www.facebook.com/The-Magdalens-270858956593256). Another pub that majors on a wide range of well-kept real ales and bottled beers. Dog- and child-friendly, large garden. Traditional pub games, newspapers and Wi-Fi. *Open daily 12.00-23.00 (Sat-Sun 01.00)*.

4 The Navigation 1 Canal Road, Ripon HG4 1QN (01765 600030; www.facebook.com/thenavigationinnripon). Close to the basin, this welcoming, friendly local serves real ales and food *L and E*. Family-friendly, outside seating. Quiz *Thu*. Traditional pub games, sports TV and Wi-Fi. *Open Tue-Thu 14.00-23.30 & Fri-Mon 12.00-23.30 (Fri-Sat 00.30)*.

5 The Forge Canal Wharf, Bondgate Green, Ripon HG4 1AQ (01765 698249; https://www.facebook.com/TheForgeRipon). Sandwiches, pies and pasties. Home-made cakes, tray bakes and honey. *Open Mon-Sat 08.00-15.30 (Sat 14.30)*.

WORKING ON SHIFTING SANDS

Our roads are now overcrowded – everyone who uses them knows this. In a region where there is much heavy industry, and good access to water transport, it makes sound sense to move bulk goods by barge. Acaster's Water Transport, Swinefleet, Goole DN14 8DR, who, amongst other activities, once transported newsprint from Goole to the Yorkshire Evening Press in York (regrettably, this now goes by road), is a small family business which manages to survive in an uncertain world. Graham Acaster and his wife often work in Goole Docks on *Little Shifta* and *Little Shuva*. Acaster's have also adapted their boats *River Star*, *Twite* and *Poem 24* at Waddington's yard to create a 600-ton barge, taking the name *River Star*. In spite of our national reluctance to use modern water transport, Acasters remain stoically cheerful and optimistic, and totally devoted to the cause. For the sake of the environment, let us hope they remain in business, and that others join them.

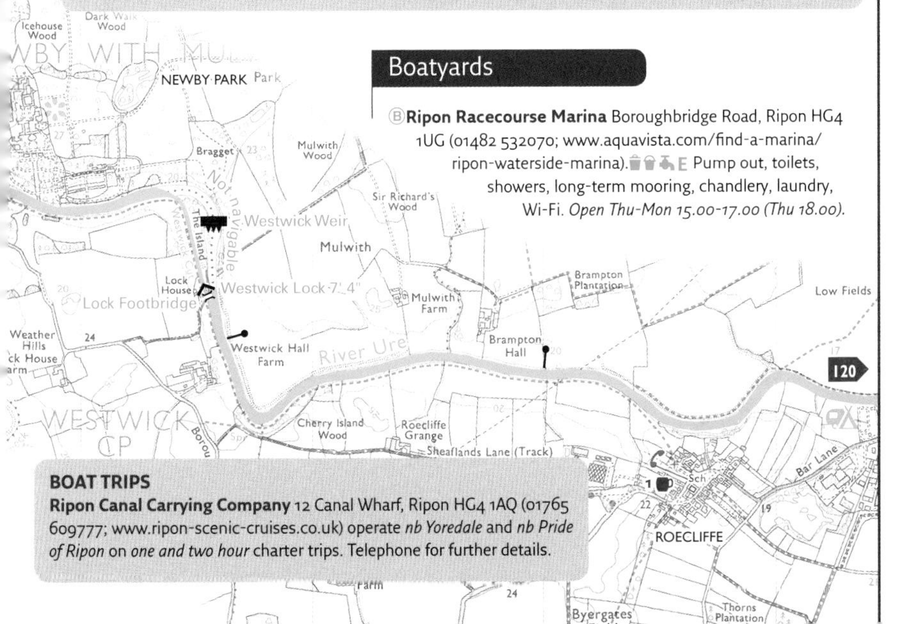

Boatyards

Ripon Racecourse Marina Boroughbridge Road, Ripon HG4 1UG (01482 532070; www.aquavista.com/find-a-marina/ripon-waterside-marina). E Pump out, toilets, showers, long-term mooring, chandlery, laundry, Wi-Fi. *Open Thu-Mon 15.00-17.00 (Thu 18.00)*.

BOAT TRIPS

Ripon Canal Carrying Company 12 Canal Wharf, Ripon HG4 1AQ (01765 609777; www.ripon-scenic-cruises.co.uk) operate *nb Yoredale* and *nb Pride of Ripon* on *one and two hour* charter trips. Telephone for further details.

Boroughbridge

The navigation swings under Arrows Bridge and the busy A1(M) as it makes its approach to Boroughbridge, passing the marina and finally entering Milby Cut, leaving the weir stream to the south. The town lies beyond the weir stream, and imposes little, but there are good moorings, a *sanitary station, pump out, showers and toilets,* so a stop to explore is worthwhile. Beyond the town is open country as the river gently winds through pleasant farmland.

Pubs and Restaurants (pages 119-120)

1 **The Crown Inn** Bar Lane, Roecliffe, York YO51 9LY (01423 322300; www.crowninnroecliffe.co.uk). A long building, with low ceilings, dating from 16th C, serving real ale and food from an à la carte menu *Mon-Sat L and E & Sun 12.00-18.00.* Real fires. B&B. *Open daily 12.00-23.00 (Sun 21.00).*

2 **The Fox and Hounds** Skelton Road, Langthorpe, Boroughbridge, York YO51 9BZ (01423 325239; www.facebook.com/Fox-Hounds-Langthorpe-114507863311020). Originally a cottage with an adjacent granary. Real ale and food available *Mon-Fri 17.00-21.00 & Sat-Sun all day from 09.00.* Dog- and child-friendly, garden. Traditional pub games, newspapers and Wi-Fi. *Open Mon-Tue 16.00-23.00 & Wed-Sun 12.00-23.00 (Fri-Sat 01.00).*

3 **The Grantham Arms** Milby, Boroughbridge, York YO51 9BW (01423 323980; www.granthamarms.co.uk). Canalside pub serving real ale and freshly prepared bar meals *Mon-Fri L and E & Sat-Sun 12.00-21.30 (Sun 20.00).* Dog- and child-friendly, garden. Newspapers and Wi-Fi. B&B. *Open daily 12.00-00.00.*

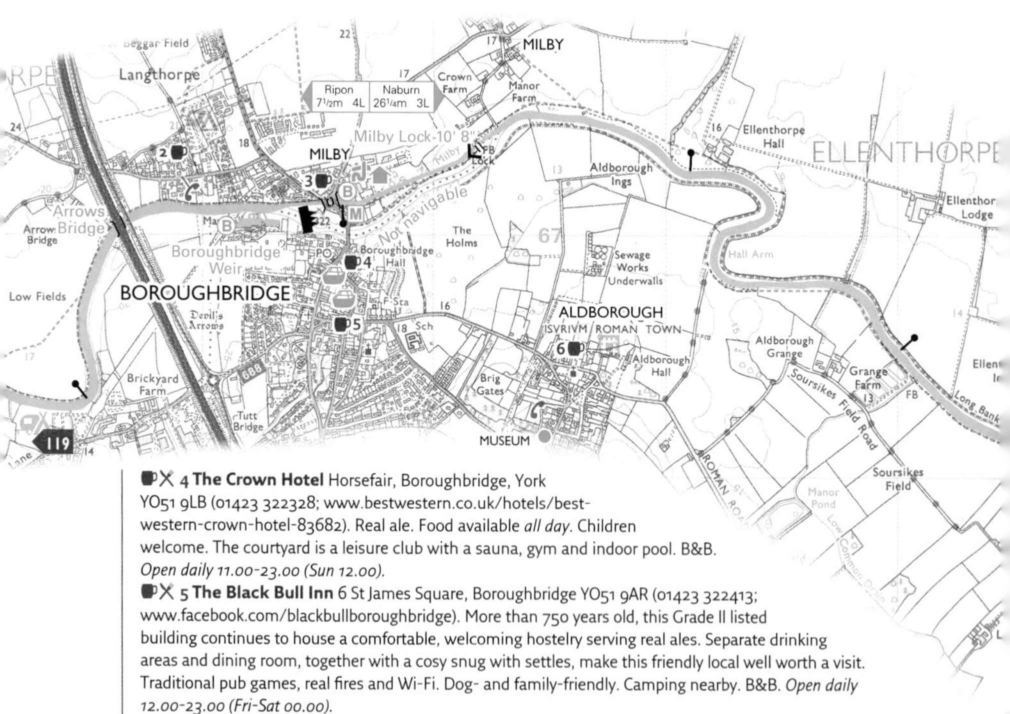

4 **The Crown Hotel** Horsefair, Boroughbridge, York YO51 9LB (01423 322328; www.bestwestern.co.uk/hotels/best-western-crown-hotel-83682). Real ale. Food available *all day.* Children welcome. The courtyard is a leisure club with a sauna, gym and indoor pool. B&B. *Open daily 11.00-23.00 (Sun 12.00).*

5 **The Black Bull Inn** 6 St James Square, Boroughbridge YO51 9AR (01423 322413; www.facebook.com/blackbullboroughbridge). More than 750 years old, this Grade II listed building continues to house a comfortable, welcoming hostelry serving real ales. Separate drinking areas and dining room, together with a cosy snug with settles, make this friendly local well worth a visit. Traditional pub games, real fires and Wi-Fi. Dog- and family-friendly. Camping nearby. B&B. *Open daily 12.00-23.00 (Fri-Sat 00.00).*

6 **The Ship Inn** Low Road, Aldborough, Boroughbridge, York YO51 9ER (01423 322749; www.shipinnaldborough.com). A beamy 14th-C inn with an open fire, serving real ale, and bar and restaurant meals and snacks *Tue-Sun L and E (not Sun E).* Dog- and child-friendly *(until 21.00)* garden. Real fires and Wi-Fi. *Open Mon-Thu L and E & Fri-Sun 11.30-23.00 (Sun 22.30).*

7 **Hideaway Inn** at the Dunsforth Lower Dunsforth, York YO26 9SA (01423 320700; www.hideawaykitchen.co.uk). Large and welcoming country inn, with open fires, mainly catering for fishermen, golfers, walkers and race-goers. Food available *Thu-Fri L (from 10.00) and E & Sat-Sun 10.00-21.00 (Sun 17.30).* Dog- and family-friendly, garden. Real fires and Wi-Fi. *Open Thu-Sun 10.00-22.00 (Sun 12.00).*

Boatyards

Ⓑ**Boroughbridge Marina** Valuation Lane, Boroughbridge YO51 9LJ (01423 323400; www.bbmarina.co.uk). E (Pump out at CRT facilities block 300yds away). Long-term, and visitor moorings, slipway, gas, chandlery, boat sales, toilets, showers, fuel available nearby, laundrette, marine engineering, facilities for narrowboat lifting, solid fuel, *24 hour* security, barbecue and picnic facilities, day boat hire. *Open Mon-Sat 09.00-17.00 & Sun 10.00-16.00.*

Ⓑ**Canal Garage** Milby Road, Boroughbridge YO51 9BL (01423 322318; www.canalgarageboroughbridge.co.uk). D Gas, engine repairs and service.

Boroughbridge

N. Yorks. PO, tel, stores, baker, delicatessen, hardware, butcher, chemist, library, farm shop, takeaways, fish & chips, garage. The Crown Hotel, just up the road from the bridge, used, when the town sat astride the Great North Road, to have stabling for 100 horses. The first mail coach passed through in 1789, but now the A1 thankfully bypasses the town. Boroughbridge was the 44th of some 400 settlements established by the Normans and their successors between 1066 and 1348 as part of a plan to unite their new kingdom, and served as the port for Knaresborough, 7 miles away. The present river bridge dates from between 1562 and 1784, having been continually repaired during that period. It replaced an earlier wooden structure, which in turn had replaced a ford downstream near Milby. The well, in the Market Place, is 250ft deep.

Tourist Information Centre 1 Hall Square, Boroughbridge, YO51 9AN (01423 323373/322956; www.visitharrogate.co.uk/things-to-do/boroughbridge-tourist-information-centre-p1209821). Telephone for opening times.

Battle of Boroughbridge 1322 Rebel barons led by the Earl of Lancaster struggled with Edward II's supporters for control of the bridge over the River Ure. Eventually Lancaster was taken to his own castle at Pontefract, where he was executed.

Battle of Myton 1319 North of Swale Nab. Known as the white battle from the number of churchmen who were involved. While Edward II was holding Berwick-upon-Tweed under siege, an army of Scots infiltrated into the north of England. They met a hastily assembled English force at Myton and defeated them. Heavy losses were incurred on the English side with some 3000 killed, including 300 priests.

Aldborough

N. Yorks. Tel. A Georgian village less than a mile from Boroughbridge, with a May pole, restored in 1999, on the green. It was once the walled Roman town of *Isurium Brigantum*, and before that *Iseur*, built by the ancient Britons. It functioned for the Romans as the civitas, or civilian capital of the Brigantes, a tribe who occupied most of what is now Yorkshire and Lancashire. Once enclosed by mighty red sandstone walls, perhaps 20ft high, the remains are modest but interesting.

Aldborough Roman Site Aldborough, Boroughbridge, York YO51 9ES (01423 322768; www.english-heritage.org.uk/visit/places/aldborough-roman-site). Relics gathered from the Roman town. Museum and grounds *open Apr-Sep, Sat-Sun 10.00-18.00.* Charge. Telephone or visit website to confirm winter opening. Suitable for picnics.

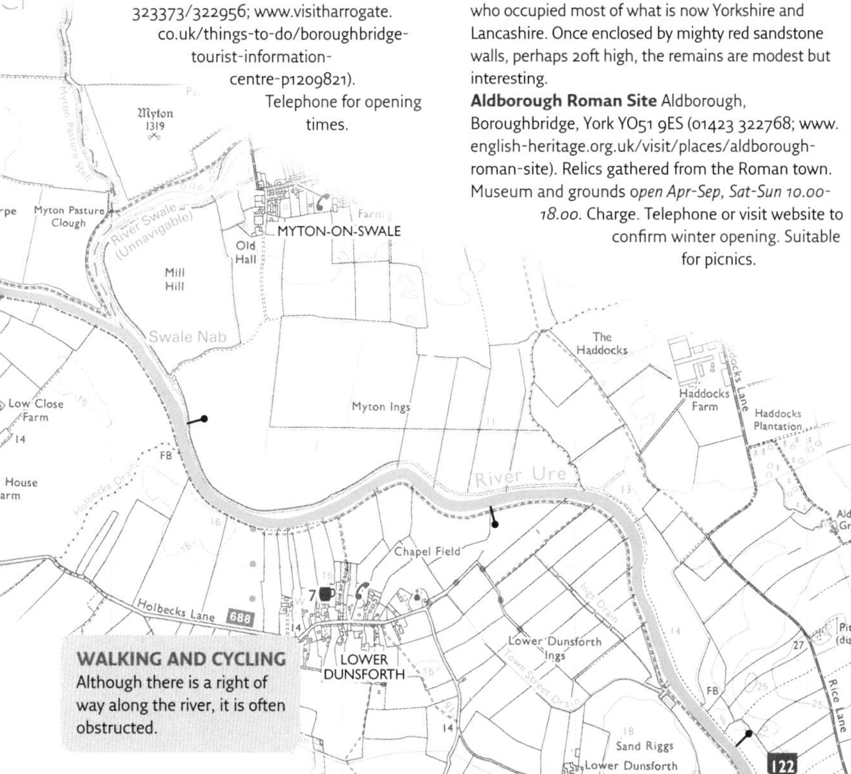

WALKING AND CYCLING
Although there is a right of way along the river, it is often obstructed.

Linton Lock

The river continues to meander gently through quiet, unprepossessing countryside with villages scattered alongside, but never actually on its banks. The rickety toll bridge at Aldwark provides the only river crossing on this stretch, emphasising its remote nature. Just before the river turns east at Cuddy Shaw Reach its name changes from Ure to Ouse, where the Ouse Gill Beck joins. To the north is Linton-on-Ouse RAF airfield, where training aeroplanes come and go noisily during the week, shattering the peace of an otherwise quiet area. The navigation falls through Linton Lock, leaving a fine large weir and salmon leap to the south. There are useful *boater services*, plus a *pub/restaurant*, here. The river then turns sharply to the west of Newton-on-Ouse to pass the extensive and well-tended grounds of Beningbrough Park and Hall, rich with trees and beautifully landscaped. As the river widens to accept the River Nidd, the outstandingly attractive and interesting village of Nun Monkton, and its splendid church, is passed.

NAVIGATIONAL NOTES

1. The Aldwark Scout Activity Centre operate in the vicinity of Aldwark Toll Bridge so keep a good look out for small craft in the area.
2. Keep right over to the north bank below Linton Lock, using the buoyed channel, to avoid shoals.

WALKING AND CYCLING

The towpath is virtually non-existent on this stretch, apart from through Beningbrough Park. From *Apr-Oct weekends* a pedestrian ferry service runs across the river from a point approximately 100yds downstream of Nidd Mouth.

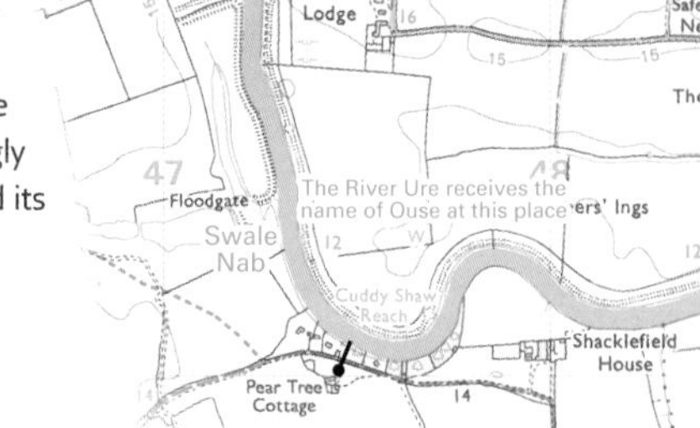

Pubs and Restaurants

1 The Aldwark Arms Aldwark, Alne, York YO61 1UB (01347 838324; www.aldwarkarms.co.uk). Village inn serving real ales and food *Mon-Fri L and E & Sat-Sun 12.00-21.00 (Sun 19.00)*. Dog- and child-friendly, garden. Real fires and Wi-Fi. *Open Mon-Fri L and E, Sat 11.00-23.00 & Sun 12.00-20.00.*

2 The Lockhouse Café Linton-on-Ouse, York YO30 2AZ (01347 848844; www.facebook.com/pages/category/Restaurant/The-Lock-House-545004482188793). Pub/café, riverside in the old lock keeper's house serving food. Takeaway service. Children welcome, lockside seating. *Open Tue-Thu L and E, Fri-Sat 11.00-21.30 (Sat 10.00 & Sun 10.00-18.30.*

3 The Dawnay Arms Moor Lane, Newton-on-Ouse, York YO30 2BR (01347 848345; www.thedawnayatnewton.co.uk). Real ales, together with home-cooked food available *Tue-Sat L and E & Sun L* are served in this delightful 18th-C listed building. Children and dogs welcome; large riverside garden with moorings. Newspapers, real fires and Wi-Fi. Camping. *Open Tue-Sun L and E (not Sun E).*

4 The Blacksmiths Arms Cherry Tree Avenue, Newton-on-Ouse, York YO30 2BN (01347 848249; www.facebook.com/blacksmithsnewton). Opposite the church, this warm and friendly pub offers real ale and unpretentious home-cooked food *Mon-Thu E; Fri L and E and Sat-Sun all day.* Dog- and family-friendly, garden. Traditional pub games, real fires, sports TV and Wi-Fi. *Open Mon-Thu E; Fri L and E & Sat-Sun 12.00-23.00.*

5 The Alice Hawthorn The Green, Nun Monkton, York YO26 8EW (01423 330303; www.thealicehawthorn.com). Real ale is available in this handsome village inn, and food is served in the bar, dining room or restaurant *Tue E; Wed-Sat L and E & Sun 12.00-15.30.* Children welcome and there is a garden. Camping by arrangement. *Open Wed-Fri L and E & Sat-Sun 12.00-23.30 (Sun 15.30).*

- **Aldwark**
  N. Yorks. PO box, tel. The pretty pebble and brick church was built to an original design in 1846–53 by E. B. Lamb.
- **Linton-on-Ouse**
  N. Yorks. Tel, stores, off-licence. A village totally overwhelmed by the adjoining RAF airfield.
- **Newton-on-Ouse**
  N. Yorks. The church of All Saints was built in 1849 for Miss Dawnay by G. T. Andrews. The base of the tower dates from the 12th C: the top is finished with a fine recessed spire.
  Beningbrough Hall Coach Road, Beningbrough, York YO30 1DD (01904 472027; www.nationaltrust.org.uk/beningbrough-hall-gallery-and-gardens). A very fine Georgian house built in 1716, where most of the rooms have no electric light. With one of the most impressive baroque interiors in England, the room settings are atmospheric with over 100 portraits and wood-carvings on loan from the National Portrait Gallery. Also on view is a glimpse of life 'downstairs', in the Victorian laundry. Art exhibitions, children's play area, beautiful gardens. Beningbrough Hall was featured as 'Biddenborough Hall' in an episode of the *Darling Buds of May* TV series. *Open Mar–Oct, Tue–Sun 12.00–17.00 (garden and restaurant 10.30) and summer holiday Mon. Very limited winter opening* – telephone for details.
- **Nun Monkton**
  N. Yorks. PO box, tel. Following the Norman conquest the village, together with other surrounding estates, was given to the Norman knight Osbern de Arches. It was one of Osbern's descendants, William de Arches, who chose this site at the junction of the rivers Nidd and Ouse to found a priory of Benedictine nuns dedicated to the Blessed Virgin Mary. Today only the nun's chapel survives as the church of St Mary. Built 1153–80 in Early English style, there is a late Norman porch and some very fine arcading above plain lower windows, access to which is gained via a staircase in the north west angle. Between the windows are 12 niches, which probably once contained effigies of the apostles. Set into the floor beneath the present altar is the pre-Reformation stone altar, with five crosses cut into it, thought to represent the five wounds of Christ. The church is quite properly considered to be one of the finest in Yorkshire, and will amply repay a visit. The village green has a splendid May pole, and a fine duck pond.

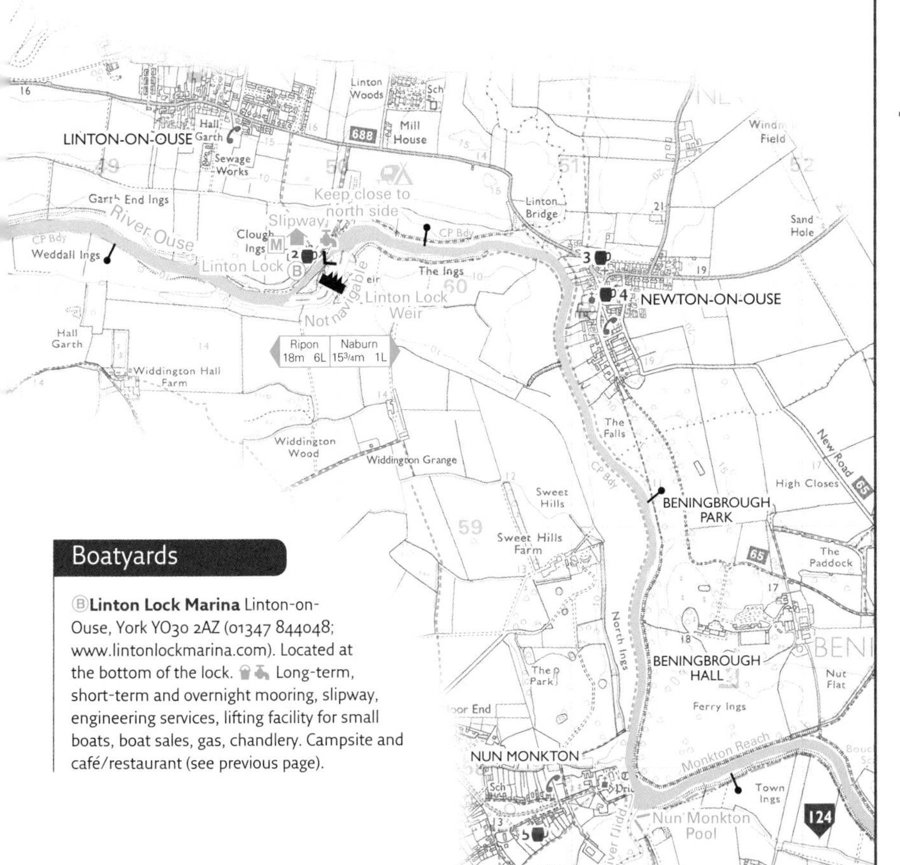

Boatyards

Ⓑ **Linton Lock Marina** Linton-on-Ouse, York YO30 2AZ (01347 844048; www.lintonlockmarina.com). Located at the bottom of the lock. Long-term, short-term and overnight mooring, slipway, engineering services, lifting facility for small boats, boat sales, gas, chandlery. Campsite and café/restaurant (see previous page).

Nether Poppleton

The river continues its isolated course towards York, passing through characteristically flat, but pleasant, countryside and flirting only briefly with the village of Nether Poppleton, before it enters the outer reaches of the City of York. The course of the river is now much wider and more substantial than near Ripon as it gathers tributaries on its passage to the sea. However, during periods of prolonged rainfall its potential for flooding is considerable: as it enters the City of York flood defences become more conspicuous.

- **Beningbrough**
  N. Yorks. PO box, tel. A remote farming settlement by the river.
- **Overton**
  N. Yorks. A tiny settlement around Overton Manor, which the abbots of St Mary, York once used as their major country house. The moat can still be traced, at the north end of the village, and a farmhouse near the church re-used the stones.
- **Nether Poppleton**
  N. Yorks. PO, tel, stores, butcher, off-licence, station (distant). A commuter village for York, most attractive by the river. The small church of St Everilda, at the far eastern end, is of Norman origin, with relics of 14th- and 15th-C glass in the east window. There are also some fine monuments to the Huttons: Sir Thomas, 1620, is depicted kneeling; Ursula, her husband and another woman, c.1640, are smaller but also kneel; Anne, 1651, is less formal, with more movement in the figure.
- **Skelton**
  N. Yorks. PO, tel. The church of St Giles is a superb example of Early English work, built c.1240, by the masons who had worked on York Minster, for Walter de Gray, Archbishop of York. Neatly constructed from magnesian limestone, there is no tower – just a bellcote separating the nave from the chancel. Toolmarks left by the masons can be seen inside, together with their marks. It was restored 1814–18 by Henry Graham, who was nineteen when the work started.

Pubs and Restaurants

1 The Lord Nelson Inn 9 Main Street, Nether Poppleton, York YO26 6HS (01904 785056; www.facebook.com/The-Lord-Nelson-Pub-138797579503917). A handsome brick-built pub serving real ale. Food is available *E*. Dog- and family-friendly, garden. Traditional pub games and sports TV. *Open Mon-Thu 17.00-23.00, Fri 15.00-00.00 & Sat-Sun 12.00-00.00 (Sun 23.00).*

WALKING AND CYCLING

There is a right of way on the north bank from Beningbrough to Rawcliffe.

BOAT TRIPS

YorkBoat The Boatyard, Lendal Bridge, York YO1 7DP (01904 628324; www.yorkboat.co.uk). Comfortable city and country sightseeing cruise boats leave from Lendal Bridge and King's Staith, for a *45-minute* river trip with commentary running from *mid Feb–late Nov*. Charge. All boats have a licensed bar and most serve tea and coffee and other refreshments. Themed cruises and charters. Self-drive motorboats for hire.

York

The River Ouse makes its passage through York, where all the major sights are tightly enclosed within the city walls, and none are more than a short walk away from the moorings. Trip boats ply back and forth, their commentaries adding to the general hub-bub of a working city and popular tourist venue. To the south of Skeldergate Bridge the River Foss joins from the east, and, whilst the entrance seems inviting and the first mile-and-a-half is navigable, there are no official moorings on the Foss, and the passage through the lock can be expensive unless the IWA volunteers are used (see below). The riverside to the south of the city is extremely pleasant as you pass under the attractive Millennium Bridge, its cable-stayed structure inspired by bicycle spokes. Look out, on the east bank, for the Roman Well, then swing round under the A64 and pass the extremely pleasant Bishopthorpe Palace and grounds. Enjoy what view there is to the west as you leave behind a very large sewage works on the east bank, then pass under Naburn Bridge to once again enter open countryside.

RIVER FOSS

York City Council, 9 St Leonard's Place, York YO1 2ET (01904 551550). The river is navigable for just over 1½ miles from Blue Bridge, until the depth disappears before a low pipe bridge. The lock size is 112' x 20'. Craft over 36' long will be unable to wind. Do not enter the lock unless the flood lights are showing green. IWA volunteers are also operating the lock *during summer months* (without charge). *Between May and Sep a minimum of 12 hrs notice (24 hrs Oct – Apr) is required*; boaters must have valid insurance documents on board and, as water levels are crucial, lock sharing is preferred. Contact 07588 236597 leaving your name, name of boat and mobile telephone number on the *24 hr* answering service, or email castle.mills@waterway.org.uk. There are no official moorings on the River Foss in York.

NAVIGATIONAL NOTES

1. The most pleasant pleasure craft moorings in York are at Museum Gardens, between Scarborough Railway Bridge and Lendal Bridge. However, THE RIVER CAN RISE VERY RAPIDLY, following heavy rain in its extensive catchment area covering the Yorkshire Dales. In recent times it has been known for the Ouse to go from normal summertime levels, to well above the upper walkway alongside Museum Gardens, literally overnight.
2. Therefore, visitors to the city should carefully monitor the Environment Agency Floodline, together with the weather forecasts covering the catchment area, and not be guided solely by the prevailing weather in York. In the event of predicted flooding the boater has five choices, AS SECURING YOUR BOAT TO A FIXED (AND STEPPED) STRUCTURE, IN THE THESE CIRCUMSTANCES, HAS THE POTENTIAL TO SINK IT:
   a) Move downstream, below Ouse Bridge, and moor at the vertical walls of either King & Queens Staith. However, during recent periods of heavy summer flooding in the city, both Staiths have been submerged under several feet of water, rendering mooring potentially dangerous.
   b) Head downstream to York Marine Services at Bishopthorpe or York Marina near Naburn having first contacted them to request a safe haven mooring (see Boatyards page 127). These are, respectively, approximately ¾ and 1 hour away.
   c) Head downstream to Naburn Lock and secure to the pontoon moorings above the lock – journey time approximately 1½ hours. There is, however, limited space here.
   d) Head upstream to Linton Lock (approximately 2½ hours away) and secure to the pontoon moorings either above or below the lock.
   e) Drop back to the York Boat pontoon moorings immediately below Lendal Bridge. This is a strategy only to be employed in an extreme emergency, as these are commercial moorings and not licensed for pleasure craft.

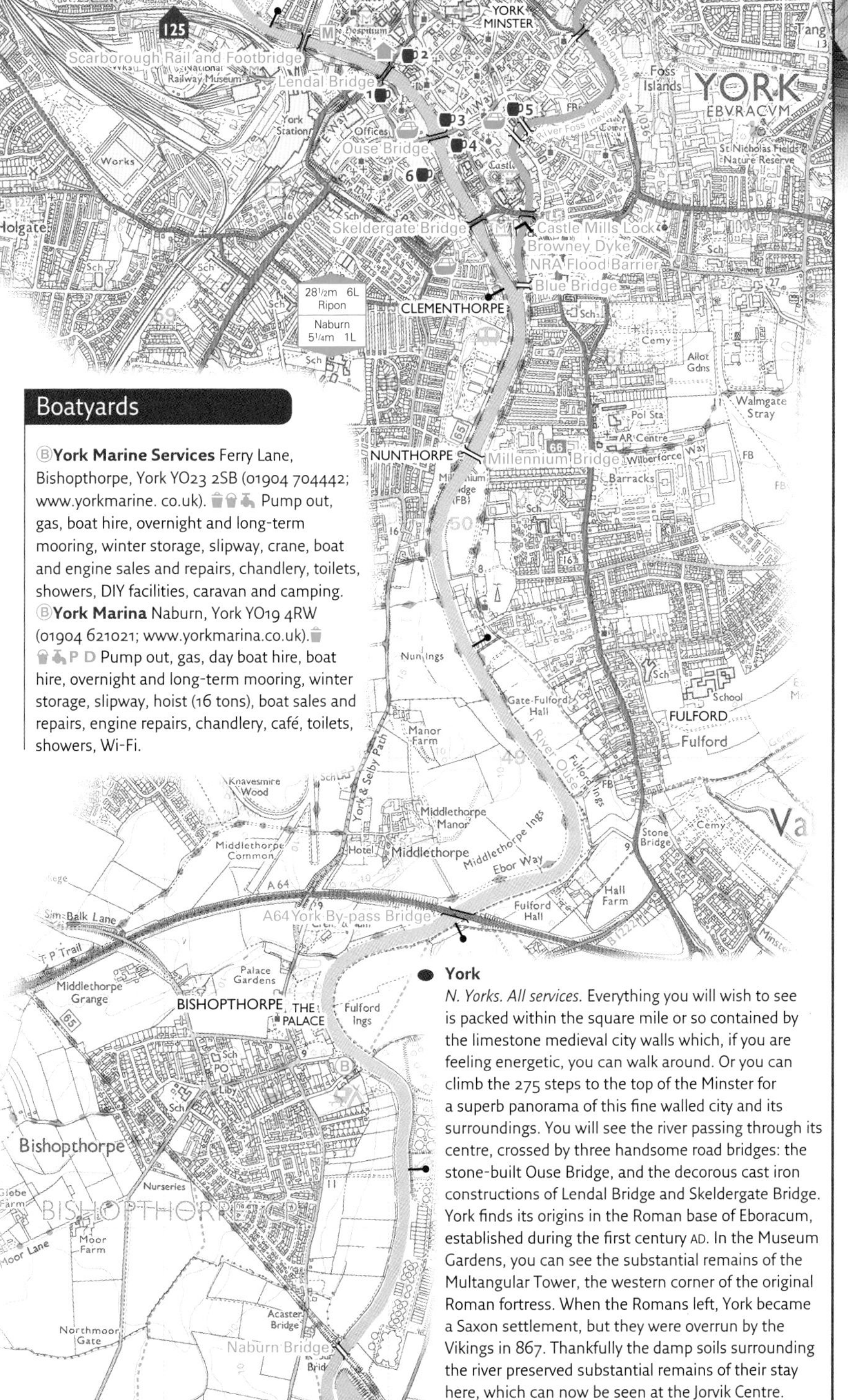

Boatyards

Ⓑ **York Marine Services** Ferry Lane, Bishopthorpe, York YO23 2SB (01904 704442; www.yorkmarine. co.uk). Pump out, gas, boat hire, overnight and long-term mooring, winter storage, slipway, crane, boat and engine sales and repairs, chandlery, toilets, showers, DIY facilities, caravan and camping.

Ⓑ **York Marina** Naburn, York YO19 4RW (01904 621021; www.yorkmarina.co.uk). P D Pump out, gas, day boat hire, boat hire, overnight and long-term mooring, winter storage, slipway, hoist (16 tons), boat sales and repairs, engine repairs, chandlery, café, toilets, showers, Wi-Fi.

York

N. Yorks. All services. Everything you will wish to see is packed within the square mile or so contained by the limestone medieval city walls which, if you are feeling energetic, you can walk around. Or you can climb the 275 steps to the top of the Minster for a superb panorama of this fine walled city and its surroundings. You will see the river passing through its centre, crossed by three handsome road bridges: the stone-built Ouse Bridge, and the decorous cast iron constructions of Lendal Bridge and Skeldergate Bridge. York finds its origins in the Roman base of Eboracum, established during the first century AD. In the Museum Gardens, you can see the substantial remains of the Multangular Tower, the western corner of the original Roman fortress. When the Romans left, York became a Saxon settlement, but they were overrun by the Vikings in 867. Thankfully the damp soils surrounding the river preserved substantial remains of their stay here, which can now be seen at the Jorvik Centre. Following the Norman conquest in 1066, William the Conqueror built two wooden towers to guard the Ouse. The present cathedral was begun in the early part of the 13th C, and was completed some 250 year later. After Charles I made York his northern headquarters in 1639, the Parliamentarians laid it siege in 1644 and, following the Battle of Marston Moor fought 6 miles to the west, Charles' garrison capitulated on the understanding that none of the city's fine religious buildings be desecrated. York's 19th-C history is centred upon the birth of the railways and the prosperity this new means of transport brought to the city. Shoppers can enjoy the vast array of shops in the streets by the Minster, and of course visit the Shambles, a narrow cobbled street which was once filled with butchers, but is now a good place for souvenirs. The university opened in 1963, reviving the city's reputation as a seat of learning.

Bar Convent Museum 17 Blossom Street, York YO24 1AQ (01904 643238; www.bar-convent.org.uk). The country's oldest active convent, founded in 1686. The dome of the chapel was remarkably hidden under a pitched roof. The present buildings are Georgian. Museum *open Mon-Sat 10.00-17.00*. Free. *Also* café *(open from 07.45)*, shop, guest house and conference rooms.

Cliffords Tower Tower Street, York YO1 9SA (01904 646940; www.english-heritage.org.uk/visit/places/cliffords-tower-york). There is a a good view of the city from the top of this tower, the last remaining part of York Castle, which once stood in Jewbury, where the city's Jews lived. In 1190 they were attacked by townsfolk complaining about loan repayments, and took refuge in the tower. There they committed mass suicide rather than convert to Christianity. Telephone or visit website to confirm opening times. Charge.

Fairfax House Castlegate, York YO1 9RN (01904 655543; www.fairfaxhouse.co.uk). Built in 1762, this superb town house houses the Terry collection of furniture and clocks. Special 18th-C Christmas exhibition each year. *Open Tue-Sat & B Hol Mon 10.00-17.00; Sun 11.00-16.00.* Admission by guided tour *Mon 11.00-14.00 & Sun 11.00.* Charge.

Jorvik DIG St Saviour's Church, St Saviourgate, York YO1 8NN (01904 615505; www.digyork.com). This attraction offers a unique archaeological adventure, as visitors excavate Roman, Viking, medieval and Victorian finds themselves. All visits are accompanied by archaeologists and are timed. Pre-booking (telephone or online) is advised, although you can just turn up and join a tour. *Open daily 10.00-17.00.* Charge.

Jorvik Viking Centre 15-17 Coppergate, York Yo1 9WT (01904 543400; www.jorvik-viking-centre.co.uk). The superbly re-created Viking town of Jorvik, discovered whilst excavating the Coppergate Shopping Centre and now superbly displayed. Sit in a time-car to journey back in time through 1000 years of English history, culminating at the Viking port discovered on this site. Journey along a Viking street surrounded by the smell of wood smoke and pigs, listening to the sounds of herring being unloaded, together with an informative commentary. *Open Easter-Oct, daily 09.00-17.00; Nov-Easter daily 10.00-16.00.* Visitors are advised to call 01904 615505 or visit the website to pre-book.Charge.

The York Dungeon 12 Clifford Street, York YO1 9RD (01904 632599; www.thedungeons.com). Branding, boiling, roasting and beheading of people are just a few of the attractions of this startling place, which is definitely *not recommended for the squeamish*. The story of Guy Fawkes is also vividly re-told including, of course, his torture and execution. Telephone or visit website for opening times and details of special events. Charge.

National Railway Museum Leeman Road, York YO26 4XJ (0844 815 3139; www.nrm.org.uk). Near York railway station. This is reputedly the world's largest railway museum, housed in two vast hangars, and whilst there are of course many superb locomotives, the exhibits illustrate rail travel in its broadest sense. Here you will see photographs, paintings, ceramics, models, ticket displays and the reproduction of a section of the Channel Tunnel. Locomotives on display include the *Agenoria*, which hauled coals in Staffordshire from 1829, and the splendid *Mallard*, which reached a speed of 126mph in 1938, still the world record for a steam locomotive. In the South Hall a replica station includes Queen Victoria's royal carriage, plus the carriage used by Queen Elizabeth II until 1977. Background recordings keep the railway atmosphere at a peak. Tours, demonstrations and rides. *Open daily 10.00-1800.* Free. Restaurant, gift shop.

Treasurer's House Minster Yard, York YO1 7JL (01904 624247; www.nationaltrust.org.uk/treasurers-house-york). A Jacobean façade on a house of which much was built in the 17th C, on the site of a Roman road. It was at one time owned by Frank Green, an industrialist and obviously intensely practical man: he put nails into the floor to remind servants where the furniture should stand. Walled garden, tearoom, art gallery and ghosts of Roman soldiers. *Open mid Feb-Oct, Sat-Thu 11.00-16.30* by guided tour only. Charge. Tea room.

Merchant Adventurers' Hall The Hall, Fossgate, York YO1 9XD (01904 654818; www.theyorkcompany.co.uk). One of York's finest timbered buildings, with a fine undercroft and a beautifully panelled hall. Museum. *Open Mar-Oct, Mon-Thu 09.00-17.00, Fri-Sat 09.00-15.30, Sun 11.00-16.00; Nov-Feb, Mon-Thu 10.00-16.00 & Fri-Sat 10.00-15.30.* Charge.

York Minster Deangate, York YO1 7HH (0844 939 0011; www.yorkminster.org). Earliest records of a religious building near this site relate to a wooden church, recorded by the Venerable Bede as being built by the Saxons in AD627. The present Minster was begun by Archbishop Walter de Gray, and completed in 1472, after 250 years' work. Built on a truly grand scale, it is 524ft long and 249ft wide (by volume, it is the largest cathedral in the country), topped by a central tower 234ft tall, completed about 1730. This tower needed remedial work in 1967, when serious weaknesses were found. The work, however, revealed a rich hoard of Roman and Saxon treasures, many of which are now displayed in the Undercroft Museum, along with all other aspects of the Minster's history. There are over 100 stained-glass windows spanning a period of 800 years, making the interior surprisingly light and airy. The earliest glass is in the second window on the left from the west door of the nave, and dates from c.1150. There is also a funeral procession of monkeys to look out for. Fine carvings around the capitals, the east window with Old and New Testament illustrations, and the stone choir screen, carved with England's rulers from William I to Henry VI, are other delights. In 1984, following some controversial statements made by the Bishop of

Durham, the roof of the south transept was struck by lightning, causing considerable damage and invoking comment about the wrath of God. This was repaired incorporating designs submitted by *Blue Peter* viewers. Every hour a priest asks visitors to stop their sightseeing and pray. Excellent free tours can be taken, leaving from the information desk. *Open Mon-Sat 09.00-17.00 & Sun 12.45-17.00.* Charge.

York Castle Museum The Eye of York, York YO1 9RY (01904 687687; www.yorkcastlemuseum.org.uk). A fascinating array of objects and displays kept in two 18th-C prisons, one of which includes the cell where Dick Turpin spent his last night. Reconstructions of a Victorian pub, Kirkgate, a Fancy Repository and a toyshop are packed full of fascinating artifacts. Many visitors will remember similar 1950s front rooms, complete with a television. *Open year round, daily 09.30-17.00. Closed Xmas and New Year.* Charge. Gift shop, coffee shop.

Theatre Royal St Leonard's Place, York YO1 7HD (01904 623568; www.yorktheatreroyal.co.uk). Shakespeare, ballet, opera and large popular productions. Café and restaurant.

Tourist Information Centre 1 Museum Street, York YO1 7DT (01904 550099; www.visityork.org). *Open Mon-Sat 09.00-17.00 & Sun 10.00-16.00.*

NAVIGATIONAL NOTES

Water, elsan disposal, refuse disposal and moorings are available at Museum Gardens in York - just upstream of Lendal Bridge on the north bank - *Apr-Sep*. A CRT watermate key is required. However, see Navigational Notes on page 126.

WALKING AND CYCLING

There is no continuous towpath on this section, although there is a fine riverside walk through York. The walk around the longest city wall in Britain should be undertaken if at all possible. Allow about 4 hours, and be prepared to make the link from Skeldergate Bridge to Monk Bar by road, via the Castle Museum, Coppergate, The Shambles and Goodramgate. You will also have to link Bootham Bar and Lendal Bridge. You will see many of the city's finest sights on the journey. Details of several walks around the city can be obtained from: Walking in the Countryside Around York, City of York Council, 9 St. Leonard's Place, York YO1 7ET (01904 551608; walking.cycling@york.gov.uk). In York 15 per cent of the population cycle to work compared with a national average of 3 per cent, so you can feel at home here on a bicycle. Maps detailing all of York's cycle routes are available from cycle retailers, libraries and City of York Council *(details above)*. The York to Beningbrough cycle route is a 9-mile ride from the city centre, initially traffic-free and with the last 5 miles along quiet lanes. It is part of the National Cycle Network route from Hull to Middlesbrough. Start from the railway station side of Lendal Bridge. You can also ride the old railway path to Selby, passing the old Terry's chocolate factory. Start from the railway station side of the Ouse Bridge at the junction of Skeldergate and Micklegate. Cycle Heaven (01904 622701/630378; www.cycle-heaven.co.uk) provides cycle hire, sales and repairs at York Station and sales and repairs at 2 Bishopthorpe Road, York YO23 1JJ (01904 636578/651870).

Pubs and Restaurants (page 127)

There are many fine pubs in York, including:

1 The Maltings Tanners Moat, near Lendal Bridge, York YO1 1HU (01904 655387; www.maltings.co.uk). An atmospheric small pub, voted Cask Ale Pub of Great Britain twice, and which runs its own beer festivals each year (telephone for details). Real ales and draught ciders. Bar meals are available *Mon-Fri 12.00-14.00, Sat and Sun 12.00-16.00. Outside seating*, dog-friendly and *regular* live music. *Open Mon-Sat 11.00-23.00 & Sun 12.00-22.30.*

2 The Old Bank 6-12 Lendal, York YO1 8AA (01904 541284; www.graduateyork.co.uk). A peaceful source of good food and drink by day, it becomes the haunt of a younger clientele by night. Real ales, real cider and food available *daily 10.00-21.00. Thu* quiz. Dog- and child-friendly, outside seating. Sports TV and Wi-Fi. *Open Sun-Thu 10.00-23.00 (Sun-Mon 22.00) & Fri-Sat 10.00-00.00.*

3 Yates's Wine Lodge Church Lane, Low Ousegate, York YO1 9QT (01904 613569; www.weareyates.co.uk/york). Riverside wine bar where meals are available *all day 09.00-21.00*. Some outside seating in the courtyard and DJ *Thu-Sun*. Family-friendly and Wi-Fi. *Open Sun-Thu 10.00-22.00 (Thu 23.00) & Fri-Sat 10.00-02.00 (Fri 01.00).*

4 The Kings Arms Kings Staith, York YO1 9SN (01904 659435). The last surviving remnant of the Water Lanes, this is also York's famous flooding pub, with water levels over the last 100 years recorded. Stone floors, brick walls, exposed beams and open fires (when the water level drops). Bar meals *L*. Outside seating. Moorings.

5 The Bluebell 53 Fossgate, York YO1 9TF (01904 654904). Over 200 years old, this pub is reputed to have the smallest and oldest interior in York. Six real ales are usually on tap. Real cider. Cheeseboard with selection of local cheeses available. Dog-friendly and traditional pub games. *Open 11.00 (Sun 12.00).*

6 The Cock & Bottle 61 Skeldergate, York YO1 6DS (01904 654165). Reputedly York's most haunted pub, and it serves real ale. Traditional pub games, real fires and sports TV. *Open Mon-Thu 16.00; Fri 15.00 & Sat-Sun 12.00. Closes 23.00 (Fri 23.30).*

WALKING AND CYCLING
There is a right of way on the west bank, between Acaster Malbis and Acaster Selby.

Naburn Locks

Having left the excitement of York, the river resumes its quiet passage through unassuming countryside, passing Naburn and Acaster Malbis on its way to Naburn Locks. Here the elegant Canal & River Trust buildings, swing bridges and crane create a fine riverside scene, marking the start of the tidal river and a gradual change in surroundings. There are also *toilets* and *showers* and a full range of *boater services*. Now the intimacy of the upper river is slowly replaced by bare banks and more open countryside around the tidal waters. Bell Hall, just half a mile south of the lock, was built in 1680, and is a fine example of its period. Moreby Park, also on the east bank, provides almost a mile of pleasing parkland and relief from the generally flat countryside. Acaster Selby, a small farming settlement, lies inconspicuously behind a bend as the river continues its languorous route south.

NAVIGATIONAL NOTES

1 The River Ouse is tidal below Naburn Lock so craft can only pass through the lock on a flood tide. Where possible please give the lock keeper *24 hrs notice* on 01904 728500. High Water Naburn is approximately 4 hours after HW Hull.

2 The Trent Series Charts, published by The Boating Association (www.theboatingassociation.co.uk; info@theboatingassociation.co.uk), are detailed charts of the tidal Ouse (and the tidal and non-tidal Trent) and are available to buy online. Also from CRT lock keepers. Charge.

3 CRT also publish useful guidance for boaters at www.canalrivertrust.org.uk/about-us/our-regions/north-east-waterways/planning-a-safe-passage-on-river-tees-and-river-ouse. This includes contact details for all moveable bridges and manned locks.

Naburn
N. Yorks. Tel. A charming and compact brick-built village nestling on a bend in the river. The church of St Matthew, built in 1854, stands separately to the south, with the famous locks a mile further on. The large Banqueting House, by the lock, was built 1823-4 as a meeting place for members of the Ouse Navigation Company.

Acaster Malbis
N. Yorks. PO box, tel. A pretty but nondescript village, with caravan parks at each end. A half-mile to the north is the large 14th-C church of the Holy Trinity, with its fine weatherboarded Victorian bell turret and spire. Look for the pretty stained glass in the east window, c.1320, and the effigy of John Malbis, from about the same time, in the south chapel. The pulpit is an elaborate 17th-C piece.

Acaster Selby
N. Yorks. A small farming settlement around what is left of Acaster Hall, built c.1670.

Boatyards

Ⓑ **Acaster Marine** Waterline Industrial Estate, The Airfield, York YO23 2UY (01904 702049; www.acastermarine.co.uk). Riverside yard just upstream of Naburn Locks. Long-term mooring, winter storage, slipway, 16-tonne crane, boat and engine sales and repairs, toilets, DIY facilities.

Pubs and Restaurants

1 The Blacksmiths Arms Main Street, Naburn, York YO19 4PN (01904 623464; www.blacksmithsarmsnaburn.com). Very comfortable and friendly pub, which for over 300 years was a blacksmith's shop. The bar has a fine collection of plates and teapots, and you can enjoy a pint here, or retreat into a cosy alcove. Real ales, and good bar meals *daily 12.00-20.00*. Dog- and child-friendly; large garden. Traditional pub games, newspapers, real fires and Wi-Fi. *Regular* live music. Camping nearby. B&B. *Open daily 12.00-23.00 (Fri-Sat 00.00).*

2 The Ship Inn Moor End, Acaster Malbis, York YO23 2UH (01904 703888; www.facebook.com/shipinnacaster). A large, stylish and haunted 17th-C coaching house, once used by Oliver Cromwell's men, and now a popular venue for visitors by road and river. Real ales and bar meals *Mon-Thu 12.00-20.00 (Mon-Thu 17.00) & Fri-Sun 12.00-21.00 (Sun 17.00). No food Mon-Tue in winter.* Dog- and child-friendly, garden. Newspapers, real fires and Wi-Fi. Camping. B&B. *Open 12.00-23.00 (Sun 22.30). Mon-Tue in winter 16.00.*

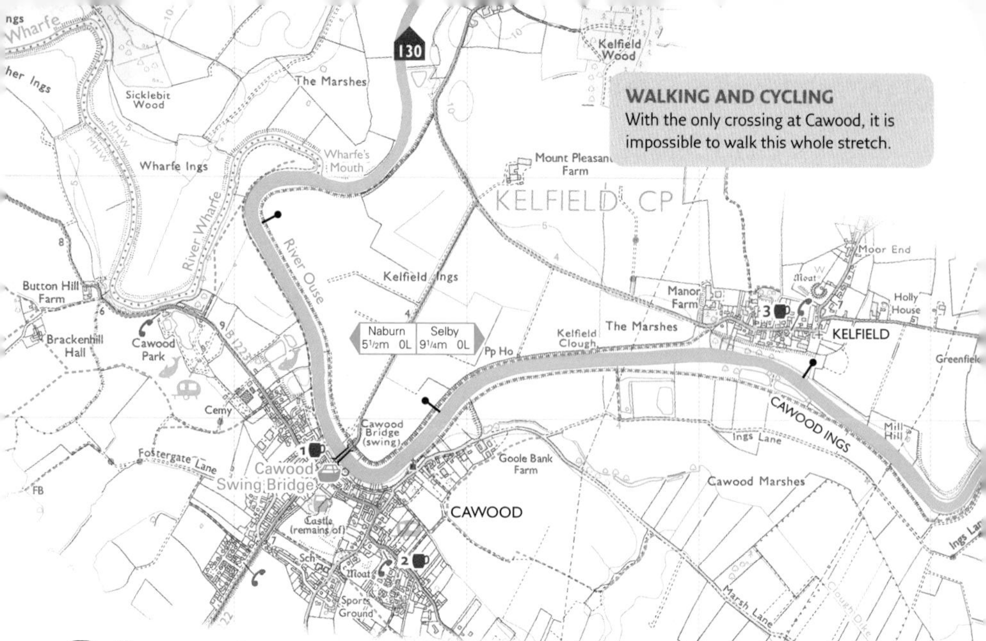

WALKING AND CYCLING
With the only crossing at Cawood, it is impossible to walk this whole stretch.

Cawood

The Ouse now starts to gather momentum as the River Wharfe, coming down from Tadcaster, joins from the west *(see below)*. Sweeping eccentrically past Cawood, the Ouse passes under the only river crossing on this section. To check headroom under Cawood Swing Bridge contact the bridge keeper on 01757 703692 before planning passage. Enclosed by flood banks and surrounded by rich farmland, the river now pursues an isolated course, with towns and villages showing a healthy respect by keeping their distance.

- **Cawood**
N. Yorks. PO, tel, stores. A pretty red brick and tile village, with narrow streets, nestling on the south bank and joined to the north by the swing bridge. A castle owned by the Archbishops of York once stood here, dating from AD930. Cardinal Wolsey visited, and was arrested here in 1530 for high treason. His fate is recalled in the nursery rhyme 'Humpty Dumpty'. All that now remains is a white stone gate house, dating from the first half of the 15th C. It has been renovated by the Landmark Trust and is available for lets (01628 825925). The Church of All Saints stands to the east of the village, and has a fine Perpendicular tower containing a monument to George Mountain, Archbishop of York, who diedin 1623.

- **Kelfield**
N. Yorks. Tel. Seeming to ignore the river totally, this village contains a chapel dated 1852, beautifully converted into a house.

- **Riccall**
N. Yorks. PO, tel, stores, off-licence, takeaway. The church of St Mary has a Norman doorway, dating from 1160, and Norman arcading from the 13th C. The south door is 12th C.

- **Barlby**
N. Yorks. Tel, stores, chemist, library, fish & chips, garage. Bypassed by the A19, Barlby, in places, still resembles a village, although it pays no heed to the river. Look out for Barlby Pinfold, a restored animal pen dating from feudal times. The stores are *open daily 06.30-21.00 (Sun 07.00)* and sell a range of hot and cold snacks, tea and coffee.

Pubs and Restaurants

1 The Ferry 2 King Street, Cawood YO8 3TL (01757 268515; www.facebook.com/TheFerryInnAllNew). Heavily beamed 16th-C hostelry, overlooking the river and swing bridge, serving real ales and food *Thu-Sun L and E (not Sun E).* Riverside garden; dog- and family-friendly. *Regular* live music, quizzes and entertainment. Traditional pub games, newspapers, real fires, sports TV and Wi-Fi. *Open Mon-Wed 16.00-22.00 (Mon 20.00) Thu-Sat 12.00-01.00 (Thu 23.00) & Sun 12.00-22.00.*

2 The Castle Inn 7 Wistowgate, Cawood, Selby YO8 3SH (01757 242837; www.thecastleinncawood.com). You can enjoy three real ales here and meals are available in the restaurant and conservatory *Mon-Fri L and E & Sat-Sun 12.00-21.30 (Sun 18.00).* Family-friendly and real fires. Garden and camping nearby. *Open Mon-Thu 12.00-23.00 & Fri-Sun 12.00-00.00 (Sun 22.00).*

3 The Grey Horse Main Street, Kelfield, York YO19 6RG (01757 248339). Real ale and bar meals. Children welcome. Garden.

NAVIGATIONAL NOTES

1. Although in theory the River Wharfe is navigable for nine miles to Tadcaster Weir, this is not advisable without local knowledge. The lower reaches are not particularly attractive and shallows around Ulleskelf – known locally as 'huts' – are just one of the problems you may encounter. Winding at Tadcaster is another.
2. Heading down river the first of two bridge call up points will be found 5 km above Selby Town Swing Bridges (see map). This is the point to request a bridge swing, if required, by calling the Bridge keepers on VHF channel 9 (01757 703126/01904 525558) reporting your location as Turnhead Reach. The next sign is 2 km above the Swing Bridges and marks the point to confirm the request for a swing, reporting your location as Barlby Bend. In this way it will be easier for the bridge keepers (and lock keeper – channel 74 – 01757 703182) to check on your progress and to more easily estimate the time of your arrival, thereby minimising any delay to road and rail services.
3. See Navigational Note 2 on page 134.

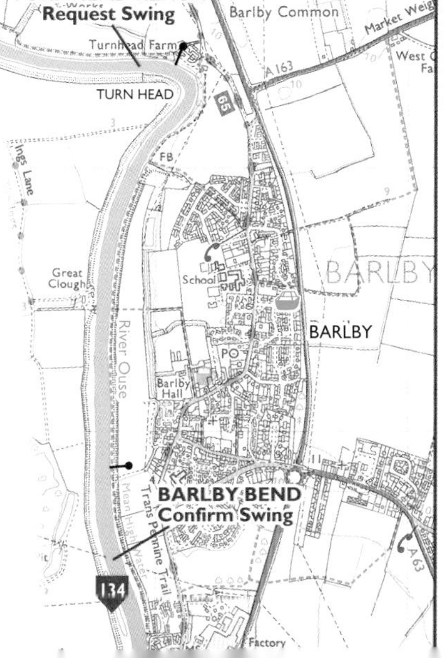

4 The Greyhound 82 Main Street, Riccall, York YO19 6TE (01757 249101; www.thegreyhoundriccall.co.uk). Friendly local serving a good selection of real ales and home-made food *Tue-Sun L and E (not Sat-Sun E)*. Dog- and family-friendly, garden. Traditional pub games, newspapers, live music, real fires, sports TV and Wi-Fi. Camping. B&B. *Open 12.00-00.00 (Sun 23.30). Winter Tue-Fri 15.00.*

5 The Hare & Hounds 8 Silver Street, Riccall, York YO19 6PA (01757 248255; www.facebook.com/TheHareHounds8). Real ale and bar meals. Children welcome. Sports TV. *Open Mon-Thu L and E (not Mon L) & Fri-Sun 12.00-23.30 (Sun 22.30).*

6 Burro Restaurant Old Riccall Mill, Landing Lane, Riccall YO19 6TJ (01757 249146; www.burrorestaurant.co.uk). Highly regarded restaurant providing authentic Italian dining in a relaxed and friendly atmosphere. All food freshly prepared and sourced locally wherever possible. Children welcome. *Open Mon-Sat 12.00-22.00 (Fri-Sat 23.00) & Sun 12.00-21.00.*

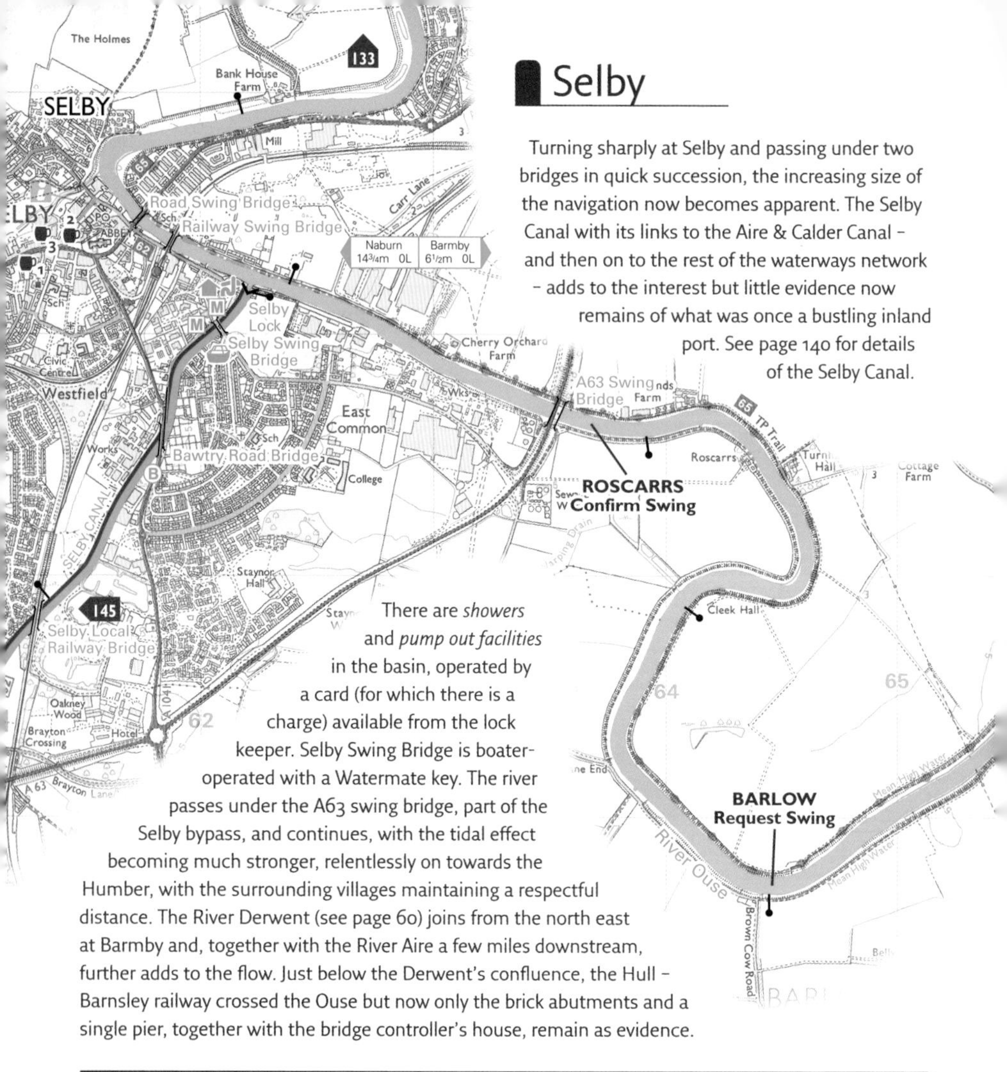

Selby

Turning sharply at Selby and passing under two bridges in quick succession, the increasing size of the navigation now becomes apparent. The Selby Canal with its links to the Aire & Calder Canal – and then on to the rest of the waterways network – adds to the interest but little evidence now remains of what was once a bustling inland port. See page 140 for details of the Selby Canal.

There are *showers* and *pump out facilities* in the basin, operated by a card (for which there is a charge) available from the lock keeper. Selby Swing Bridge is boater-operated with a Watermate key. The river passes under the A63 swing bridge, part of the Selby bypass, and continues, with the tidal effect becoming much stronger, relentlessly on towards the Humber, with the surrounding villages maintaining a respectful distance. The River Derwent (see page 60) joins from the north east at Barmby and, together with the River Aire a few miles downstream, further adds to the flow. Just below the Derwent's confluence, the Hull – Barnsley railway crossed the Ouse but now only the brick abutments and a single pier, together with the bridge controller's house, remain as evidence.

NAVIGATIONAL NOTES

1. The Ouse is now becoming a powerful river with a strong tidal effect. Navigation should not be attempted without the requisite experience and a suitably equipped craft.
2. Selby Railway Swing Bridge is left in the closed position and any vessel requiring a swing *06:00-22:00* should contact the bridge keeper on VHF radio channel 9 or by telephoning 01904 718028/0330 858 7749. *For night-time* operation boaters must book *at least 24hrs in advance*.
3. Heading up river the first of two bridge call up points will be found 5 km below Selby Town Swing Bridges (see map). This is the point to request a bridge swing, if required, by calling the Bridge keepers on VHF channel 9 (01757 703125) reporting your location as Barlow. The next sign is 2 km below the Swing Bridges and marks the point to confirm the request for a swing, reporting your location as Roscarrs. In this way it will be easier for the bridge keepers (and lock keeper – channel 74 – 01757 703182) to check on your progress and to more easily estimate the time of your arrival, thereby minimising any delay to road and rail services.
4. The Selby Bypass Bridge keeper can be contacted on 01757 703692 and would appreciate *24hrs notice* for a swing.
5. Note that High Water Selby is approximately 2 hours after HW Hull.
6. Visitor moorings are available in Selby Basin. A transit licence is available for craft on River Registration to use the canals between Selby and Keadby on the Trent (missing Trent Falls).

● **Selby**

N. Yorks. All services. Away from the River Ouse, this is a handsome market town, dominated by its sparkling abbey. The present road bridge was built in 1970, and became toll-free in 1991: it replaced an earlier structure which had stood since 1791.

Selby Abbey The Crescent, Selby YO8 4PU (01757 703123; www.selbyabbey.org.uk). Founded for the Benedictines, as a result of Benedict's vision of three swans landing on a river coming to fruition here. The east window shows the family tree of the Kings of Israel and dates from the 14th C. Below the south east window is the grave slab of Laurence Selby, abbot from 1486–1504. Notice that the three swans seen by Benedict are featured in a shield by his shoulder. *Open daily 09.00–16.00, although if there is a ceremony taking place some of the abbey will be cordoned off to visitors.*

Selby Park Selby. A very pleasant 5 acres of trees and plants, with a children's play area, picnic tables, mini-golf and bowls. *Open Mon–Fri 10.00–21.00, Sat and Sun 10.00–17.00.*

Selby Market Selby. Over 150 stalls, food and entertainment in front of the Abbey. *Every Mon 08.00–15.30 and a smaller market takes place on Sat.*

Visitor Centre 52 Micklegate, Selby YO8 4EQ (0845 0349543). Located in Selby Library. *Open daily.*

● **Hemingbrough**

N. Yorks. PO, tel. The very tall slender spire of the church of St Mary can be seen for miles across the flat Yorkshire countryside, standing fully 189ft high.

Drax Power Station Drax, Selby YO8 8PH (01757 618381; www.draxpower.com). This is Europe's largest coal-fired power station, producing 10 per cent of England's electricity. However, increasingly it is relying on biomass to replace some of the coal previously employed. Opened in 1973 it dominates the area for miles around. Guided tours for groups only, by prior arrangement.

● **Barmby on the Marsh**

N. Yorks. PO box, tel. Village with some Georgian houses hemmed in by the rivers Ouse and Derwent.

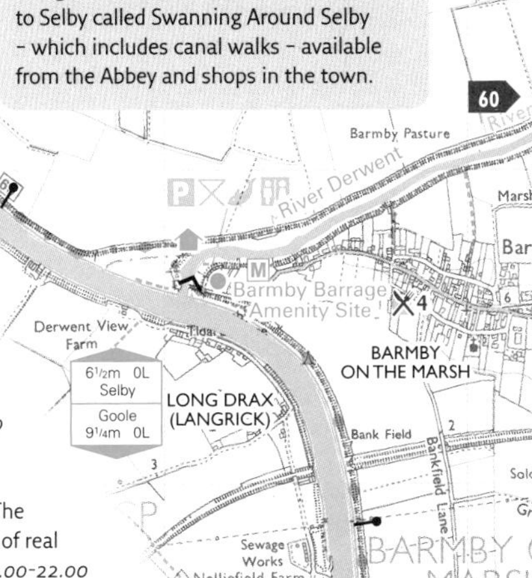

WALKING AND CYCLING

The towpath is continuous on this section, along the north bank. There is a Guide to Selby called Swanning Around Selby - which includes canal walks - available from the Abbey and shops in the town.

Pubs and Restaurants

1 The Giant Bellflower 47a Gowthorpe, Selby YO8 4HF (01757 293020; www.jdwetherspoon.com/pubs/all-pubs/england/north-yorkshire/the-giant-bellflower-selby). Converted from a furniture shop and named after a plant found growing on the river bank, this hostelry sells keenly-priced real ale, real cider and food *daily 08.00-23.00.* Family-friendly, outside seating. Real fires and Wi-Fi. *Open 08.00-00.00 (Fri-Sat 01.00).*

2 The George Inn Market Place, Selby YO8 4NS (01757 707355; www.thegeorgeinn-selby.co.uk). Real ale and food available *daily 08.00-21.00.* Family-friendly, garden. Sports TV and Wi-Fi. *Open 08.00-23.00 (Fri-Sat 01.00).*

3 The Blackamoor 6 Finkle Street, Selby YO8 4DS (07908 205324; www.facebook.com/theblackamoor). The main bar features live music *Fri-Sat* and good selection of real ale throughout the week. Karaoke *Thu. Open Mon-Fri 11.00-22.00 (Thu-Fri 03.00) Sat 11.00-04.00 & Sun 12.00-22.00.*

4 Lorenzo's Italian Restaurant High Street, Barmby on the Marsh, Goole DN14 7HT (01757 633827; www.lorenzositalian.co.uk). Well presented, tasty food featuring all the Italian favourites. Great pizzas and friendly staff. Children welcome. Takeaway service. *Open daily 12.00-21.00 (Fri-Sat 22.00). Bar opens at 12.00.*

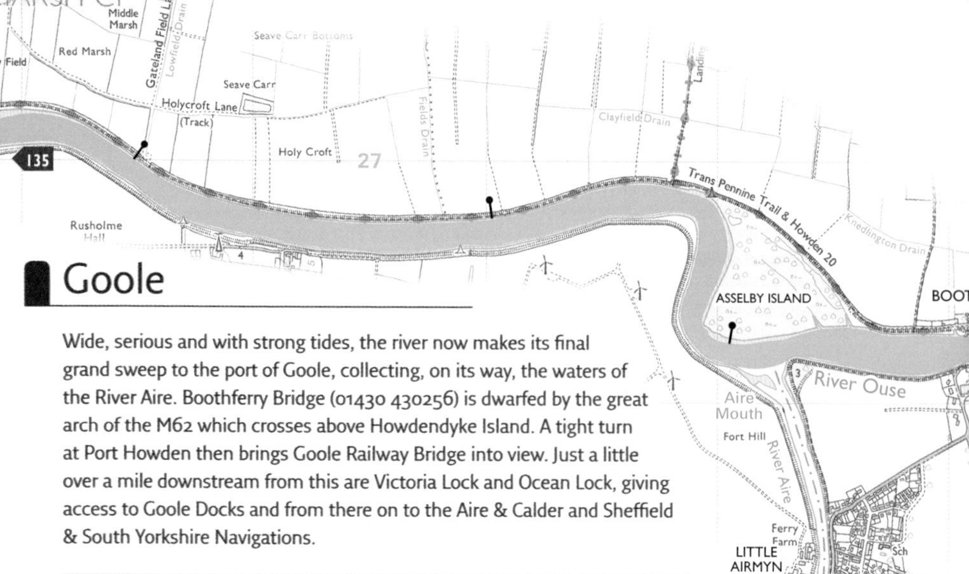

Goole

Wide, serious and with strong tides, the river now makes its final grand sweep to the port of Goole, collecting, on its way, the waters of the River Aire. Boothferry Bridge (01430 430256) is dwarfed by the great arch of the M62 which crosses above Howdendyke Island. A tight turn at Port Howden then brings Goole Railway Bridge into view. Just a little over a mile downstream from this are Victoria Lock and Ocean Lock, giving access to Goole Docks and from there on to the Aire & Calder and Sheffield & South Yorkshire Navigations.

NAVIGATIONAL NOTES

1 The Ouse is now a working river, with large craft and a strong tidal effect. Navigation should not be attempted without the requisite experience and a suitable craft. Cruising notes are available free of charge from Selby Locks (01757 703182) and Naburn Locks (01904 728500). The lock keeper at Goole will willingly offer advice and information on navigating the tideway. For their part boaters must inform Associated British Ports (ABP) that they are on the river and make their position known (*see* note 2). ABP maintain a continuous watch on channel 14.

2 At the west end of South Dock, Goole, the navigation is under the jurisdiction of ABP. Contact them on VHF radio channel 14 – call *Goole Docks* – or by telephoning 01482 327171. Boats using Ocean Lock and the tideway **must carry VHF radio and have at least two people on board**.

3 To the west of this point ocean-going shipping is manoeuvring and contact must be made with Ocean Lock Control before entering the docks.

4 Overnight mooring will incur a substantial charge and temporary mooring, whilst awaiting a lock or bridge swing, is only permitted if the crew are in attendance. Mooring on any pier whilst on the tideway (unless awaiting a lock) will also incur a charge.

5 Lock operating times are *2½ hours before high tide and 1 hour after* for which no charge is made. Outside these times special pens are always available on payment of a fee. High Water Goole is approximately 1 hour after HW Hull.

6 The Trent Series Charts, published by The Boating Association (www.theboatingassociation.co.uk; info@theboatingassociation.co.uk), are detailed charts of the tidal Ouse (and the tidal and non-tidal Trent) and are available to buy online. Also from CRT lock keepers. Charge.

7 It is approximately 7 miles from Swinefleet to Trent Falls. ABP's jurisdiction extends from the mouth of the Humber to Gainsborough on the Trent and Skelton Railway Swing Bridge (aka Hook Railway Bridge) on the Ouse, which can be contacted on VHF channel 9 – or by telephoning 01430 430012. Above this point the river falls under the jurisdiction of CRT who publish useful guidance for boaters at www.canalrivertrust.org.uk/about-us/our-regions/north-east-waterways/planning-a-safe-passage-on-river-tees-and-river-ouse. This includes contact details for all moveable bridges and manned locks.

Pubs and Restaurants

1 The Percy Arms 89 High Street, Airmyn, Goole DN14 8LD (01405 780792; www.thepercyarmsairmyn.co.uk). Cosy village pub with open fires. Real ale. Meals available *Mon-Fri L and E; Sat 12.00-20.30 & Sun 12.00-15.00*. Family-friendly, children's play area and garden. Newspapers and Wi-Fi. *Open Mon-Sat 11.30-23.00 (Sat 00.00) & Sun 11.30-20.00.*

2 The Viking Western Road, Goole DN14 6RG (01405 765671; www.hungryhorse.co.uk/pubs/east-riding-yorkshire/vikings). Family-oriented eatery, serving real ale with food available *09.00-22.00 (Sun 21.00)*. Family-friendly with children's play area, garden. Traditional pub games, sports TV and Wi-Fi. *Open 09.00-23.00 (Fri-Sat 00.00).*

See also **Pubs and Restaurants** on page 27

Boatyards

Ⓑ**Goole Boathouse** The Timber Pond, Dutch Riverside, Goole DN14 5TB (01405 763985; www.gooleboathouse.co.uk). **DE** Gas, pump out, secure overnight and long-term moorings *(6' max draught)*, chandlery, dry dock, slipway, winter storage, engine repairs, blacking, welding, licensed clubhouse.

Ⓑ**Viking Marine** Albert Street, Goole DN14 5SY (01405 765737; www.vikingmarine.co.uk). **D** Mooring, Gas, 16-tonne crane, boat and engine sales, winter storage, maintenance and repair service, chandlery. Approved Honda main dealer (outboards and generators). Closed *Sun*.

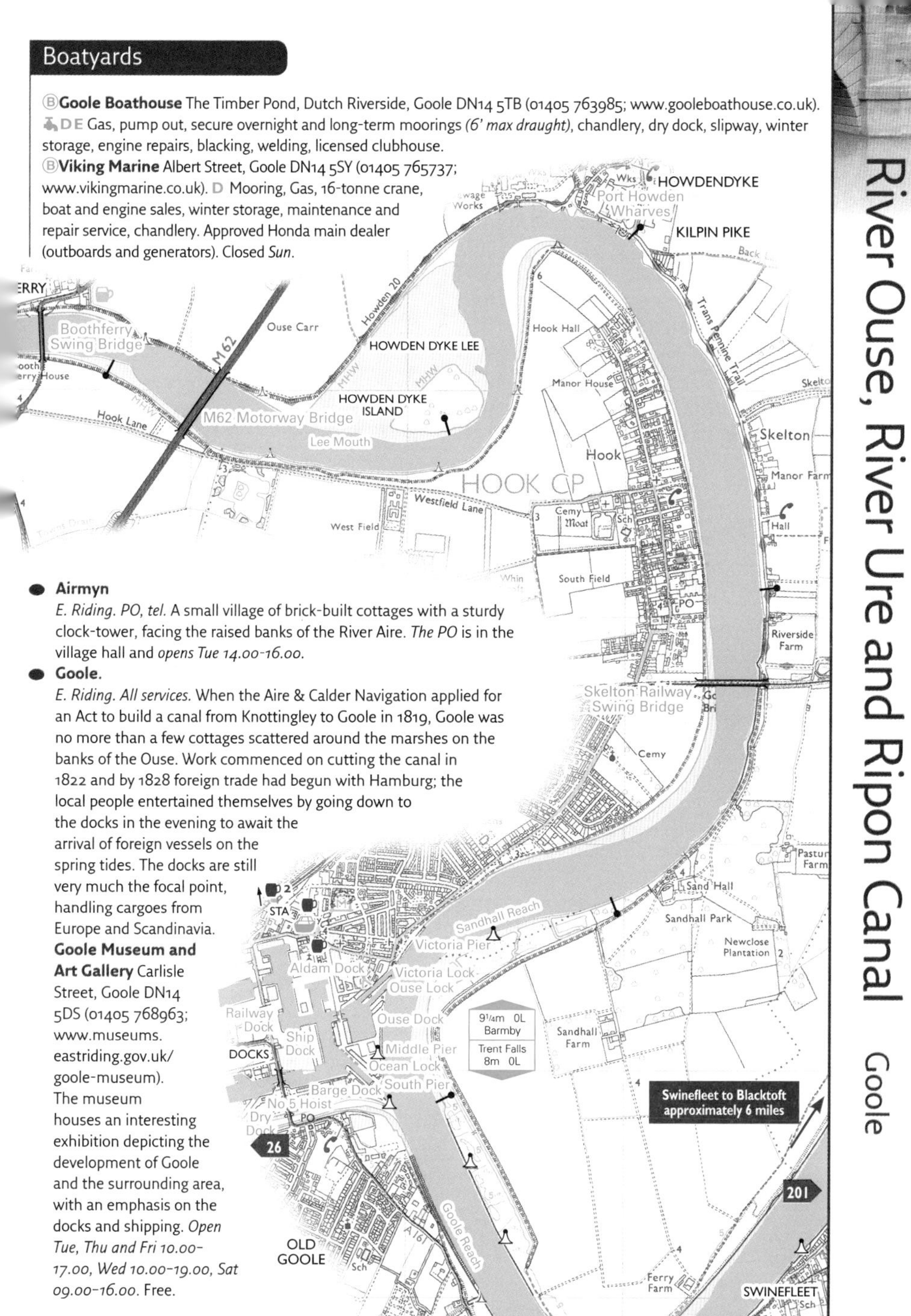

- **Airmyn**
  E. Riding. PO, tel. A small village of brick-built cottages with a sturdy clock-tower, facing the raised banks of the River Aire. *The PO* is in the village hall and *opens Tue 14.00-16.00.*
- **Goole.**
  E. Riding. All services. When the Aire & Calder Navigation applied for an Act to build a canal from Knottingley to Goole in 1819, Goole was no more than a few cottages scattered around the marshes on the banks of the Ouse. Work commenced on cutting the canal in 1822 and by 1828 foreign trade had begun with Hamburg; the local people entertained themselves by going down to the docks in the evening to await the arrival of foreign vessels on the spring tides. The docks are still very much the focal point, handling cargoes from Europe and Scandinavia.
  Goole Museum and Art Gallery Carlisle Street, Goole DN14 5DS (01405 768963; www.museums.eastriding.gov.uk/goole-museum). The museum houses an interesting exhibition depicting the development of Goole and the surrounding area, with an emphasis on the docks and shipping. *Open Tue, Thu and Fri 10.00-17.00, Wed 10.00-19.00, Sat 09.00-16.00.* Free.

Departing Ocean Lock, Goole.

SELBY CANAL

MAXIMUM DIMENSIONS

Bank Dole Junction, Knottingley, to junction with the River Ouse, Selby
Length: 78' 6"
Beam: 16' 6"
Draught: 4'
Headroom: 8'

MANAGER

0303 040 4040
enquiries.yorkshireandnortheast@canalrivertrust.org.uk

MILEAGE

Bank Dole Junction, Knottingley to:
Haddlesey Flood Lock: 6½ miles
Selby, junction with the River Ouse: 11¾ miles

Locks: 4

Bank Dole and West Haddlesey locks give access to river sections of the navigation. River level gauge boards indicate conditions as follows:

GREEN BAND - Normal river levels safe for navigation.

AMBER BAND - River levels are above normal. If you wish to navigate the river section you are advised to proceed on to and through the next lock.

RED BAND - Flood conditions unsafe for navigation. Lock closed.

CRT publish useful guidance for boaters navigating the tidal Ouse at www.canalrivertrust.org.uk/about-us/our-regions/north-east-waterways/planning-a-safe-passage-on-river-tees-and-river-ouse.

In 1774 the Aire and Calder Navigation Company obtained an Act to construct a navigation from the River Aire at Haddlesey to the Ouse at Selby. This was not, however, the first attempt to improve communication by navigable waterways in the area. During the 17th C local industry had transported goods by packhorse along the Hambleton Causeway to Selby Dock from where they were shipped to their destination. When the Aire was eventually made navigable to small vessels, Selby's trade declined. For some 70 years the traders battled with the difficulties that navigating the Aire presented until, in 1770, there were rumours that there was to be a new canal created, covering some 23½ miles and linking Leeds directly to Selby. The proprietors of the Aire & Calder Company soon realised the gravity of this threat. In making a connection with a tidal waterway at each end of its navigation, the Leeds and Liverpool Canal Company could very soon put the Aire & Calder Canal Company out of business. The latter employed the services of John Smeaton and William Jessop in the hope of eliminating the tideway on the river. Instead an Act was finally secured in 1774 which took the shortest and cheapest option. That was a direct route from the Aire's lowest lock at Haddlesey to Selby, a mere 5½ miles. The navigation opened on 29 April 1778. It was built to Jessop's design and cost £20,000. As a result Selby flourished. The town was in the enviable position of being at the junction of two great waterways and at a point where river, canal and road met. The manufacturers of the West Riding were able to send goods directly to Hull and London as well as being within more easy access of York and Leeds. By 1821 one-third of the people living in Selby were making their living from the waterways. The town was busy with ship and boat building, rope and sail making, flax dressing and linen manufacture. Industries in Leeds, Castleford and Knottingley improved, to all of which Selby had direct access. The building of a customs house at Selby enabled traffic to go straight out into the North Sea without having to stop at Hull to complete the necessary paperwork. The 8 acres of land around the lock were thriving with a counting house, rigging house, tarring house and sailmaker's shop. A small cut was made parallel with the Ouse where smaller vessels could be kept for transhipment of goods from larger vessels on the river. A sailing packet left Selby every Monday for Hull, returning Thursday if weather conditions permitted. The fare was two shillings return, with food available on board at a cost of sixpence for men and fourpence for ladies. As trade increased, so did the amount of traffic and the size of loads carried on the navigation. The one shortcoming of the quick and cheap construction of the canal, namely the shallow draught of only 3' 6", proved to be its downfall. The Aire & Calder Canal Company was under fire from merchants and traders, all dissatisfied by the lack of capacity that the navigation offered for larger vessels. The rise in the production of coal from the Selby coalfield highlighted a serious deficit in the capacity of larger vessels and soon the company was under pressure to provide an alternative course. By 1826 the new and deeper canal from Knottingley to Goole was in operation and trade on the Selby Canal, although not entirely abandoned, suffered greatly as a consequence.

Today the canal is used solely for leisure and recreational purposes. The acquisition of the River Ouse by Canal & River Trust has resulted in the Selby Canal being promoted as a through-route to the city of York. Since 1988 boating numbers have rocketed, with a peak of 2000 craft passing through Selby Lock annually. The towpath forms part of the Selby Horseshoe Walk – www.selby.gov.uk/sites/default/files/Documents/Selby_Horseshoe_v2.pdf. A recent canal Corridor Study has recognised the potential of the canal in creating a linear urban park. At present the industries which line its banks are turning their backs on the water, but an imaginative scheme set to reverse this trend promises to inject some life and create a valuable recreational resource along the banks of the canal. It is hoped that before too long Selby's canal will once again be recognised for the important role it once played in the life of the town.

Selby Lock, Selby

Beal

The navigation from Knottingley provides a welcome escape from the intensive industry of the area. However, the concentration required to navigate safely on the commercial waterways cannot be abandoned, as the Aire adopts a fairly tortuous course as it meanders across more open countryside towards Haddlesey. Care needs to be taken on the countless bends until the navigation changes course at Haddlesey Lock.

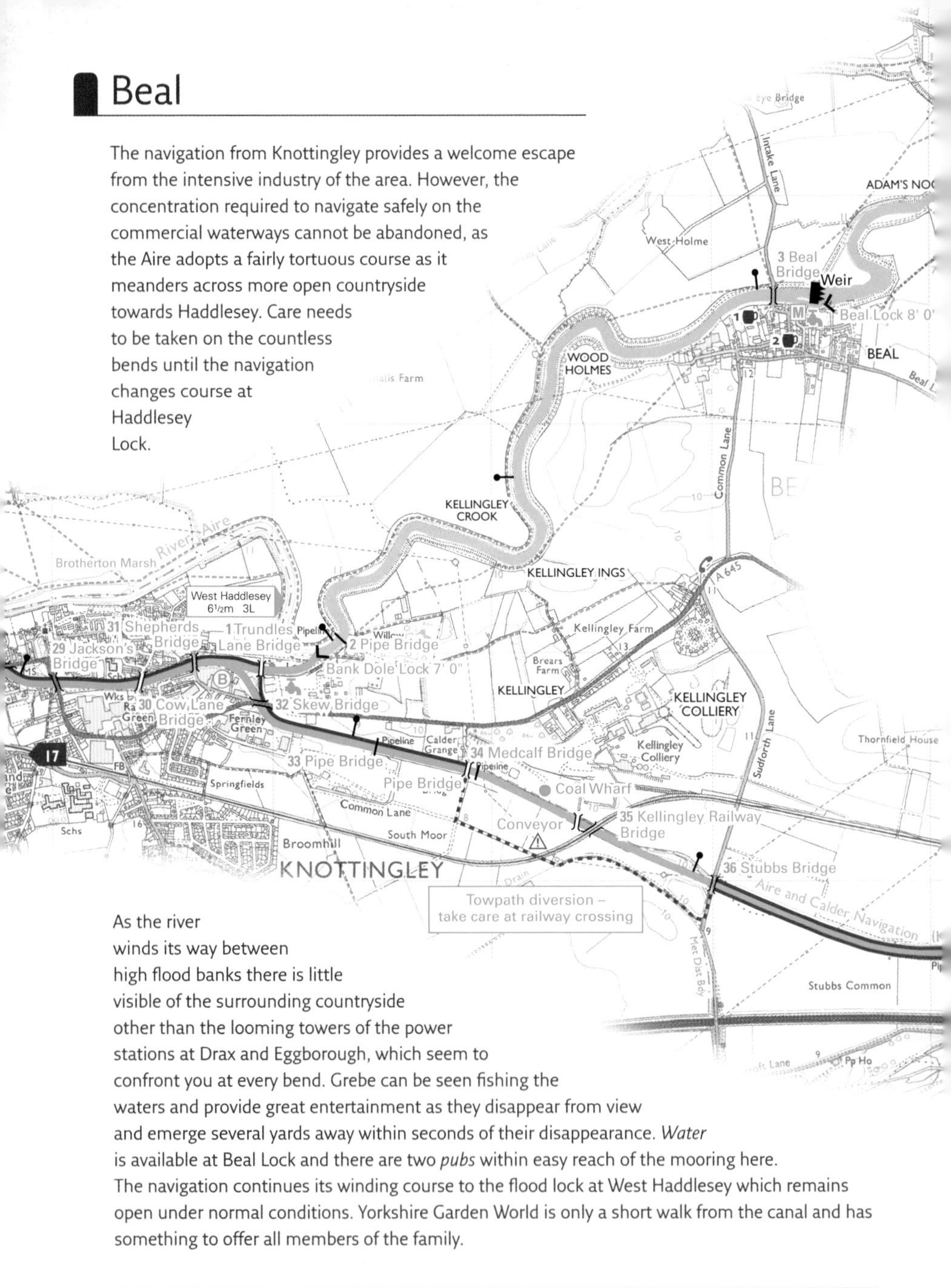

As the river winds its way between high flood banks there is little visible of the surrounding countryside other than the looming towers of the power stations at Drax and Eggborough, which seem to confront you at every bend. Grebe can be seen fishing the waters and provide great entertainment as they disappear from view and emerge several yards away within seconds of their disappearance. *Water* is available at Beal Lock and there are two *pubs* within easy reach of the mooring here. The navigation continues its winding course to the flood lock at West Haddlesey which remains open under normal conditions. Yorkshire Garden World is only a short walk from the canal and has something to offer all members of the family.

NAVIGATIONAL NOTES

Bank Dole Lock is unmanned. Temporary mooring is available on the river alongside all locks, although the landing stages should be approached with care. Vigilance is required locking up as the paddles are quite fierce. Caution should also be exercised on entering the lock at West Haddlesey as the wind can easily catch the boat, forcing it against the approach wall.

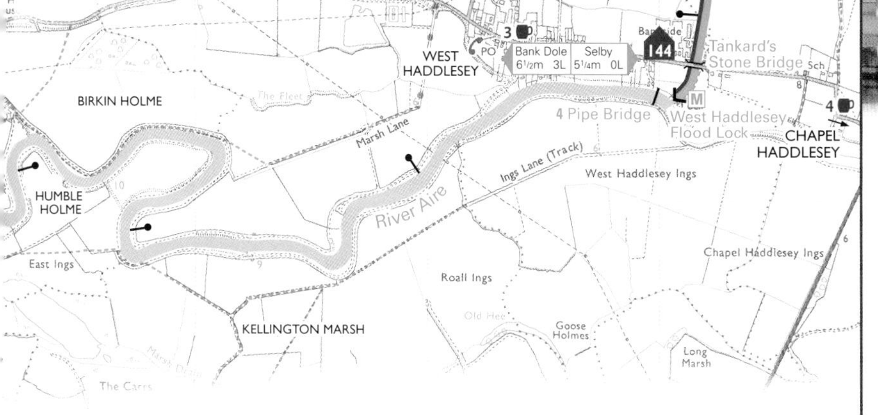

Pubs and Restaurants

1 The Jenny Wren Main Street, Beal DN14 0SS (01977 309862). A selection of real ales are served in the old taproom little changed in 60 years. Food is available *Sun 12.00-19.00. Real fires. Open Mon-Sat 16.00-00.00 (Sat 14.00) & Sun 12.00-00.00.*

2 The Kings Arms Marsh Lane, Beal DN14 0SL (01977 607180). Bar and restaurant serving real ale. Generous Generous portions of home-made food are served *Mon-Sat L and E & Sun 12.00-17.00.* Family-friendly. *Open 12.00-23.00.*

3 The George and Dragon Main Street, West Haddlesey YO8 8QA (01757 228198; www.facebook.com/george.westhaddlesey). Real ale is served from the bar where you can enjoy an open fire and home-cooked food *Wed-Sat 17.30-20.30 & Sun 12.00-16.00.* Dog-friendly, garden. Traditional pub games, live music, sports TV and Wi-Fi. Camping. B&B. *Open Mon-Fri 17.00-00.00 (Fri 01.00) Sat 14.00-01.00 & Sun 12.00-22.30.*

4 The Jug Inn Hirst Road, Chapel Haddlesey, Selby YO8 8QQ (01757 270718; www.facebook.com/Janemickburns). A regular choice of real ale is dispensed in this traditional village country pub with heavily beamed ceilings and open fires. Freshly prepared, home-made food is available *Tue-Sat L and E & Sun 12.00-16.00.* Real cider. Dogs welcome, garden. *Open Tue-Sun 12.00-23.00 (Tue 16.00).*

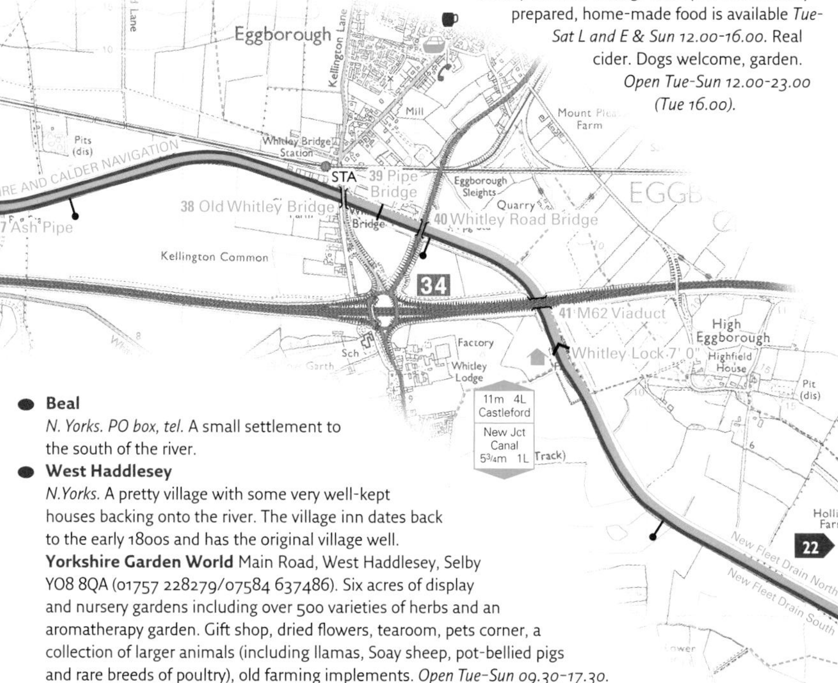

Beal
N. Yorks. PO box, tel. A small settlement to the south of the river.

West Haddlesey
N.Yorks. A pretty village with some very well-kept houses backing onto the river. The village inn dates back to the early 1800s and has the original village well.

Yorkshire Garden World Main Road, West Haddlesey, Selby YO8 8QA (01757 228279/07584 637486). Six acres of display and nursery gardens including over 500 varieties of herbs and an aromatherapy garden. Gift shop, dried flowers, tearoom, pets corner, a collection of larger animals (including llamas, Soay sheep, pot-bellied pigs and rare breeds of poultry), old farming implements. *Open Tue-Sun 09.30-17.30.* Charge for gardens and animals.

Selby

Leaving West Haddlesey and the River Aire (once navigable to Airmyn and junction with the River Ouse) behind, the navigation now enters the Selby Canal, whose course provides a welcome contrast. The rich vegetation on both banks changes with the seasons but is never without interest. The towpath, which follows the north bank, is popular with the local people and the banks are well-populated with fishermen, particularly during competition time when the short stretch to Selby may attract as many as 1000 competitors! Several old milestones can be seen along the bank marking the distance from the River Ouse. Just to the north of Burton Bridge is Burton Hall, built on the site of a medieval manor, and beyond it the wooded hill of Brayton Barff which provides excellent views over the Vale of York to Selby. Barff is an ancient British name for barrow or burial place. There is an excellent *pub* in Burn and a *mooring* at Burn Bridge, providing access to Brayton to the north, where there are further *pubs*, two *stores, a post office, a butcher and a garage*. The graceful 15th-C spire of St Wilfrid's Church at Brayton can be seen across the fields. Passing under Selby Local Railway Bridge, which carried the old East Coast Main Line, the canal enters the short industrial corridor into Selby basin. The railway, which once headed directly north from Selby, had to be diverted to the west to avoid subsidence due to the newly opened deep mines to the north east of the town. Selby Swing Bridge is boater-operated with a Watermate key and can only be used during *daylight hours*. There are *toilets, showers* and *pump out facilities* in the basin operated by a Smart card available from the lock keeper.

WALKING AND CYCLING

The towpath is in excellent condition for both walking and cycling between Selby Lock and Burn Bridge but is better suited to walking beyond here. There is a Guide to Selby called Swanning Around Selby – which includes canal walks – available from the Abbey and shops in the town or downloadable at www.selbycivicsociety.org.uk/uploads/selby_civic_society/files/Swanning_Around_Selby_v05(1).pdf.

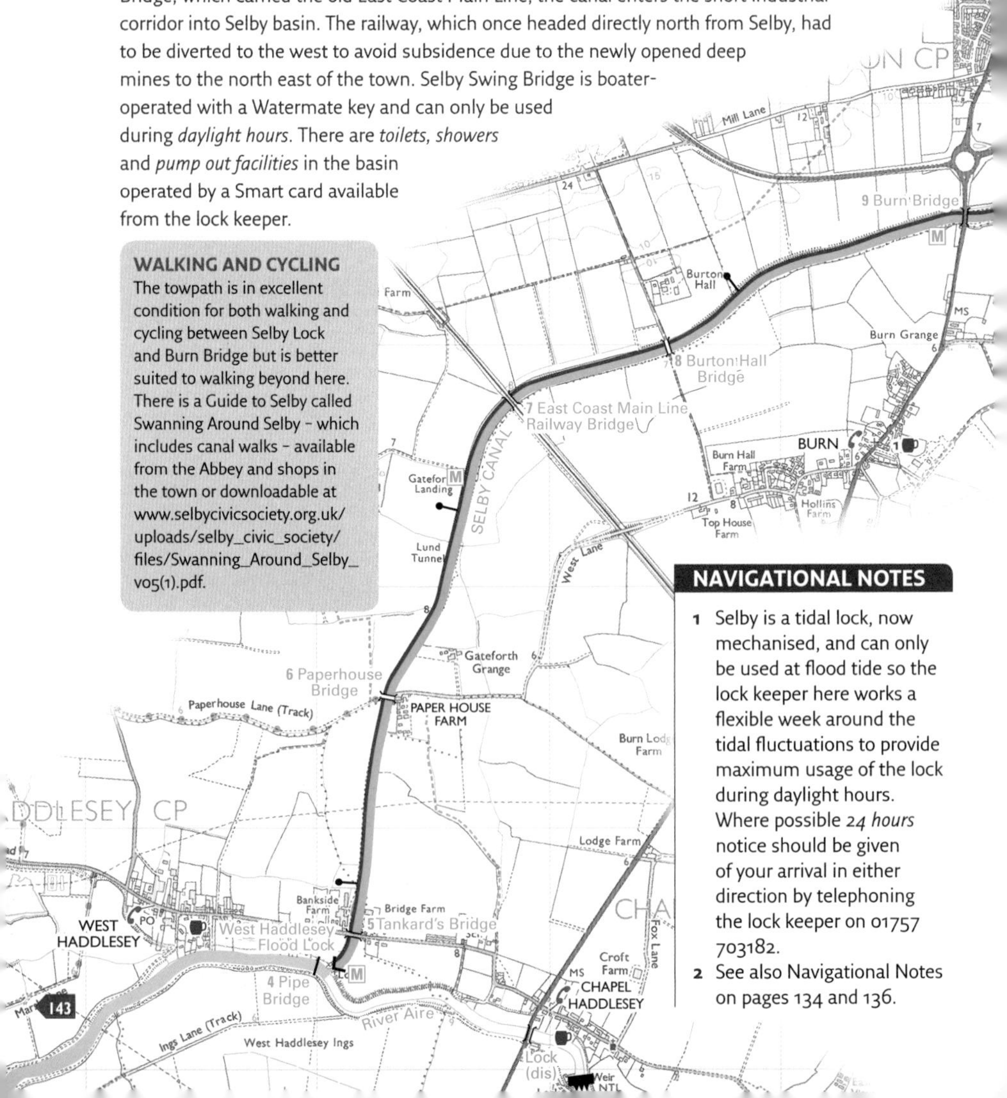

NAVIGATIONAL NOTES

1 Selby is a tidal lock, now mechanised, and can only be used at flood tide so the lock keeper here works a flexible week around the tidal fluctuations to provide maximum usage of the lock during daylight hours. Where possible *24 hours* notice should be given of your arrival in either direction by telephoning the lock keeper on 01757 703182.

2 See also Navigational Notes on pages 134 and 136.

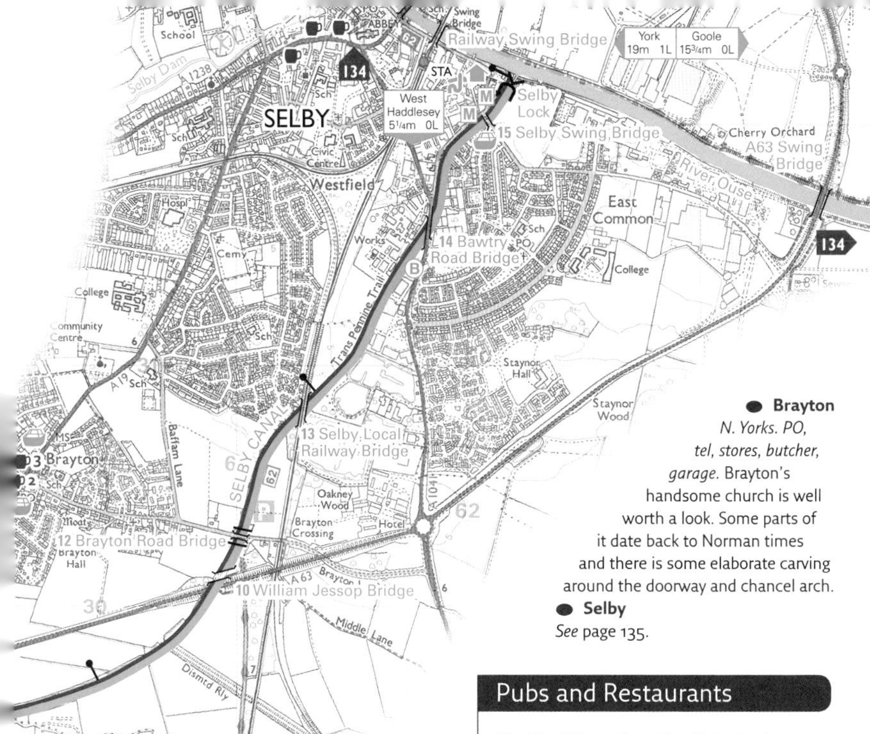

Brayton
N. Yorks. PO, tel, stores, butcher, garage. Brayton's handsome church is well worth a look. Some parts of it date back to Norman times and there is some elaborate carving around the doorway and chancel arch.

Selby
See page 135.

Boatyards

Ⓑ**Selby Boat Centre** Bawtry Road, Selby YO8 8NB (01757 212211; www.selbyboatcentre.co.uk). D E Pump out, gas, gas installations, overnight moorings, long-term moorings, boat painting, welding services.

Ⓑ**DB Marine** Bawtry Road, Selby YO8 8NB (01977 678160; www.db-marine.co.uk). Builders of narrowboats, wide-beams and Dutch barges. Boat repair, servicing and restoration. Joinery, boat electrics, blacking, painting. *Emergency call out.*

Pubs and Restaurants

1 The Wheatsheaf Inn Main Road, Burn, Selby YO8 8LJ (01757 270614; www.wheatsheafburn.co.uk). Perfect place to stop for refreshment. Real ale and home-made food *every day L and Wed-Sat 18.30-20.30.* Excellent malt whisky selection which can be sampled amidst 578 Squadron memorabilia and a host of knick-knacks collected and donated by customers over the years. Traditional pub games, live music, newspapers, real fires and sports TV. Beer garden and children and dogs welcome. Wi-Fi. *Open daily 12.00-23.00 (Fri-Sat 00.00).*

Try also: **2 The Grey Horse** Doncaster Road, Brayton YO8 9HD (01757 702719) and **3 The Swan** Doncaster Road, Brayton YO8 9EG (01757 703870; www.enterpriseinns.com/run-a-pub/pubs/Pages/swan-inn-brayton.aspx).

For pubs in Selby see page 135.

BURSTING AT THE SEAMS

It is difficult to conceive whilst cruising quietly around the waterways of Yorkshire that underground there was once the largest coal mining complex in Europe. Only the effects of subsidence remind us of the extensive activity which took place below. The mines which comprised the Selby coalfield extracted some 11 million tons of coal, and provided work for 4000 people. Shafts sunk in the 1960s and 1970s at a cost of £1 billion extend eastwards towards the North Sea at a depth of 700ft, some seams measuring two or three miles in length. In spite of it once being the most modern and productive complex in Europe, this high tech operation still chose to employ the cleanest and most environmentally-friendly mode of transport at one of its collieries – the canal. In 1996 Kellingly Colliery celebrated the transportation of the 35-millionth ton of coal by barge to Ferrybridge Power Stations. However, since the demise of Hargreaves (who operated the highly efficient tugs and coal carrying pans) it would appear that what little remains of the coal traffic will be transferred onto the road and rail system at a significant environmental cost.

Mooring at Barnby Dun

SOUTH YORKSHIRE NAVIGATIONS

MAXIMUM DIMENSIONS

Sheffield to Rotherham
Length: 60' 0"
Beam: 15' 1"
Headroom: 10'
Draught: 4' 3"
Locks from Rotherham to the bottom of the Tinsley Flight are longer and will pass narrowboats up to approximately 70'

Rotherham to Sykehouse
Length: 198'
Beam: 20'
Headroom: 10' 6"
Draught: 8' 2"

Bramwith to Keadby
Length: 61' 8"
Beam: 17'
Headroom: 10' 6"
Draught: 7' 3"

New Junction Canal
Length: 215'
Beam: 22' 6"
Headroom: 10' 10"
Draught: 9'

MANAGER

0303 040 4040
enquiries.yorkshireandnortheast@canalrivertrust.org.uk

MILEAGE

SHEFFIELD Basin to:
Rotherham: 6 miles, 15 locks
Swinton Junction: 12 miles, 18 locks
Doncaster Lock: 21½ miles, 23 locks
Bramwith Junction: 28 miles, 24 locks
Thorne: 33 miles: 26 locks
Crowle Wharf: 39½ miles, 26 locks
KEADBY, junction with River Trent: 43 miles

Locks: 27

SOUTHFIELD JUNCTION, junction with Aire & Calder Canal: 33½ miles

Locks: 25

Four separate waterway developments combine to make up the South Yorkshire Navigations. Prior to their improvement, trade with the industrial heartland of South Yorkshire was by horse and cart to Bawtry, and then by the natural line of the River Idle into the Trent and on into the Humber estuary. The River Don was largely given over to powering water wheels along its upper length, whilst its lower reaches split into two channels west of Thorne and drained into the Trent. In 1627 Cornelius Vermuyden was employed to drain Hatfield Chase and the Isle of Axholme. His scheme involved blocking one of the River Don's outlets into the Trent, thereby forcing all its waters into the tidal River Aire. This was unsuccessful and resulted in flooding, making what had been an already difficult river navigation into a hazardous one. A new channel, the Dutch River, was cut east from the River Don into the Ouse. This improved drainage, but not navigation.

Upstream, the river between Doncaster and Mexborough had, by 1729, been considerably improved, with complete navigation to Tinsley, four miles from Sheffield, a reality by 1751. All goods to and from Sheffield for shipment by water travelled by road between a river wharf at Tinsley and the city. It was not until 1815 that an Act of Parliament was obtained to build a canal into the city centre. The Sheffield Canal was opened on 22 February 1819. For the first time the city was linked directly to the sea, via the Trent and Humber. The Trent link had in fact been made 17 years earlier, with the construction of the Stainforth & Keadby Canal, which bypassed the tidal reaches of the old Dutch River.

The navigation declined until 1888, when the Sheffield & South Yorkshire Navigation Company was formed, and improvements made. The Straddle Warehouse built over Sheffield Basin dates from this period, as did the negotiations with the Aire & Calder Navigation to link Sheffield directly to the port of Goole and the more northerly coalfields. These negotiations resulted in the opening of the New Junction Canal on 2 January 1905. In 1983 the navigation was upgraded to the 700-tonne Eurobarge standard as far as Rotherham. Unfortunately, with no established traffic, the annual tonnage of goods carried is now just a fraction of the record one million tonnes achieved in 1951 and the navigation's future now seems to be firmly in the area of leisure and recreation.

Sheffield

The restored Sheffield Basin is dominated by the impressive Straddle Warehouse, built on columns over the water in 1895 by the South Yorkshire Navigation Company. Immediately behind this stands the Grain Warehouse, beyond which is the original Terminal Warehouse of 1819, standing an imposing seven storeys high. Leaving the basin *(showers and toilets)* the canal initially curves away beneath a railway bridge. Bridge 6, Bacon Lane, built in 1819, was also known as Needle's Eye, due to the problems its narrow width posed. The sharp-eyed will be able to spot evidence of boats having been forced through with a crowbar. It is now renowned as the place where the *Full Monty* was filmed. Staniforth Road Bridge provides useful access to pubs, *cafes, restaurants and shops* on Attercliffe Road, as does Darnall Road Aqueduct, known locally as T'Acky Dock! At Greenland Road Bridge the towpath crosses to the north side of the canal. The water here was once polluted, but this has now been eliminated and wildlife has recovered well. Fishermen can be seen along the banks, as can clumps of Michaelmas daisies, toadflax and valerian. Ahead the canal enters the top lock of the Tinsley Flight (*toilets* and *showers* here), and descends under the shadow of a massive steel viaduct carrying the M1 across the valley. A total of 11 locks, with tranquil wide pounds and open views, lower the navigation from its summit level, with the bright-green domed roofs of the Meadow Hall shopping centre dominating the outlook to the west. The canal joins the River Don at Halfpenny Bridge, and bends sharply right after passing the head of a large weir. Three locks, almost equally spaced, continue the descent towards Rotherham. The chamber of Rotherham Lock is quite tiny – retaining the original keel length of 61' 6" – and looks very pleasant in front of the court house, where barristers and defendants alike can be seen crossing the canal to the car park. There then follows a very tight right turn before the waterway seems almost to burrow underground and snake through the heart of the town.

WALKING AND CYCLING

The towpath is constantly undergoing improvement and upgrading and is now used by the Trans Pennine Trail along most of the section between Meadow Hall and Rotherham. Built very much as an industrial waterway, the South Yorkshire Navigation does not lend itself particularly to walking and cycling. Cycling maps of Sheffield can be downloaded from www.cyclesheffield.org.uk along with some detailed route descriptions. A pleasant five-mile walk can be found at www.alltrails.com/trail/england/south-yorkshire/penistone-line-sheffield-five-weirs.

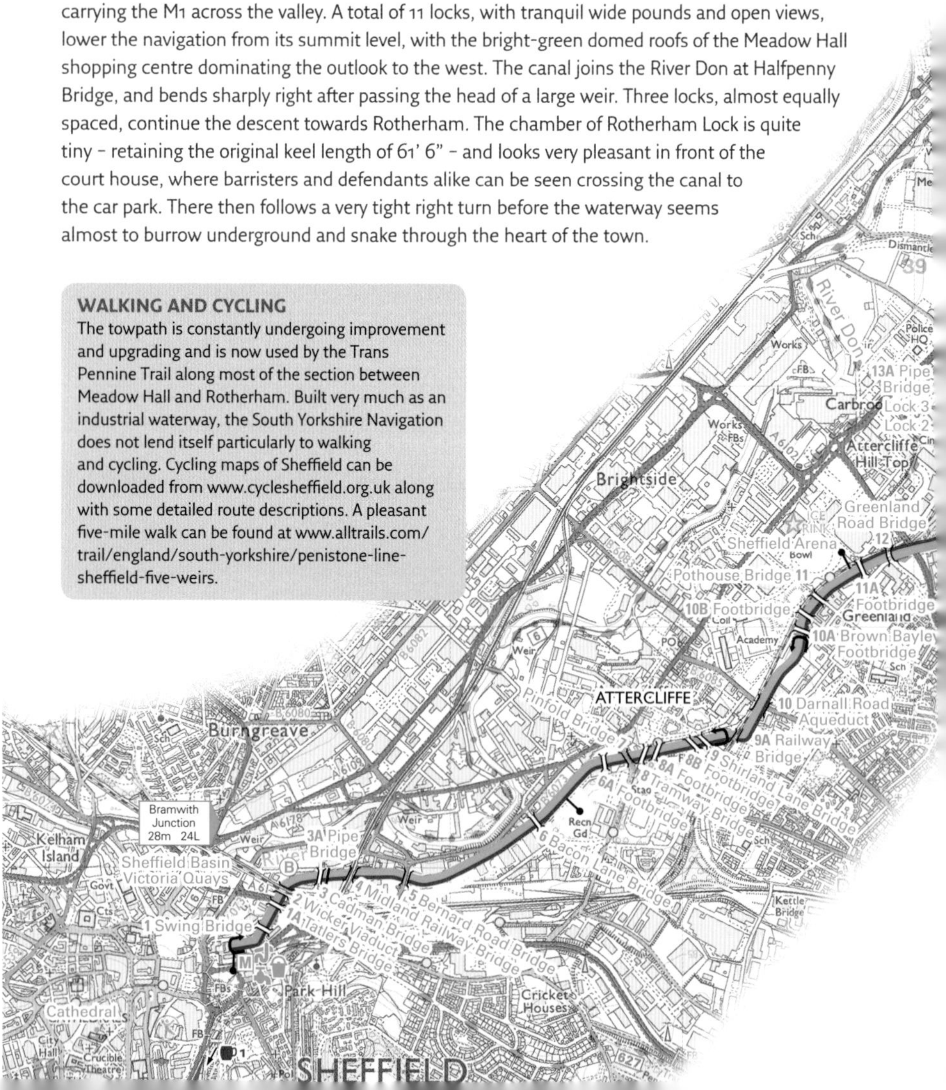

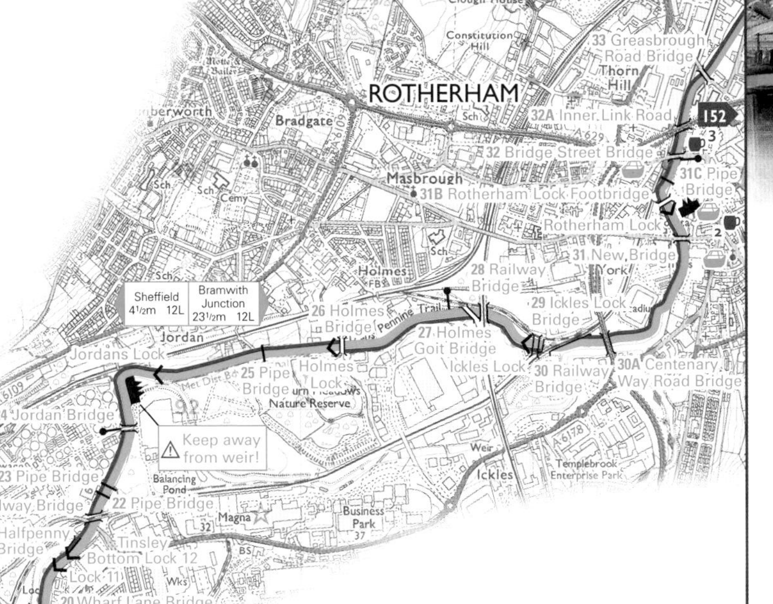

Boatyards

Ⓑ **CV Marine** Victoria Quays, Sheffield S2 5SY (0114 276 7111; www.cvmarine.co.uk). E Gas, pump out, solid fuel, short and long-term mooring, engine sales and repairs, boat sales and repairs, chandlery, books, maps and gifts, café, showers, toilets, Wi-Fi.

Ⓑ **Jonathan Wilson Boatbuilders** Victoria Boatyard, Sussex Street, Sheffield S4 7YY (0114 278 1234/07815 904721; www.tylerwilsonboats.com). Long-term mooring, slipway, crane, boat building, boat and engine sales and repairs, chandlery, toilets, DIY facilities, hull blacking.

NAVIGATIONAL NOTES

1. Although it is possible to moor at several points along this stretch of waterway, it is advisable to use Sheffield Basin for an overnight stop. The swing bridge at the entrance to the Basin requires a Watermate key and a windlass.
2. Passage through the Tinsley Flight (S9 2FN) requires assistance from one of the lock keepers who are on duty *daily 08.00–16.00 throughout the year.* No boat longer than 60' 0" may now use these locks. Telephone 07710 175488 (or 0303 040 4040 if no reply) *and ensure that you give 24 hours notice.* This also effectively applies to Jordans, Holmes and Ickes Locks so also inform the lock keeper of your intention to use these locks.
3. From Tinsley to Doncaster Town Lock you are entering a river navigation with a series of artificial cuts. Many of the locks are accompanied by large weirs, so keep a sharp lookout for signs which direct you safely into the locks.
4. Once the river level rises 2ft above normal (gauging sticks are fixed at the top and bottom of all locks) pleasure craft may well experience difficulty due to the current, floating debris and the pull at weirs. Seek advice from CRT staff before proceeding.
5. All locks require a Watermate key for operation; Holmes and Ickles Locks require a windlass. Obey the traffic light signals.
6. All weirs are protected by weir booms – keep well away.

Sheffield

S. Yorks. All services. Sheffield is England's fourth largest city and owes its world-famous reputation to the manufacture of steel, cutlery and silverware. The unique landscape into which Sheffield was built, steep hills sliced by deep-cut valleys, contributed to its importance during the Industrial Revolution. Five rivers facilitated the operation of water wheels, and hills rich in iron ore made Sheffield a natural pioneer of the steel industry. Today the city bustles with life, and new shopping complexes merge with the existing Georgian and Victorian architecture to give a lively mix. Overhead the two-car units of the Supertram shuttle back and forth, and the station close to the Canal Basin makes access to this excellent means of transport quite easy. Tudor Square brings together the internationally famous Crucible Theatre with the Lyceum Theatre, restored to its former Victorian splendour (from Park Square, by the Canal Basin, walk along Commercial Street, then turn left into Arundel Gate to find them). Also nearby are the award-winning Ruskin Gallery and Graves Art Gallery. Just across Exchange Street an open market is useful for supplies.

Town Hall Pinstone Street, Sheffield S1 2HH. Built in 1897 and designed by Mountford, the town hall has a clock tower, 210ft high, crowned with a statue of Vulcan, Roman God of Fire. There is a sculptured frieze outside depicting the industries of Sheffield.

Cutlers' Hall Church Street, Sheffield S1 1HG (0114 276 8149; www.cutlers-hall-sheffield.co.uk). Built in 1832, the Cutlers' Hall houses the Cutlers' Company collection of silver. Tours for parties. Telephone for details.

Millennium Galleries Arundel Gate, Sheffield S1 2PP (0114 278 2600; www.museums-sheffield.org.uk/museums/millennium-gallery/home). A venue for art and design, bringing major exhibitions to the city. Paintings, drawings and prints of John Ruskin, plus a craft and design gallery. *Open daily 10.00-17.00 (Sun 16.00).* Free. (charge for some exhibitions).

Weston Park Museum Western Bank, Sheffield S10 2TP (0114 278 2600; www.museums-sheffield.org.uk/museums/weston-park/home). The museum contains the largest collection of Sheffield Plate in the world and has a unique section devoted to cutlery. Also Bronze Age antiquities, local geology and wildlife gallery. *Open Mon-Sat 10.00-17.00, Sun 11.00-16.00. Closed 25, 26 December and 1 January.* Free. Touch sessions available for visually impaired people. Café and shop.

Cathedral of St Peter & St Paul Opposite the Cutlers' Hall in Church Street, Sheffield S1 1HA (0114 275 3434; www.sheffieldcathedral.org). A largely 15th-C church with 12th-C foundations and an interesting extension incorporating a new glass and steel porch, elevated to cathedral status in 1914. Five years later it was decided to enlarge the building, whilst retaining much of the original, to designs by Sir Charles Nicholson. Visitors will enjoy the stained-glass windows depicting local history and the Chaucer window in the Chapter House. *Open daily.* Guided tours can be arranged.

Kelham Island Museum Alma Street, Sheffield S3 8RY (0114 272 2106; www.simt.co.uk). Set upon an island in the River Don, this museum takes you through Sheffield's industrial past, with a chance to see craftsmen at work. A trail takes you past the only surviving Bessemer Converter, George Stephenson's first reversing-link engine, a grand-slam bomb, a Spitfire crankshaft and a 150hp Crossley gas engine. The River Don Engine (a 12,000bhp engineering wonder) is usually in steam twice a day. *Open Mon-Thu 10.00-16.00, Sun 11.00-16.45.* Charge. Café and shop.

Abbeydale Industrial Hamlet Abbeydale Road South, Sheffield S7 2QW (0114 236 7731; www.simt.co.uk). Four miles south west of the city centre. A superb example of industrial archaeology which displays a restored community, built around a water-powered scythe and steel works on a site used for iron forging for at least 500 years. *Open Mon-Thu 10.00-16.00 & Sun 11.00-16.45.* Café and shop. Bus from the High Street (continuation of Commercial Street, off Park Square). Charge.

Bishop's House Norton Lees Lane, Sheffield S8 9BE (0114 255 7701; www.bishopshouse.org.uk/index.php/visit-us). A timber-framed Bishop's house of 15th-C origins with 16th- and 17th-C additions. Other displays include Sheffield in Tudor and Stuart times and changing local history exhibitions. *Open Sat-Sun 10.00-16.00 & Mon-Fri* for pre-booked groups only. Charge. Bus from the Transport Interchange, opposite the BR station in Pond Street, south of Park Square. Free.

Crucible Theatre 55 Norfolk Street, Sheffield S1 1DA (0114 249 6000; www.sheffieldtheatres.co.uk). Studio theatre. The World Snooker Championships are held here each year.

Tourist Information Centre Sheffield no longer has a public tourist information service. All available information can be accessed at www.welcometosheffield.co.uk/visit.

Rotherham

S. Yorks. All services. An attractive town set amidst the industrial heartland of South Yorkshire where the buildings, although dating from a variety of periods, integrate well to form a coherent town centre. A part of the medieval town plan remains while the old town hall, in its new guise of an arcade, presents a fine renovation. In ancient times Rotherham was an important seat of learning, the College of Jesus being founded in 1482 by Archbishop Thomas and surviving until the Dissolution. The pinnacled tower of All Saints Church dates from 1409, and the remainder was almost entirely constructed during the same century. Its position, whilst maintaining an intimate contact with the town, is nevertheless imposing. Standing on the remaining four arches of the bridge which spans the River Don, the Chapel of Our Lady was built in 1483 and again fell victim to the Dissolution, after which it variously became an almshouse, a prison and a tobacconist's. It was finally restored and re-consecrated in 1924 and forms a very attractive feature in the lower part of the town. The key is available from the verger of All Saints, nearby.

Rotherham's modern growth dates from 1746 when Samuel Walker, a former schoolmaster, established its first ironworks. Coal mining developed, as well as the production of brass, steel, rope and glass, yet it is probably for the production of quality steels, in the form of fine-edge tools, that the town is best known.

Clifton Park Museum Clifton Lane, Rotherham S65 2AA (01709 336633; www.cliftonparkrotherham.co.uk/museum). A collection containing gemstones and examples of Rockingham and other local pottery can be seen here, in a house dating from 1783. Loan exhibitions of paintings. Roman remains from Templeborough can be seen in the park, opened by the Prince of Wales in 1891 and which covers an area of 56 acres. Café. *Open Mon-Fri 10.00-17.00; Sat 09.30-17.00 & Sun (Apr-Oct) 13.30-16.30.* Free (charge for some exhibitions).

Magna Science Adventure Centre Sheffield Road, Templeborough, Rotherham S60 1DX (01709 720002; www.visitmagna.co.uk). Housed in a former steelworks, this is an interactive centre, where you can experience the full power of the natural elements: air, water, fire and earth. Shoot with a water cannon, dodge lightning, feel what it is like to fly, use water power to launch a rocket, control a JCB and explode a rock face. *Open daily 10.00-17.00.* Charge. Restaurant, café, shop.

Meadowhall Shopping Centre Above Lock 9 on Tinsley Flight, Sheffield S9 1EP (0333 313 2000; www.meadowhall.co.uk). An immense indoor shopping mall accessible from above Lock 9 on the Tinsley Flight. *Open Mon-Fri 10.00-21.00, Sat 09.00-20.00, Sun 11.00-17.00.* Restaurants and bars.

Elsecar Heritage Centre Wath Road, Elsecar, Barnsley S74 8HJ (01226 740203; www.elsecar-heritage-centre.co.uk). Access by train from Sheffield. Follow the signs from Elsecar Station. These Victorian engineering workshops dating from the early 1800s have been transformed into an exciting centre, containing the Darwin Iron Works, the Elsecar Power House, The National Bottle Collection and the Elsecar Steam Railway. *Open daily 10.00-16.00. Closed Xmas and New Year.* Charge. Tearooms.

Tourist Information Centre 26 High Street, Rotherham, South Yorkshire, S60 1PP (01709 255752; www.yorkshire.com/view/attractions/rotherham/rotherham-tourist-information-centre-1164923).

ART GALLERIES IN SHEFFIELD

Graves Leader House, Surrey Street, Sheffield S1 2LH (0114 278 2600; www.museums-sheffield.org.uk/museums/graves-gallery/home). A fine collection of English watercolours, drawings and prints, European paintings and Old Masters (16th-C to present). Coffee bar. *Open Tue & Thur-Sat 11.00-16.00 and Wed 13.00-18.00.* Free.

Ruskin Collection Millennium Gallery, Arundel Gate, Sheffield S1 2PP (0114 278 2600; www.museums-sheffield.org.uk/museums/millennium-gallery/exhibitions/current/ruskin-collection). A fine collection of minerals, plaster casts and architectural details, paintings, watercolours, illuminated manuscripts and books collected by John Ruskin for the people of Sheffield. Craft gallery. *Open Mon-Sat 10.00-17.00 and Sun 11.00-16.00.* South west of Park Square.

Pubs and Restaurants (pages 148-149)

There are many pubs and restaurants in Sheffield, but few are close to the navigation.

1 The Sheffield Tap Platform 1b, Sheffield Station, Sheaf Street, City Centre, Sheffield: Central S1 2BP (0114 273 7558; www.sheffieldtap.com). Originally the first class waiting room for Sheffield Midland Station, rescued from years of neglect in 2009, this brewery tap serves up to 10 real ales from within its sumptuous neo-Grecian surroundings. (the on-site brewery, in the former dining room, is also on view). Dog- and family-friendly, outside seating. Wi-Fi. *Open 11.00-23.00 (Fri-Sat 00.00).*

2 The Bluecoat The Crofts, Rotherham S60 2DJ (01709 539500; www.jdwetherspoon.com/pubs/all-pubs/england/south-yorkshire/the-bluecoat-rotherham). Originally a charity school, deriving its name from the colour of the uniform worn by its pupils, this popular pub now serves inexpensive real ales; cask cider and food *daily 08.00-23.00.* Family-friendly, outside seating. Quiz *Wed.* Traditional pub games, sports TV and Wi-Fi. *Open 08.00-00.00 (Fri-Sat 01.00).*

3 The Bridge Inn 1 Greasebrough Road, Rotherham S60 1RB (01709 836818). Built in 1930, using stone from the original 18th-C pub of the same name, this popular hostelry serves real ales with an emphasis on local micro-breweries. Dog-friendly. Traditional pub games and sports TV. *Regular* events. *Open 12.00-23.00 (Fri-Sat 00.00).*

Swinton

The exit from Rotherham is marked by a very large expanse of water before Rawmarsh Road Bridge, beyond which the Rotherham Cut eventually rejoins the River Don. There is a useful retail park (*including chemist and DIY stores*) accessed from beside Eastwood Footbridge 39B. When Eastwood Locks were combined on the upper site the river was re-aligned along the old canal bed. The new lock, opened on 1 June 1983 by the then Chairman of BWB (now CRT), and called Sir Frank Price Lock in his honour (it is now Eastwood Lock), completed the modernisation to the 700-tonne barge standard of the South Yorkshire Navigations. There are good *moorings* here, with *toilets, showers and electricity*. It is worth noting, however, that from Sheffield the navigation has remained virtually unchanged since its original construction, a lasting tribute to its designers. At Aldwarke Lock a short channel bypasses the weir and a new concrete flyover has taken over from Wash Lane Bridge. Built in 1834, this listed structure bears the marks of much abuse from both barges and road traffic alike. The navigation now follows the course of the River Don, twisting and turning between high and often tree-lined banks, passing gaunt modern factory complexes, largely engaged in specialist steel manufacture. All discharges from these works are now carefully monitored for purity and to this end brightly coloured booms surround each outfall, containing their emissions for regular testing by the Environment Agency.

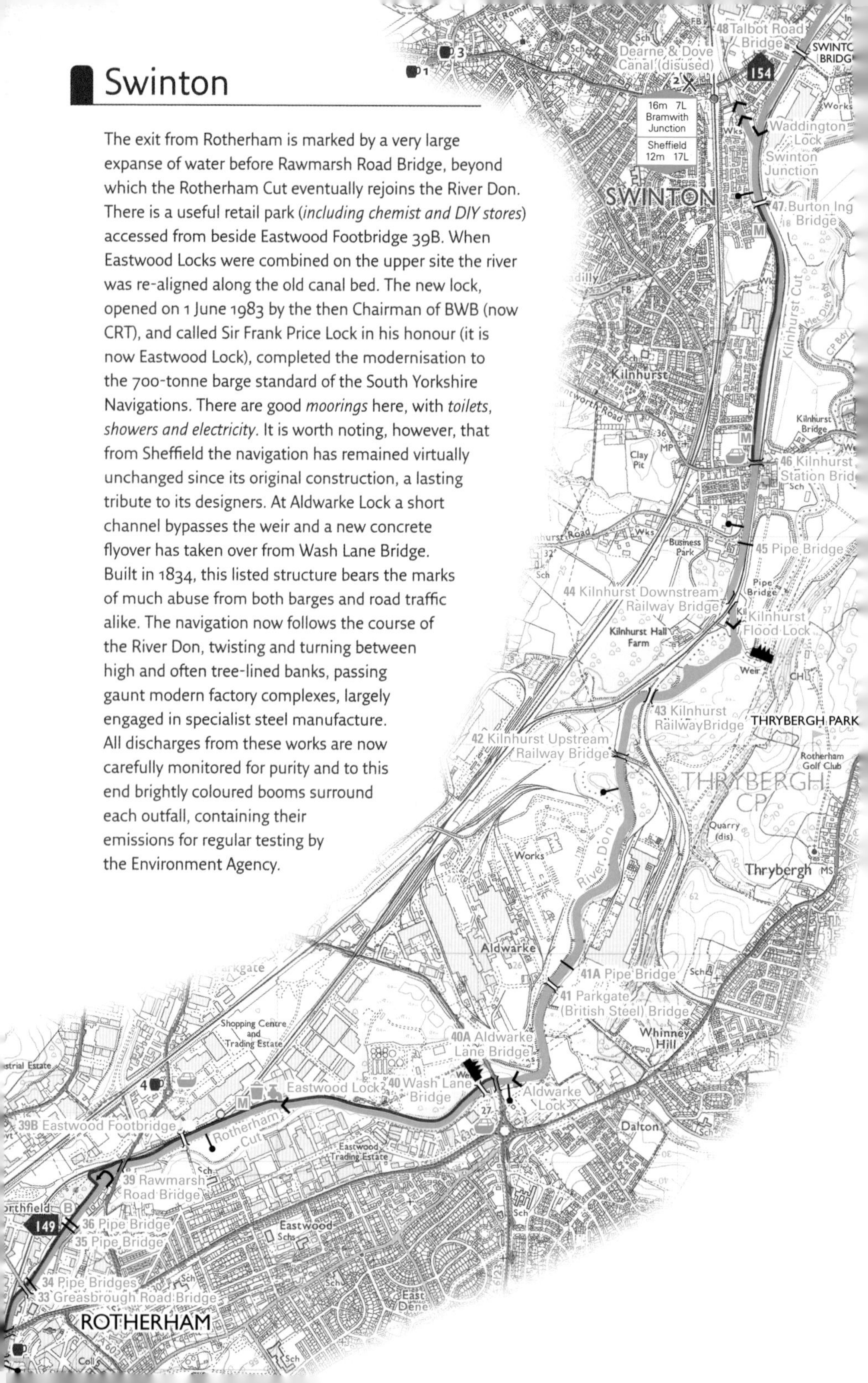

Within recent memory the Don was fast becoming one of the most polluted rivers in Europe, but stringent control measures have reversed this trend and fishing on this stretch of water is now quite popular. Overlooked to the east by Thrybergh Park, it is not at all unpleasant. Kilnhurst Cut is entered at Kilnhurst Flood Lock, where the towpath crosses the river – without the benefit of a bridge, barge horses were obliged to use flat-decked chain ferries. At Hooton Road Bridge there is reasonable *mooring, stores (open long hours) an off-licence and a takeaway.* To the east Hooton Common, criss-crossed with hedges and trees, rises to a more distant skyline. Once a tar works and a colliery lined the left bank, the former receiving the bulk of its deliveries by barge from local town gas works, before natural gas made these plants redundant. At Swinton Junction, the remains of the Dearne & Dove Canal climbs the locks off the mainline towards Barnsley. Waddington's boats throng the junction in a jumble of boilers, pipes and cranes, using the first pounds of the closed canal as a dry dock. The lock on the main line here was renamed Waddington Lock in recognition of the contribution that E.V. Waddington's barges once made to the life of the navigation.

NAVIGATIONAL NOTES

There is currently regular oil traffic on the South Yorkshire Navigations to Rotherham, operating once or twice a week. Stone loaded from Cadeby Quarry (*see* map page 155) is also transported along the waterway. Therefore, moor only at recognised mooring sites, using fixed rings or bollards, and keep a good lookout when underway.

- **Eastwood**
  S. Yorks. Tel, stores, chemist, butcher, takeaways. A suburb of Rotherham, with an excellent variety of corner shops dotted throughout the streets.
- **Kilnhurst**
  S. Yorks. Tel, stores, takeaway. A nondescript village merging into the conurbation linking Mexborough with Rotherham. Once the site of an ironworks and, more recently, a colliery, both now closed down. It was also known for the production of earthenware pottery.
- **Swinton**
  S. Yorks. PO, tel, chemist, takeaways, fish & chips, garage, station. Once a busy junction and boat building centre, it still forms an interesting canal settlement. Here the Dearne & Dove Canal left the mainline and provided a route to Barnsley and thence via the Barnsley Canal to Wakefield. Together they made up the southern loop of the so-called Yorkshire Ring. Both waterways have long since fallen into disrepair but ambitious plans, by the Barnsley, Dearne & Dove Canals Trust (01924 373866; www.bddct.org.uk) have been mooted to re-open them.
- **Swinton Junction**
  Swinton, Rotherham (www.bddct.org.uk). Here the Dearne & Dove Canal left the mainline and provided a route to Barnsley and thence via the Barnsley Canal to Wakefield. Together they made up the southern loop for the so-called Yorkshire Ring. Both waterways have long since fallen into disrepair but ambitious plans have been mooted to re-open them. Once a busy waterway junction and boat building centre, it still forms an interesting canal settlement, worthy of exploration.

Pubs and Restaurants

1 **The Rockingham Tap** 12 Rockingham Road, Swinton S64 8ED (www.facebook.com/RockinghamTap). Small, cosy micropub serving real ales, tea and coffee, pies and bar snacks. Local breweries take precedence. Dog- and family-friendly, covered patio. *Regular* live music and Wi-Fi. *Open Mon-Wed 13.00-21.00 & Thu-Sun 12.00-23.00 (Sun 22.00).*

2 **Cinamon Indian Restaurant** 24 Station Street, Swinton S64 8PP (01709 578513; www.cinamon-indiancuisine.co.uk). Welcoming restaurant serving authentic Indian cuisine *daily from 17.30-23.00.* Takeaway service.

3 **The Gate Inn** 114 Church Street, Swinton S64 8DQ (01709 571724; www.sizzlingpubs.co.uk/thegateinnswinton). Real ales and food available *all day* in this family orientated pub. Inexpensive children's menu. Quiz *Tue, Thu and Sun*. Beer garden, traditional pub games and sports TV. *Open daily 09.00-23.00.*

4 **The Story Teller** Stadium Way, Parkgate, Rotherham S60 1TG (01709 529383; www.greeneking-pubs.co.uk/pubs/south-yorkshire/story-teller). Family-friendly establishment serving food *daily 12.00-21.00 (Sun 20.30).* Beer garden, sports TV and Wi-Fi. *Open Mon-Sat 11.00-23.00 & Sun 11.30-22.30.*

Conisbrough

The fruits of EU land reclamation grants have been in evidence between Sheffield and here, in the form of both landscaping and tree planting, as the concept of waterways as linear parks comes close to reality. Cadeby Quarry makes regular use of the waterway to transport stone and boaters should be on the look out for barges unloading and manoeuvring immediately to the north of the railway bridge. The canal then passes Sprotbrough Flash, with woodland on the opposite bank. There are attractive *moorings* above Sprotbrough Lock which, being on the river, are prone to flooding after heavy rain.

Boatyards

Ⓑ **Tulleys Marine Services** Boatyard, Northfield Road, Rotherham S60 1RR (01709 836743; www.tulleys-marine.co.uk). D Gas, overnight and long-term mooring, winter storage, slipway, hoist, boat building, boat and engine sales and repairs, toilets, DIY facilities.

Ⓑ **Yorkshire Narrowboats** Nursery Lane, Sprotbrough DN5 7NB (07831 862607; www.yorkshirenarrowboats.com). Boat fitting out, boat hire.

The Earth Centre

In 1990 Jonathan Smales, who was working on an idea for a museum of the millennium, decided that the derelict (though ecologically reclaimed) 400 acre site of Denaby Main Colliery beside the River Don, at Conisbrough, would provide the ideal location. His fundamental plan was to offer visitors fun with an underlying message of sustainable development and regeneration. Ultimately, this was realised in the form of a Planet Earth Gallery, a Wilderness Play Area, a Water and Nature Works and a variety of garden eco-systems funded, in 1995, by a £41.6 million grant from the Millennium Commission, making this one of its Landmark Projects. It was finally completed in May 2001, with more attractions being added as additional grant sources were successfully tapped. Although underpinned by educational visits, initial high visitor numbers were not sustained and in October 2004 it was put into the hands of administrators, prompting the Guardian to observe that: "Following Earth Centre progress was a roller coaster ride of false starts, wild hopes and dashed plans." In 2008 it featured substantially in the re-make of the BBC television series Survivors and again, a year later, in the sequel. Annual care and maintenance costs to Doncaster Council, of £200,000, forced the sale of the site and in March 2011 it was bought by Kingswood. This outdoor education firm have completed a multi £million refurbishment scheme, re-opening the Centre in 2012 as an activity base for school children. They see their scheme forming a natural continuation of the site's heritage as a centre for learning, with a focus on environmental sustainability and already hosts one of Europe's largest solar panels. To the cynical, it can also be viewed as maintaining the site's tradition for effortlessly soaking up large sums of money.

NAVIGATIONAL NOTES

Do not on any account moor in the manoeuvring bay beside the supermarket, immediately north of Double Bridge, as commercial craft require all the available space for navigation at this point.

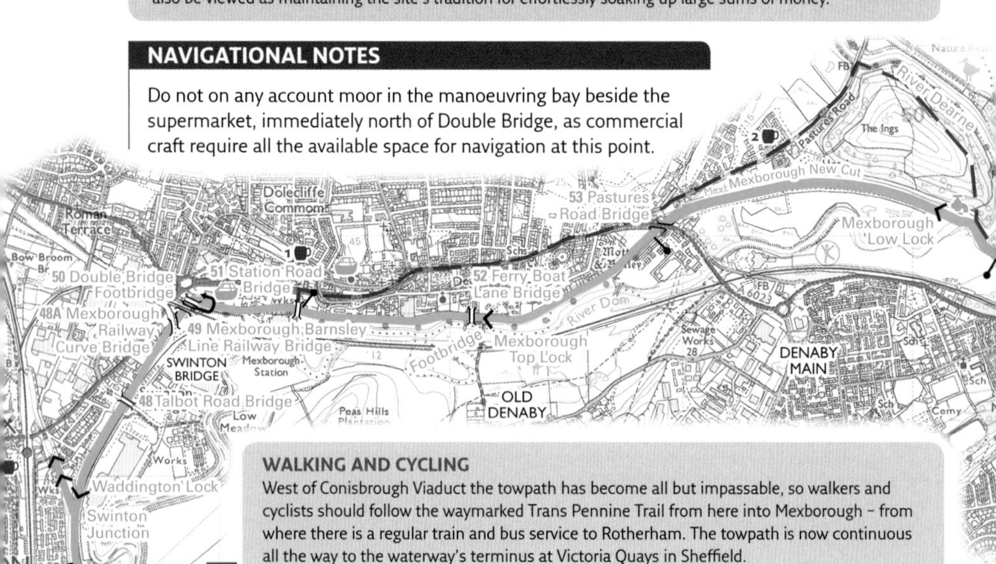

152

WALKING AND CYCLING

West of Conisbrough Viaduct the towpath has become all but impassable, so walkers and cyclists should follow the waymarked Trans Pennine Trail from here into Mexborough – from where there is a regular train and bus service to Rotherham. The towpath is now continuous all the way to the waterway's terminus at Victoria Quays in Sheffield.

Pubs and Restaurants

1 The Concertina Band Club 9a Dolcliffe Road, Mexborough S64 9AZ (01709 580841). North of Station Road Bridge, *The Tina* as it is affectionately known locally, serves its own real ale (amongst others) brewed in the cellar beneath the bar. This unique establishment was home to a concertina band for many years. Pool room and pub games. Dogs welcome and patio beer garden. *Open daily L and E.*

2 Pastures Lodge Pastures Road, Mexborough S64 0JJ (01709 579599; www.pastureslodge.co.uk). A large hotel, featuring well-known entertainers and bands, dispensing real ale and food *daily 11.45-21.00 (Fri-Sat 21.30).* Family-friendly, indoor and outdoor playgrounds. Wi-Fi. B&B. *Open 11.00-23.30 (Sun 23.00).*

3 The Cadeby Pub and Restuarant Main Street, Cadeby, Doncaster DN5 7SW (01709 864009; www.cadebyinn.com). Fine village pub, with open fires, in a converted farmhouse. Serves real ale and a wide range of food *Mon-Sat L and E & Sun 12.00-18.00.* Real cider. Family-friendly, garden. Newspapers, sports TV and Wi-Fi. *Open 11.00-23.00.*

4 The Boat Inn 1 Nursery Lane, Sprotbrough, Doncaster DN5 7NB (01302 858500; www.vintageinn.co.uk). Former coaching house, where Sir Walter Scott reputedly wrote Ivanhoe, this hostelry now serves real ale and food *all day.* Open fires *in winter,* courtyard eating *in summer.* Dog- and child-friendly. *Open Mon-Sat 11.30-23.00 (Sat 11.00) & Sun 11.00-22.30.*

5 The Ivanhoe Melton Road, Sprotbrough, Doncaster DN5 7NS (01302 853130). ½ mile from the river at the top of the village. Lively, comfortable pub overlooking the cricket Pitch. Real ale. Garden and traditional pub games. *Open Mon-Thu L and E, Fri-Sat 11.30-23.00 & Sun 12.00-22.30.*

- **Mexborough**
  S. Yorks. All services. The tiny church of St John the Baptist has a 13th-C tower arch. Gardens and a fine reconstructed archway face the canal.
- **Conisbrough**
  S. Yorks. All services. A relatively attractive town.
  Conisbrough Castle Castle Hill, Conisbrough, Doncaster DN12 3BU (01709 863329; www.conisbroughcastle.org.uk). A Norman castle - c.1185 - with a circular keep capped by a conical wooden roof, superbly sited 90ft above the River Don. Excellent visitor Centre. *Opening times vary throughout the year* so telephone or visit the website for details. Shop. Charge.
- **Sprotbrough**
  S. Yorks. PO, tel, stores, chemist, baker. A useful source of provisions as the stores are *open Mon-Sat 06.00-22.00 & Sun 07.00-21.00.* Sir Walter Scott is reputed to have written part of *Ivanhoe* here. The church of St Mary dates from the 13th C, and is well worth a visit. In the chancel floor are brasses to William Fitzwilliam, 1474, who left £40 towards the building of the church tower.

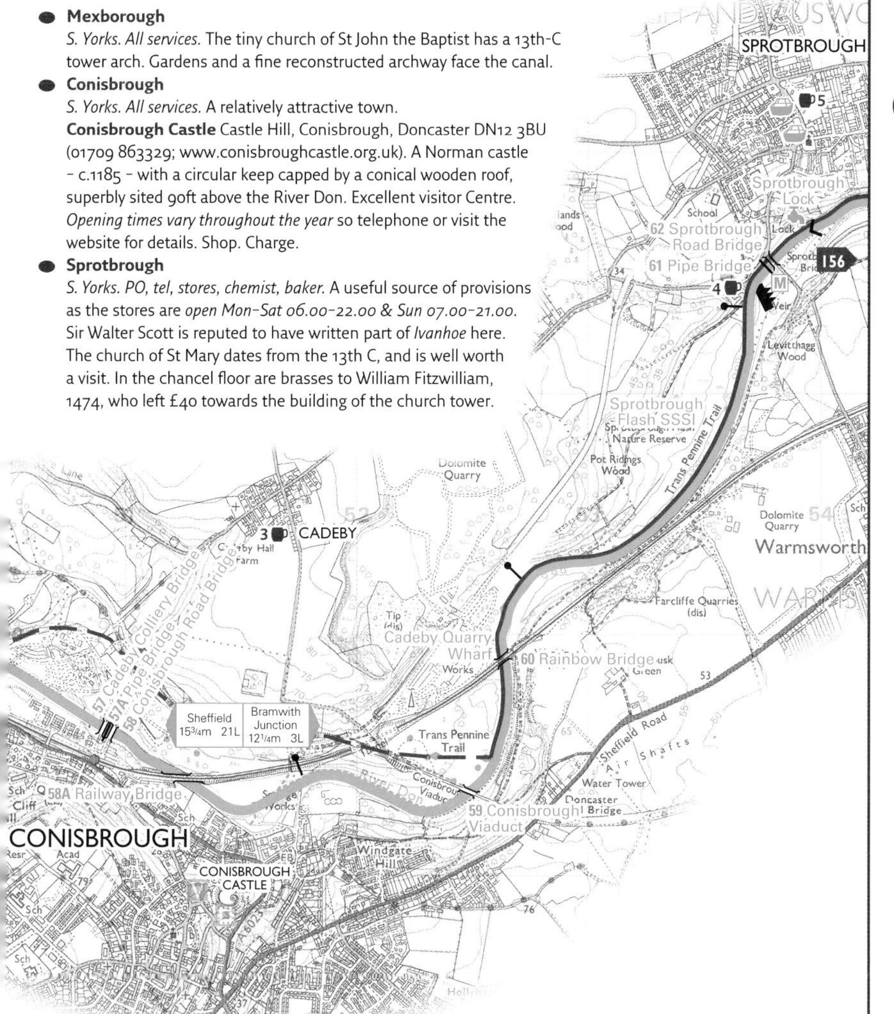

Doncaster

The waterway now enters a pleasant tree-lined valley, only briefly intruded upon by the noise of motorway traffic crossing overhead on the slender Don viaduct. Passing beneath two iron-girdered railway bridges, the waterway sweeps around wide bends towards Doncaster. Just before Doncaster Town Lock the navigation finally parts company with the River Don, although the river is never far away for many miles to come. Ahead lies a jumble of transport systems as road crosses railway, which in turn crosses the canal, all just beyond Doncaster Town Lock. Then the navigation is in Doncaster, widening out opposite the church. The town centre is a short walk to the east, where there is a large *market place*, with some excellent seafood stalls, and the expansive Frenchgate Shopping Centre and a *supermarket*. There is a *laundrette* in Beckett Road, 5 minutes' walk to the west. As you leave the town, factories sprawl around the outside sweep of a wide bend, while all the time the River Don hugs the left-hand bank, obscured by flood embankments. There is little of interest between the centre of Doncaster and Long Sandall Lock, with its tower-shaped control cabin looking down on manicured lawns and neat flower beds. There is a *picnic site* and a self-operated *pump out* here. Dickens stayed in Long Sandall in 1857 and described nearby Doncaster as being thronged with 'horse-mad, betting-mad, drunken-mad, vice-mad crowds'. Some say the area is quieter now.

Pubs and Restaurants

There is a wide range of pubs in Doncaster, suiting all tastes. These are a selection close to the navigation:

1 The Corner Pin 145 Saint Sepulchre Gate West, Doncaster DN1 3AH (01302 340670; www.facebook.com/pages/category/Beer-Bar/Corner-Pin-109566590525498). Close to the town centre, behind the station, this popular pub serves a range of real ales (often from local micro-breweries). Dog- and child-friendly *(until 17.00)* outside seating area. Traditional pub games, newspapers, sports TV and Wi-Fi. *Open daily 12.00-23.00 (Sun 00.00).*

2 The Red Lion 37-38 Market Place, Doncaster DN1 1NH (01302 732120; www.jdwetherspoon.com/pubs/all-pubs/england/south-yorkshire/the-red-lion-doncaster). A lively pub, one wall devoted to depicting winners and jockeys in the post-war St Leger, serving a wide range of real ales, real cider and food *07.00-23.00*. Family-friendly, courtyard seating. Traditional pub games, sports TV and Wi-Fi. B&B. *Open Mon-Sat 07.00-00.00 (Fri-Sat 01.00) & Sun 07.00-23.30.*

3 Doncaster Brewery Tap 7 Young Street, Doncaster DN1 3EL (01302 376436; www.facebook.com/donnybrewery). Devoid of TV and loud video games, this hostelry encourages conversation and the quaffing of their range of excellent real ales, together with a perry and several real ciders. Dog-friendly. Traditional pub games, newspapers and Wi-Fi. *Open Tue-Thu 17.00-23.00 & Fri-Sun 12.00-23.00 (Sun 17.00).*

4 Tut 'n' Shive 6 West Laith Gate, Doncaster DN1 1SF (01302 360300; www.greeneking-pubs.co.uk/pubs/south-yorkshire/tut-n-shive). Good ales and fine company feature in profusion in this friendly local, handy for the canal. Outside seating. Newspapers, sports TV and Wi-Fi. *Open Mon-Sat 11.00-23.00 (Fri-Sat 00.00) & Sun 12.00-23.00.*

5 The Plough 8 West Laith Gate, Doncaster DN1 1SF (01302 738310; www.facebook.com/TheLittlePlough). Featured in CAMRA's National Inventory of Historic Pub Interiors, the décor of this hostelry – known locally as The Little Plough – dates from 1934. Today it serves real ales *11.00-23.00 (Fri-Sun 00.00)* together with outside seating, traditional pub games, real fires, sports TV and Wi-Fi.

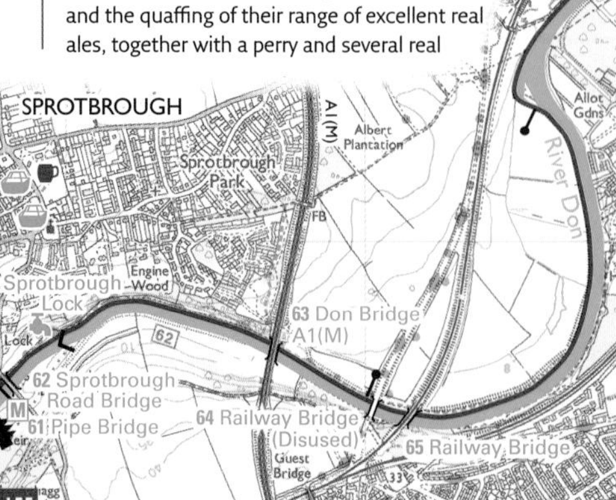

WALKING AND CYCLING

Details of walks in the Doncaster area can be found at www.doncaster.gov.uk/maps/walking-map while details of the local Walking Festival are available at www.getdoncastermoving.org/walking. There are usually more than 20 organised walks, such as the 4-mile Sprotbrough and Cusworth Millennium Walk, a stroll round Highfields Country park and the more challenging Beating the Bounds walk. From Long Sandall Lock walkers and cyclists should follow the waymarked signs to complete their journey into Doncaster.

NAVIGATIONAL NOTES

Long Sandall Lock: When locking upstream keep away from the top gates to avoid excessive turbulence. Similarly, boats below the lock should keep well clear of the bottom gates when it is emptying. This applies to Sykehouse Lock as well.

● **Doncaster**
S. Yorks. All services. Once the site of a Roman station - Danum - the town became an important industrial centre in the 19th C; the home of a large railway and carriage works and ringed by a girdle of mining villages. Exploited for almost a century, the pits of the South Yorkshire Coalfield yielded open-cast coal to the west, whilst to the east of a dividing ridge of magnesian limestone, deep mines were sunk. In the early part of the 19th C, when the town was largely an agricultural community straddling the Great North Road, its High Street was regarded as the finest along the route between London and Edinburgh. Alas, most of the buildings of the last 50 years pay little regard to the original character. One consistent link with the past is, however, provided by the annual St Leger horse race, first run in 1776, and pre-dating the Derby by two years. There is a large market to the east of the canal.

Parish Church of St George (Doncaster Minster) Church Street, Doncaster DN1 1RD (01302 323748; www.doncasterminster.org). Built to a design by George Gilbert Scott in 1858 on an almost cathedral scale (the crossing tower is fully 170ft tall), it replaced a medieval church burnt down in 1853. A very fine example of Victorian Neo-Gothic. *Open to visitors Mon-Fri 10.30-15.30; Sat 11.00-14.00 & Sun for services.*

Mansion House 45 High Street, Doncaster DN1 1BN (01302 734032; www.doncaster.gov.uk). An impressive civic building designed by James Paine and finished in 1748. *Open Apr-Dec roughly twice a month*; for afternoon tea *monthly* and the *occasional* tea dance. Details and tickets for the Tourist Information Centre. Otherwise by appointment (made via the number above).

Doncaster Museum and Art Gallery Chequer Road, Doncaster DN1 2AE (01302 734293; www.doncaster.gov.uk). Opened in 1964, it contains relics from the Roman station, early town documents, costumes, paintings, ceramics and silver, archaeological and natural history displays, and the regimental collection of the King's Own Yorkshire Light Infantry. *Open Wed-Fri 10.00-16.30 & Sat-Sun 10.30-16.00.* Free.

Cusworth Hall, Museum and Park Back Lane, Doncaster DN5 7TU (01302 782342; www.doncaster.gov.uk). The Georgian house (rebuilt and then altered by James Paine in the 1740s) set in landscaped parkland, contains a museum which illustrates South Yorkshire's history, industries, agriculture and social life. Shop and tea rooms. *Open Mon-Wed 10.00-16.30 & Sat-Sun 10.30-16.15.* Charge.

Brodsworth Hall and Gardens Brodsworth, Doncaster DN5 7XJ (01302 722598; www.english-heritage.org.uk/visit/places/brodsworth-hall-and-gardens). About 5 miles north west of Doncaster, off the A635, and worth the effort. A rare example of a Victorian country house which has survived, largely unaltered, with much of its original furnishings and decorations intact. It was built during the 1860s, and retains a faded grandeur which speaks of an opulent past. The gardens are delightful. *Open Apr-Oct, Tue-Sun 13.00-16.30.* Gardens *open 10.00-17.00;* winter gardens *only 11.00-16.00.* Charge. Tearoom and shop. Telephone 01709 515151; or visit www.travelsouthyorkshire.com for details of buses from Doncaster.

Tourist Information Centre 1 Priory Place, Doncaster DN1 1BN (01302 734309; www.visitdoncaster.com). *Open Mon-Fri 09.30-17.00 & Sat 10.00-15.30.*

Stainforth

At Sandall Grove there is a tiny, though delightful, hotch potch of a church, nestling beside a farmyard, beyond which Barnby Dun comes into view. There is a *shower block* with facilities for the disabled at this pretty village.

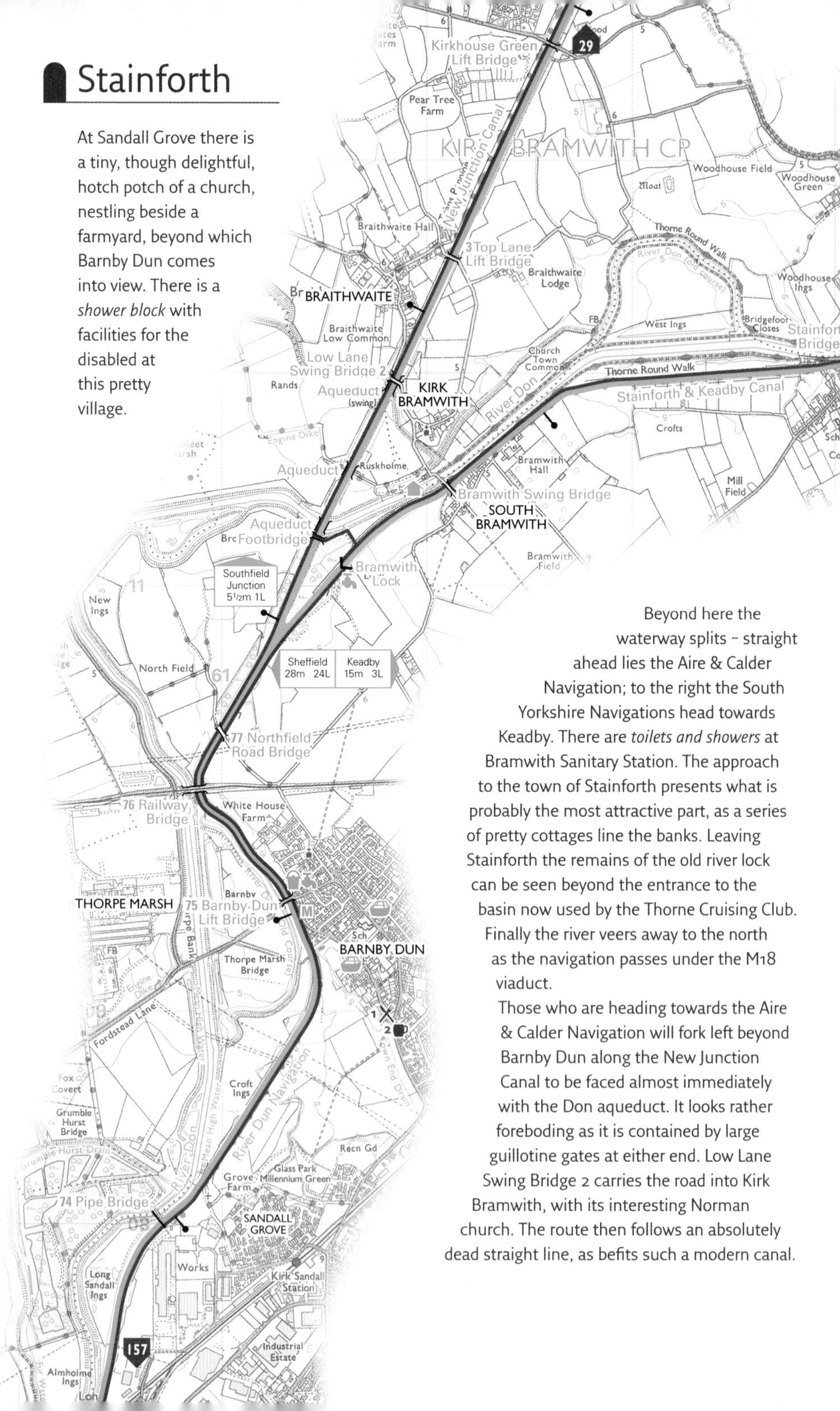

Beyond here the waterway splits – straight ahead lies the Aire & Calder Navigation; to the right the South Yorkshire Navigations head towards Keadby. There are *toilets and showers* at Bramwith Sanitary Station. The approach to the town of Stainforth presents what is probably the most attractive part, as a series of pretty cottages line the banks. Leaving Stainforth the remains of the old river lock can be seen beyond the entrance to the basin now used by the Thorne Cruising Club. Finally the river veers away to the north as the navigation passes under the M18 viaduct.

Those who are heading towards the Aire & Calder Navigation will fork left beyond Barnby Dun along the New Junction Canal to be faced almost immediately with the Don aqueduct. It looks rather foreboding as it is contained by large guillotine gates at either end. Low Lane Swing Bridge 2 carries the road into Kirk Bramwith, with its interesting Norman church. The route then follows an absolutely dead straight line, as befits such a modern canal.

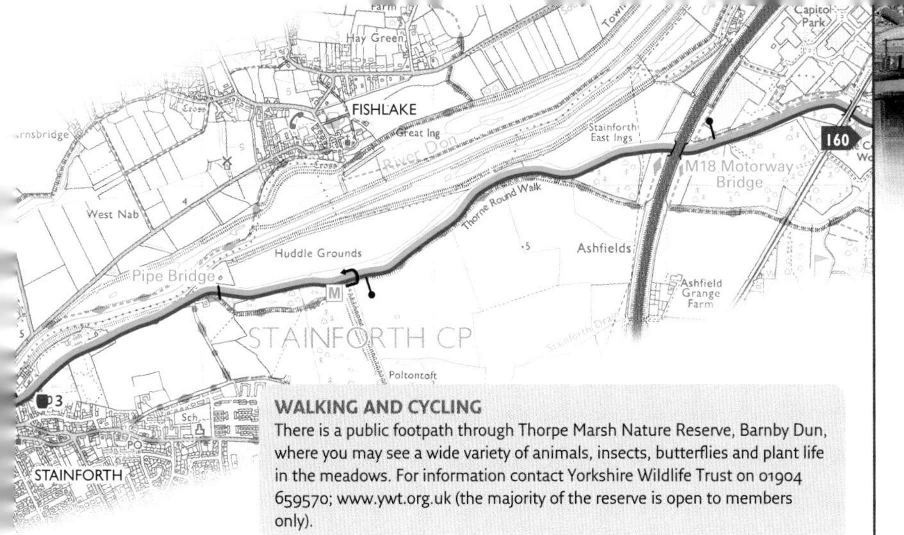

WALKING AND CYCLING

There is a public footpath through Thorpe Marsh Nature Reserve, Barnby Dun, where you may see a wide variety of animals, insects, butterflies and plant life in the meadows. For information contact Yorkshire Wildlife Trust on 01904 659570; www.ywt.org.uk (the majority of the reserve is open to members only).

Barnby Dun

S. Yorks. PO, tel, stores, chemist, butcher, baker, off-licence, farm shop, takeaways, fish & chips. An attractive village laid out along one side of the canal on slightly rising ground. Once a picturesque mix of old cottages, more recent infilling threatens to overpower the original village and turn it into a Doncaster suburb. It is reported that the once boggy marshland around the village yielded a surprising find: the vertebrae of a whale. From the Lift Bridge (*toilets and showers*) a walk along the street, which almost parallels the canal, will be rewarded by an excellent *farm shop* selling fresh local produce, a *Thai restaurant* and a *pub*. The church of St Peter and St Paul is a virtually intact example of 14th-C work, with some remarkable gargoyles. It is well worth a visit. The shop is *open daily 07.00-21.00.*

Stainforth

S. Yorks. All services - station 1 mile distant. An unprepossessing town strung out along the main road south of the canal.

NAVIGATIONAL NOTES

1. All locks and moveable bridges can be boater-operated using a CRT Watermate key.
2. A windlass is needed to operate Bramwith Lock.
3. Bramwith Lock has two chambers. Check to see whether in fact the lock is in use before operating.

Pubs and Restaurants

1 **Amazing Thai Restaurant** Top Road, Barnby Dun, Doncaster DN3 1BD (07760 284598; www.amazingthairestaurant.co.uk). The interior presents a striking contrast with the typical pub exterior, enhanced by the warmth of the welcome from the friendly, helpful staff who are happy to assist you in your choice of dishes, which are prepared from herbs and spices imported directly from growers in Thailand. Children welcome. *Open Tue-Sun 17.30-22.30 & B. Hol Mon.*

2 **The Olive Bar & Grill** 1-3 Station Road, Barnby Dun DN3 1HA (01302 891403; www.olivebarandgrill.co.uk). Contemporary eatery and bar with a menu that includes burgers, salads and steaks cooked on volcanic rocks. *Open Mon-Thu 15.00-22.00 & Fri-Sun 12.00-23.00 (Sun 21.00).*

3 **The New Inn** New Inn Lane, Southbank, Stainforth DN7 5AW (01302 618591; www.facebook.com/New-Inn-468444669843763). Overlooking the Stainforth & Keadby Canal, just east of Stainforth Bridge, this recently refurbished hostelry dispenses real ales and food *Mon-Thu L and E; Fri-Sat 12.00-20.00 & Sun 12.00-16.00.* Family-friendly, garden, and moorings. Live music, sports TV and Wi-Fi. *Open 12.00-23.00 (Fri-Sat 00.30).*

NEW JUNCTION CANAL

This waterway, completed in 1905, provides a link between the South Yorkshire Navigations and the Aire & Calder Navigation. It is 5½ miles long and completely straight all the way, the monotony being broken only by a series of swing and lift bridges. There are aqueducts at each end of the long corridor formed by the navigation, the one in the south carrying the canal over the River Don. The Don Aqueduct is equipped with tall guillotine gates, which serve either to isolate the canal in times of flood, or to facilitate repairs. Moorings are available beside Sykehouse Lock and Sykehouse Lift Bridge but there are no facilities. (*see* page 29).

Thorne

Staniland Marina, immediately beyond the railway bridge, provides both safe *moorings* and a range of *services*, Thorne town centre being only 1/4 mile away. Beyond Thorne Bridge there are further *moorings*, available to visitors, at the marina. On leaving the town the landscape again opens up and a rich, fertile plain borders the navigation. Boaters will no doubt enjoy operating Wykewell Lift Bridge, which, together with the road barriers and flashing red lights, is controlled by pressing the appropriate buttons in the grey box. At Moores Swing Bridge a line of farms can be seen to the north of the canal. Here there is still evidence of the old strip system of farming, where each dwelling is backed by a long narrow strip of land. These units of land would vary in size according to the type of soil and the lie of the land. The one-acre strip (220yds long by 22yds wide) was a rarity in most parts of the country, farms generally possessing strips much smaller than this. Much of the land along the length of the navigation from Stainforth to Keadby was prone to seasonal flooding and consequently benefited greatly from the drainage schemes established during

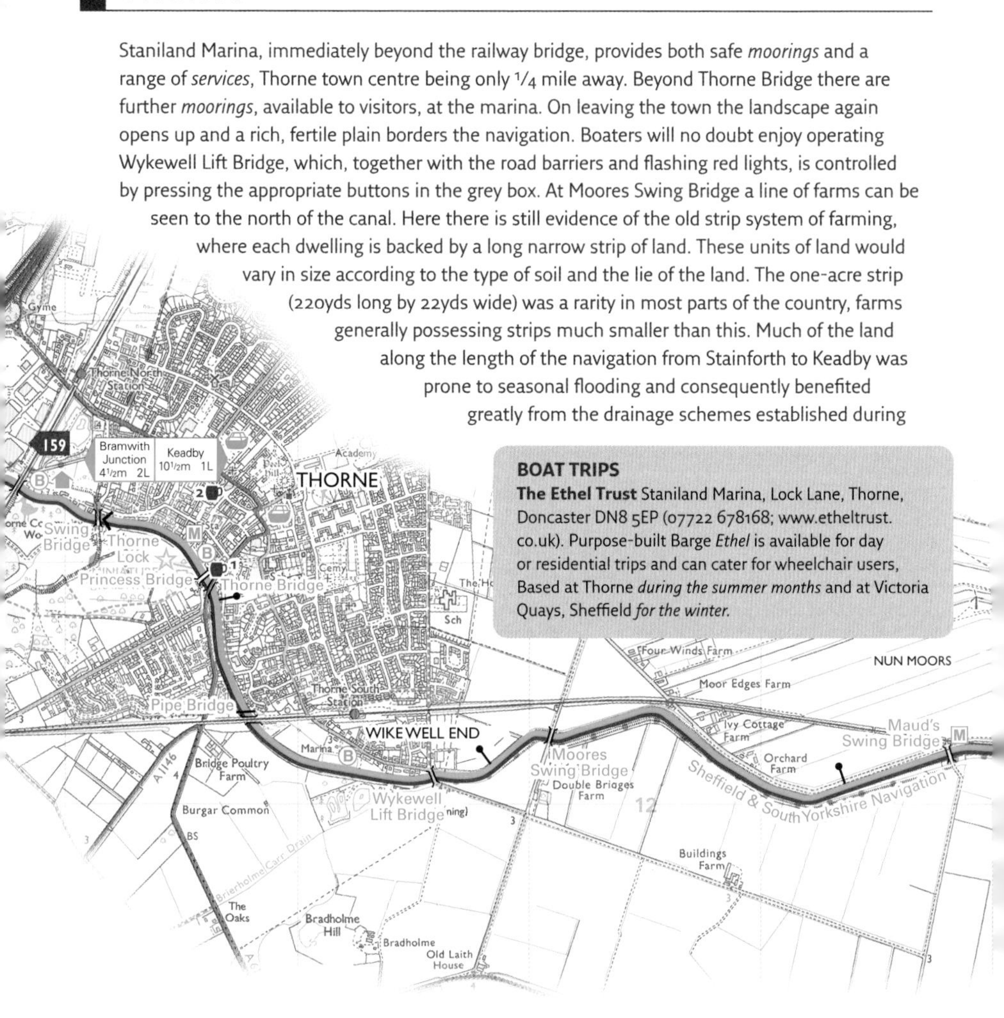

BOAT TRIPS

The Ethel Trust Staniland Marina, Lock Lane, Thorne, Doncaster DN8 5EP (07722 678168; www.etheltrust.co.uk). Purpose-built Barge *Ethel* is available for day or residential trips and can cater for wheelchair users. Based at Thorne *during the summer months* and at Victoria Quays, Sheffield *for the winter.*

Thorne

S. Yorks. All services. A small brick-built market town with an attractive pedestrian precinct around Finkle Street. Thorne's early industries were rope making, sacking and weaving with a canal traffic of coal, pig iron and stone. The town was in fact dependent on the river and the canal for its water supply, the only boreholes supplying Darley's brewery and the workhouse. Regettably the brewery ceased to function as such in 1986. St Nicholas' church displays a variety of 13th-C work, including the south doorway and an unbuttressed west tower.

Pubs and Restaurants

There are many pubs in Thorne. The following are right by the navigation:

1 The Canal Tavern South Parade, Thorne, Doncaster DN8 5DZ (01405 813688; www.canaltavernthorne.co.uk). Canalside at Princess Bridge, serving food *Mon-Sat L and E & Sun L* carvery. Garden. *Open daily 11.00-23.00.*

2 The Windmill Inn 19 Queen Street, Thorne DN8 5AA (01405 812866). Friendly community pub serving real ales which usually includes one from a local brewery. Large beer garden. Dogs welcome in conservatory. Traditional pub games, sports TV and Wi-Fi. *Open Mon-Sat 14.00 & Sun 12.00.*

the 17th C. Herons abound in this area, and grebe can also be seen along the more overgrown sections of the waterway, where their floating nests are anchored to the reeds. Only 100 years ago these birds had been all but exterminated in England due to fashionable Victorian ladies wishing to display not just the odd feather, but occasionally the entire plumage, in their hats. At Maud's Bridge, again boater-operated, instructions for its operation are to be found on the white box. Now the railway adds some excitement by joining the canal and running along the north bank to Medge Hall and Crook o'Moor Swing Bridge, where it moves briefly away only to rejoin the line of the navigation at Godnow Bridge.

Boatyards

Ⓑ **Staniland Marina** Lock Hill, Thorne DN8 5EP (01405 816992; www.stanilandmarina.co.uk). D Pump out, gas, overnight and long-term mooring, winter storage, slipway, hoist, boat sales and repairs, chandlery, toilets, showers, laundrette, DIY facilities. Clubhouse bar with restaurant. Marina *open Mon-Sat 09.00-17.00 & Sun 10.00-16.00*. Clubhouse *open Wed-Fri 18.00-00.00 & Sat-Sun 12.00-00.00.*

Ⓑ **Thorne Boat Services** South Parade, Thorne, Doncaster DN8 5DZ (01405 814197; www.thorneboatservices.co.uk). (toilets and showers next door) D Pump out gas, boat repairs, engine sales and repairs, chandlery, books and maps. *Emergency call out service.*

Ⓑ **Blue Water Marina** South End, Thorne, Doncaster DN8 5QR (01405 813165; www.bluewatermarina.co.uk). D Pump out, gas, overnight and long-term mooring, slipway, boat sales, toilets, showers, limited chandlery, winter storage, blacking, solid fuel. *Closed Mon-Tue.*

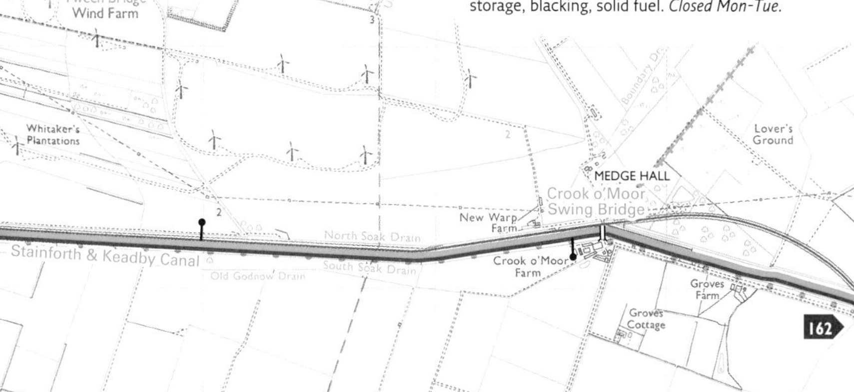

Richard Dunston Ltd

Richard Dunston moved to Thorne, from Torksey on the Trent, in 1858 and set up a boatyard constructing wooden, clinker-built boats on the north bank of the Stainforth & Keady Canal, just below Thorne Lock. His philosophy was one of self-sufficiency so the yard made everything from blocks, masts and spars through to boat hooks, oars and sail covers. He also spawned a thriving rope-making industry in Thorne, producing sheets and halyards in coir, manilla, hemp and cotton for rigging the sailing barges of the time. He valued the local timber, sawn by hand, in the construction of his vessels, some of which carried cargoes of up to 80 tons. Initially clinker built, later designs were of carvel construction and by the end of the C19th his designs had been standardised on the Sheffield Keel and the Humber Sloop, the latter able to carry nearer 100 tons. Richard was succeeded by his son Thomas, who died in 1910, and control of what was then a thriving yard passed to his 20 year old son, who wasted little time in steering production into the then, new field of iron and steel fabrication. Keadby Lock - at 22' 6" wide - together with the depth of the canal, limited the size of craft they could build, so a second yard was acquired in 1932 at Hessle, on the north bank of the Humber, just west of Hull. A great number of very diverse ships were built at the two yards, from Clyde Puffers through to Admiralty tugs. Indeed, at the height of the Second World War they were turning out one tug every six days - producing a total of 159 vessels - having originally pioneered the concept of all-welded ships. The company was sold in 1985 and the Thorne yard was closed down. Shipbuilding continued at Hessle until 1994 when the shipyard went into liquidation.

Keadby

The village of Crowle can be reached from either Godnow Swing Bridge or Crowle Bridge. It is a mile to the north, and is worth the walk since it has a selection of *shops* and *pubs*, and an interesting church. In 1747 the body of a woman was found nearby in the peat moor, buried upright at a depth of 6ft. From her sandals it appeared that she had been there for several centuries, but was remarkably well preserved. Just beyond Crowle Station there is evidence of the site of the old Axholme Joint Railway Bridge, demolished in 1972. The bridge must have proved an impressive landmark, consisting of four brick archways and a circular brick abutment upon which the railway pivoted through 90 degrees, thus allowing the passage of the tall-sailed keels. Ahead lies the long straight to Keadby. It is not without excitement, however, as immediately beyond Vazon Swing Bridge there is a remarkable railway bridge, skewed across the canal only a couple of feet above the water (see page 195 for more details). Built in 1925, the bridge is supposedly one of only three of its kind in Europe. In order to allow the passage of boats, winches slide the bridge deck sideways, so clearing the navigation and, by a further series of wire cables and pulleys, winch the deck back into place. The entire operation is controlled from the nearby signal box. Once beyond the bridge the canal passes the rebuilt Keadby Power Station which, together with the new wind farm, dominates the north bank. Ahead is Keadby Swing Bridge and Lock, allowing entry into the tidal Trent. There are *showers* and *toilets* and *moorings* are available before the swing bridge.

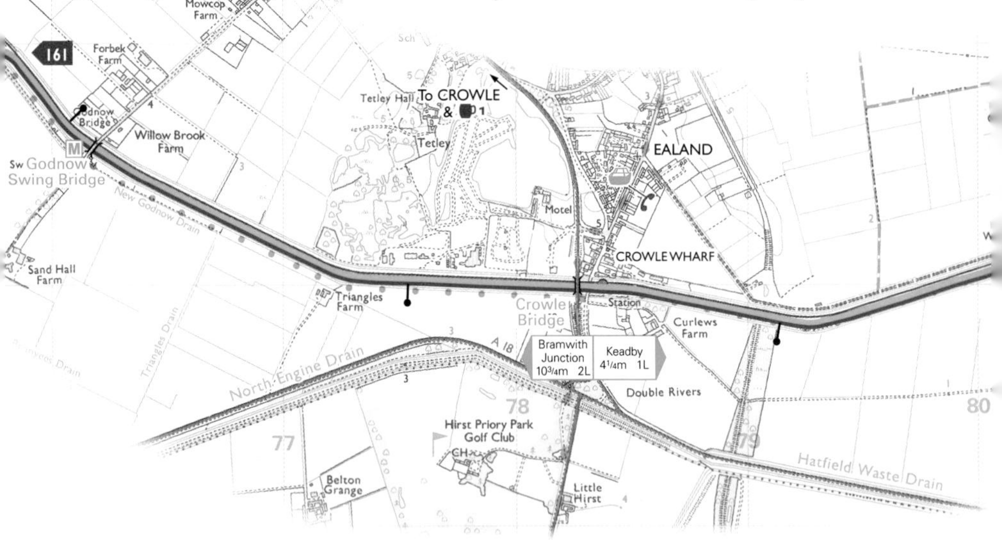

NAVIGATIONAL NOTES

1. Keadby Lock is 77' 8" x 22' 6" although longer craft can be admitted when the tide makes a level. Draught may be limited by the build up of silt at the mouth of the lock.
2. Commercial river traffic operates on VHF Channel 6 upstream of Keadby Bridge on the River Trent. VHF users should monitor this channel to establish the whereabouts of large craft on the river. Keadby Lock operates on channel 74.
3. *See* note 5 on page 196 and notes 2 and 4 on page 193.
4. Toot your horn when approaching Vazon Sliding Railway Bridge. Operational *24 hrs a day*.
5. The lock keeper at Keadby should be contacted on 07733 124611 or 01724 782205 giving *at least 24 hours notice*. If unattended contact CRT on 0303 040 4040.
6. In order to secure your boat safely whilst using Keadby Lock, bow and stern ropes should be at least 25' in length.

- **Crowle**
Humberside. All services - station 1 mile distant beside the waterway. A straggling village one mile north of the canal. There are some attractive Georgian houses in the vicinity of the church. The Market Square retains some of its character and is dominated by the elaborate Victorian façade of the old ballroom, now used for discos. The church of St Oswald is a handsome structure containing much Norman work, and some fine incised doorways. During the restoration of the tower in 1840 an Anglo-Saxon cross shaft, probably inspired by the Vikings and some 7ft in length, was found over a doorway. It is believed to date from the 11th C and now stands at the back of the church.

- **Ealand**
Humberside. PO, tel, stores, off-licence, station. A small settlement next to the canal. There are some pretty cottages in the village, and a station. *Gas* is available from the stores.

- **Keadby**
Humberside. PO, tel, stores, off-licence, fish & chips, station. All facilities are approximately ½ mile south of the lock. A dull settlement which has declined since the Stainforth & Keadby Canal ceased to carry commercial traffic. The only real activity is provided by craft navigating the tidal Trent and the commercial vessels unloading at the river wharfs.

Pubs and Restaurants

There are now no pubs close to this stretch of the waterway and for refreshment the boater must either take a walk or a taxi. However the following hostelries are well worth making the effort for:

1 **The Red Lion** 36 North Street, Crowle DN17 4NE (01724 711611; www.redlioncrowle.co.uk). 1¼ miles north of the canal. Lively village pub serving real ale and incorporating the Spice Village Indian takeaway. Live music, real fires and sports TV. Children welcome. *Open Mon-Thu 12.00-23.30 (Mon-Tue 15.00) & Fri-Sun 12.00-00.00 (Sun 23.30).*

2 **Take A Gander** High Street, Burringham DN17 3NA (01724 639661; www.facebook.com/TAGander). Two miles over the Trent via Keadby Bridge and then turn right - see map on page 197. Describing itself as 'a bar and eatery' this unusually named establishment serves appetising meals based on seasonally available local produce. Majoring on the rustic feel - exposed brick and stonework, a plethora of old oak beams and posts - there is a pleasant ambiance, though currently no real ale. Food is available *Tue-Sat 12.00-20.00 (Fri-Sat 20.30) & Sun 12.00-16.00.*

3 **The Ingleby Arms** Amcotts DN17 4AJ (01724 782385). 2¼ miles: follow the road north along the bank of the Trent. Friendly, welcoming village local serving highly regarded food *Wed E; Thu-Sat L and E & Sun 12.00-21.00.* Children and dogs welcome. Garden and children's play area. *Open Wed-Sat L and E (not Wed L) & Sun 12.00-23.00.*

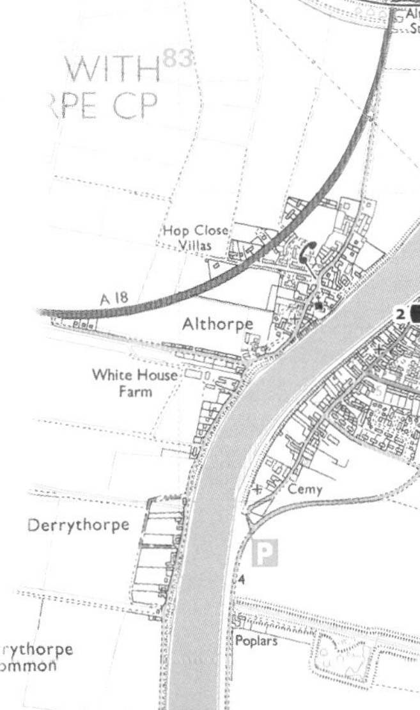

RIVER TRENT

MAXIMUM DIMENSIONS

Shardlow to Meadow Lane Lock, Nottingham
Length: 81'
Beam: 14' 6"
Headroom: 8'

Meadow Lane Lock to Gainsborough
Length: 165'
Beam: 18' 6"
Headroom: 13'

MANAGER

0303 040 4040
enquiries.eastmidlands@canalrivertrust.org.uk

The numbered red markers on the mapping represent the CRT kilometre posts visible along the river bank from Nottingham to Gainsborough.

MILEAGE

DERWENT MOUTH to:
Cranfleet Lock: 2¾ miles
Beeston Lock: 7 miles
Meadow Lane Lock, Nottingham: 12 miles
Gunthorpe Bridge: 22 miles
Fiskerton: 29¾ miles
Newark Castle: 35½ miles
Cromwell Lock: 40½ miles
Dunham Bridge: 53 miles
TORKSEY Junction: 57 miles
Littleborough: 60¼ miles
GAINSBOROUGH Bridge: 67 miles
WEST STOCKWITH: 71¾ miles
KEADBY Junction: 84¼ miles
TRENT FALLS: 93¾ miles

Locks: 12

The River Trent is a historic highway running for about 100 miles from the Midlands to the Humber ports and the North Sea, and has long been of prime economic and social importance to the areas through which it flows. It is thought that as long ago as the Bronze Age the Trent was part of the trade route from the Continent to the metal-working industry in Ireland. The Romans recognised the value of the river as a route to the centre of England from the sea. In about AD 120, in the time of Emperor Hadrian, they built the Foss Dyke canal to link the Trent valley with Lindum Colonia (now Lincoln), the River Witham and the Wash. The Trent later acted as an easy route for the Danish invaders, who penetrated as far as Nottingham. In about AD 924 Edward the Elder expelled the Danes from Nottingham and built the first bridge there. The second bridge at Nottingham was built in 1156 (some 20 years earlier than Old London Bridge) and lasted 714 years. Its remains can still be seen. The third bridge was built in 1871 and forms the basic structure of today's Trent Bridge. The first Act of Parliament to improve the Trent as a navigation was passed in 1699. In 1783 an Act authorised the construction of a towpath, thus allowing for the first time the passage of sail-less barges. Ten years later the Trent Navigation Company's engineer drew up a comprehensive scheme to build locks and weirs, to increase the depth in certain reaches and build a number of training walls to narrow and thus deepen the channel. In 1906, the Royal Commission on Inland Waterways adopted it as the official future plan, authorising locks at Stoke Bardolph, Gunthorpe, Hazleford and Cromwell. The works were completed in 1926. Trade soon increased fourfold.

At its peak in the 19th C and early 20th C, the Trent formed the main artery of trade for the East Midlands, connecting with the South Yorkshire Navigations, the Chesterfield Canal, the Fossdyke, the Grantham Canal, the Erewash Canal, the River Soar Navigation and the Trent & Mersey Canal. Although it remains connected today to all but the Grantham Canal, the large trade between these waterways dwindled away with railway competition and in particular as a result of railway ownership of most of those connecting waterways. Today there is no scheduled commercial carrying from gravel pits along the tidal Trent, although sporadic traffic does penetrate as far up river as Newark bound, largely, for Staythorpe Power Station.

The Trent remain a useful through route for pleasure craft, easy to navigate and with many interesting Connections. Canal & River Trust have improved facilities for pleasure craft with landing stages at locks, moorings and easier lock operating systems.

Thrumpton

Downstream from Derwent Mouth *(see Books 3 and 4)*, the navigation goes through Sawley Cut, avoiding the weir to the north, by the M1 bridge. Near the head of the cut is a flood lock, which under most conditions is open. Beyond this lock and the main road bridge is a wide stretch of waterway, where both banks are crowded with moored boats. Just at the tail of Sawley Locks (a pair - both now mechanised with a keeper in attendance Fri-Mon - 07717 802543) is a large railway bridge over the river which once carried oil and coal trains to Castle Donnington and Willington power stations. There are *recycling facilities* here and at Trent Lock. To the east the cooling towers of the huge Ratcliffe Power Station are clearly visible, but they are discreetly tucked away behind Red Hill and their intrusion into the landscape is thus minimised. Trent Lock marks the junction of the Erewash Canal with the River Trent, while at the wooded Red Hill is the mouth of the River Soar. It is important not to get lost here, for there is a large weir just downstream of the railway bridges. Boats aiming for Nottingham should bear left at the big sailing club house, entering Cranfleet Cut. A pair of protective flood gates will be passed, then another railway bridge (the line disappearing into the decorative tunnel portal through Red Hill), another long line of moored motor cruisers (many belonging to the Nottingham Yacht Club) and an attractive white accommodation bridge. There are *recycling facilities* at Sawley, Trent and Cranfleet Locks. At the end of the cut is Cranfleet Lock; from here one may enjoy a view of the woods hiding Thrumpton Park. The old lock house at Cranfleet is now the headquarters of the Nottingham Yacht Club. Steep wooded slopes rise behind Thrumpton, while the towers of the power station still overlook the whole scene. Below Thrumpton, the river winds through flat land, passing the village of Barton in Fabis.

Pubs and Restaurants (pages 166-167)

1 **The Navigation** 143 London Road, Shardlow DE72 2HA (01332 792918; www.facebook.com/navigationinnshardlow). Built to serve the inland port of Shardlow, this pub now dispenses real ale and food *Mon-Sun E & Sat-Sun L*. Dog- and child-friendly, garden. Real fires and camping. *Open daily 16.00-23.00 (Sat-Sun 12.00).*

2 **The Coffee Kiosk** Sawley Lock House, Sawley NG10 3AD (0115 972 7551). Coffee with a view! Friendly service and a perfect location in which to enjoy tea, coffee, ice-creams, sandwiches and light meals. Dogs welcome. *Open Wed-Sat 11.00-16.30.*

3 **The Plank & Leggit** Tamworth Road, Sawley, Long Eaton NG10 3AD (0115 972 1515; www.hungryhorse.co.uk/pubs/nottinghamshire/plank-leggit). Real ale with food available *Mon-Sat 12.00-22.00 & Sun 11.30-21.00*. Beer garden with indoor and outdoor play areas. Dogs welcome in garden. *Open Mon-Sat 11.00-23.00 & Sun 11.30-22.30.*

4 **Harrington Arms** 392 Tamworth Road, Sawley Long Eaton NG10 3AU (0115 973 2614; www.oldenglishinns.co.uk/our-locations/the-harrington-arms-long-eaton). 400-year-old, heavily beamed pub, 1/4 mile from Sawley Marina, serving an extensive selection of meals *available all day*. Excellent real ale selection. Children welcome, large garden. Newspapers and real fires. *Open daily 11.00-23.00 (Fri-Sat 00.00).*

5 **The Nag's Head** Wilne Road, Sawley, Long Eaton NG10 3AL (0115 973 2983). Village local serving real ale and good value, home-cooked food *L and E*. Dog- and family-friendly. Traditional pub games and newspapers. *Open Mon-Sat 11.00-23.00 (Fri-Sat 00.00) & Sun 12.00-23.00.*

6 **The White Lion** 352 Tamworth Road, Sawley, Long Eaton NG10 3AT (0115 946 3061; www.facebook.com/WhiteLionSawley). Traditional pub games, real ales and real cider. Pizzas *Fri-Sat E*. Children and dogs welcome, garden. No machines. Newspapers, real fires and Wi-Fi. *Open Mon-Fri 14.00-23.30 & Sat-Sun 12.00-23.30.*

7 **The Trent Lock** Lock Lane, Long Eaton NG10 2FY (0115 972 ; www.facebook.com/Thetrentlock). Formerly the Navigation Inn. Large, popular, family pub with a garden and play area. Real ales and food available *all day*. Moorings. *Open daily 12.00-23.00 (Sun 22.30).*

8 **The Steamboat Inn** Lock Lane, Long Eaton NG10 2FY. (0115 946 0356; www.facebook.com/The-Steamboat-Pub-Restaurant-608774959201508). On the Erewash Canal. Built by the canal company in 1791, when it was called the Erewash Navigation Inn, it is now an upmarket canalside pub and restaurant. Real ale available. Food served *L and E*. Dog- and child-friendly, garden. Traditional pub games and camping nearby. *Open 11.00-23.00 (Sat 00.00).*

9 **Lock House Tea Rooms** Lock Lane, Trent Lock, Long Eaton NG10 2FY (0115 972 2288). Chintzy tea rooms with a twist, offering a wide variety of teas and homemade food. Outside seating overlooking the lock. Dogs welcome. *Open Wed-Sun from 10.00; closing times vary from 16.00 to 18.00 depending on the day and season.*

● **Sawley**
Notts. PO, tel, stores, takeaways, fish & chips, baker station (Long Eaton). The tall church spire attracts one across the river to Sawley, and in this respect the promise is fulfiled, for the medieval church is beautiful and is approached by a formal avenue of lime trees leading to the 600-year-old doorway. Otherwise Sawley is an uninteresting main road village on the outskirts of Long Eaton.

● **Sawley Cut**
In addition to a large marina and a well-patronised mooring site, the Derby Motor Boat Club have a base on the Sawley Cut. All kinds of boats are represented here: canal boats, river boats and even seagoing vessels. It is certainly no place to be passing through on a summer Sunday late-afternoon, for there will be scores of craft queuing up to pass through the locks after spending the weekend downstream.

● **Trent Lock**
A busy and unusual boating centre at the southern terminus of the Erewash Canal *(see Book 3)*. There are two boatyards, two pubs and a tearoom here.

● **Thrumpton**
Notts. Tel. This little village beside the Trent is, like so many other places on the river, a dead end.

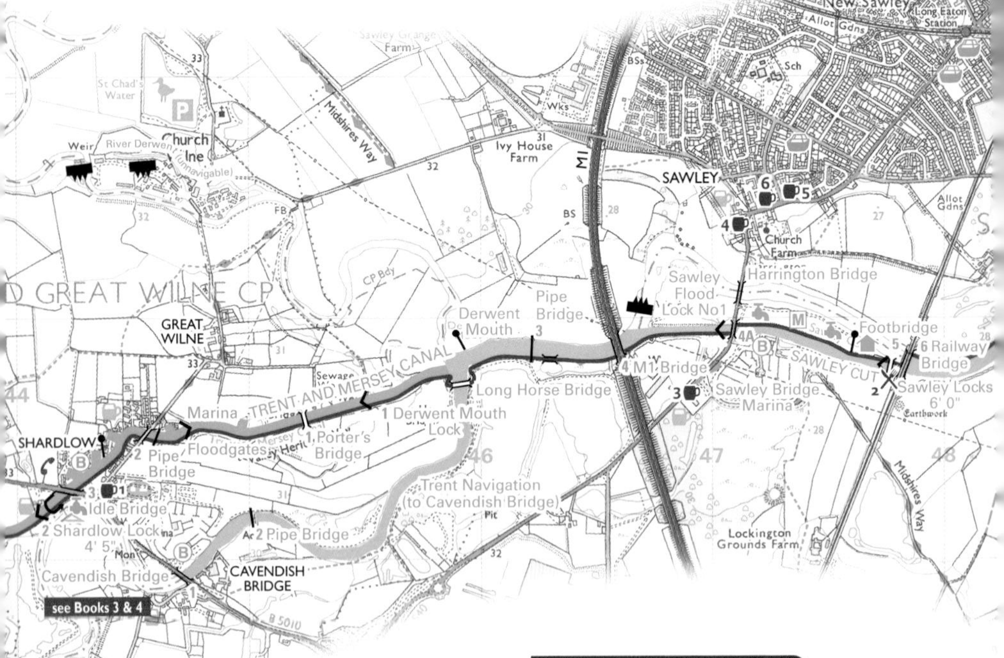

Motorists only go there if they have good reason to. Hence Thrumpton is a quiet and unspoilt farming village, with new development only up at the far end. Although the impressive Hall is hidden away at the west end of the village, its large uncompromising gateway serves to remind the villagers what they are there for. The tiny church, with its narrow nave and a tower, was built in the 13th C but restored in 1872 by the well-known architect G.E. Street, at the expense of Lady Byron. The single street winds past it down to the river – there used to be a ferry here.

Thrumpton Hall Thrumpton NG11 0AX (0115 983 0410/07796 956556; www.thrumptonhall.com). Basically a James I mansion built around a much older manor house. The Hall is famous for its oak staircase, which dates from the time of Charles II. The ground-floor rooms are well-used, and elegantly decorated; the grounds are delightful, encompassing a backwater off the River Trent. The house is private and used as a wedding location. Gardens *open Wed 11.00–15.00* but telephone in advance to confirm.

● **Barton in Fabis**
Notts. Tel. A small and isolated village, composed mainly of modern housing and set well back from the river. The 14th-C church seems unbalanced in several respects; it has a great variety of styles. The building has, however, considerable charm, being light, and attractively irregular. It contains several monuments to the Sacheverell family.

Boatyards

Ⓑ✕**Redhill Marine Ltd** Redhill Marina, Ratcliffe on Soar, Nottingham NG11 0EB (01509 672770; www.redhill-marine.co.uk). Gas, overnight and long-term mooring, winter storage, crane, slipway, hoist, boat sales and repairs, engine sales and repairs, boat refurbishment, chandlery, DIY facilities, toilets, general store, café, camping.

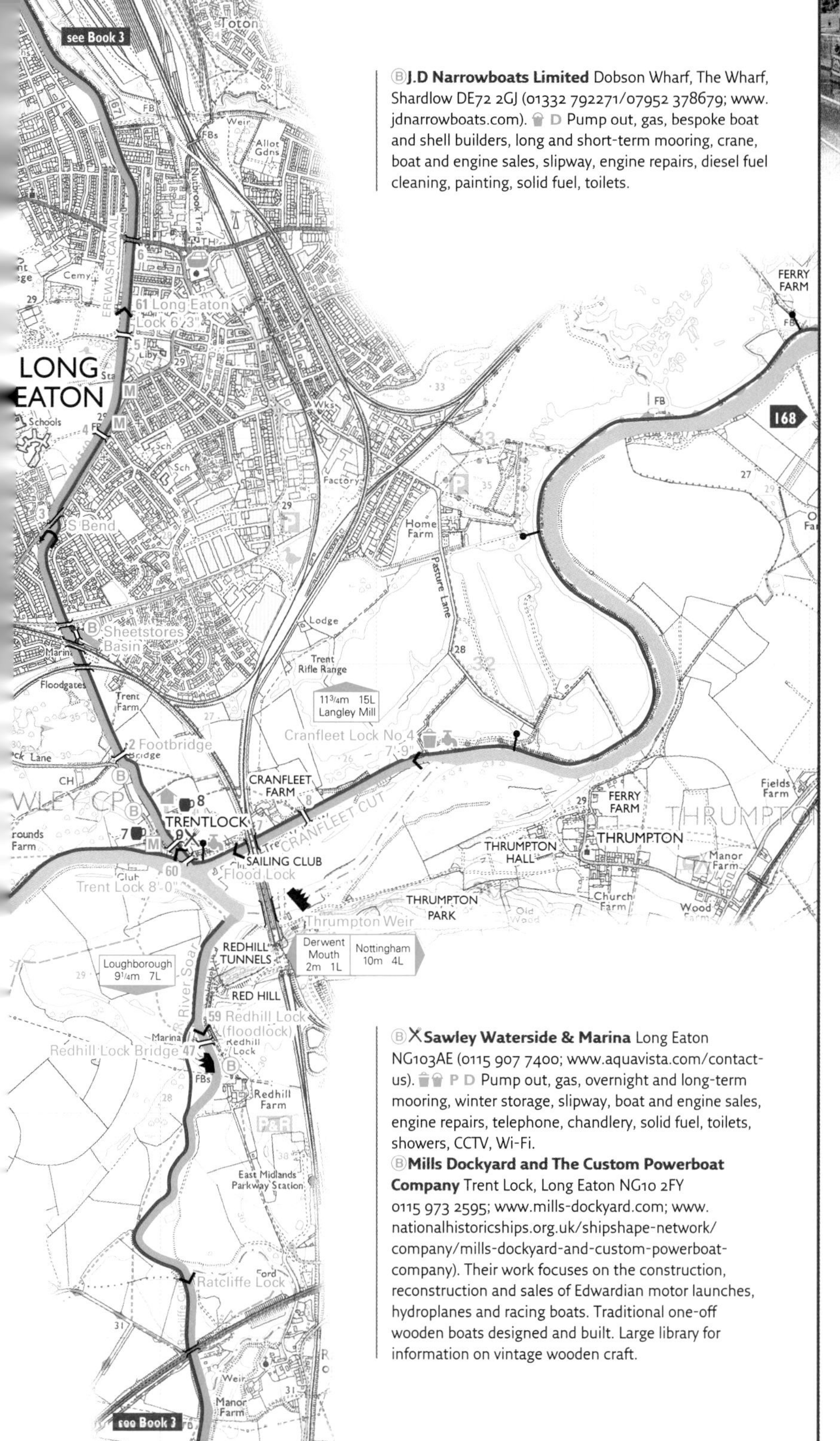

Ⓑ **J.D Narrowboats Limited** Dobson Wharf, The Wharf, Shardlow DE72 2GJ (01332 792271/07952 378679; www.jdnarrowboats.com). D Pump out, gas, bespoke boat and shell builders, long and short-term mooring, crane, boat and engine sales, slipway, engine repairs, diesel fuel cleaning, painting, solid fuel, toilets.

Ⓑ **Sawley Waterside & Marina** Long Eaton NG103AE (0115 907 7400; www.aquavista.com/contact-us). P D Pump out, gas, overnight and long-term mooring, winter storage, slipway, boat and engine sales, engine repairs, telephone, chandlery, solid fuel, toilets, showers, CCTV, Wi-Fi.

Ⓑ **Mills Dockyard and The Custom Powerboat Company** Trent Lock, Long Eaton NG10 2FY 0115 973 2595; www.mills-dockyard.com; www.nationalhistoricships.org.uk/shipshape-network/company/mills-dockyard-and-custom-powerboat-company). Their work focuses on the construction, reconstruction and sales of Edwardian motor launches, hydroplanes and racing boats. Traditional one-off wooden boats designed and built. Large library for information on vintage wooden craft.

Nottingham

The river winds on towards Nottingham passing the picturesque Barton Island (keep to the west of it), the old gravel pits of the Attenborough Nature Reserve and many sailing boats; this is clearly a popular stretch of the river. To the south runs a ridge of hills on which stands Clifton Hall. At the marina you should keep to the north side of the river to avoid the weir and enter Beeston Lock (where there are *showers* and *toilets*). This introduces the Beeston Canal or Beeston Cut which bypasses an unnavigable section of the River Trent. The canal passes first a housing estate and then Boots Estate, followed by Players' Horizon Factory designed by Arup Associates. East of the A52 bridge, the canal passes Lenton Chain. This marks the end of the short Beeston Canal for at this point the Nottingham Canal used to flow in from the north. The junction was called Lenton Chain because the Trent Navigation Company used to lock their

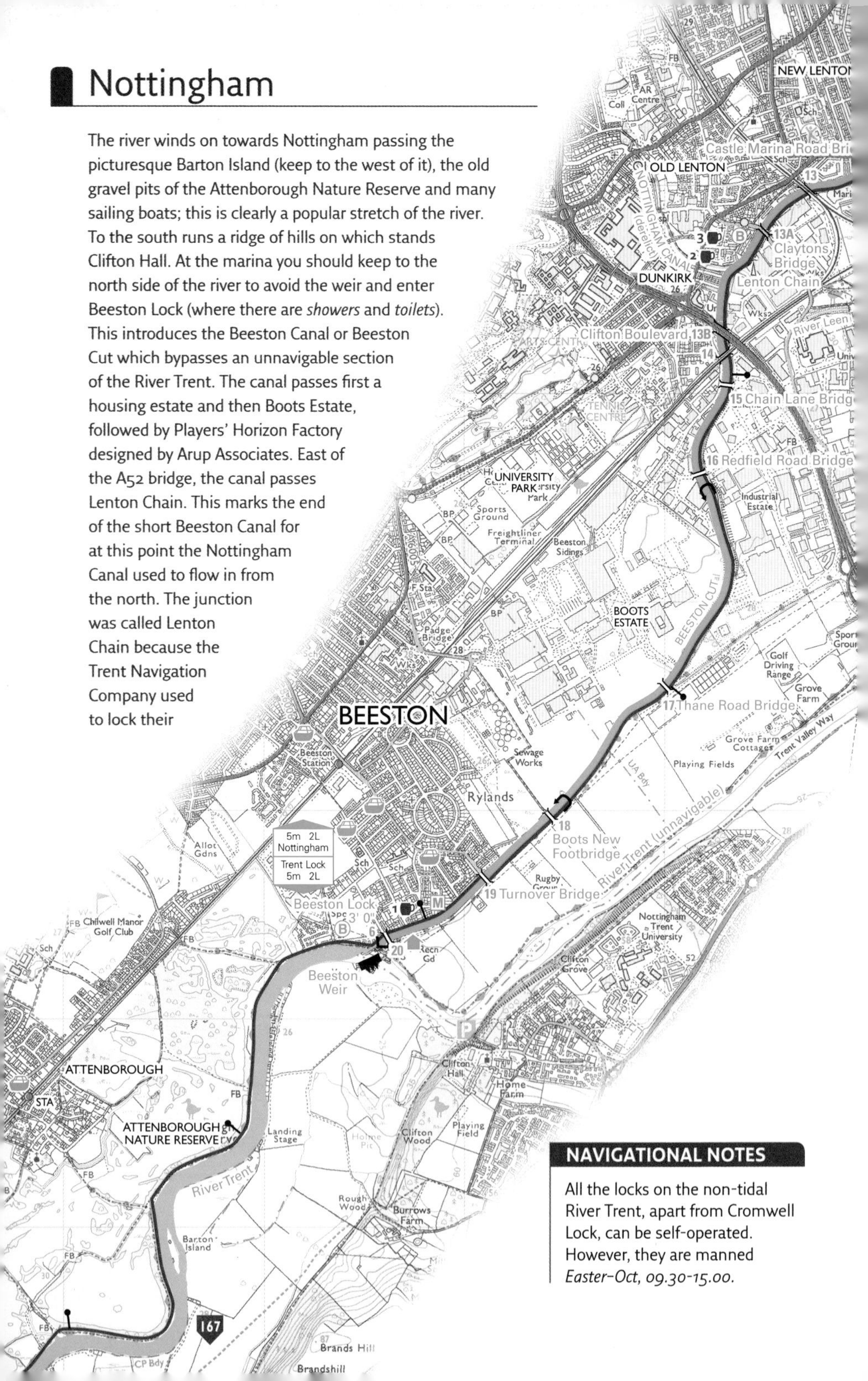

NAVIGATIONAL NOTES

All the locks on the non-tidal River Trent, apart from Cromwell Lock, can be self-operated. However, they are manned *Easter–Oct, 09.30-15.00.*

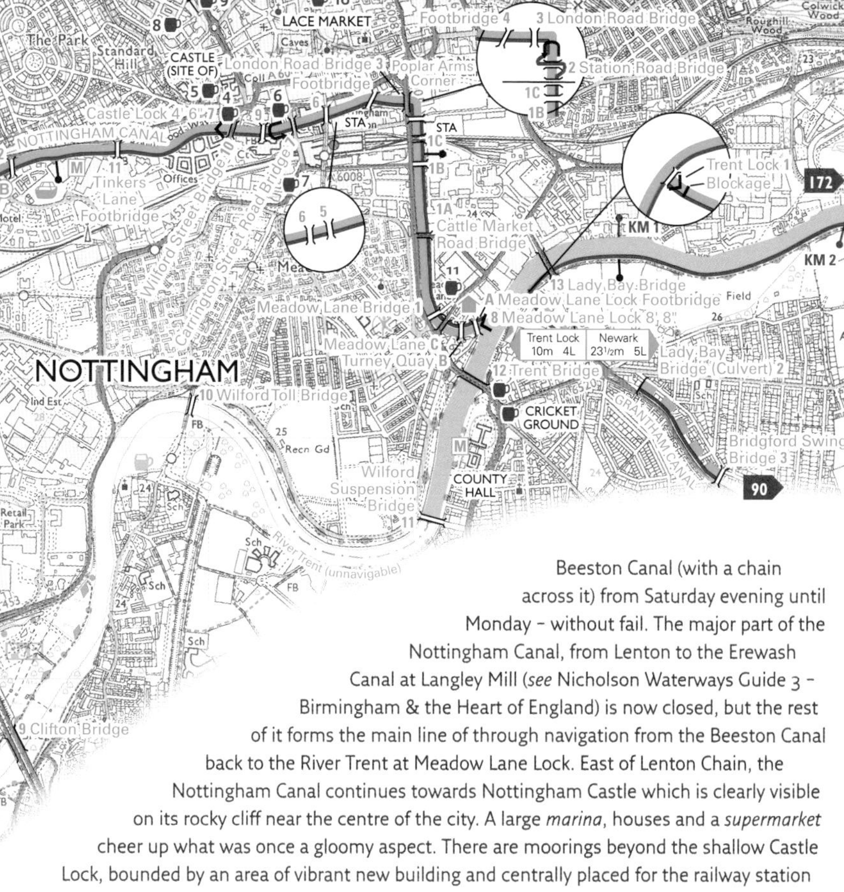

Beeston Canal (with a chain across it) from Saturday evening until Monday – without fail. The major part of the Nottingham Canal, from Lenton to the Erewash Canal at Langley Mill (*see* Nicholson Waterways Guide 3 – Birmingham & the Heart of England) is now closed, but the rest of it forms the main line of through navigation from the Beeston Canal back to the River Trent at Meadow Lane Lock. East of Lenton Chain, the Nottingham Canal continues towards Nottingham Castle which is clearly visible on its rocky cliff near the centre of the city. A large *marina*, houses and a *supermarket* cheer up what was once a gloomy aspect. There are moorings beyond the shallow Castle Lock, bounded by an area of vibrant new building and centrally placed for the railway station and city centre. Approaching Poplar Arms corner, once hemmed in by massive stone viaducts: a memorial to the Great Central Railway, the waterway opens out and makes a sharp turn at what was once a junction and progresses in a cutting, grassed and tidied up, towards Meadow Lane Lock and the River Trent. Upstream the river is navigable for a short distance above Trent Bridge (good moorings on County Hall steps) but the main navigation is to the east. Near Meadow Lane Lock is the Notts County football ground, while on the opposite side of the river is the Trent Bridge cricket ground with Nottingham Forest football stadium next to it. Below the latter is the entrance lock to the Grantham Canal now undergoing complete restoration (*see* page 90).

Boatyards

Ⓑ **Beeston Marina** 1A The Quay, Riverside Road Beeston, Nottingham NG9 1NA (0115 922 3168; www.beestonmarina.com). D E Gas, overnight mooring, long-term mooring, winter storage, slipway, 7-tonne crane, chandlery, engine sales and repairs (including outboards), books, maps and gifts, groceries, solid fuel, café, bar, telephone, Wi-Fi. *Open daily 08.30–17.00.* Riverside Bar and Boathouse Café.

Ⓑ **Trevethicks Boatyard** Canal Wharf, Gregory Street, Old Lenton, Nottingham NG7 2NP (0115 978 3467). Traditional boat builders, boat repairs, welding, dry dock, boat restoration, painting and sign writing.

Ⓑ **Nottingham Castle Marina** Marina Road, Castle Marina Park, Nottingham NG7 1TN (0115 941 2672; www.castlemarinas.co.uk/marinas/nottingham). D Pump out, gas, overnight and long-term mooring, slipway, wet dock, chandlery, books, maps and gifts, boat sales, solid fuel, toilets, showers, laundry and drying room. *Open Mon–Fri 09.30–17.00 & Sun and B Hols 10.00–16.00.*

Attenborough Nature Centre Barton Lane, Attenborough, Nottingham NG9 6DY (0115 972 1777; www.attenboroughnaturecentre.co.uk). Worked out gravel pits, once derelict and unsightly, are now providing an interesting habitat for plant and animal life. There are comprehensive nature trails and a wooden observation hide. Designated SSSI. Café. Visitor Centre. *Open Mon-Fri 09.00-17.00 & Sat-Sun 09.00-18.00 (winter 16.00); access to reserve 07.00-dusk.* Free.

Beeston Lock

Nottingham. A splendidly kept lock where facilities are available for boats. The pretty cottages and the little backwater off the canal are a hint of its past importance; until some years ago there used to be a lock down into the river here, at right angles to the present lock. The river channel used to be navigable - by shallow-draught vessels - from here down to Trent Bridge, the Beeston Canal being cut to connect with the Nottingham Canal and to afford access into the middle of the town. But now the river is unnavigable as a through route and the canal is the only way.

Nottingham

Notts. All services. The city's prosperity derives largely from the coal field to the north, and the long-established lace industry. John Player & Son made all their cigarettes here and Raleigh turned out bicycles for the world. The city centre is busy and not unattractive - there is an imposing town hall in Slab Square - but little of the architecture is of note. Modern developments are encouraging, however, notably the superb Playhouse Theatre and the appearance of a variety of theme festivals spread throughout the year.

Nottingham Contemporary Weekday Cross, Nottingham NG1 2GB (0115 948 9750; www.nottinghamcontemporary.org). One of the largest contemporary art spaces in the UK. *Open Tue-Sun 10.00-18.00 (Sun 17.00).* Café, bar.

Brewhouse Yard Museum Castle Boulevard, Nottingham NG7 1FB (0115 876 1400; www.nottinghamcastle.org.uk/explore/museum-of-nottingham-life-at-brewhouse-yard). Re-created shops, period rooms and a shopping street from between the wars. *Open Sat-Sun 12.00-16.00 & B Hols.* Charge.

City of Caves Drury Walk, Upper Level, Broadmarsh Shopping Centre, Nottingham NG1 7LS (0115 988 1955; www.cityofcaves.com). A unique honeycomb of caves open for a variety of different tours *Mon-Fri 10.30-16.00 & Sat-Sun 10.00-16.00. Advanced booking advisable for all tours.*
No wheelchair and pushchair access. Shop. Charge.

The Galleries of Justice High Pavement, Lace Market, Nottingham NG1 1HN (0115 952 0555; www.galleriesofjustice.org.uk). A major crime and punishment experience. Visitors assume the identity of real 19th-C criminals, take part in a trial, visit the cells and finally the gallows. New civil law and children's activity centres. *Open daily 10.30-16.00.* Tours comprise a mix of audio and performance tours - telephone for further details). Pre-booking advisable. Shop and café. Charge.

Lakeside Arts Centre University Park, Nottingham NG7 2RD (0115 846 7777; www.lakesidearts.org.uk). Attractive lakeside walks, two cafés, affordable craft items and a broad spectrum mix of theatre, dance, exhibitions and concerts. Museum *open Tue-Sat 11.00-17.00 & Sun 12.00-16.00.*

Nottingham Castle Friar Lane, Off Maid Marian Way, Nottingham NG1 6EL (0115 915 3700; www.nottinghamcity.gov.uk). William the Conqueror's castle, which was notorious as the base of Robin Hood's unfortunate enemies while King Richard I was away crusading, has been destroyed and rebuilt many times during its tumultuous history. (It was a Yorkist stronghold in the Wars of the Roses and it was here that Charles I raised his standard in 1642, starting the Civil War.) Though the original secret caves beneath the castle still exist and can be visited on a guided tour, the present building dates only from 1674. It now houses the city's **Museum and Art Gallery** which includes fine displays of English pottery, silver and glass together with a collection of 17th-, 18th- and 19th-C paintings by artists including Rosetti, Le Brun and Nottingham artists Bonington and Sandby. Also the exciting interactive Circle of Life gallery. Café and shop. *Open daily 10.00-17.00.* Charge.

Nottingham Goose Fair Forest Recreation Ground, outskirts of Nottingham City Centre, just off Mansfield Road/A60, Nottingham (www.nottinghamgoosefair.co.uk). The Goose Fair is now a conventional funfair but on a gigantic scale. It features traditional entertainments like boxing bouts (challengers invited to fight the house champ) as well as the usual mechanical fairground delights. The fair's original site was in the town centre but now it is out on the Forest Recreation Ground, a mile to the north east (served by buses). The fair takes place in the *first week of Oct* and it is advisable to get there before the *Saturday*, when the prices are doubled.

Nottingham Playhouse Wellington Circus, Nottingham NG1 5AF (0115 941 9419; www. nottinghamplayhouse.co.uk). Box office *open Mon-Sat 10.00-20.00; Sun and B Hols 2 hours before a performance.* Wide variety of theatre, a stunning Sky Mirror sculpture by Anish Kapoor in the forecourt, exhibitions. Bar.

Nottingham Tourism Centre 1-4 Smithy Row, Nottingham NG1 2BY (0844 477 5678; www.visit-nottinghamshire.co.uk/plan-a-visit/tourist-info). *Open Mon-Sat 09.30-17.30.*

WILDLIFE

The River Trent has historically been heavily polluted: water taken directly from the Trent has not been used as a drinking supply in living memory. However, as money is invested in the quality of the river water, the situation is changing. After becoming all but extinct in England (particularly the Midlands) since the late 1990s, the number of *otters* around the Trent and its tributaries has been steadily increasing. Otters are superbly adapted to an amphibious lifestyle and their dives can last for several minutes. They feed mainly on fish.

Pubs and Restaurants (pages 168-169)

1 The Boat & Horses 137 Trent Road, Beeston NG9 1LP. (0115 779 5327; www.boatandhorsesbeeston.co.uk). Once a changeover station for barge horses, this fine old pub serves real ale and food *Mon-Sat 12.00-18.00 (Fri 20.00) & Sun 12.00-16.00*. Dog- and child-friendly, garden. Traditional pub games, newspapers, sports TV and Wi-Fi. *Open Mon-Sat 12.00-23.30 (Fri-Sat 00.00) & Sun 12.00-22.30.*

2 The Johnsons Arms 59 Abbey Street, Lenton, Nottingham NV7 2NZ (0115 978 6355; www.facebook.com/thejohnsonarms). Friendly establishment serving real ale, real cider and food *Mon-Sat L and E & Sun 12.00-17.00*. Dogs welcome, garden. Traditional pub games, newspapers and Wi-Fi. *Open daily 12.00-23.00 (Fri-Sat 23.30).*

3 The Boat Inn Priory Street, Lenton, Nottingham NG7 2NX (0115 978 0267; www.facebook.com/pages/category/Pub/The-Boat-Inn-Priory-Street-Lenton-557463188104603). A 'proper' pub dispensing real ale and real cider surrounded by naval memorabilia. Food available *Mon-Sat L and E (not Sat E)*. Dog- and child-friendly *(until 17.30)* garden. Traditional pub games and Wi-Fi. *Open 12.00-23.00 (Fri-Sat 00.00).*

4 The Navigation 6 Wilford Street, Nottingham NG2 1AA (0115 837 1930; www.facebook.com/thenavinn). Real ale and bar snacks available *Mon-Fri 12.00-17.00*. Canalside by Castle Lock. Real ale. Bar food available *Sun-Mon 12.00-18.00 & Tue-Sat 12.00-21.00*. Canalside seating and mooring below the lock. *Regular* live music and Wi-Fi. Dog-friendly. *Open 11.00-23.00.*

5 Ye Olde Trip to Jerusalem 1 Brewhouse Yard, Nottingham NG1 6AD (0115 947 3171; www.triptojerusalem.com). Set into the cliff face below the castle, this is allegedly the oldest inn in England and is not without atmosphere. Real ale together with food served from an extensive menu *11.00-22.00 including breakfast*. Dog-friendly, courtyard seating. Traditional pub games, real fires and Wi-Fi. *Open 11.00-23.00 (Fri-Sat 00.00).*

6 Fellow Morton & Clayton 54 Canal Street, Nottingham NG1 7EH (0115 924 1175; www.fellowsmortonclayton.co.uk). Set in the old Fellows, Morton & Clayton warehouse, this establishment serves a selection of real ales and good value, traditional pub food *Mon-Sat 10.00-21.00 & Sun 12.00-19.00*. Real cider. Patio seating, traditional pub games, newspapers, large screen TV and Wi-Fi. *Open Mon-Sat 10.00-00.00 & Sun 12.00-22.30.*

7 The Vat & Fiddle 12-14 Queens Bridge Road, Nottingham NG2 1NB (0115 985 0611; www.castlerockbrewery.co.uk/pubs/vat-and-fiddle). Close to the railway station. Traditional pub serving a wide selection of real ales, malt whiskies and real cider. Bar meals served *daily 12.00-20.00 (Sun 17.00)*. Dog- and child-friendly *(until 21.00)* outside seating. Traditional pub games, newspapers and Wi-Fi. *Open Mon-Fri 10.00-23.00 (Fri 00.00) & Sat-Sun 11.00-00.00 (Sun 23.00).*

8 The Round House Royal Standard Place, The Park, Nottingham NG1 6FS (0115 924 0120). With its impressive ceiling mural and nude-adorned walls, this is an interesting pub in which to enjoy real ales, often from local breweries. The highly-regarded food is served *Tue-Sun L and E (not Sun E)*. Dog-friendly, amphitheatre seating. Wi-Fi. *Open Tue-Sat 12.00-23.00 (Fri-Sat 00.00) & Sun 12.00-18.00.*

9 The Dragon 67 Long Row West, Nottingham NG1 6JE (0115 941 7080; www.the-dragon.co.uk). A relaxed atmosphere in which to enjoy real ale and home-made food that has never seen a microwave. Food available *Mon-Thu 12.00-21.00 & Fri-Sun 12.00-17.00*. Outside seating, newspapers and Wi-Fi. Dog-friendly. *Open Sun-Thu 12.00-23.30 & Fri-Sat 12.00-01.00.*

10 The Crosskeys 15 Byard Lane, Nottingham NG1 2GJ (0115 941 7898; www.crosskeysnottingham.co.uk). On the edge of the Lace Market, this friendly pub serves real ale and food *daily 12.00-21.00 (Sun 20.00)*. Newspapers, sports TV and Wi-Fi. *Open 09.00-23.00 (Fri-Sat 01.00).*

11 The Trent Navigation 17 Meadow Lane, Nottingham NG2 3HS (0115 986 5658; www.trentnavigation.com). Comfortable pub with its own brewery, serving real ales from its range, together with guests, and home-cooked food *Mon-Tue L and E & Wed-Sun 12.00-21.00 (Sat-Sun 20.00)*. Real cider. Dog-friendly, patio seating. Traditional pub games (cards), newspapers, sports TV and Wi-Fi. *Regular* live music. *Open Sun-Thu 12.00-23.00 (Sun 22.30) & Fri-Sat 12.00-00.00 (Sat 11.00).*

Stoke Bardolph

Downstream from the railway bridge, the wide river soon leaves Nottingham behind and enters pleasant countryside. On the north bank are many boating centres and the Colwick racecourse. On the south side an exploration of the landscaped area will reveal the magnificent rowing course at Holme Pierrepont. Downstream are Holme Lock and sluices *(recycling facilities)*; the lock is on the south side (0115 981 1197). This section serves to establish the Trent's attractive rural character as it continues to sweep along through Nottinghamshire. Passing under a railway bridge (the Nottingham-Grantham line), one sees a very steep escarpment of tree-covered hills, effectively cliffs, rising out of the water. Radcliffe on Trent is concealed in the woods by the bend, but access is difficult. It is better to move on, down to the delightfully secluded Stoke Lock (0115 987 8563/07887 787353), where there are *full boater services (including recycling) and toilets*. The lock island is covered with trees. Below the lock, the river bends northwards and crosses over to the other side of the valley, leaving behind the woods and cliffs. At Burton Joyce the river rebounds from the side of the valley and turns east again. The water meadows that accompany the river serve to keep at bay any inroads by modern housing.

Pubs and Restaurants

1 **The Manvers Arms** Main Road, Radcliffe on Trent, Nottingham NG12 2AA (0115 933 2404; www.starpubs.co.uk/pubs/manvers-arms-radcliffe-trent). A beautiful appointed hostelry offering a welcoming and relaxed atmosphere, together with a selection of real ales. Appetising food is available *Mon-Sat L and E & Sun 12.00-18.00*. Dog-friendly, garden. Traditional pub games and live music *Thu*. Newspapers, real fires, sports TV and Wi-Fi. *Open 12.00-23.00 (Fri-Sat 00.00)*.

2 **The Royal Oak** Main Road, Radcliffe on Trent, Nottingham NG12 2FD (0115 933 5659; www.facebook.com/RoyalOakPubKitchen). Cosy, village local dispensing a selection of real ales and food daily 12.00-21.00 (Sun 17.00). Dog- and family-friendly, outside seating. Newspapers, real fires, sports TV and Wi-Fi. *Open 12.00-23.00 (Sat 11.00)*.

3 **The Ferry Boat Inn** Stoke Bardolph, Nottingham NG14 5HX (0115 987 1232; www.hungryhorse.co.uk/locations/ferry-boat-inn). Real ale and bar food available daily 11.00-22.00 (Sat-Sun 10.00). Large heated courtyard popular with its indoor and outdoor play areas. Garden and Wi-Fi. *Open 10.00-23.00*.

Try also: 4 **The Lord Nelson** Chestnut Grove, Burton Joyce, Nottingham NG14 5DN (0115 931 1800; https://www.molefacepubcompany.co.uk/the-lord-nelson.html), 5 **The Cross Keys** Main Street, Burton Joyce, Nottingham NG14 5DX (0115 931 3286; www.crosskeysburtonjoyce.co.uk/index) and 6 **The Wheatsheaf Inn** Church Road, Burton Joyce, Nottingham NG14 5GB (0115 931 3298; www.chefandbrewer.com/pubs/nottinghamshire/the-wheatsheaf).

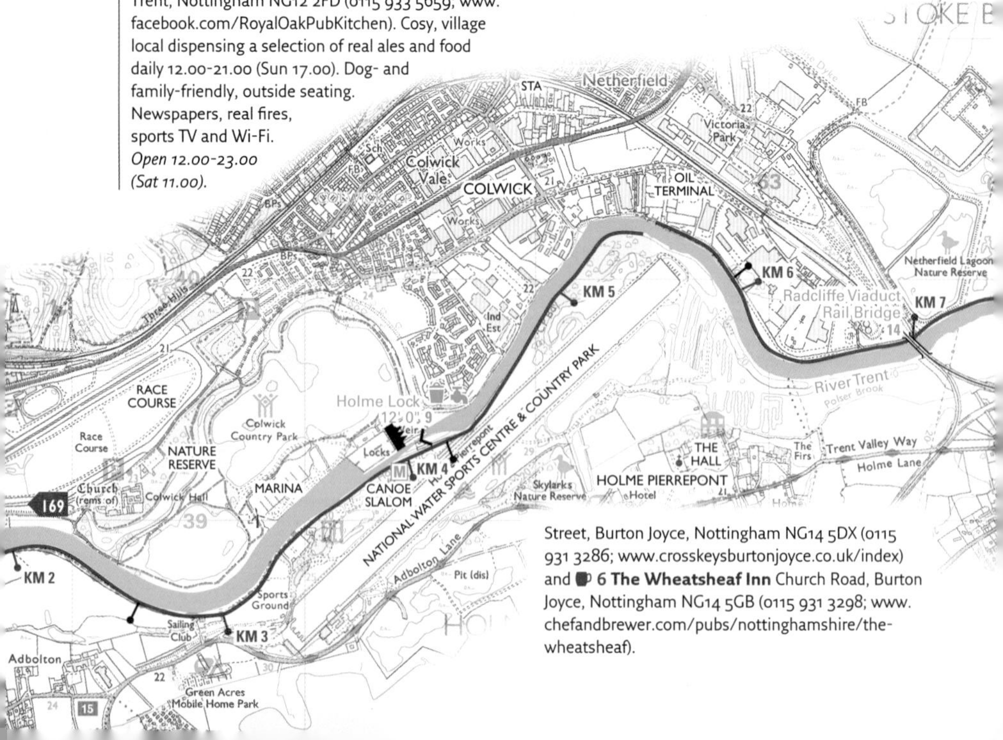

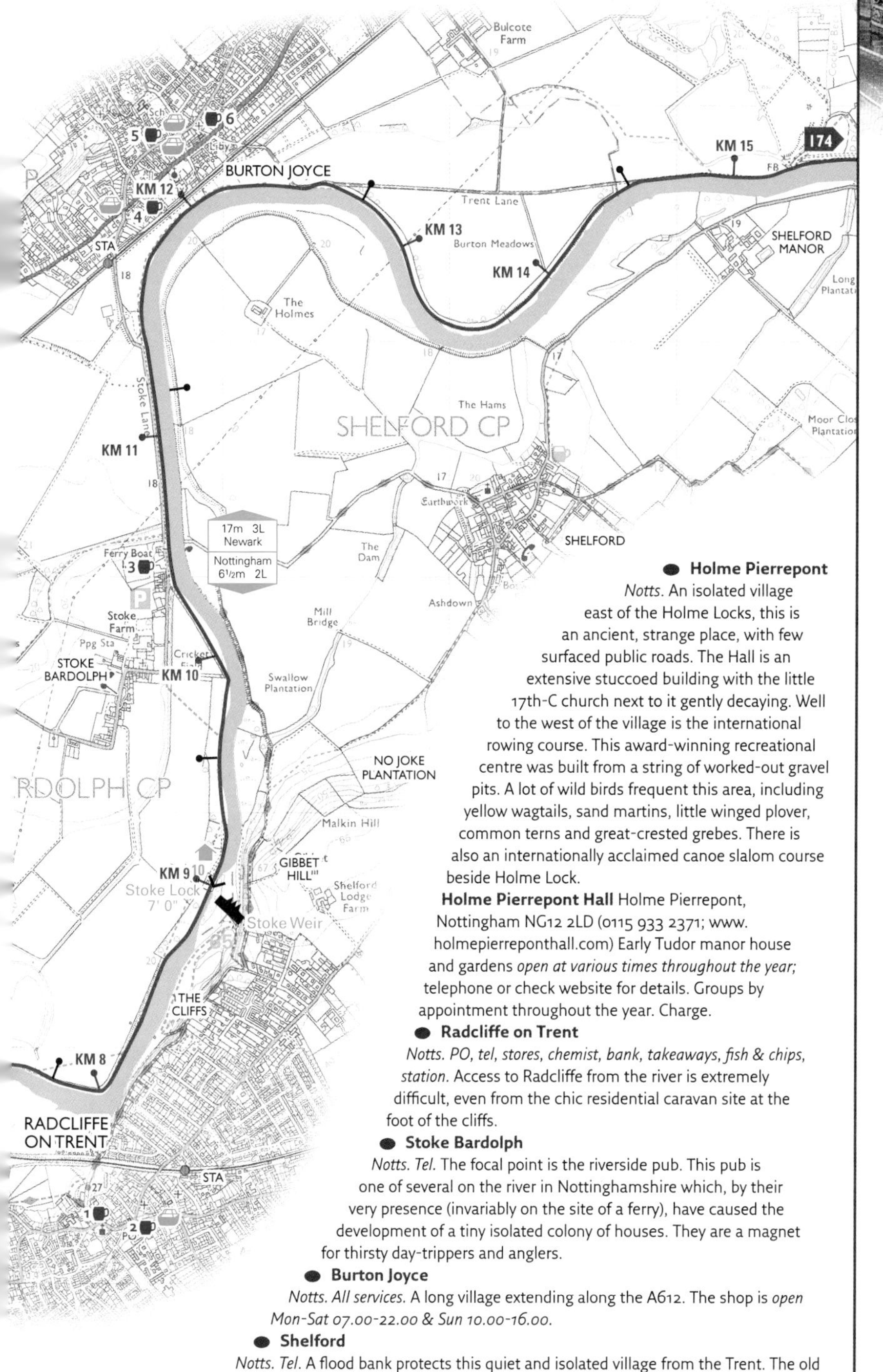

● Holme Pierrepont

Notts. An isolated village east of the Holme Locks, this is an ancient, strange place, with few surfaced public roads. The Hall is an extensive stuccoed building with the little 17th-C church next to it gently decaying. Well to the west of the village is the international rowing course. This award-winning recreational centre was built from a string of worked-out gravel pits. A lot of wild birds frequent this area, including yellow wagtails, sand martins, little winged plover, common terns and great-crested grebes. There is also an internationally acclaimed canoe slalom course beside Holme Lock.

Holme Pierrepont Hall Holme Pierrepont, Nottingham NG12 2LD (0115 933 2371; www.holmepierrepontenhall.com) Early Tudor manor house and gardens *open at various times throughout the year;* telephone or check website for details. Groups by appointment throughout the year. Charge.

● Radcliffe on Trent

Notts. PO, tel, stores, chemist, bank, takeaways, fish & chips, station. Access to Radcliffe from the river is extremely difficult, even from the chic residential caravan site at the foot of the cliffs.

● Stoke Bardolph

Notts. Tel. The focal point is the riverside pub. This pub is one of several on the river in Nottinghamshire which, by their very presence (invariably on the site of a ferry), have caused the development of a tiny isolated colony of houses. They are a magnet for thirsty day-trippers and anglers.

● Burton Joyce

Notts. All services. A long village extending along the A612. The shop is *open Mon-Sat 07.00-22.00 & Sun 10.00-16.00.*

● Shelford

Notts. Tel. A flood bank protects this quiet and isolated village from the Trent. The old church has a wide Perpendicular tower which commands the Trent valley. There is a pub, but there is no obvious mooring place for boats to be left on the river.

Hoveringham

This is a stretch in which the presence of big old riverside *pubs* has far more effect on the river scene than do the villages that they represent. Passing Shelford Manor, one arrives at the sleek arches of Gunthorpe Bridge – the only road bridge over the river in the 24 miles between Nottingham and Newark. *Gas is available* beside the A4097, ¼ mile north of the bridge. To the east of the bridge are the grand houses up on the hills of East Bridgford. Boats heading downstream should keep left to enter the mechanised Gunthorpe Lock (*recycling facilities* – 0115 966 3821/07887 787353) and avoid the foaming weir. On the west bank, just below the bridge, there is a CRT *visitor mooring pontoon (depth limited to 2' 6")*, while above the lock there is *water, a sanitary station, showers and toilets*. The next five or six miles below Gunthorpe are probably the most beautiful and certainly the most dramatic on the whole river. On the east side, the wooded cliffs rise almost sheer from the flat valley floor to a height of 200ft, allowing here or there the presence of a strip of fertile land on which cattle graze. Only at two places does a track manage to creep down the perilous slope to the river; otherwise, access is impossible. On the west side, by contrast, the ground is flat for miles, across to the other side of the valley. The river continues along its superb isolated course, with the forested cliffs of the Trent Hills striding along the river's east bank, while on the other side the flat plain of the valley rolls away through green fields and quiet Nottinghamshire villages. Unseen up on the plateau to the east is the big Syerston Airfield, now little used. Hazelford Ferry Hotel, now a residential care home, is on the left bank near an island in the river; boats should keep west of the island to reach Hazelford Lock (01636 830312/07887 787352). There are private and CRT *pontoon moorings* beside the old hotel, and further *moorings*, together with an attractive *barbecue area*, below the lock. Below the old hotel a ferryman plies across the river for fishermen, and there is also power boat activity in the area *at weekends*.

173

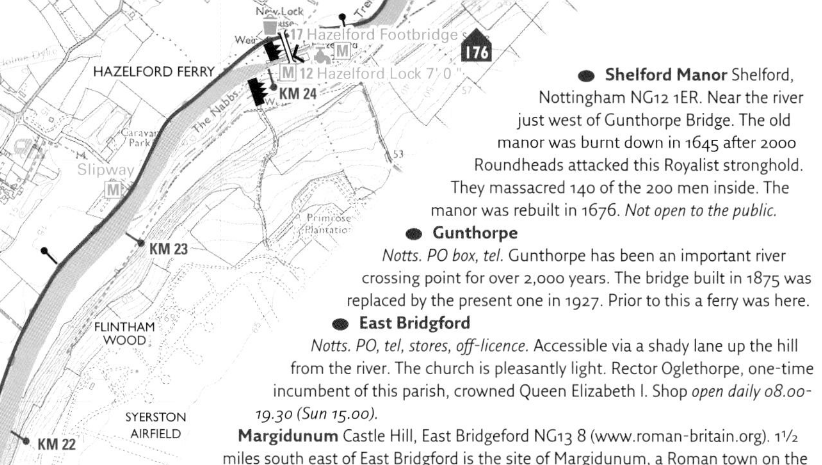

● **Shelford Manor** Shelford, Nottingham NG12 1ER. Near the river just west of Gunthorpe Bridge. The old manor was burnt down in 1645 after 2000 Roundheads attacked this Royalist stronghold. They massacred 140 of the 200 men inside. The manor was rebuilt in 1676. *Not open to the public.*

● **Gunthorpe**
Notts. PO box, tel. Gunthorpe has been an important river crossing point for over 2,000 years. The bridge built in 1875 was replaced by the present one in 1927. Prior to this a ferry was here.

● **East Bridgford**
Notts. PO, tel, stores, off-licence. Accessible via a shady lane up the hill from the river. The church is pleasantly light. Rector Oglethorpe, one-time incumbent of this parish, crowned Queen Elizabeth I. Shop *open daily 08.00-19.30 (Sun 15.00).*

Margidunum Castle Hill, East Bridgeford NG13 8 (www.roman-britain.org). 1½ miles south east of East Bridgford is the site of Margidunum, a Roman town on the Fosse Way (the straightest road in England). Margidunum was probably located here to guard the ford at East Bridgford.

● **Hoveringham**
Notts. PO box, tel. A village intimately linked with the gravel extraction industry.

● **Bleasby**
Notts. PO box, tel, stores, off-licence, station. Gas is available at the caravan site (07979 878568) approximately 500 yds up the lane from the Hazelford Residential Care Home.

Pubs and Restaurants

1 Tom Browns Brasserie The Old School House, Trentside, Gunthorpe, Nottingham NG14 7FB (0115 966 3642; www.tombrowns.co.uk). Restaurant/bar serving real ales and an imaginative range of excellent food *daily L and E (not Sun E)*. This establishment is set in an old Victorian schoolhouse. Afternoon tea can *be booked Tue-Sat 12.00-15.00.* Outside seating. *Open daily 12.00-23.00.*

2 The Unicorn Hotel Trentside, Gunthorpe, Nottingham NG14 7FB (0115 966 3612; www.unicornhotelpub.co.uk).This riverside hotel serves real ales and food *daily 12.00-22.00 (Sun 21.00).* Children welcome, canalside seating. *Occasional* live music and Wi-Fi. B&B. *Open Mon-Sat 11.00-23.00 & Sun 12.00-22.30.*

3 Biondi Bistro Gunthorpe Lock, Trentside, Gunthorpe NG14 7FB (0115 966 4833; www.biondi-bistro.com). Describing itself as a Bistro-Caffe-Bar, located in an attractive setting beside the lock, this establishment offers alfresco, courtyard dining *daily 10.00-16.00.* Breakfast menu.

4 Ferry Farm Park and Restaurant Boat Lane, Hoveringham, Nottingham NG14 7JP (0115 966 4512; www.ferryfarm.co.uk). Quality lunches, snacks and cream teas in conjunction with a farm park featuring rare breeds, animals to pet, children's adventure playground; assault course and slides for all ages and large indoor soft play area. Telephone for *opening times.* You may take your own alcoholic refreshment for which a small corkage charge will be made.

5 The Waggon & Horses Gypsy Lane, Bleasby NG14 7GG (01636 830283; www.thewaggonbleasby.co.uk). ½ mile north of Hazelford ferry. Delightful, and very friendly, village local serving well-kept real ales and inexpensive, traditional pub food *Wed-Fri L and E (not Wed L) & Sat-Sun 12.00-21.00 (Sun 15.30).* "No gimmicks or electronic games, just good conversation and banter." Dogs welcome, garden. Traditional pub games, newspapers, real fires and Wi-Fi. Camping nearby. *Open Mon-Wed 17.00-23.00 & Thu-Sun 12.00-23.00 (Fri-Sat 00.00).*

6 Manor Farm Tea Shoppe Station Road, Bleasby NG14 7FX (01636 831316; www.manorfarmteashoppe.co.uk). A range of light meals made from fresh local produce and delicious cream teas, together with shepherds hut B&B. *Open Wed-Sun 09.00-16.00.*

Try also: **7 The Royal Oak** Main Street East Bridgeford NG13 8PA (01949 21092; www.theroyaloakeb.co.uk/contacts), **8 The Reindeer** Main Street, Hoveringham NG14 7JR (0115 934 6071; www.reindeer-hoveringham.co.uk) and **9 The Black Horse Inn** 29 Main Street, Caythorpe, Nottingham NG14 7ED (0115 966 3520).

Boatyards

Ⓑ**Gunthorpe Marina Trentside** Trentside, Gunthorpe, Nottingham NG14 7FB (0115 966 4283). Pump out, gas, narrowboat hire, long-term mooring, winter storage, café, maps and gifts. Incorporating The Lighthouse Club.

Ⓑ**Gunthorpe Leisure Boats Ltd** Trentside, Gunthorpe NG14 7FB (07854 004333; www.gunthorpeleisureboats.co.uk). *Gunthorpe Belle* and *Gunthorpe Star* are available for skippered cruises or self-drive hire. Telephone for further details.

Newark-on-Trent

Beyond Hazelford Lock the steep Trent Hills dwindle away and the river leaves the woods (near the battlefield of East Stoke) for Fiskerton. Downstream of Fiskerton, the river sweeps round past the parkland at Stoke Hall. The site of a 4-acre Roman fort is on the nearby Fosse Way. At Farndon, a pleasant riverside village with sailing clubs on either side and a small ferry, there is a CRT *mooring pontoon*. The boat population is further increased by the use of some old gravel pits just north of Farndon as a mooring site for pleasure boats. Navigators must be especially careful to avoid the large Averham Weir which takes the main channel of the Trent to Kelham and round the north side of Newark. Boats heading downstream should keep right, steering by the 240ft spire of Newark church. The waterway immediately becomes narrower east of this weir. This is the Newark Branch which takes boats straight into the middle of the town. On the way into Newark, the navigation passes an old windmill, a boatyard at the mouth of the River Devon (pronounced 'Deevon'), some extensive old maltings, and a restored warehouse (now a museum and brasserie) with the words Trent Navigation Company in faded lettering on the side. Opposite is the CRT repair yard, followed by Newark Town Lock (01636 702226/07887 754487) and then below is the Waterways Office. Alongside the town lock are the remains of the old lock, half of which is now used as a mooring for pleasure boats while the rest is a covered dry dock. The townscape at this point is dominated by the north west wall of the ruined Newark Castle. Nearby is a splendid old seven-arched stone bridge. The size of the arches limits the width of boats which can use the navigation but this bridge is listed as an ancient monument and so cannot be altered to accommodate bigger vessels.

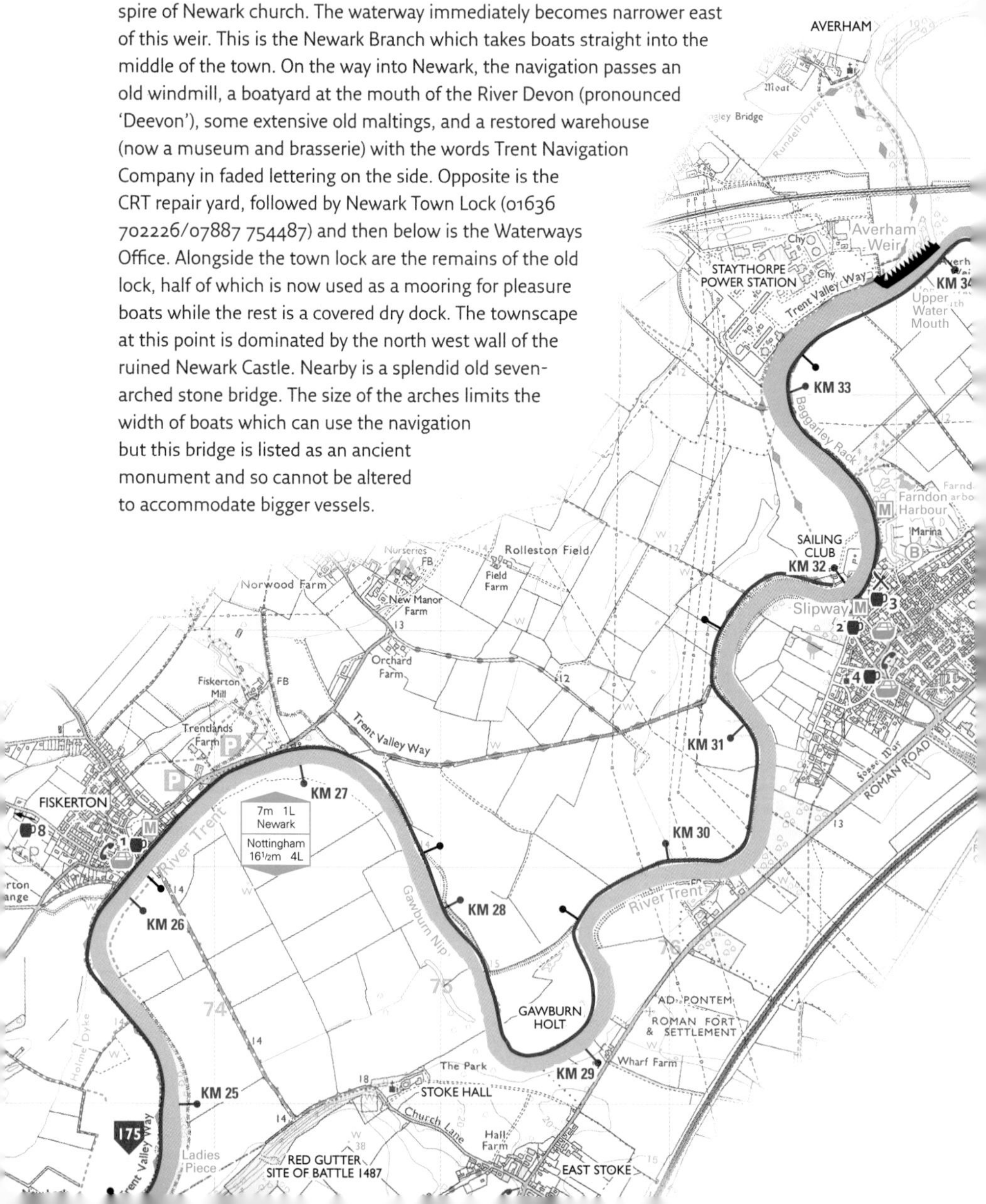

BOAT TRIPS
Newark Castle Line Ltd
Cuckstool Wharf, Castle Gate, Newark NG24 1BG (01636 362303; www.rivertrip.co.uk). *M.V.Sonning* sails from just below Newark Town Lock *Mar-Oct, daily during summer* if the weather is fair. Pleasure, charter and themed trips. Drinks and refreshments available. Telephone or visit the website for details.

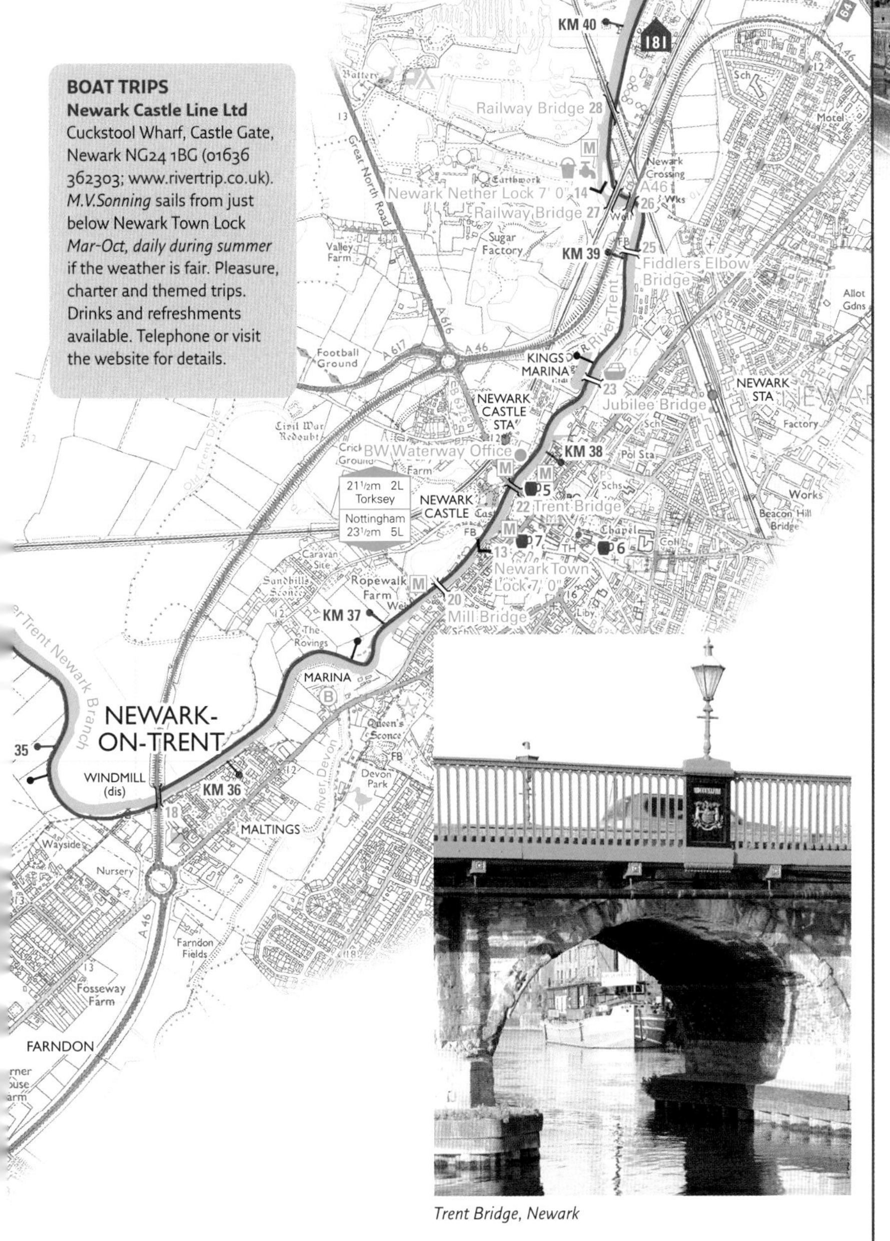

Trent Bridge, Newark

Just through the bridge is Town Wharf which is a useful *temporary mooring* site when space is available. Beyond here the navigation passes the oldest and most interesting industrial buildings in Newark – an old ironworks, more redundant maltings, a brewery (now only a distribution centre) and a glueworks giving off a smell of old leather. Gradually these buildings, or their sites, are undergoing renovation and wholesale redevelopment. A weir follows this to the left, then a right bend under a railway bridge, and one arrives at Newark Nether Lock (01636 703830/07887 754486) with a smart new lock keeper's cottage nearby. East of the lock, the navigation rejoins the main channel of the River Trent and proceeds north eastward under the graceful modern road bridge carrying the Newark bypass.

● **Fiskerton**
Notts. PO, station. Charming riverside village with excellent access for boats. Although the normal river level is well below the wharf, all the buildings along the splendid front are carefully protected from possible flood by stone walling or a bank of earth.

● **Southwell**
Notts. Three miles north west of Fiskerton, this very attractive country town is well worth visiting in order to see its minster. The minster was founded at the beginning of the 12th C by the Archbishop of York, and is held by many to be one of the most beautiful Norman ecclesiastical buildings in England. Its scale is vast for Southwell, but it is set well back from the houses and is in a slight dip so it does not overawe the town centre, in spite of the two western towers and the massive central tower. Chief among the treasures inside the building are the naturalistic stone carvings in the late 13th-C chapter house, and the wooden carvings of the choir stalls.

● **Farndon**
Notts. PO, tel, stores, off-licence. A local ferry still transports the fishermen to the far side of the river in this attractive village. The pub makes it a popular spot in summer as do the sailing boats. Extensive renovation of the 14th-C church in 1891 revealed a stone coffin containing a Saxon bronze sword. The shop is *open Mon-Fri 06.00-21.00; Sat 07.00-21.00 & Sun 07.30-21.00.*

● **Newark**
Notts. All services. Two stations. Newark is magnificent, easily the most interesting and attractive town on the Trent, and it is very appealing from the navigation. Situated at the junction of two old highways, the Great North Road and the Fosse Way, the town is of great historical significance. During the Civil War it was a Royalist stronghold which was besieged three times by the Roundheads between March 1645 and May 1646. The defensive earthworks or sconces constructed by the Royalists are still visible. Today Newark, like everywhere else, is large, busy and surrounded by industry and modern housing. But the town centre is intact and still full of charm. Elsewhere antique stalls, markets and warehouses attract a steady flow of bargain hunters and collectors to the town. However, it is only the decaying, riverside maltings that give a hint of its past significance within the brewing industry.

British Horological Institute Upton Hall, Upton, Newark NG23 5TE (01636 813795; www.bhi.co.uk). Library, training and educational centre for all those interested in matters horological together with a fascinating museum open to the public. Housed in Upton Hall, built in 1828, the museum displays the original 'Six Pip' generator and the actual watch worn by Captain Scott on his final, disastrous expedition, amongst many other gems. Tearoom. *Open to members during office hours; group visits by appointment; open day when clocks change.* Charge. Partial disabled access. Regular bus service from Newark.

Church of St Mary Magdalene Market Place, Newark NG24 1JS (01636 704513). The enormous spire is all that one can see of this elegant church from the market place, for the buildings on one side of the square hide the body of the structure. Inside, the church is made light and spacious by soaring columns and a magnificent 15th-C east window in the chancel. The building was begun in 1160 and completed about 1500. It is rich in carving, but one of the church's most interesting features is a brass made in Flanders to commemorate Alan Fleming, a merchant who died in 1375. The monument is made up of 16 pieces of metal and measures 9ft 4ins by 5ft 7ins - one of the biggest of its type in England.

Market Place Newark. It is worth making a point of visiting Newark on market day to view the scene in the colourful old market. In opposite corners of the square once stood two ancient pubs: one of them, the White Hart, now resited elsewhere in the town, was built in the 15th C and is the oldest example of domestic architecture in the town; the other is the Clinton Arms where W. E. Gladstone made his first speech in 1832. He later became Prime Minister.

National Civil War Centre 14 Appleton Gate, Newark NG24 1JY (01636 655765; www.nationalcivilwarcentre.com). Newark was vital because it lay at the crossroads of the Great North Road and the Fosse Way and provided an important crossing point over the River Trent. Find out how this conspired to project the town into the forefront of the conflict. Shop. *Open Apr-Sep 10.00-17.00 & Oct-Mar 10.00-16.00.* Charge.

Newark Heritage Barge 24 The Weavers, Newark NG24 4RY (07971 589612; www.newarkheritagebarge.com). A floating interpretation centre established in the last intact Trent size dumb barge. It aims to show working life on the river in the Newark area, through the comprehensive archive that the project leaders are gradually building up. It depicts how barges were built and repaired, shows how important Newark was as the base of the Newark Navigation Company (later British Waterways) and encourages visitors to interact with exhibits, by adding their own memories and photographs, to an archive for the benefit of future generations. Telephone for *details of opening times.*

Newark Castle Castlegate, Newark NG24 1BG (www.newark-sherwooddc.gov.uk). Only a shell remains, the one intact wall overlooking the river. The first known castle on this site was constructed c.1129, probably for Alexander, Bishop of Lincoln. The present building was started in 1173, with various additions and alterations in the 14th, 15th and 16th C - notably the fine oriel windows. King John died here in October 1216, soon after his traumatic experience in the Wash. The castle was naturally a great bastion during the Civil War sieges and battles that focused on Newark. When the Roundheads eventually took the town in 1646, they dismantled the castle. The ruins and the grounds are *open daily.* Free.

Newark Gilstrap Centre Castlegate, Newark NG24 1BG (0300 500 8080; www.nottinghamshire.gov.uk/celebrate/venues/the-gilstrap). *Open Mon-Fri 09.00-16.30.*

Newark Town Hall Museum Town Hall, Market Place, Newark NG24 1DU (01636 680333; www.newarktownhallmuseum.co.uk). Newark town's treasures, which include paintings, furniture and ceramics, ceremonial items, civic gifts and the town's charters. *Open all year Mon-Sat 10.30-15.30. Closed B Hols.*

Tourist Information Centre 14 Appleton Gate, Newark NG24 1JY (01636 655765; www.experiencenottinghamshire.com/general-and-tourist-information/visitor-gateway-newark-p576431). *Open daily 10.00-16.00.*

Boatyards

Ⓑ✕🍷 **Farndon Marina** North End, Farndon, Newark NG24 3SX (01636 705483; www.farndonmarina.co.uk). D P E Pump out, gas, overnight mooring, long-term mooring, winter storage, slipway, crane (25 tonnes), chandlery, books, boat repairs, boat fitting out, DIY facilities, electrical repairs, boat sales, engine sales and repairs (including outboards), toilets, showers, laundrette, restaurant. CRT licensing. Boat transport by road.

Ⓑ**Kings Marina** Mather Road, Newark NG24 1FW (01636 678549; www.aquavista.com/contact-us). D E Pump out, gas, overnight mooring, long-term and visitor mooring, chandlery, toilets, showers, laundry. Grocery shop close by.

Ⓑ**Newark Marina** 26 Farndon Road, Newark NG24 4SD (01636 704022; www.newark-marina.co.uk). D Gas, overnight mooring, long-term mooring, winter storage, crane (40 tonne), chandlery, books and maps, gifts, boat building and fitting out, DIY facilities, boat sales and repairs, inboard and outboard engine sales and repairs, toilets and showers.

Pubs and Restaurants (pages 176-177)

✕ 1 **The Bromley at Fiskerton** Main Street, Fiskerton NG25 0UL (01636 830789; www.bromleyatfiskerton.com). An attractive riverside pub, set beside the old wharf, with superb country views and serving real ale. Food is available *from 11.30 daily*. Outside seating overlooking the river and moorings. Family-friendly, traditional pub games, newspapers and Wi-Fi. Camping nearby. *Open daily 11.00-00.00.*

✕ 2 **The Riverside Pub and Kitchen** North End, Farndon NG24 3SX (01636 710990; www.distinctiveinns.co.uk/the-riverside). Popular riverside pub, serving real ale. Fresh, modern British cuisine served *daily 10.00-21.30*. Family-friendly, garden. Wi-Fi. There is a slipway available in front of the pub. Charge. *Open Mon-Sat 11.30-23.00 (Fri-Sat 00.00) & Sun 12.00-22.30.*

✕ 3 **The Farndon Ferry** off Wyke Lane, Farndon NG24 3SX (01636 676578; www.farndonferry.co.uk). Bar and restaurant serving fresh food, sourced locally where possible *daily 12.00-20.30*. Also real ales and continental beers. Live music *Sun*. Outside seating for the *summer*; open fires for *winter*. Moorings, free for patrons (book in advance). *Open 10.00-23.00 (Fri-Sat 00.00).*

✕ 4 **The Rose and Crown** Main Street, Farndon, NG24 3SA (01636 680498; www.facebook.com/roseandcrownfarndon). Local pub dispensing real ale and home-made bar meals *daily 12.00-20.00 (Sun 17.00)*. Dog- and family-friendly, garden. Traditional pub games, newspapers, sports TV and Wi-Fi. *Open Mon-Tue 15.00-23.30, Wed-Sat 12.00-00.00 & Sun 11.00-23.00.*

5 **The Castle Barge** The Wharf, Newark NG24 1EU (01636 677320; www.castlebarge.co.uk). Floating pub in a 94ft former Spiller's grain barge. The lower deck provides an atmospheric bar with lots of polished wood and an interesting display of pictures. However, many prefer to sit outside in the summer and enjoy the river. Real ales and reasonably priced bar snacks with seasonal specials available *daily 12.00-19.00*. Morning coffee *from 11.00* and *daily* special offers. Dog- and family-friendly. *Regular* music. Newspapers and Wi-Fi. *Open daily 10.00-00.00 (Mon-Tue 23.00).*

6 **The Fox & Crown** 4-6 Appletongate, Newark NG24 1JY (01636 605820; www.castlerockbrewery.co.uk/pubs/fox-and-crown). A wide selection of real ales, speciality bottled beers and over 20 traditional ciders vie for the drinkers' attention in this town-centre pub. Also inexpensive food *L and when open*. Dog- and child-friendly, beer garden. Traditional pub games, *regular* live music, newspapers, sports TV and Wi-Fi. *Open Sun-Mon and Wed-Thu 15.00-23.00 & Fri-Sat 12.00-22.00.*

✕ 7 **The Prince Rupert** 46 Stodman Street, Newark NG24 1AW (01636 918121; www.facebook.com/ThePrinceRupert.Newark). This timber-framed pub, dating from 1452, has recently been renovated to a high standard and now serves a range of real ales, real cider and food *Mon-Fri L and E & Sat-Sun 12.00-21.00 (Sun 20.00)*. Dog-friendly, outside seating. *Regular* live music, newspapers, real fires and Wi-Fi. *Open Mon-Sat 11.00-23.00 (Fri-Sat 01.00) & Sun 12.00-23.00.*

✕ 8 **The Full Moon Inn** Main Street, Morton, Newark NG25 0UT (01636 830251; www.thefullmoonmorton.co.uk). Licensed for civil ceremonies, this hostelry also dispenses real ale and food *L and E (not Sun E)*. Dog- and family-friendly: outdoor play area and indoor toy cupboard. Traditional pub games, live music, newspapers, real fires and Wi-Fi. *Open Mon-Thu L and E, Fri 11.00-23.00 & Sat-Sun 10.00-23.00 (Sun 22.00).*

Cromwell Lock

From Newark, the Trent follows a generally northerly course towards the Humber, which is still over 50 miles away owing to the very sweeping and tortuous line of the river. The villages of North Muskham and Holme face each other across the water and used to be connected by ferry. A mile or more below Holme is Cromwell Lock *(toilets, showers, recycling facilities)* and Weir. On 28 September 1975 ten volunteers of the 131 independent parachute squadron of the Royal Engineers lost their lives here whilst taking part in Expedition Trent Chase. Cromwell has always been a significant place on the river; in the 8th C a bridge was built at this point. The lock here marks the beginning of the tidal section of the Trent, so navigation north of it requires a very different approach.

NAVIGATIONAL NOTES

1 Cromwell Weir is the largest on the Trent. It is buoyed and has a safety boom. All boats should keep to the west side of the river. The lock too is truly enormous; it is mechanised, and there is a lock keeper on duty *daily 08.00-16.00* (01636 821213/07887 754485). Boaters must book *at least 24 hours in advance* to be guaranteed passage. For passage outside these designated times contact the lock keeper.

2 Boaters intending to break their passage to Torksey Lock, by staying on the pontoon mooring at Dunham, are requested to inform the lock keeper at Cromwell to avoid alarm at their non-arrival at Torksey. Similarly should you change your plans and subsequently stop at Dunham please contact a lock keeper to avoid unnecessary concern for your safety.

3 The occasional commercial river traffic operate on VHF channel 6 upstream of Keadby Bridge and it is useful for VHF users to monitor this channel to establish the whereabouts of large craft.

Navigating the Tidal Trent

A suitable boat is essential: proper navigation lights (compulsory on all the navigable Trent) and safety equipment (including an anchor and cable) is also compulsory. Navigation Notes are available from www.canalrivertrust.org.uk. The Trent Series Charts, published by The Boating Association, are detailed charts of the tidal Trent (and the tidal Ouse and non-tidal Trent) and are available from www.theboatingassociation.com. Also from CRT (above) and lock keepers - charge. Deep-draughted boats should beware of shoals at low water (especially on neap tides above Gainsborough) and should avoid the inside of bends. The river banks are unsuitable for mooring and there are few wharves; those that remain are largely for commercial craft. There are excellent, though limited, pontoon moorings north of Gainsborough Arches. Navigators who are more used to canals and non-tidal rivers will be more likely to treat the tidal Trent as a link route with the Fossdyke & Witham Navigation, the Chesterfield Canal, the South Yorkshire Navigations or the Humber Estuary. They should plan their trip with an eye to the tide table. The best approach is either to use a Hull tide table (available from local boatyards, fishing shops and newsagents) bearing in mind that the Trent floods for only about 2¼ hours and ebbs for the remainder of the 12-hour period or, if in doubt, to ask the CRT lock keepers at the various junctions along the river. The relevant telephone numbers are: Cromwell Lock 01636 821213/07887 754485; West Stockwith Lock 01427 890204/07884 238780; Torksey Lock 01427 718202/07884 238781; Keadby Lock 01724 782205/07733 124611. In most cases it is advisable to plan your journey so that the tide is running with you, but bear in mind the lock operating times.

Pubs and Restaurants

1 **The Lord Nelson** Gainsborough Road, Winthorpe, Newark NG24 2NN (01636 707705; www.lordnelsonwinthorpe.co.uk). Real ales and real cider. Home-cooked bar and restaurant meals available *daily, L and E*. Children welcome in garden and restaurant. Log fires, leather sofas and exposed beams. Live music *Fri*. Wi-Fi. *Open Tue-Sun 12.00-23.00 (Sun 20.00).*

2 **The Muskham Ferry** Ferry Lane, North Muskham, Newark NG23 6HB (01636 704943; www.muskhamferry.com). Riverside pub with mooring for patrons, fronted by a garden. Real ales together with inexpensive home-cooked food available *L and E*. Children and dogs welcome. Traditional pub games and newspapers. *Open daily 12.00-23.00.*

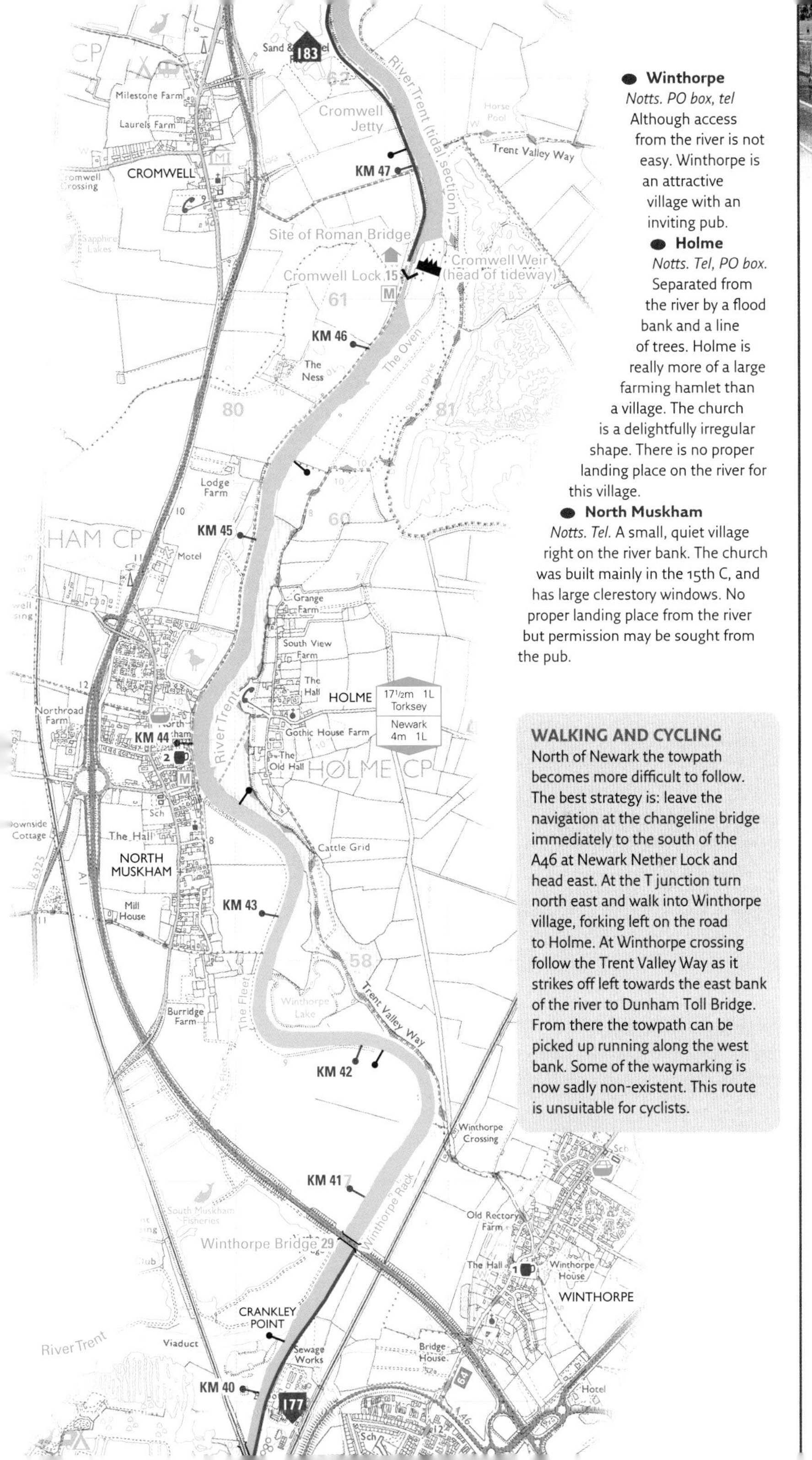

Winthorpe
Notts. PO box, tel
Although access from the river is not easy. Winthorpe is an attractive village with an inviting pub.

Holme
Notts. Tel, PO box.
Separated from the river by a flood bank and a line of trees. Holme is really more of a large farming hamlet than a village. The church is a delightfully irregular shape. There is no proper landing place on the river for this village.

North Muskham
Notts. Tel. A small, quiet village right on the river bank. The church was built mainly in the 15th C, and has large clerestory windows. No proper landing place from the river but permission may be sought from the pub.

WALKING AND CYCLING

North of Newark the towpath becomes more difficult to follow. The best strategy is: leave the navigation at the changeline bridge immediately to the south of the A46 at Newark Nether Lock and head east. At the T junction turn north east and walk into Winthorpe village, forking left on the road to Holme. At Winthorpe crossing follow the Trent Valley Way as it strikes off left towards the east bank of the river to Dunham Toll Bridge. From there the towpath can be picked up running along the west bank. Some of the waymarking is now sadly non-existent. This route is unsuitable for cyclists.

Sutton on Trent

This is a typical stretch of the upper section of the tidal Trent. The river meanders along its northward course, flanked by flood banks and with no bridges. The land is largely grazed as permanent pasture nurtured by the high summer water table maintained by the winter flood (now of course contained). Evidence of an ancient landscape is glimpsed, often on the inside of a sweeping bend, in the form of isolated stretches of hedgerow. These are rich in an abundance of species including ash, willow, wild roses and hawthorn - a picture of white blossom in springtime. Apart from these tantalising views there is little to see save for occasional narrowboat or cruiser. Elsewhere the land yields a vast quantity of glacial gravel quarried for building and road construction. The village of Sutton on Trent is near this wharf; so is a large converted windmill. On the east bank are the remains of New Besthorpe Wharf which used to feed gravel from the adjacent pit into waiting barges, the traffic now lost to 'rationalisation'. The Trent valley was once rightly called the powerhouse of England: electricity generating stations operating within sight of the river used to generate more than a quarter of all electricity consumed in England and Wales. This area made an ideal site for power stations with its plentiful supply of water for steam production, as well as for cooling the spent steam once it has passed through the generating turbines. A large reserve of coal to fire the boilers was also available, until relatively recently, from the nearby East Midlands coalfield, although several of the power stations are now converted to gas. Most of them have been built since 1950, and their huge cooling towers stand out as prominent features on an otherwise largely agricultural landscape. Approximately half of all the electricity generated in the Trent Valley was transmitted, via the Supergrid of overhead power lines, to London, which as a large consumer is nevertheless poorly situated for large-scale power production. Whilst waste cooling water was returned to the river, the vast output of fly ash has been used to fill nearby spent gravel pits. In an imaginative scheme it has also, in conjunction with soil from sugar beet washings, been used to reclaim worked-out clay pits at a Peterborough brickworks. These have then been returned to agricultural use. In most cases mooring along the tidal Trent is not recommended.

Pubs and Restaurants

1 **The Lord Nelson Inn** 35 Main Street, Sutton on Trent, Newark NG23 6PF (01636 821885; www.lordnelsonpub.co.uk). Formerly the Memory Lane, this is a comfortable, cosy inn and restaurant serving real ales and food *Wed-Sat 12.00-21.00 (Sat 10.00) & Sun 12.00-16.00. Sat* brunch. Dog- and family-friendly, garden. Children's play area and conservatory. *Regular* live music, sports TV and Wi-Fi. Camping. B&B. *Open Sun-Fri 12.00-23.00 (Mon-Tue 16.00) & Sat 10.00-23.00.*

WALKING AND CYCLING

Under the 1792 Trent River Navigation Act hauling rights were granted in return for an annual rent. Since the 1930s craft using the river have been self-propelled and these rights have not been exercised. Custom and practice has led to paths following the flood banks rather than the water margins. CRT's legal rights are for maintenance access only, whilst they also have an obligation to maintain and erect the numerous clapper gates as necessary. On the tidal stretch of the Trent it is often possible to follow a marked footpath on either flood bank (and in some cases a minor road); therefore the towpath indicated on the map represents only the most straightforward, continuous route. In practice this offers excellent opportunities for walkers, and a combination of routes can be devised following a mix of river bank, the Chesterfield Canal towpath, country lanes and footpaths. The Trent Valley Way - further information at www.trentriverstrust.org/trent-valley-way - also parallels the river and meets the canal at Cooper's Bridge No 80. Unfortunately there is no guide for this long-distance walking trail currently in print although members of the Long Distance Walking Association can download information at www.ldwa.org.uk/ldp/members/show_path.php?path_name=Trent+Valley+Way. The bridleways along the Trent also offer the adventurous cyclist plenty of scope, although the numerous clapper gates can become somewhat irksome.

Sutton on Trent
Notts. PO box, delicatessen, library, garage. This pretty village is close to Carlton Wharf. The almost oriental white cap of a converted windmill, typical of this area, can be seen from the river. The stores are open *daily 07.00-22.00.*

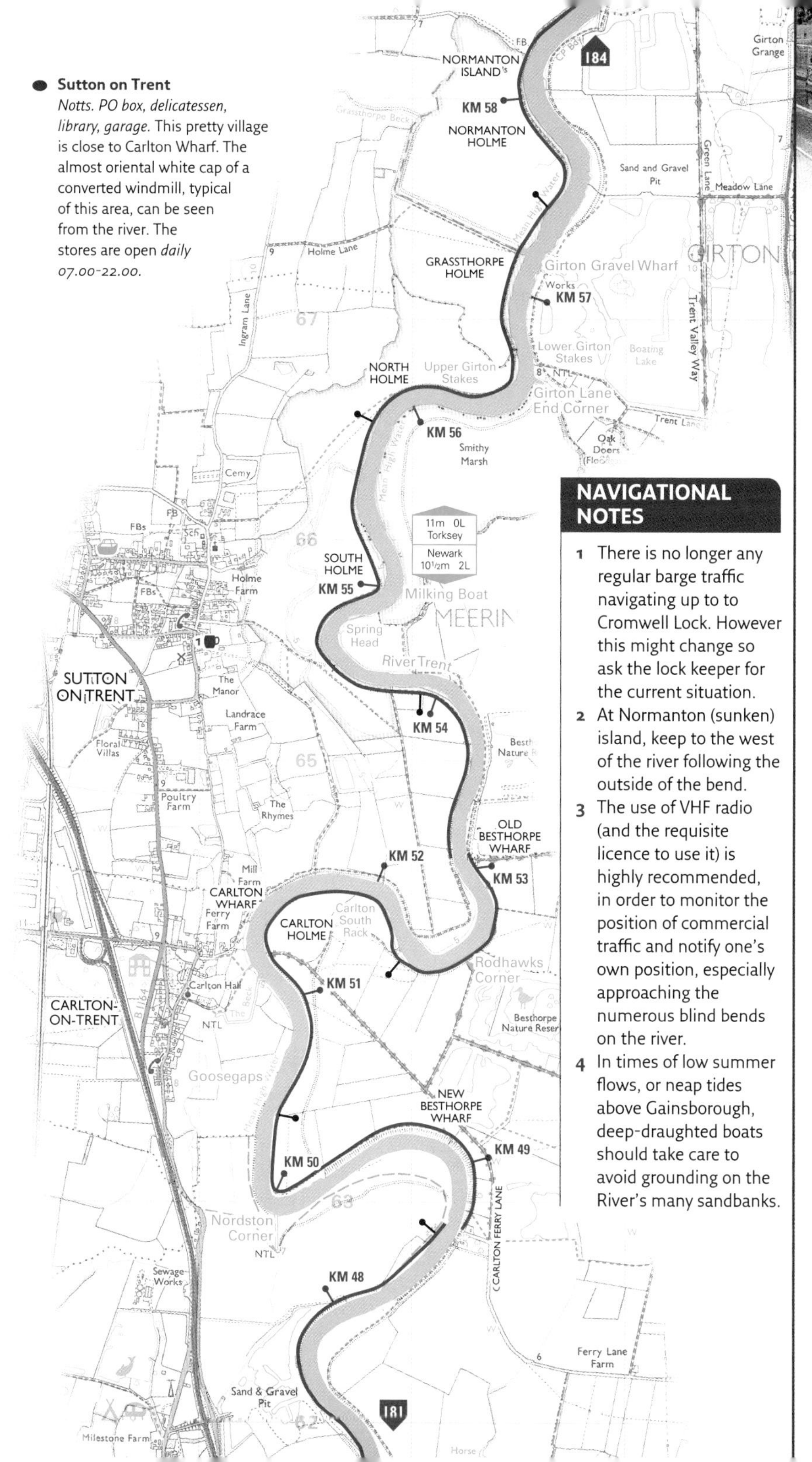

NAVIGATIONAL NOTES

1. There is no longer any regular barge traffic navigating up to to Cromwell Lock. However this might change so ask the lock keeper for the current situation.
2. At Normanton (sunken) island, keep to the west of the river following the outside of the bend.
3. The use of VHF radio (and the requisite licence to use it) is highly recommended, in order to monitor the position of commercial traffic and notify one's own position, especially approaching the numerous blind bends on the river.
4. In times of low summer flows, or neap tides above Gainsborough, deep-draughted boats should take care to avoid grounding on the River's many sandbanks.

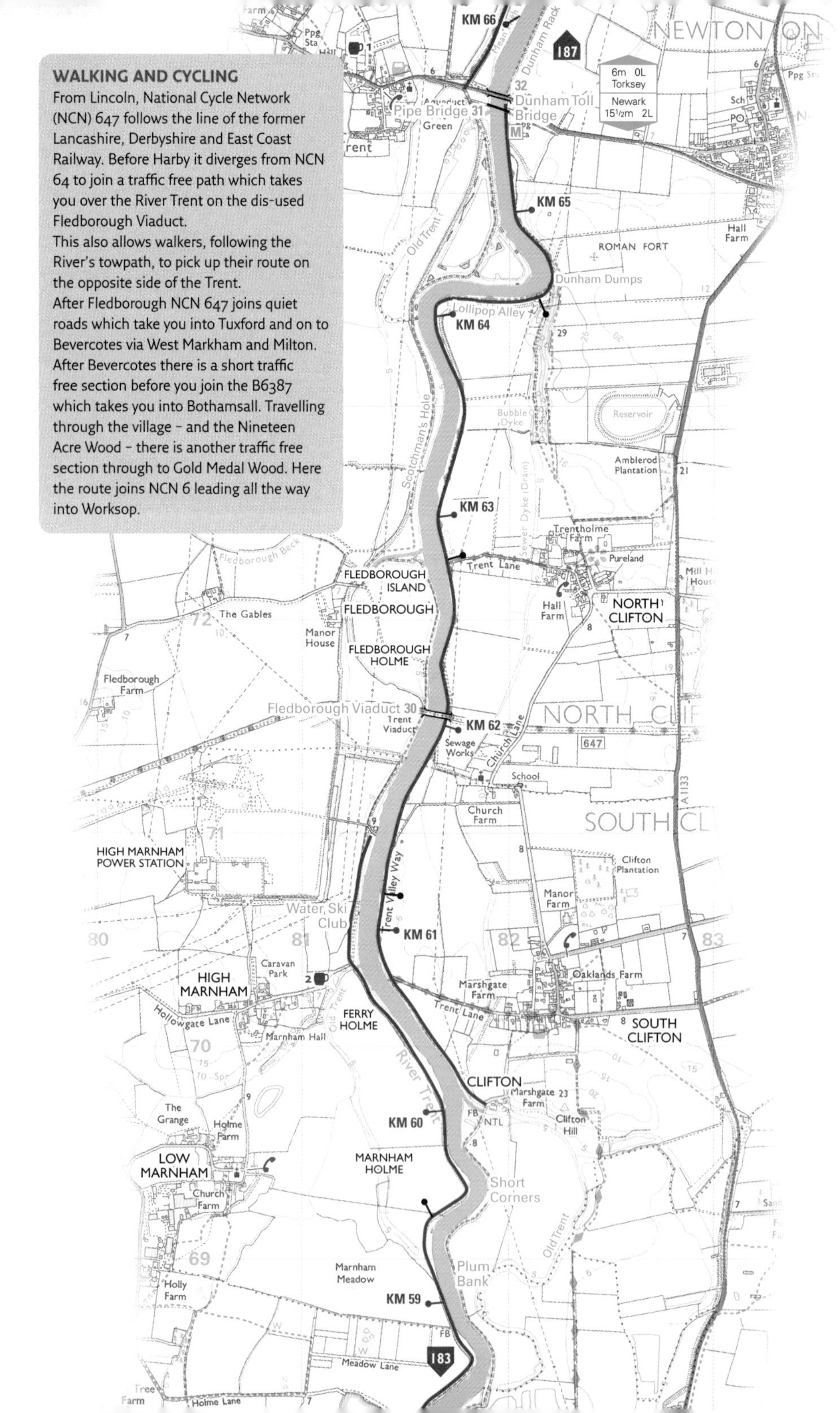

WALKING AND CYCLING

From Lincoln, National Cycle Network (NCN) 647 follows the line of the former Lancashire, Derbyshire and East Coast Railway. Before Harby it diverges from NCN 64 to join a traffic free path which takes you over the River Trent on the dis-used Fledborough Viaduct.

This also allows walkers, following the River's towpath, to pick up their route on the opposite side of the Trent.

After Fledborough NCN 647 joins quiet roads which take you into Tuxford and on to Bevercotes via West Markham and Milton. After Bevercotes there is a short traffic free section before you join the B6387 which takes you into Bothamsall. Travelling through the village – and the Nineteen Acre Wood – there is another traffic free section through to Gold Medal Wood. Here the route joins NCN 6 leading all the way into Worksop.

Dunham Bridge

The river wriggles around Plum Bank and Short Corners on its approach to High Marnham, passing the course of the Old Trent river. High Marnham was at one time two hamlets: Ferry Marnham and Church Marnham. The old Hall which stood between them was demolished in 1800. It was the property of the Cartwright family who held many claims to fame. Dr Edmund Cartwright invented the power loom which revolutionised the weaving industry. One of his brothers was the engineer responsible for the construction of the Ramper Road leading into Newark over raised arches. Another was an admiral in Lord Nelson's navy. Near the railway viaduct is the isolated church of St George, situated equidistant between North and South Clifton in order to serve both parishes. North Clifton once had the use of a ferry which was free to its inhabitants. 1½ miles further, the river describes a sharp S-bend as it passes a welcome little ridge of hills, pleasantly wooded. But the ridge fades away as one reaches Dunham Toll Bridge (the present structure replacing one built in 1832) and the iron aqueduct that precedes it. Once a market town, Dunham was notorious for its flooding. The Trent frequently caused buildings to be awash with up to 10ft of water. As a consequence most of the inhabitants were boat owners in order to maintain communications during the floods. Recent flood protection measures have, hopefully, made such events a thing of the past. The countryside resumes its flat and rather featureless aspect, while the river now forms the border between Nottinghamshire and Lincolnshire (as far downstream as West Stockwith). From Stapleford to Dunham the river is a birdwatcher's paradise of water meadows, pools and marshes. *Mooring* is available on a CRT pontoon at Dunham, just upstream of the bridge on the east bank.

NAVIGATIONAL NOTES

At Fledborough (sunken) island, steer a line between the middle of the river and the west bank.

Pubs and Restaurants

1 **The White Swan** Main Street, Dunham on Trent, Newark NG22 0TY (01777 228307; www.facebook.com/thewhiteswandunhamontrent). An attractive village hostelry serving real ale, real cider and food *daily 12.00-21.00*. Dog- and family-friendly, outdoor play area. *Regular* music nights. Quiz *Mon. Open 12.00-23.00.*

2 **The Brownlow Arms** High Marnham, Newark NG23 6SG (01636 822505; www.facebook.com/the-Brownlow-arms-high-marnham-124136702282). This family pub, with a large garden and children's play area, serves real ales and food *L and E (not Mon L)*. Dog- and family-friendly, garden. Traditional pub games, real fires and sports TV. Boat launching facilities. Telephone for details. Also Camping. *Open Mon-Fri L and E (not Mon L) and Sat-Sun 12.00-23.00 (23.30).*

QUAY STRATEGY

Navigating the tidal Trent, the boater is constantly aware of the potential - both present and future - to move large bulk loads effortlessly. Evidence of the river's past glory as a waterways highway can be found at every tortuous twist and turn in the form of decaying wharves and abandoned jetties. The waterfront at Gainsborough, once heaving with barge traffic - often moored as many as three-deep - jostling for position to load or unload, is now moribund, locked in by concrete flood defences. This apparent shame at a past prosperity, one that was largely water-generated, is a telling indictment on the importance now attached to what was arguably the original form of green transport. Logic, it would appear, is completely lacking in a system that eschews the economies and scale of water transport in favour of diesel guzzling lorries. But, on reflection, is it? The more diesel consumed, the more revenue for the government. The greater the number of lorries cluttering up the roads, the greater the income from the road fund licence. Could it be that in promoting the benefits of water transport the chancellor is at risk of shooting himself in the foot or, possibly, in economic terms somewhere far more painful?

Torksey

At Laneham the traveller will enjoy a little relief from the Trent's isolation. Here there is a church and a few houses on a slight rise near the river. A farmhouse on the river bank was built on the site of the old manor. The cellars in the building are reputed to date back even further than this to the time when the land belonged to the palace of the Archbishops of York. To the north of the village, yet another power station - Cottam - appears as the river turns back on itself to the south before swinging northwards again at the junction of the Fossdyke Navigation (marked by a pumping station). The lock up into the Fossdyke is just through the road bridge, *mooring* is below the bridge and there is gas at the caravan site, together with *a pub* and a *petrol station* (*provisions* can be purchased from the pub). Torksey offers a haven for the boater navigating the tidal Trent with *72-hour pontoon moorings, water and toilets,* together with a *barbecue area.* There is also an excellent *tearoom* at the lock - for further information on Torksey *see* page 66. Nearing the railway viaduct at Torksey, one sees the gaunt ruin of Torksey Castle standing beside the river. As at Newark, the façade that faces the Trent is the most complete part of the building, for the rest has vanished. (The castle has been abandoned since the 16th C.) For the first 15ft or so from the ground, the castle is built of stone - above this it is dark-red brick. In most cases mooring on the tidal Trent is not recommended.

NAVIGATIONAL NOTES

Boaters intending to break their passage to Cromwell Lock, by staying on the pontoon mooring at Dunham, are requested to inform the lock keeper at Torksey to avoid alarm at their non-arrival at Cromwell. Similarly should you change your plans and subsequently stop at Dunham, please contact a lock keeper to avoid unnecessary concern for your safety. The relevant telephone numbers are:

Cromwell Lock: 01636 821213/07887 754485
Torksey Lock: 01427 718202/07884 238781

Laneham

Notts. Tel. Originally Lanum, the parish is divided into two areas, Church Laneham, also known as Laneham Ferry, and Laneham itself, the two being little more than half a mile apart. The church of St Peter is well worth a visit. Its wonderful Norman doorway, heavily decorated with chevron, herringbone and sunflower patterns, still contains the original Norman door, hanging on the very hinges on which it was mounted in the 11th C. The tower was once used as a watch tower over the Trent ferry. The ringing chamber of the tower contains 25 wedding rings or cheeses. These date back to the period between 1813 and 1840 when it became the custom for couples married at the church to pay the ringers a sage cheese or five shillings each for the privilege of having their initials placed in a ring.

Pubs and Restaurants

X 1 **Torksey Tearoom** The Lock House, Torksey LN1 2EH (01427 717923). Beside the lock, this establishment is rightly famed for its sausage rolls, homemade cakes and pastries, superb teas and coffees and for its jams and pickles. Also snacks, ices and a Civil Ceremony Licence! *Open 5 days a week 11.00-16.00 (closed Mon & Fri).*

2 **The White Swan** Newark Road, Torksey LN1 2EJ (01427 718653; www.facebook.com/whiteswantorkseylock). Near the lock. A local village pub, popular with boaters and fishermen. Real ale is served, along with food *Mon-Sat L and E (not Mon & Thu L) and Sun 12.00-16.00.* Children welcome, and there is a play area and garden. Traditional pub games, real fires and sports TV. Basic provisions available. Dog-friendly. *Open 12.00-23.00 (Mon, Tue & Thu 16.00).*

X 3 **The Ferry Boat Inn** Church Laneham, Retford DN22 0NQ (01777 228350; www.ferryboatpub.co.uk). Temporary moorings below the caravan park give access to this friendly pub which is just a short walk up from the river. Real ale is served as well as home-made food *Tue-Sun 12.00-20.00 (Sun 17.00).* Dog- and family-friendly, outside seating. Traditional pub games, live music, real fires, sports TV and Wi-Fi. Camping. *Open Tue-Sat 12.00-22.00 (Fri-Sat 00.00) & Sun 12.00-21.00.*

WALKING AND CYCLING

Torksey Railway Bridge, unused since the last train rumbled over it in 1959, has been given a new lease of life carrying a permissive footpath across the Trent, thereby eliminating an 11-mile round trip for walkers and cyclists. Opened in 1849, this rare example of a steel, tubular girder structure was designed by Sir John Fowler, co-designer of the illustrious Forth Railway Bridge. Its two 130ft spans once carried the Sheffield & Lincolnshire Railway, later to become part of the Grand Central Railway, and the structure has subsequently been listed as Grade II*. However, this did not prevent it joining the Buildings at Risk Register so this recent resurrection is a timely intervention. Incidently, back in 1849, it took Sir John four months to convince the Railway Commissioners as to the integrity of the bridge's construction, before they would finally allow the first train across. The passage of time has surely vindicated the virtues of his design.

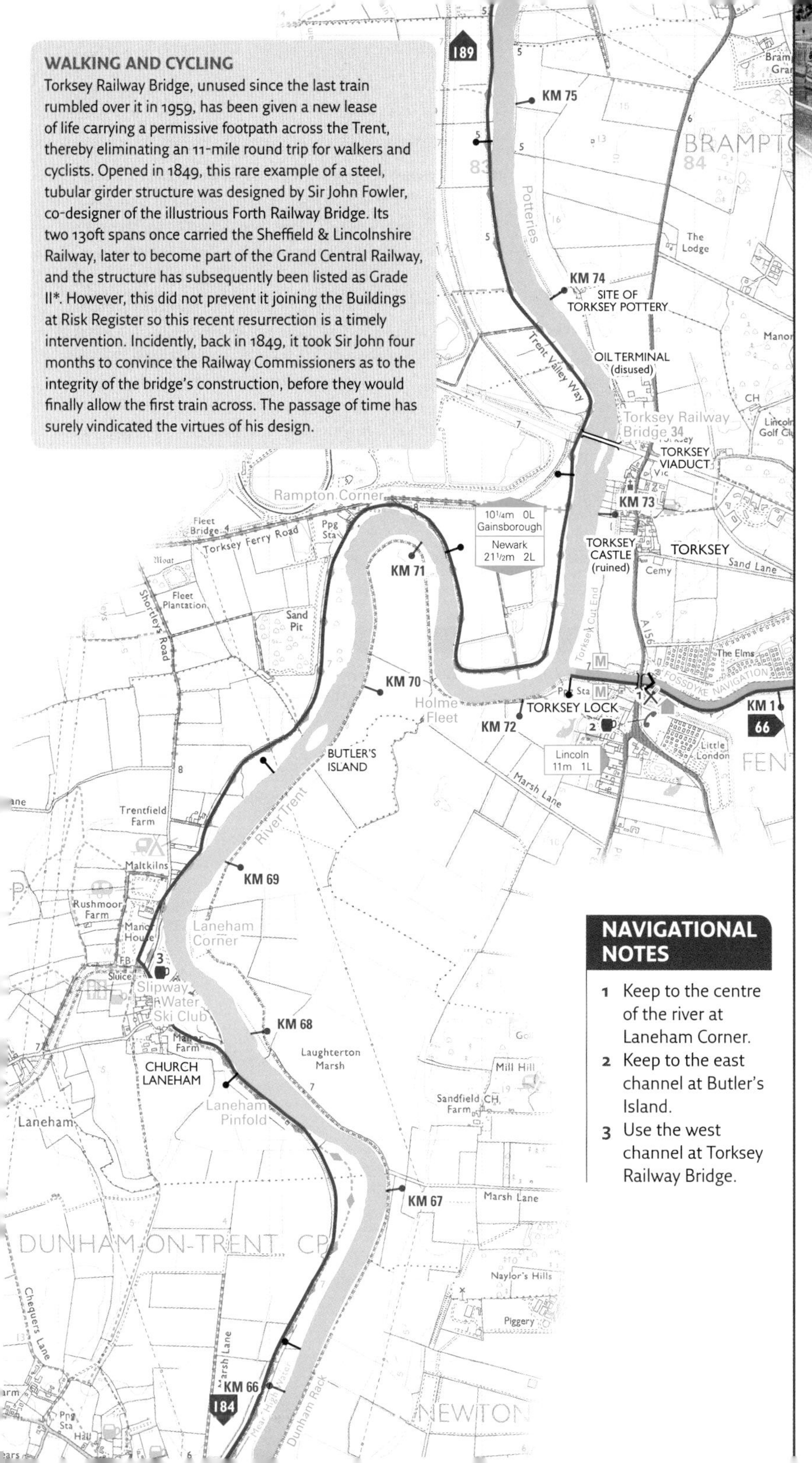

NAVIGATIONAL NOTES

1. Keep to the centre of the river at Laneham Corner.
2. Keep to the east channel at Butler's Island.
3. Use the west channel at Torksey Railway Bridge.

Littleborough

From Cottam, the river continues to wind northwards towards Gainsborough. This is not as dull a stretch as those further south. A windmill marks the exaggeratedly named Trent Port, which is in fact the wharf for the small village of Marton. Speedboats operate from here, but owners of any larger boats will once again find it difficult to land. Marton was important in Saxon times because of its position near the ford where a Roman road (now the A1500) crossed the Trent. This ford marked the western boundary of the ancient kingdom of Lindsay. Many historians believe that Saint Paulinus baptised some of the first Saxon Christians here in AD627. The church of St Margaret has evolved around an early Saxon church, side aisles being added to the original structure. The tapering Anglo-Saxon tower still reveals some fine herringbone masonry. In 1904 it was discovered that the entire structure was unsafe as it had been built on foundations only two feet deep made of sand and pebbles. The next place of interest is Littleborough, a tiny riverside settlement. Fortunately boats may moor temporarily at the floating jetty. Below Littleborough is a beautiful reach with steep wooded hills rising from the water's edge on the Lincolnshire side. The attractive brick and stone building set in the parkland is called Burton Château. A little further downstream, another clump of trees on the east bank at Knaith conceals a former nunnery and chapel, but mooring is only just possible here. On towards Gainsborough, the cooling towers of West Burton Power Station stand out prominently in the flat landscape on the west side of the river.

NAVIGATIONAL NOTES

Approaching Marton Mill corner from the south, the channel is on the inside (to the west) of the corner and moves across to the outside (to the north) as the river swings west.

- **Knaith**
  Lincs. Temporary mooring just possible. Among the trees is the Hall and an interesting old church with a Jacobean pulpit. Both were part of a nunnery dissolved in 1539. The Hall was the birthplace of Thomas Sutton, who founded Charterhouse School and Hospital.
- **Littleborough**
  Notts. An attractive hamlet with reasonably good access from the river. The little church stands on a slight rise; it is a delightfully simple Norman structure and incorporates much herringbone masonry. It is assumed from various finds, including the perfectly preserved body of a woman dug up in the graveyard, that this was the site of the Roman camp Segelocum. The paved ford dating from the time of Emperor Hadrian became visible during a drought in 1933. King Harold's army crossed this ford on its way to Hastings in 1066.

BREAKFAST AT POTTERIES

Viewed from the wheelbox of a sand-carrying barge, the Romans and their ilk were untidy fellows. Clearly they thought nothing of tossing their rubbish into the river - to make a ford or empty a failed kiln - and might be considered the forerunners of the contemporary litter lout. A heavily-laden barge lumbers down this river with difficulty, banging the bottom on even the most generous ebb, unsure where she'll finally come to rest to await the next flood tide. History's cast-offs do nothing to help the situation and invariably result in an unscheduled halt, mid-river. Piling stones on the river bed, to form a ford, might have seemed a good idea to the Romans at the time. It is not, however, an opinion widely shared amongst barge skippers of today. Littleborough doubtless offers plenty to excite the archaeologist with its wealth of antiquity, whilst a short distance upstream, connoisseurs of porcelain can wax lyrical about the decorative output from the 19th-C Torksey Pottery. The common thread lies in the debris ejected into the tideway (commemorated in the name of this reach), making it a sure-fire resting place for loaded barges and an enforced bed and breakfast stop for their crew.

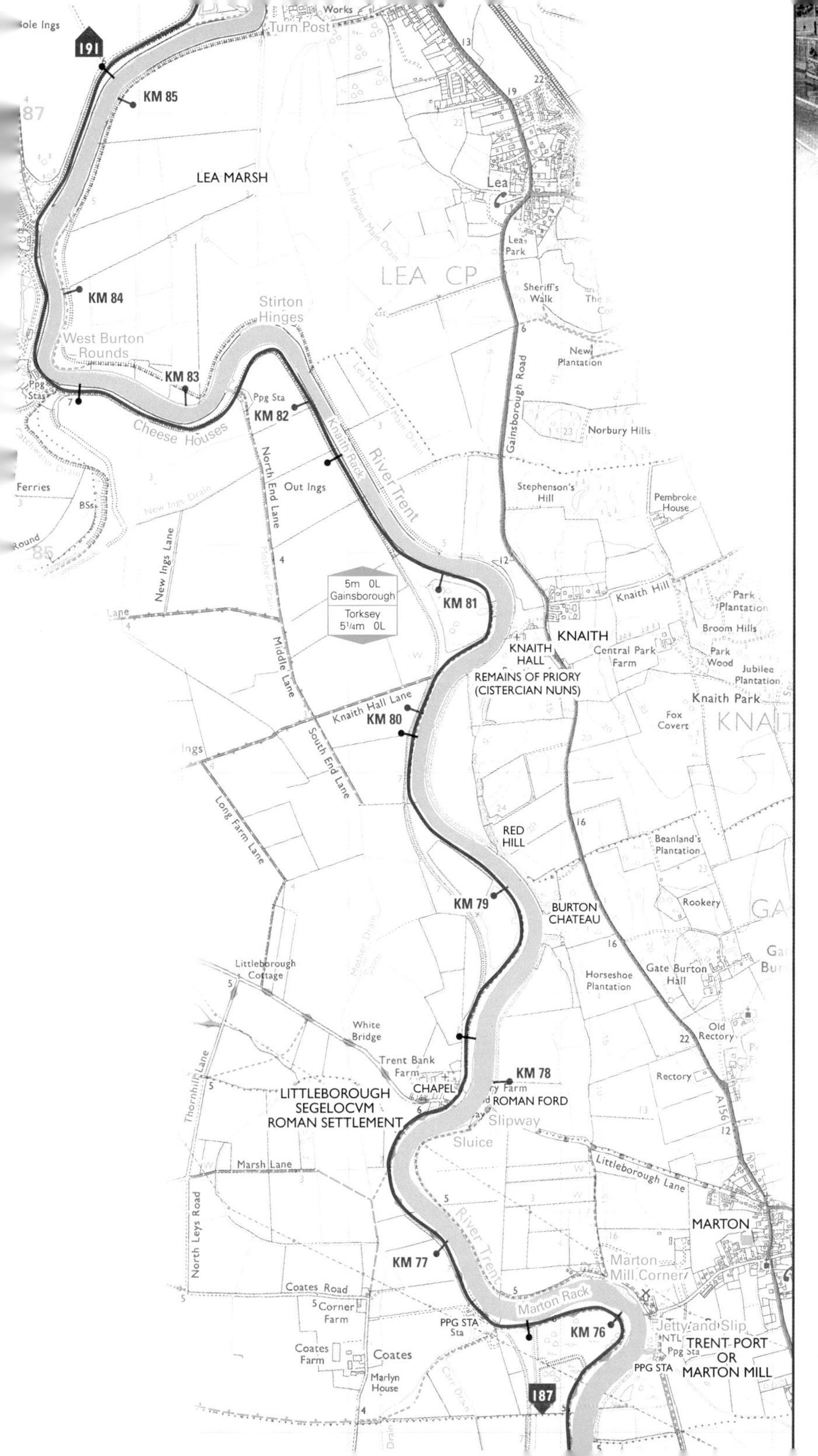
191
KM 85
LEA MARSH
Lea
Lea Park
LEA CP
Sheriff's Walk
KM 84
Stirton Hinges
West Burton Rounds
KM 83
Ppg Sta
KM 82
Cheese Houses
Knaith Rack
River Trent
Gainsborough Road
New Plantation
Norbury Hills
Out Ings
North End Lane
New Ings Lane
Stephenson's Hill
Pembroke House
Ferries
5m 0L Gainsborough
Torksey 5¼m 0L
KM 81
Knaith Hill
Park Plantation
Broom Hills
KNAITH
KNAITH HALL
Central Park Farm
Park Wood
Jubilee Plantation
REMAINS OF PRIORY (CISTERCIAN NUNS)
Middle Lane
Knaith Hall Lane
KM 80
Knaith Park
Fox Covert
South End Lane
Long Farm Lane
RED HILL
Beanland's Plantation
Rookery
KM 79
BURTON CHATEAU
Littleborough Cottage
Horseshoe Plantation
Gate Burton Hall
White Bridge
Old Rectory
Trent Bank Farm
KM 78
Rectory
Thornhill Lane
LITTLEBOROUGH SEGELOCVM ROMAN SETTLEMENT
CHAPEL
ROMAN FORD
Slipway
Sluice
Marsh Lane
Littleborough Lane
North Leys Road
MARTON
KM 77
Marton Mill Corner
Coates Road
Corner Farm
Marton Rack
PPG STA
KM 76
Jetty and Slip
TRENT PORT OR MARTON MILL
Coates Farm
Coates
Marlyn House
187

Gainsborough

The river moves away from the wooded slopes, passes the power station (the northernmost on the river) and heads for Gainsborough, which is clearly indicated by a group of tall flour mills. Below the railway bridge, the river bends sharply before reaching these mills, the bridge at Gainsborough and the desolate wharfs. With the completion of the new flood defences, much of this area has been changed into an attractive riverside walk with an imaginatively landscaped area just below Gainsborough Arches. Further north, handy for the town, there is a secure *pontoon mooring* accessed with a Watermate key. The town is set entirely on one side of the river, and is worth visiting. It was once a centre for heavy engineering and home to Marshall Tractors, manufacturers of the famous traction engines and the firm where L.T.C. Rolt (author and inland waterway campaigner) was first introduced to steam propulsion.

NAVIGATIONAL NOTES

1. Below Gainsborough Arches the River Trent ceases to be under the jurisdiction of CRT and is controlled by the Humber Navigation by-laws. These are administered by Associated British Ports (ABP) from whom a copy may be obtained by telephoning 01482 327171/212191 (www.humber.com).
2. ABP require all vessels navigating within their jurisdiction **TO HAVE A MINIMUM CREW OF TWO AND CARRY VHF RADIO**. It is regarded as an essential aid to navigating tidal, commercial waterways, as it allows the boater to know the whereabouts of other craft, and to maintain contact with lock keepers who listen out on channels 16 and 74-working on channel 74. See note on page 180 for telephone contact.
3. CRT request that boaters give lock keepers along the tidal river *24 hours' notice* of passage. Always seek advice from lock keepers and respect their skill and experience.
4. The Trent Series Charts, published by The Boating Association (www.theboatingassociation.co.uk), are detailed charts of the tidal Trent (and the tidal Ouse and non-tidal Trent) and are available from their website. Also from CRT lock keepers. Charge.
5. The Aegir, or tidal bore, a tidal wave of between 1ft and 5ft in height, and breaking at the sides, may be encountered between Keadby and Torksey. It is normally only seen on spring tides of over 25ft (Hull), and arrives at the same time as the flood, although there can be a variation of half an hour each way. If you are on the river, keep a watch for it, and meet it head on, facing straight downstream and in the middle of the river. If you are anchored, use twice the normal length of warp. If you are moored, try to tie up to a pontoon mooring or large craft, which will itself rise and fall with the wave.

● **Gainsborough**
Lincs. All services, two stations. Gainsborough is best seen from the river, where the old wharves and warehouses serve as a reminder of the town's significance as a port in the 18th and 19th C. Once qualifying as Britain's furthest inland port, there is now no evidence of the boats (of up to 850 tonnes deadweight) that used to carry animal feedstuffs, grain, fertilisers and scrap metals. Elsewhere industrial sprawl and Victorian red-brick housing tend to obscure the qualities of this old market town. There are several Victorian churches, but All Saints retains its Perpendicular tower. Gainsborough was a frequent battleground during the Civil War and George Eliot described it as St Ogg's in *The Mill on the Floss*.
All Saints Parish Church Church Street, Gainsborough DN21 2JR (01427 611036). *Open during daylight hours.* Café *open Mon-Sat.*
Gainsborough Old Hall Parnell Street, Gainsborough DN21 2NB (01427 677348; www.gainsborougholdhall.com). An attractive manor house in the centre of town, now a folk museum: it contains a medieval kitchen and Great Hall. Here Henry VIII met Catherine Parr, later his sixth wife, who was the daughter-in-law of the house. The Pilgrim Fathers also met here. *Open Mar-Oct, Mon-Fri 10.00-17.00 & Sat-Sun 10.30-17.00; Nov-Feb, Mon-Fri 10.00-16.00 & Sat-Sun 10.30-16.00.* Charge.
Model Railway Museum 23 Florence Terrace, Gainsborough DN21 1BE (01427 615367; www.gainsboroughmodelrailway.co.uk). *Telephone for opening times.*
Old Nick Theatre 31 Spring Gardens, Gainsborough DN21 2AY (01427 810616; www.gainsboroughtheatrecompany.com). *Telephone for performance details and bookings.*
Trinity Arts Centre Trinity Street, Gainsborough DN21 2AL (01427 676655/676676; www.microsites.lincolnshire.gov.uk/tac). Box office *open Wed-Fri 10.00-14.00 & Sat 09.30-13.00.*

West Lindsey Leisure Centre The Avenue, Gainsborough DN21 1EP (01427 615169; www.everyoneactive.com). *Open Mon–Fri 07.00–22.00, Sat–Sun 08.00–20.00.* **Gainsborough Tourist Information Centre** Guildhall, Marshall's Yard, Gainsborough DN21 2NA (01427 676666; www.visitlincolnshire.com).

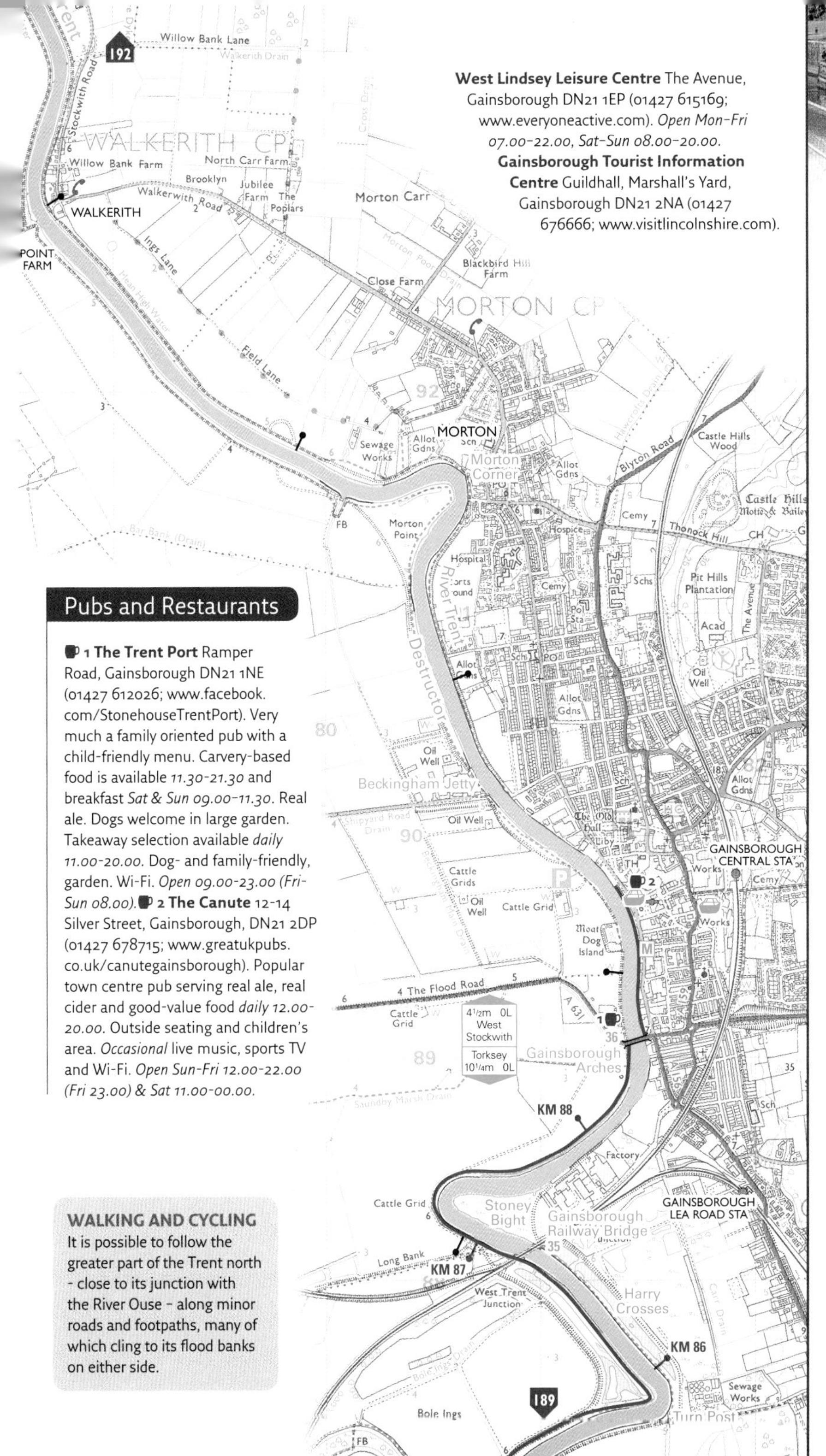

Pubs and Restaurants

1 The Trent Port Ramper Road, Gainsborough DN21 1NE (01427 612026; www.facebook.com/StonehouseTrentPort). Very much a family oriented pub with a child-friendly menu. Carvery-based food is available *11.30–21.30* and breakfast *Sat & Sun 09.00–11.30*. Real ale. Dogs welcome in large garden. Takeaway selection available *daily 11.00–20.00*. Dog- and family-friendly, garden. Wi-Fi. *Open 09.00–23.00 (Fri–Sun 08.00)*.

2 The Canute 12–14 Silver Street, Gainsborough, DN21 2DP (01427 678715; www.greatukpubs.co.uk/canutegainsborough). Popular town centre pub serving real ale, real cider and good-value food *daily 12.00–20.00*. Outside seating and children's area. *Occasional* live music, sports TV and Wi-Fi. *Open Sun–Fri 12.00–22.00 (Fri 23.00) & Sat 11.00–00.00.*

WALKING AND CYCLING

It is possible to follow the greater part of the Trent north - close to its junction with the River Ouse - along minor roads and footpaths, many of which cling to its flood banks on either side.

West Stockwith

On leaving Gainsborough the river passes the jetty of the Trent Wharfage Group on the left. This was once the destination of the large coasters which occasionally plied the Trent above Gunness, where they discharged cargoes of ferro-metals, timber, fertilisers, bulk chemicals and animal feeds. They were able to carry loads of up to 1250 tonnes at a time, shipped from as far away as Sweden. Then the navigation bends sharply to the left, passing Moreton Wharf with its old Flemish gables and new housing, winding its way past the hamlet of Walkerith towards West Stockwith. Immediately after the sharp right-hand bend in the river (below Farmers Jetty) the entrance lock into the Chesterfield Canal is visible on the left, giving access into the basin with its *boater facilities, moorings* and friendly yacht club. Just downstream from the basin the River Idle, barricaded in by steel flood doors, joins the Trent beside West Stockwith's unusual

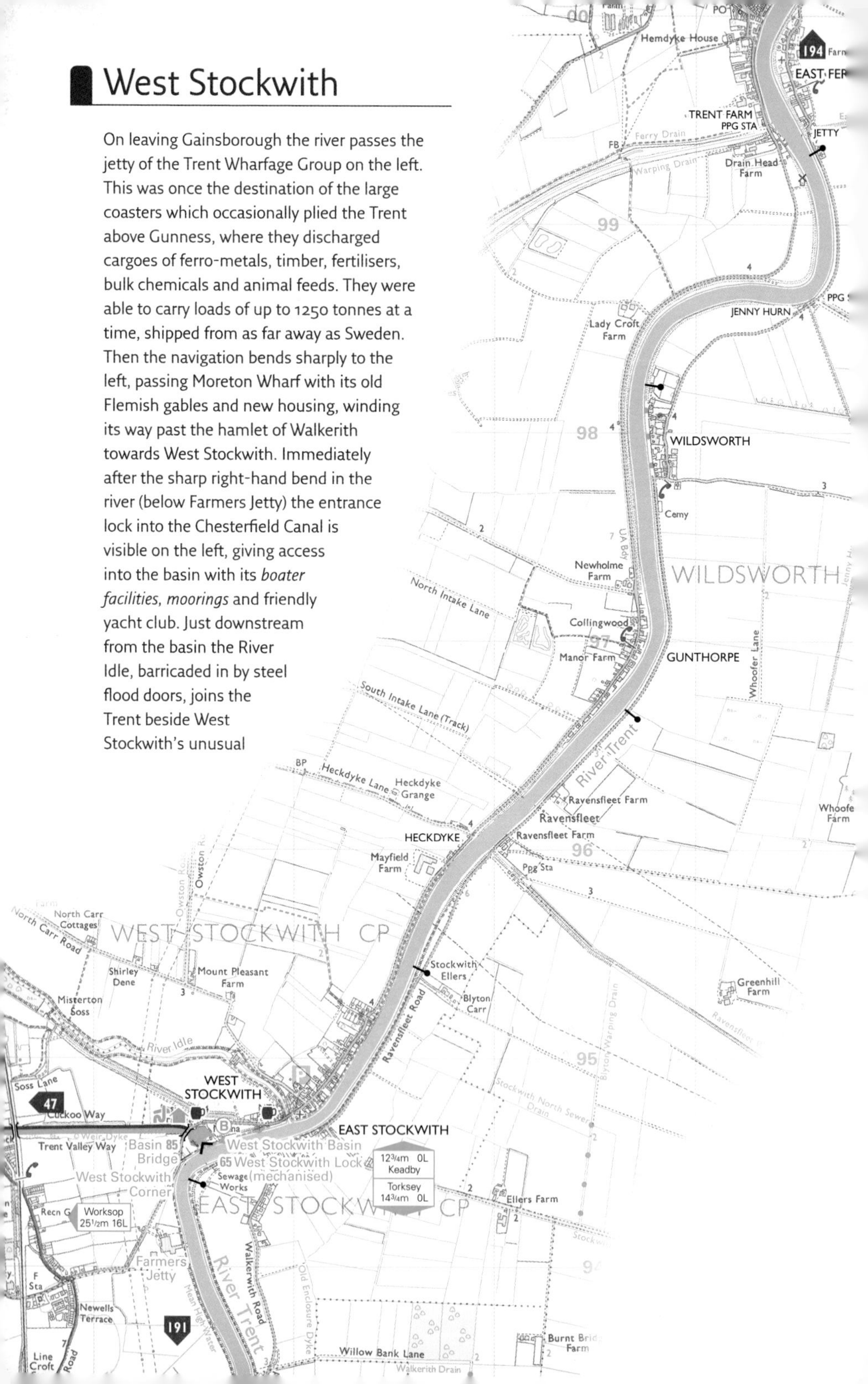

18th-C Georgian church. This was once the main highway from the industrial areas of South Yorkshire, terminating at a large wharf in Bawtry. Goods travelled to and from the town by horse and cart and, before the development of the River Don as a reliable navigation, were dependent upon the River Idle for onward transport. In draining the Isle of Axholme in the 17th C, Cornelius Vermuyden modified the course of the Idle and drastically reduced its effectiveness as a navigable waterway. From the river, West Stockwith, now a conservation area, presents a closed-in, almost intimate, aspect with its many tall three-storey buildings. It is possible to catch the occasional tantalising glimpse into the village up tiny passages, or ginnels, running between the houses. Once a thriving boat building community - there were five boatyards only 100 years ago - West Stockwith had a population of 5,000 in the 1880s; it is now reduced to 240. The brick-built church, looking more like a chapel capped with a squat bell tower, is one of only three of its kind and was completed in 1722. Inside the plasterwork is classic Adam. *See* page 47 for further details on the village. Leaving West Stockwith the Trent follows a comparatively straight course passing the isolated hamlets of Gunthorpe and Wildsworth, barely visible to the boater hidden as they are below the river's flood banks. All this area bordering the river was, in AD886, part of the Danelaw, and place names with *by* and *thorpe* endings are of Viking derivation. A sense of isolation and independence persists into the 21st C from a time when the Wash, the Trent and the Humber effectively cut this area off from the remainder of the country. In those times the inhabitants identified more with Denmark, Holland and the sea than with the rest of England.

NAVIGATIONAL NOTES

1. Entering the Chesterfield Canal from the Trent can be tricky due to the tidal flow across the entrance to the lock. A leaflet is available from CRT 0303 040 4040 (and from most Trent locks) with instructions on how to access the lock safely - or contact the lock keeper. The lock accepts craft up a maximum size of 72' x 17' 6". The lock is keeper-operated (give as much prior notice as possible by telephoning 01427 890204/07884 238780) and passage can usually be made
   2½ hours before to 4½ hours after high water. By coincidence, flood (when the tide ceases ebbing and turns to come back in) at Stockwith is almost the same time as high water at Hull. The flood runs for approximately 2½ hours and the direction of flow changes very rapidly.
2. Keepers at all the Trent locks can be contacted on marine band VHF radio, calling channel 16, working channel 74 - the radio is not constantly manned - or by telephone using the numbers listed below:
   Cromwell Lock 01636 821213/07887 754485;
   West Stockwith Lock 01427 890204/07884 238780;
   Torksey Lock 01427 718202/07884 238781;
   Keadby Lock 01724 782205/07733 124611.
   Commercial river traffic operates on channel 6 upstream of Keadby Bridge and it is useful for VHF users to monitor this channel to establish the whereabouts of large craft.
3. Deep-draughted commercial traffic, especially coasters, require the deepest channel on the navigation at all times. Be prepared to give way to allow for this and do not necessarily expect to pass port to port when meeting craft head on.
4. Boaters intending to break their passage to Cromwell Lock, by staying on the pontoon mooring at Dunham, are requested to inform the lock keeper at West Stockwith to avoid alarm at their non-arrival at Cromwell. Similarly, should you change your plans and subsequently stop at Dunham, please contact a lock keeper to avoid unnecessary concern for your safety.

Owston Ferry

The conical tower of an old windmill on the left bank has been restored as part of a spacious new dwelling on a fairly grand scale – even to the point of having a helipad sited on an adjacent field. This feature, very much of the 21st C, contrasts strongly with the mellow buildings of Owston Ferry directly ahead. As the channel swings to the right, the pleasing scale of the riverside houses becomes apparent. Skilfully constructed using local brick and tile, they are both solid and graceful in appearance. There is something reminiscent of a Dutch painting in the views over the river seen from the lower part of the village. The church, standing a little way from the waterway, is largely medieval, but with early 19th-C Gothic additions, and inside there is an attractive rood screen dating from 1897. Although modern executive dwellings have crept into the village, generally by way of infill, it is the largely three-storey, Dutch-influenced buildings that still predominate. At Robin Hood's Well to the north west, Roman coins have been found, indicating that this is a settlement of some antiquity. Flowing northwards the river regains its isolation amidst the flat, fertile countryside behind the flood banks. Throughout history this area has been known as the Isle of Axholme – once a wetland prone to seasonal flooding and in ancient times a forest, heath and then marsh. It is a tract of low, flat land less than 100ft above sea level, some 5 miles wide and running for approximately 18 miles along the Trent's western bank. In 1625 a Dutchman, Cornelius Vermuyden, was brought over to oversee the draining of the area at a cost of £56,000. The land's natural fertility was soon realised under the Dutch and French Protestant settlers that followed him, much to the disgust of the ousted native inhabitants. After lengthy litigation the land was finally divided in 1691, the locals receiving 10,532 acres and the settlers 2,868 acres. The chief town in the area is Epworth, some 4 miles west of Kelfield and famous as the birthplace, in 1703, of John Wesley, founder of Methodism. His father was rector of the parish for 59 years. Over the years the pattern of agriculture in the area has varied, reflecting a changing society. At the time when the Wesley family lived at Epworth, flax and hemp, used in the manufacture of sacking and canvas, were amongst the principal crops. Walnut trees were plentiful along the east bank of the river, the nuts gathered as a further source of income. Today intensive vegetable growing, cereals and root crops predominate.

NAVIGATIONAL NOTES

The substantial mooring dolphins located on various reaches of the navigation – e.g. north and south of the M180 bridge – are for the safety of commercial craft and not to be used by pleasure vessels. They do not provide a way ashore.

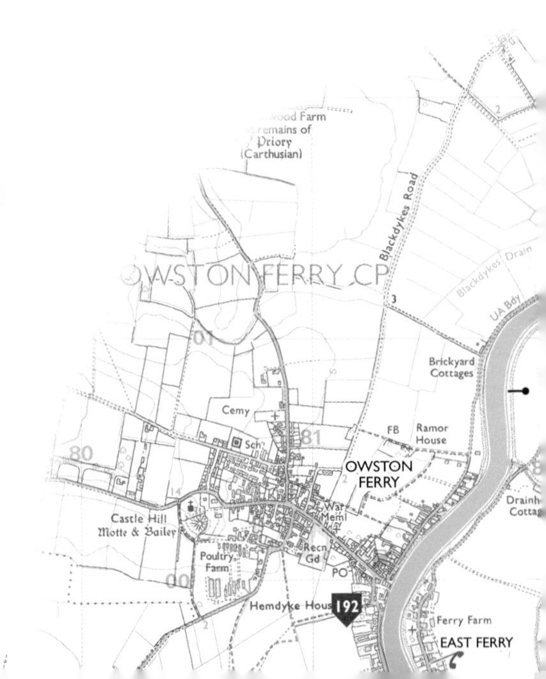

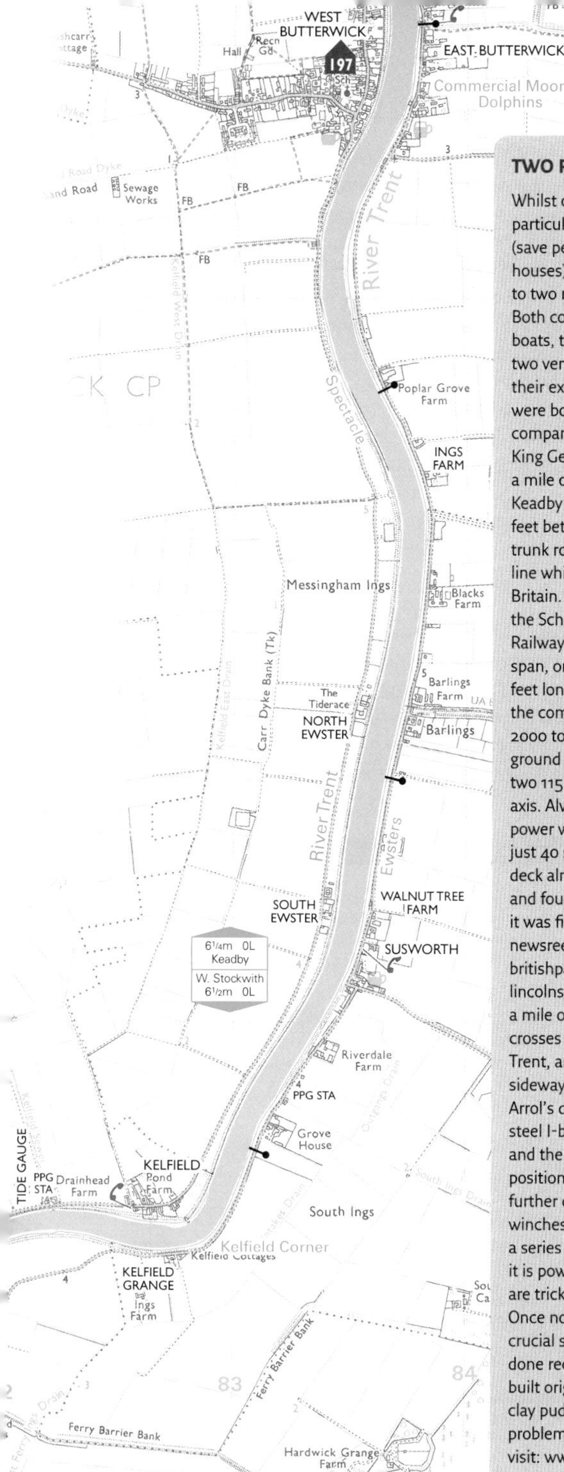

TWO ROLLING RAILROADS

Whilst on the face of it there is nothing particularly outstanding about Keadby (save perhaps for its total dirth of public houses) the settlement in fact plays host to two rather extraordinary railway bridges. Both constructed to permit the passage of boats, their designers, however, adopted two very different engineering strategies in their execution although, coincidently, they were both built by the same construction company -Sir William Arrol & Co of Glasgow. King George V Bridge spans the Trent half a mile or so upstream of the Stainforth & Keadby Canal's junction with the river. 548 feet between abutments, it carries the A18 trunk road alongside a double track railway line which sees 60% of all freight carried in Britain. It was designed by James Ball - on the Scherzer principle - for the Grand Central Railway and completed in 1916. The lifting span, on the east bank of the river, is 163 feet long and weighs 3,500 tons of which the compensating ballast tanks amount to 2000 tons. In operation it rolled around its ground based segmented 'feet,' powered by two 115 hp. electric motors mounted at its axis. Always near the point of balance, little power was required for operation which took just 40 seconds and was completed with the deck almost vertical. It was last lifted in 1956 and four years later, under Act of Parliament, it was fixed closed. This rather charming Pathé newsreel clip shows it in operation: www.britishpathe.com/video/a-novel-bridge-in-lincolnshire. Although separated by less than a mile of track, Vazon Sliding Railway Bridge crosses the canal, near its junction with the Trent, and operates by drawing the entire span sideways to rest on the bank. Built in 1925 to Arrol's design (and rebuilt in 2004) its riveted steel I-beam construction is carried on rollers, and the entire deck is winched into the open position, to allow for the passage of boats. A further combination of wire ropes and pulleys winches it back into place, where it rests on a series of jacks and wedges. Interestingly, it is powered by a bank of batteries, which are trickle charged from the mains supply. Once notorious for sticking at the most crucial stages of operation, much has been done recently to stabilise the abutments - built originally on made-up ground on the clay puddle - which were at the root of the problem. For an animation of its workings, visit: www.movablebridges.co.uk/keadby.htm.

Keadby

The twin villages of East and West Butterwick now come into view, facing each other across the river. As seems so often to be the case on the lower part of the Trent, the village to the west is larger than its eastern counterpart. West Butterwick is another village with a strong Dutch influence evident in the local buildings. It has an attractive church built in 1841 from creamy white brick, deceptively stone-like from a distance. It follows the Gothic style, and has a small octagonal spire together with period interior fittings. In contrast, East Butterwick is a plain place with a small church built in 1884 at a cost of £500. It was once described as being 'surrounded by root crops and often by fog'. Now the river begins to broaden out, passing under the M180 viaduct, built in 1978, and rising out of the flat countryside to clear the navigation. The scale of the river is such that the boater can now begin to appreciate just how major a watercourse the Trent really is – 150 miles long, with a catchment area of over 4,000 square miles. The river once flowed due east from Nottingham, discharging into the Wash. At some point in prehistory this channel became blocked and the river turned north, picking a course through the soft keuper marls, still evident in the many shoals along the navigation, to its present junction with the Ouse. Three thousand cubic feet of water a second discharge into the Humber, a volume greater than that from the Thames into the estuary. Throughout history the Trent has been exploited both as a trunk navigation and for its inherent fertility. For centuries farmers working the land beside the river have encouraged it to flood the fields during winter months, by directing its water along warping drains cut at right angles to the waterway. As the river water spread across the land the fertile sediment settled out, enriching the soil and raising the water-table to sustain rich summer grazing. North of the M180 two further villages sit opposite one another – behind flood embankments – before Keadby is reached. These are Burringham to the east, with its early Victorian brick and slate church squatting beside the river, and Althorpe to the west, where the church, with its late Perpendicular tower, nestles in with the houses. Dedicated to St Oswald, it owes its origins

NAVIGATIONAL NOTES

1. Three red lights are normally displayed at all times when Keadby Lock is not available. A green light will be shown when there is sufficient depth of water over the cill to work the lock. This is theoretically up to 7 hours after high water, but despite constant dredging a sand bar builds up in front of the lock and 5 hours is often the maximum realistic time after high water that passage can be effected.
2. Shelter passes are available from the lock keeper for non-registered craft using CRT navigations and/or moorings for a limited period.
3. All locks and bridges on CRT waterways west of Keadby Swing Bridge are now boater-operated using the Watermate key. This key is also required for access to the lock area itself. Keadby Swing Bridge *only opens 07.00-10.00 & 15.00-17.00.*
4. Due to the number of craft requiring the lock and the varying tide envelope, please give the lock keeper *48 hours'* notice of your intention to use the lock.
5. Boaters intending to break their passage to Cromwell Lock, by staying on the pontoon mooring at Dunham, are requested to inform the lock keeper at Keadby to avoid alarm at their non-arrival at Cromwell. Similarly, should you change your plans and subsequently stop at Dunham, please contact a lock keeper to avoid unnecessary concern for your safety. VHF radio frequencies: calling channel 16, working channel 74; or telephone as below:
Cromwell Lock 01636 821213/07887 754485;
West Stockwith Lock 01427 890204/07884 238780;
Torksey Lock 01427 718202/07884 238781;
Keadby Lock 01724 782205/07733 124611.
6. Boaters navigating downstream of Keadby should check that their insurance policy covers them for this passage.
7. In order to secure your boat safely whilst using Keadby Lock, bow and stern ropes should be at least 30' in length.

to Sir John Nevill whose 1483 tower and chancel are incorporated into a larger structure. Both his coat of arms, and that of the Mowbray family, appear in stone, carved on the ogee arch of the west door. Less than a mile downstream of these villages is the combined road and rail bridge, built in 1916, which was the only bridge into the Isle of Axholme before the construction of the motorway viaduct (*see* page 195). When operational, it worked on the principle of water being pumped into the large counter balance tank on the upper structure of the eastern end of the bridge. Once filled with a mass of water slightly less than the weight of the bridge, the whole edifice proceeded to tip over into the open position. Boaters should follow the channel between the right-hand pier and the bank under the lifting section of the bridge, and beware of large vessels at Gunness Wharf immediately below. A further half mile below this bridge, on the left, is Keadby Lock (for further details of Keadby *see* page 162) leading into the Stainforth & Keadby section of the South Yorkshire Navigations. The entrance is often totally obscured by coasters unloading at the wharf between the sluice at the Three Rivers outfall and the lock itself which can quite literally be immediately ahead of the bows of a large vessel.

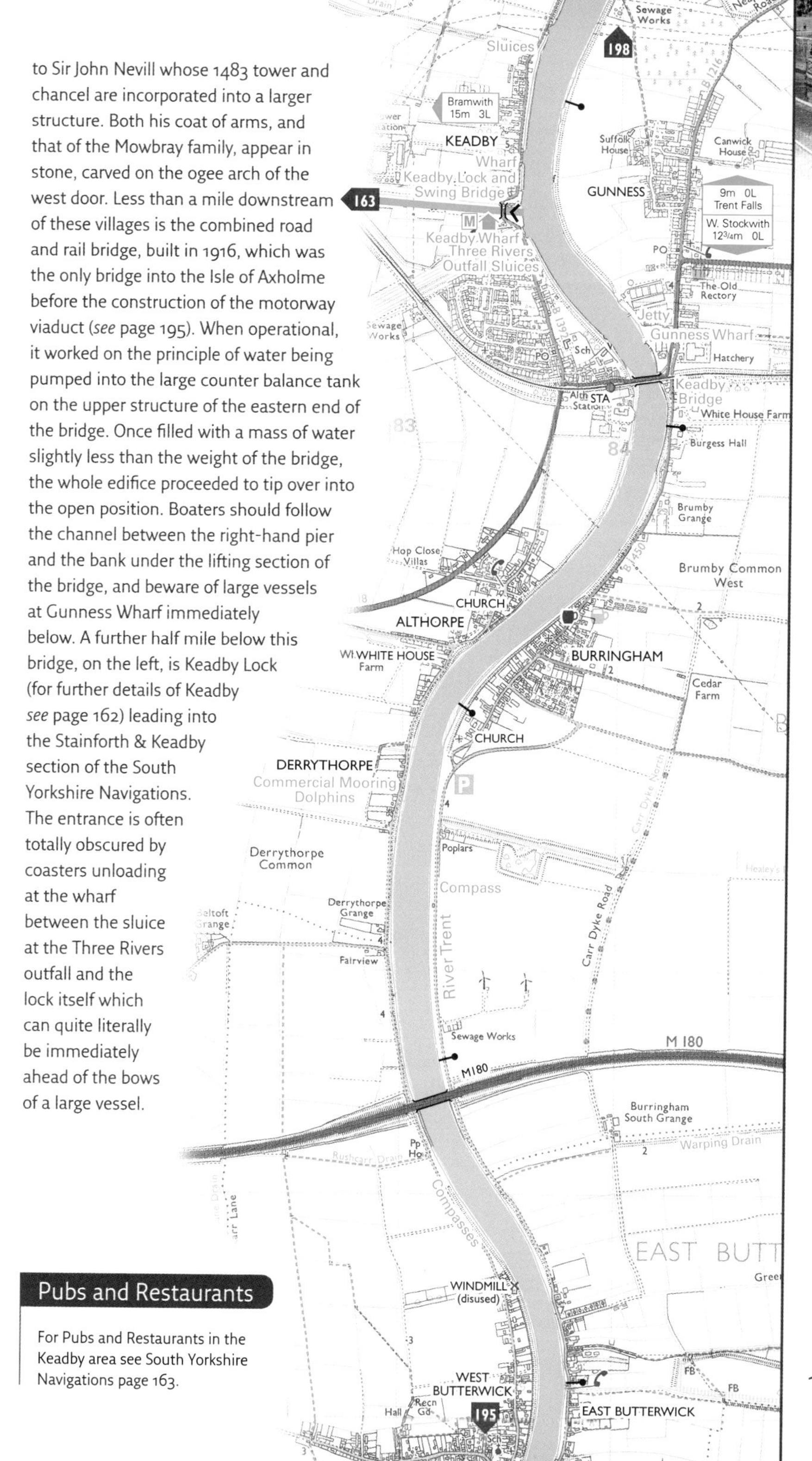

Pubs and Restaurants

For Pubs and Restaurants in the Keadby area see South Yorkshire Navigations page 163.

GARTHORPE SHORE
201
BURTON STATHER
MEDIEVAL VILLAGE OF WATERTON (site of)
Waterton Hall
Mast Hill Farm
Sewage Works
BURTON UPON STATHER
School
Carr Lane
Sewage Works
4½m 0L Trent Falls
Keadby 4½m 0L
Meredyke Rd
MERE DYKE
Burton Wood
Burton and Flixborough Drain
Cottley Hall Dyke
Livthorpe Kennels
River Trent
Flixborough Grange
FLIXBOROUGH
East Farm
Mineral Railway
Industrial Estate
AMCOTTS CP
Boskerdyke Drain
Pasture Lane
Manor House Farm
FLIXBOROUGH STATHER
Willow Holt
Middle Road
Hook House Farm
AMCOTTS
White House
Trent Side Farm
Park Ings Farm
Park Ings Store
Woodbine Cottage
Lysaght's Drain
Boskeydyke Farm
Neap House
Amcotts Hook
Skippingdale Industrial Park
Neap House Farm
Jetty
Jetties
Grove Wharf
Neap House Wharf
Ferry Road West
Crosby le Moor Farm
Grange Farm
Neap House Road
197

Burton Stather

This final section of the river is host to serious continental shipping and is punctuated by a series of bustling wharves. Coasters come and go with the tides carrying steel, coal and fertilisers and the constant activity of cranes, on the busy jetties, warms the heart of the true waterways enthusiast. It is perhaps not insignificant that the wharves are all in private ownership and, although relatively modest, they are nonetheless efficient for this and are clearly most cost-effective enterprises. It is probably unique for the boater, used to the prosaic names of inland pleasure craft, to be passing hulls bearing the cyrillic inscriptions of vessels registered in Eastern European ports - and beyond. Water depth for these craft is critical, even so close to the mouth of the river (it's not unusual for them to have no more than one foot of water under their keel) and all movements require very close correlation with the tide in conjunction with expert pilotage. Always bear this in mind and pay close attention to the requirements of any large vessel on the move. It is in these situations that VHF radio is an essential aid; or at least a comprehensive knowledge of the international sound signals. The wharves do not permit casual mooring (except in an emergency) so once past Keadby on a falling tide the boater, intending to head up the Ouse back into the inland waterways system, is, on reaching Trent Falls, committed to one of four courses of action:

1. Anchor under the lee of the training wall in the west channel, to the south of Trent Falls light.
2. Beach on Tackhammer flats.
3. Moor on Blacktoft Lay-by Jetty. *Charge.*
4. Punch the ebbing tide in the Ouse up to Goole (or beyond).

These options are examined in greater detail on the next page. Boaters passing Flixborough Stather, now predominantly engaged in steel traffic, may recall the disastrous explosion that occurred here on 1st June 1974, when it was the site of a vast chemical works which was virtually flattened by the blast. To the north, beside the outfall from Meredyke, is a silt bank which, unusually, has built up on a straight section of the river, at the approach to the bite of a bend - BEWARE. Burton Stather was built and operated by the late Victor Waddington whose barges, moored on the Aire & Calder Navigation, once clustered around the western outskirts of Goole Docks, awaiting incoming shipments of steel. Similarly his boats were to be found tied up several deep at Waddington Lock, on the Sheffield & South Yorkshire Navigations and were a living testimony to his undying commitment to water-borne transport. It was increasingly stringent crewing regulations - with particular regard to their on-board accommodation - that finally sounded the death knell on his carrying operation and today, sadly, most of his barges have been cut up. His past enthusiasm, often in the face of a less than co-operative bureaucracy, was only matched by the immense carrying capacity of his total barge fleet. He is alleged to have observed, about the perilous state of his home navigation, that 'The top's too near the bottom, the bottom's too near the top and there's nowt in between'. The unwary boater, failing to use the marked channel at Trent Falls, may well have occasion to reflect at some length on this observation.

Trent Falls

Now the steep wooded hills that have followed close to the east bank of the river start to peel away as the mouth of the Trent and its junction with the Ouse (to form the Humber) is approached. Large areas of low-lying ground – part mud flat, part rough grazing – accompany the waterway to its conclusion, only to be dwarfed by the vast acreage of water that is the confluence of these two great rivers. There is a lonely eeriness about so much water with only the village of Alkborough in the distance to suggest human habitation. Strangely enough the River Don, now confined to its sterile, straight, tidal channel at Goole, used to have one of its two mouths here, just to the south of Anchor Drain. When Vermuyden set out to drain the Isle of Axholme he unsuccessfully attempted to divert the river's entire output along its second branch, into the River Aire near Snaith. Nowhere else in Britain will the inland navigator be exposed to so much water and so little bank. Many boaters, regaled with tales of the fearsome nature of these waters, will do anything to avoid passage, but in reality, in a properly equipped boat, in the right weather conditions and with informed planning, Trent Falls can be navigated with comparative ease. Before passing Keadby, with its safe haven in the Stainforth and Keadby Canal, you should be clear about the channel (*see* reference to *Trent Series Charts*, below), the tide and weather conditions and your strategy once the Humber is reached (technically the point where Trent and Ouse meet and all points east). You should also be clear that Trent Falls is also called Trent Mouth and Apex (Apex being the name given to the lighthouse at the end of the western training wall). All three names can be heard in regular use on local shipping radio traffic. Most boaters will choose to approach Trent Falls on an ebbing tide; low-powered craft will have no option. Deep-draughted vessels will obviously plan to arrive well before low water. Only powerful boats will consider turning into the Ouse to push against the ebb to Goole. For the remainder the choices are set out below.

NAVIGATIONAL NOTES

1. Anchor in the western channel between South Trent Beacon and Anchor Drain, about 20ft out from the training wall. There is a firm bottom here and you are clear of empty sand barges risking a short cut.
2. Flat-bottomed boats can beach on Tackhammer Flats and await the flood. To perform this manoeuvre, follow the eastern channel to a point roughly mid-way between South Trent Beacon and Apex Light, turn south east at right angles to your track and head square onto the flats. The ebb will draw your stern northwards, helping to lodge the vessel securely, whilst the flood will push it southwards and help to pull you off. **Note** (a) This is not a good strategy in rough weather. The western channel anchorage provides a modicum of shelter from westerly winds. (b) If attempted at night, remember that other vessels, especially large sand barges, may also have beached, so look out for riding lights.
3. On the Ouse, west of Trent Falls (almost opposite West Ouse Beacon – the second flashing red light west of Apex Light) is Associated British Ports' (ABP) Blacktoft Lay-by Jetty which, for a fee, can be used between tides. Be prepared to share it with large commercial vessels and be sure that your vessel is powerful enough to reach it.
4. At all times read the above narrative and navigational notes in conjunction with a reputable chart such as The Trent Series Charts, published by The Boating Association (www.theboatingassociation.co.uk). Be willing to take advice from CRT lock keepers and ABP staff in Goole Docks (01482 327171). **ABOVE ALL ELSE INLAND BOATERS SHOULD NOT PASS KEADBY UNLESS THEY FULLY UNDERSTAND WHAT THEY ARE DOING.**
5. Boats navigating waterways under ABP jurisdiction (in this instance Gainsborough Arches to Skelton Railway Swing Bridge, north of Goole) **MUST CARRY VHF RADIO AND HAVE AT LEAST TWO PEOPLE ON BOARD.**
6. High Water Trent Falls is approximately 30 minutes after HW Hull.

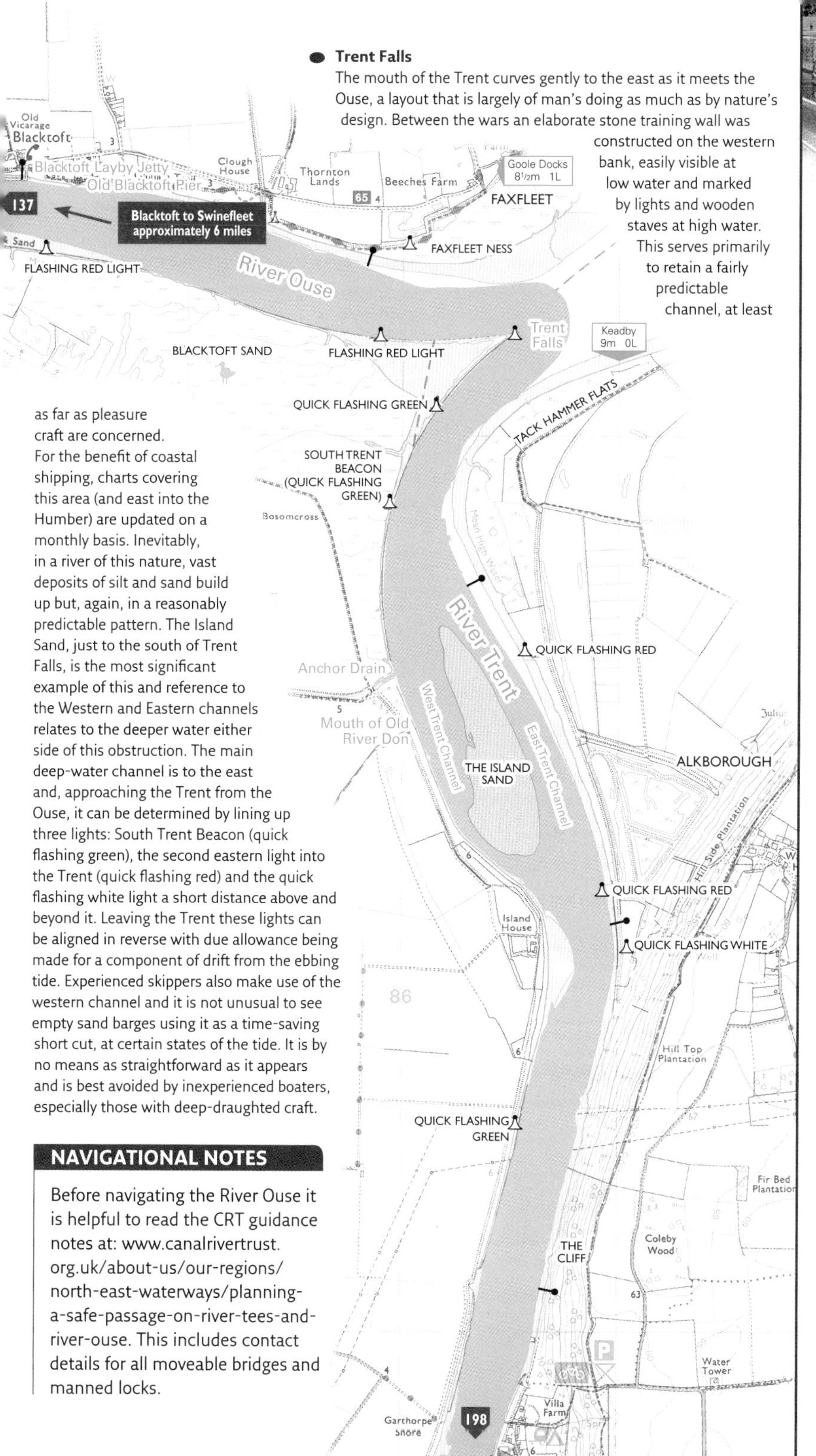

Trent Falls

The mouth of the Trent curves gently to the east as it meets the Ouse, a layout that is largely of man's doing as much as by nature's design. Between the wars an elaborate stone training wall was constructed on the western bank, easily visible at low water and marked by lights and wooden staves at high water. This serves primarily to retain a fairly predictable channel, at least as far as pleasure craft are concerned.

For the benefit of coastal shipping, charts covering this area (and east into the Humber) are updated on a monthly basis. Inevitably, in a river of this nature, vast deposits of silt and sand build up but, again, in a reasonably predictable pattern. The Island Sand, just to the south of Trent Falls, is the most significant example of this and reference to the Western and Eastern channels relates to the deeper water either side of this obstruction. The main deep-water channel is to the east and, approaching the Trent from the Ouse, it can be determined by lining up three lights: South Trent Beacon (quick flashing green), the second eastern light into the Trent (quick flashing red) and the quick flashing white light a short distance above and beyond it. Leaving the Trent these lights can be aligned in reverse with due allowance being made for a component of drift from the ebbing tide. Experienced skippers also make use of the western channel and it is not unusual to see empty sand barges using it as a time-saving short cut, at certain states of the tide. It is by no means as straightforward as it appears and is best avoided by inexperienced boaters, especially those with deep-draughted craft.

NAVIGATIONAL NOTES

Before navigating the River Ouse it is helpful to read the CRT guidance notes at: www.canalrivertrust.org.uk/about-us/our-regions/north-east-waterways/planning-a-safe-passage-on-river-tees-and-river-ouse. This includes contact details for all moveable bridges and manned locks.

INDEX

NOTES

NOTES

NOTES

NOTES